UNDERSTANDING THE OLYMPICS

The Olympic Games are unquestionably the greatest sporting event on earth, with television audiences measured in billions of viewers. By what process did the Olympics evolve into this multi-national phenomenon? How can an understanding of the Olympic Games help us to better understand international sport and society? And what will be the true impact and legacy of the London Olympics in 2012?

Understanding the Olympics answers all of these questions, and more, by exploring the full social, cultural, political, historical and economic context to the Olympic Games. It traces the history of the Olympic movement from its origins in ancient Greece, through its revival in the nineteenth century, to the modern mega-event of today. The book introduces the reader to all of the key themes in contemporary Olympic Studies, including:

- Olympic politics
- nationalism and internationalism
- access and equity
- festival and spectacle
- urban development
- political economy
- processes of commercialisation
- the Olympics and the media
- Olympic futures.

Written to engage and inform, the book includes illustrations, information boxes, chronologies and glossaries. No other book offers such a comprehensive and thoughtful introduction to the Olympic Games and therefore this is essential reading for anyone with an interest in the Olympics or the wider relationship between sport and society.

John Horne is Professor of Sport and Sociology at the University of Central Lancashire, UK.

Garry Whannel is Professor of Media Cultures at the University of Bedfordshire, UK.

Also by the authors

By both authors with Alan Tomlinson

Understanding Sport: An Introduction to the Sociological and Cultural Analysis of Sport, London: E&FN Spon, 1999

By John Horne

Sport in Consumer Culture, Basingstoke: Palgrave, 2006

Edited by John Horne and Wolfram Manzenreiter

Sports Mega-Events: Social Scientific Analyses of a Global Phenomenon, Oxford: Blackwell, 2006

Football Goes East: The People's Game in China, Japan and Korea, London: Routledge, 2004

Japan, Korea and the 2002 World Cup, London: Routledge, 2002

By Garry Whannel

Culture, Politics and Sport: Blowing the Whistle Revisited, London: Routledge, 2008

Media Sport Stars: Masculinities and Moralities, London: Routledge, 2002

Fields in Vision: Television Sport and Cultural Transformation, London: Routledge, 1992

UNDERSTANDING THE OLYMPICS

JOHN HORNE AND GARRY WHANNEL

Routledge
Taylor & Francis Group

LONDON AND NEW YORK

First published 2012
by Routledge
2 Park Square, Milton Park, Abingdon, Oxon OX14 4RN

Simultaneously published in the USA and Canada
by Routledge
711 Third Avenue, New York, NY 10017

Routledge is an imprint of the Taylor & Francis Group, an informa business

British Library Cataloguing in Publication Data
A catalogue record for this book is available from the British Library

Library of Congress Cataloging-in-Publication Data
Horne, John, 1955–
Understanding the Olympics / by John Horne and Garry Whannel.
p. cm.
1. Olympics--History. 2. Olympic Games (30th : 2012 : London, England) I. Whannel, Garry. II. Title. GV721.5.H64 2011
796.48–dc22
2011002138

ISBN: 978–0–415–55835–8 (hbk)
ISBN: 978–0–415–55836–5 (pbk)
ISBN: 978–0–203–86772–3 (ebk)

Typeset in Zapf Humanist and Eras
by Keystroke, Station Road, Codsall, Wolverhampton

Printed and bound in Great Britain by
TJ International Ltd, Padstow, Cornwall

CONTENTS

ILLUSTRATIONS

FIGURES

BOXES

PREFACE

Most books on the Olympics will feature accounts of the great moments and stars, repeating oft-told tales of Olympic mythology. Our book offers an understanding of the Olympic movement in its broader social and historical context. It provides ways of understanding the politics, the economics and the cultures within which the Olympic Games was forged and within which it grew to become the pre-eminent mega-event. We hope it will answer the questions that someone who wants to understand the Olympic Games will ask. That we are both from London and that the next Summer Olympic and Paralympic Games are to be held there is one reason, but not the only one, why we have collaborated in writing this book. As social and cultural analysts we have been observing and commenting on sporting cultures for around 30 years, and we wanted to explore the continuing fascination with the Olympic Games – neither as a celebration nor as a condemnation, but as a critical reflection. In particular we wanted to examine aspects of the Games that, we suspect, many other books will neglect.

The book is divided into three parts. The first part, 'The Olympics and London', provides answers to three broad questions. What are the main elements in the story behind London winning the right to host the 2012 Olympics? What is the International Olympics Committee (IOC), the organization that owns and protects the contemporary Olympic 'brand'? What are the main economic forces that have led to the television- and sponsor-driven commercial-isation of sport, including the Olympic Games, in the past 30 years?

Chapter 1 examines the development of the London bid since 2002 and events since the Olympic Games were awarded to London in 2005. It outlines current political tensions around costs, security and legacy. It analyses the structure of the bid, and the relationship between the Games, urban development and commerce. It examines the London Olympic Games in the context of the three previous failed bids by Britain to stage the Games since 1980. It places the successful London bid in the context of the complex political relations between the government, the London Mayor's Office, the bidding committee and subsequently the organising committee.

Chapter 2 examines the nature of the IOC, and its relationship to the other components of international sport; the nature of the bidding process; and the political economy of the Olympic movement and the sports business. It places London's Games in relation to the structure of the Olympic movement, and the ways in which it relates to the various institutions of international sport. It provides a schematic economic overview of the finances of the Olympic movement. And it analyses the peculiarly contradictory nature of the IOC in terms of its historical formation, its awkward adjustments to modernity and enterprise, and its extraordinary commercial success with one of the world's strongest brands.

Chapter 3 takes a closer look at the ways in which television has transformed the Olympics and how sponsorship became organised on a global scale. It outlines the processes by which sport's governing bodies were forced to adapt to survive. It analyses the place sport occupies within the world of television, and the significance of the role television played in creating global audiences for the Olympic Games. It traces the development of a more entrepreneurial exploitation of sponsorship by the Olympic movement. And it examines the ways in which the IOC is now attempting to cope with the challenges posed by new media.

The second part of the book, 'From out of the past', provides a look back into the past to examine the historical context of the emergence and establishment of the modern Olympic Games. The two chapters in this part seek to explain where the Olympic Games came from and how they developed during the last decade of the nineteenth century and the twentieth century.

Chapter 4 discusses the ways in which the ancient games were mythologized, in forms that provided the underpinnings of modern Olympism. It reviews attempts to establish modern multi-sport events (e.g. Penny Brookes's Much Wenlock Olympics, the Cotswold games) of which De Coubertin's was only one. It traces the ways in which mythologies of ancient Greece, the English public school system of the mid-nineteenth century, the post-1870 crisis of France, and utopian internationalism all contributed to the formation of modern Olympism. It examines the various religious underpinnings of the modern Olympic 'faith'.

Chapter 5 examines the way the early Olympic Games as a cultural form were closely linked to world's fairs and how only in the television era was the Olympics able to become a fully fledged mega-event. This chapter traces that development, examining how the Olympic Games retained elements of their origins whilst they altered in relation to other significant political and economic and cultural processes.

The third part of the book, 'The spectacle of modernity: towards a postmodern world?', is the longest. It outlines the political, economic and cultural processes that have shaped the current state of the Olympic Games. Although the Games were conceived partly as an internationalist meeting ground, from the start the tensions and rivalries between nations disrupted the aspirations of Olympism. The 1936 Games became notorious as the 'Nazi' Olympics and in the Cold War era the Games became a symbolic battleground between East and West, communism and capitalism. Chapter 6 examines the inherent contradictions of national organisation, the Cold War era, and the rise of individualism as impacting on the Olympic Games. It outlines the development and management of political tensions by the Olympic movement and the relation between the Olympic movement and great power diplomacy.

In the period between 1968 and 1984 the Games became the site of more focused symbolic political contestation in which the boycott became a significant political weapon. Chapter 7 examines the mythologising of key moments, such as the 'Black Power' salutes in the 1968 Games in Mexico, and raises questions about the process whereby symbolic politics have been marginalised in more recent Games. It examines the extent to which the Beijing Olympics marked a break with this more recent depoliticisation and assesses the future political terrain that the Olympic movement will be negotiating. And it outlines the ways in which, within the politics of bidding and hosting the games, boosters and sceptics have to articulate and negotiate issues of risk and global geopolitics.

Chapter 8 interrogates 'Olympism' in terms of concepts of festivity, spectacle and the carnivalesque, returning to a question posed by one of the authors in the 1980s: Can an event succeed in being both a spectacle and a festival (Whannel 1984)? It examines the rather problematic relation of the needs of festivity and security, the patchy history of the Cultural Olympiad, and the tendency for the noble aspirations of bidding cities to fade before the Games arrive. It concludes with a detailed examination of a striking feature of the 2012 Olympics – the vast shopping mall that occupies the space between the two stations and the Olympic Park itself. This chapter raises questions about public space, popular cultural pleasures, and Olympic legacies.

Chapter 9, the penultimate chapter, examines issues of access and equity – social class and the exclusion of professionals, the treatment of women, the composition of the IOC, race and racism, and disability sport. It examines the contrast between the rhetoric and the practice of Olympism. Women were excluded entirely from early Games, and only since the 1980s has the full programme of events begun to be opened to women. The commitment to amateurism, only abandoned since the early 1980s, gave the Games a distinct class character. The Paralympic Games, even after a long struggle for inclusion, are still staged as a separate event. The governance of the Olympics is still dominated by the European aristocracy. Major corporations, most notably NBC and its parent General Electric, are in a position to exercise a shaping influence on the development of the Games. This chapter asks the question 'Who are the games for?'

The final chapter, Chapter 10, examines urban development, tourism and the growth of concerns for establishing a sustainable legacy from hosting an Olympic Games. The escalation in the costs of staging the Games requires justification. Since Barcelona in 1992, bids have emphasised the marketing of a city as a tourist destination. But cities like London and Paris do not need the Games to attract tourists; so urban development and legacy have also become familiar terms in the bidding context. Winning the Games functions to enable a whole range of giant infrastructural projects that would otherwise struggle to win support. The Games stimulate the dreams of architects and mayors, builders and planners, leaders and entre-preneurs. 'Legacy' has become justification in the rhetoric of sports mega-event speak.

John Horne and Garry Whannel
Edinburgh and London
December 2010

ACKNOWLEDGEMENTS

Institutional and financial support for much of the research and travel upon which this book is partially based has been gratefully received from the University of Central Lancashire (JH), the University of Edinburgh (JH) and the University of Bedfordshire (GW). The libraries of these institutions and also the British Library, the National Library of Scotland, the Bibliothèque Nationale, the Bibliothèque du Centre Pompidou and the Library of New South Wales have enabled access to difficult-to-find material. So too did the archivists in the Museum of London. Financial support and support in kind were also received from the Carnegie Trust for the Universities of Scotland, the Australian Centre for Olympic Studies at the University of Technology Sydney, the University of Western Sydney, and the Government of Canada Faculty Research Programme. Unless otherwise stated, John or Garry took all the photographs in this book. We are lucky in having partners who themselves know that research is mostly fun and writing can be hell, and we thank Delia Lomax and Deborah Philips for their forbearance, support and love. We would also like to thank Joshua Wells and Simon Whitmore of Routledge for their interest in our work and their patience.

There are four groups of people John would especially like to pay acknowledgement to, who in various ways have supported this work over the past ten years or so. First are those with whom he has had the good fortune to work as co-researcher and co-author: Jean Harvey, Graeme Hayes, Wolfram Manzenreiter, Parissa Safai and David Whitson. These collaborations have resulted in ideas, information and material that are incorporated into this text in various ways. Second, are those people who have encouraged him in his work, by inviting him either to contribute to publications or to talk at conferences and other symposia, or both: Alan Bairner, Glauco Bienenstein, Anne-Marie Broudehoux, Richard Cashman, Chris Gaffney, Tony Hwang, John Karamichas, Gilmar Mascarenas, Carlos Vainer, Raquel Rolnik, John Schulz, Atsuo Sugimoto, Yoshio Takahashi and Steve Wagg. Third, are those friends who have provided him with support by making available information, providing translations or images or being prepared to discuss some of the finer points of Olympic history, despite their very busy lives: Helena Galiza, Rick Gruneau, Annette Hofmann, Shin Kawaguchi, Gerd von der Lippe, Nelma Gusmao de Oliveira, Tony Veal and Takayuki Yamashita. Fourth, but by no means least, are those students and researchers who have heard some of this before and helped him reformulate what he actually meant to say: Sadie Hollins, Michael Seibold, Jacqui Stone and Donna Wong.

Garry would like to thank Alan Tomlinson, with whom he edited *Five Ring Circus* in 1984, and who did so much to fuel his own Olympic interests; and Taylor Downing, Michael Poole and

Michael Jackson who provided journalistic contexts in which he could pursue that interest. He would also like to thank Alexis Weedon, Director of RIMAD (Research Institute for Media Art and Design) at the University of Bedfordshire; Raymond Boyle and the contributors to the special issue of *Convergence* (2010, 16: 3) devoted to Sport and New Media; members of the JOG Group (Journalism and the Olympic Games); the conference organisers who were good enough to include him, especially Robert K. Barney; colleagues and students at the University of Bedfordshire; and David Rowe of the University of Western Sydney for making him welcome and supporting his research into some aspects of the Olympics.

Conversations, interviews and chance encounters with many people over many years have fed Garry's continuing fascination with the Olympic Games. The list includes such diverse figures as Seb Coe, Sam Ramsamy, Ron Pickering, Adrian Metcalfe, John Rodda, Alec Gilady, Bruce Kidd, Keith Connor, Fanny Blankers-Koen, Wojciech Liponski, Nicos Filaretos, Michele Verdier and David Bedford. His own work on sport, culture and politics would not have been possible without fellow founders of the Centre for Sport Development Research, Jennifer Hargreaves and Ian McDonald. The work of Alina Bernstein in establishing the Media and Sport Section of the IAMCR (International Association for Media and Communication Research) has greatly strengthened our various networks. He owes thanks also to others with whom he has discussed sport, culture and politics – Joe Maguire, Toby Miller, Larry Wenner, Belinda Wheaton and Tony Veal.

In a list like this there are inevitably omissions – apologies to those people we should have included. Hopefully see you in the second edition!

ABBREVIATIONS

AAA	Amateur Athletic Association
AAC	Amateur Athletic Club
AIOWF	Association of the International Olympic Winter Sports Federations
ANOC	Association of National Olympic Committees
ANOCA	Association of National Olympic Committees of Africa
ASOIF	Association of Summer Olympic International Federations
BOA	British Olympic Association
CAS	Court of Arbitration for Sport
CCTV	China Central Television
cctv	closed circuit television
CSL	Commission for a Sustainable London 2012
DCMS	Department of Culture, Media and Sport
DEFRA	Department for the Environment, Food and Rural Affairs
EBU	European Broadcasting Union
EOC	The European Olympic Committees
FIFA	Fédération Internationale de Football Association
GFP	Games Foundation Place
GGS	German Gymnastic Society
GLA	Greater London Authority
GLC	Greater London Council
GOE	Government Olympic Executive (within DCMS)
IAAF	International Amateur Athletic Federation
IF	International Federation
ILTF	International Lawn Tennis Federation
IOA	International Olympic Academy
IOC	International Olympic Committee
IPC	International Paralympic Committee
LDA	London Development Agency
LEST	London Employment and Skills Taskforce
LOCOG	London Organising Committee of the Olympic Games and Paralympic Games
NEF	New Economics Foundation
NOC	National Olympic Committee
OB	Olympic Board
OBSG	Olympic Board Steering Group

OC   Olympic Charter
OCA   Olympic Council of Asia
OCOG   Organising Committee of the Olympic Games
ODA   Olympic Delivery Authority
OGKS   Olympic Games Knowledge Services
OLMF   Olympic Legacy Masterplan Framework
ONOC   Oceania National Olympic Committees
OPSU   Olympic Programme Support Unit
PASO   Pan-American Sports Organisation
PRC   People's Republic of China
PSA   Public Service Agreement
RSI   Red Sports International
SANOC   South African National Olympic Committee
SANROC   South African Non-Racial Olympic Committee
SCSA   Supreme Council for Sport in Africa
TCC   transnational capitalist class
TOP   The Olympic Programme
USFSA   Union des Sociétés Françaises de Sports Athlétiques
USSR   Union of Soviet Socialist Republics
WADA   World Anti-Doping Agency

TIMELINE

A selective timeline of the modern Summer and Winter Olympic Games

Year	Number	Host cities for Summer and Winter (W) Olympics	Continent	Olympic President
1896	I	Athens	Europe	Demetrias Vikelas
1900	II	Paris	Europe	Pierre De Coubertin
1904	III	St Louis	N. America	Coubertin
1906[1]		Athens	Europe	Coubertin
1908	IV	London	Europe	Coubertin
1912	V	Stockholm	Europe	Coubertin
1916[2]	VI	Berlin	Europe	Coubertin
1920	VII	Antwerp	Europe	Coubertin
1924	VIII	Paris / Chamonix (W)	Europe	Coubertin
1928	IX	Amsterdam / St Moritz (W)	Europe	Henri de Baillet-Latour
1932	X	Los Angeles / Lake Placid (W)	N. America	Baillet-Latour
1936	XI	Berlin / Garmisch-Partenkirchen (W)	Europe	Baillet-Latour
1940[3]	XII	Tokyo; Helsinki / Sapporo; Garmisch-Partenkirchen (W)	E. Asia / Europe	Baillet-Latour
1944[3]	XIII	London / Cortina d'Ampezzo (W)	Europe	J. Sigfrid Edstrom
1948	XIV	London / St Moritz (W)	Europe	Edstrom
1952	XV	Helsinki / Oslo (W)	Europe	Edstrom
1956	XVI	Melbourne[4] / Cortina d'Ampezzo (W)	Australasia / Europe	Avery Brundage
1960	XVII	Rome / Squaw Valley (W)	Europe / N. America	Brundage
1964	XVIII	Tokyo / Innsbruck (W)	E. Asia / Europe	Brundage
1968	XIX	Mexico City / Grenoble (W)	N. America / Europe	Brundage

Year	Number	Host cities for Summer and Winter (W) Olympics	Continent	Olympic President
1972	XX	Munich / Sapporo (W)	Europe / E. Asia	Brundage
1976	XXI	Montreal / Denver; Innsbruck (W)[5]	N. America / Europe	Lord Killanin
1980	XXII	Moscow / Lake Placid (W)	Europe / N. America	Killanin
1984	XXIII	Los Angeles / Sarajevo (W)	N. America / Europe	Juan Antonio Samaranch
1988	XXIV	Seoul / Calgary (W)	E. Asia / N. America	Samaranch
1992	XXV	Barcelona / Albertville (W)	Europe	Samaranch
1994		Lillehammer[6] (W)	Europe	Samaranch
1996	XXVI	Atlanta	N. America	Samaranch
1998		Nagano (W)	E. Asia	Samaranch
2000	XXVII	Sydney	Australasia	Samaranch
2002		Salt Lake City (W)	N. America	Samaranch
2004	XXVIII	Athens	Europe	Jacques Rogge
2006		Torino (W)	Europe	Rogge
2008	XXIX	Beijing	E. Asia	Rogge
2010		Vancouver-Whistler (W)	N. America	Rogge
2012	XXX	London	Europe	Rogge[7]
2014		Sochi (W)	Europe	?
2016	XXXI	Rio de Janeiro	S. America	?
2018		Annecy, Munich or Pyeongchang (W). To be decided at the IOC Session in Durban, July 2011.	Europe or E. Asia	?
2020	XXXII	To be decided at the IOC Session in Buenos Aires, July 2013.	?	?

1 This event celebrated the tenth anniversary of the first modern Games; whilst officially intercalated by the IOC, it is not numbered as an Olympic Games.
2 The VI Games (scheduled for Berlin) was not held due to the First World War, but the IOC officially counts it.
3 The XII and XIII Summer Olympic Games (scheduled respectively for Tokyo, then Helsinki before finally being called off in May 1940, and London) were not held due to the Second World War, but are officially counted by the IOC. The Winter Olympics in 1940 scheduled for Sapporo were relocated to Garmisch-Partenkirchen even after the German invasion of Poland in September 1939 before finally being called off.
4 Because of Australian quarantine laws, the equestrian events were held in Stockholm, Sweden.
5 Awarded to Denver in Colorado, the Winter Olympics were transferred to Innsbruck when Colorado residents rejected the hosting decision.
6 The IOC decided in 1986 to reschedule the Summer and Winter Games, so a new four-year cycle for the Winter Games began in 1994 with the Summer and Winter Olympics staggered two years apart.
7 Re-elected for a third four-year term, Rogge will have to stand down in 2013.

Source: adapted from Chappelet and Kubler-Mabbott (2008: 23); Greenberg (1987: 9); Hampton (2008: 20–22); Toohey and Veal (2007: 49, 199); IOC (2010).

PART I

THE OLYMPICS AND LONDON

CHAPTER 1

LONDON, THE OLYMPICS AND THE ROAD TO 2012

In 2012 London will be staging the Olympic Games for the third time, the first city to do so. This chapter examines the London bid to stage the Games and the previous unsuccessful British bids, and traces progress on the road to 2012. On 6 July 2005, on a hot humid night in Singapore, the International Olympic Committee (IOC) was about to announce the result of a two-year battle between candidate cities to stage the Olympic Games. It was 8.49 p.m., just after midday in London. The envelope was opened, and IOC President Jacques Rogge announced the winner. In the final round of voting, London had beaten Paris by 54 votes to 50. For much of the race Paris had been the strong favourite. It had been a long contest – and the bookmakers' odds favoured Paris right to the end – but the IOC had voted, and London was to stage the 2012 Olympic Games.

Wild celebrations broke out amongst the London delegation in the hall and in Trafalgar Square, whilst the Paris delegation was in despair, with recrimination and bitterness to follow. The London delegation partied on into the night. Meanwhile, in the UK four young British-Asians were making their final preparations. Many of the London delegation in Singapore would, in late morning, have been emerging from sleep as the four young men began their final London-bound journeys at dawn. Just 20 hours after the triumphant Singapore victory was announced, in London four bombs exploded – three, all around 8.50 a.m., in tube trains and one almost an hour later, on a bus, all within a mile or so of King's Cross, on the northern edge of central London. London's Olympic success dominated the news for less than a day. It made for a sombre start to the journey towards 2012. It was also a salutary reminder that security and risk management would be significant elements in the costs of staging the Games.

WHO IS RUNNING THE GAMES?

There are two main organisations involved – the London Organising Committee for the Olympic Games (LOCOG) and the Olympic Delivery Authority (ODA). LOCOG is responsible for running the Games, while the ODA is responsible for the provision of the infrastructure. More recently, an additional body, the Olympic Park Legacy Company, has been established, charged with responsibility for organising the use or disposal of Olympic facilities after the Games are over. The National Olympic Committee – in the case of the UK, the British Olympic Association (BOA) – develops the bid to stage the Games, helping to establish a bidding team, but once the bid is successful, it is necessary to establish an organising committee which must also represent the interests of the host city and country. The key stakeholders as defined in the 2012 Programme are the BOA, GLA, LOCOG, ODA and DCMS. Also involved are the five 'Host Boroughs': Greenwich, Hackney, Newham, Tower Hamlets and Waltham Forest.

How much will it cost?

It has become conventional to split Olympic finances into two elements – the cost of running the Games and the cost of providing the facilities. The budget for running the Games is based on an assumption that a share of television and sponsorship income from the IOC, ticket sales, local sponsorship and merchandising will cover running costs. The original bid specified total public funding of £3.4 billion, made up of £1.5 billion from the National Lottery, £625 million from the London council tax (provided by an Olympic levy of 38p per week), £250 million from the London Development Agency, and £1 billion from the Treasury (*Guardian* 16 March 2007).

However, in 2007 it emerged that the actual budget had soared to £9.3 billion. This is made up as follows: £2.375 billion from the original 2012 Games funding package (Lottery money and the London council tax) and in additional sums: £4.9 billion central government departments, an additional £700 million from the National Lottery, an additional £300 million from the London Mayor (not from council tax, but from reserves and LDA profits on land sales, post-Olympics) and £1.044 billion committed by central government specifically for regeneration and legacy (*Evening Standard* 15 March 2007).

Where does this money go?

A sum of £5.3 billion goes to the Olympic Delivery Authority, £2.2 billion into a contingency fund, £840 million for tax and VAT, £600 million for security and £390 million is invested in training elite athletes and the cost of the Paralympics (*Guardian* 16 March 2007). Since construction began, a substantial portion of the contingency fund has been utilised or earmarked for use. The Olympic Delivery Authority commissions project management teams who, in turn, sub-contract work to builders. The major tasks are the preparation of the site and the construction of the main stadium, the aquatic centre, a range of smaller stadiums, the Olympic Village, the media centre and the Broadcasting Centre. At the time of writing (the end of 2010), the project is ahead of schedule and under budget.

How do these costs compare with previous Games?

A quick answer might be: four times as much as Sydney 2000, almost twice as much as Athens 2004, but one-third that of Beijing 2008. However, it can be difficult to compare costs (see Preuss 2004). Every Olympic Games has its own accounting conventions, the circumstances vary from country to country, and exchange rates and differing levels of inflation complicate the calculations. The extent to which Olympic-related infrastructural costs are included or excluded varies from Games to Games. Typically, governments will try and minimise the

4

Year	City	Cost ($ millions)
1948	London	0.76
1956	Melbourne	5.4
1964	Tokyo	72
1968	Mexico City	176
1976	Montreal	1,500
1984	Los Angeles	412
1996	Atlanta	1,700
2000	Sydney	3,000
2004	Athens	7,200
2008	Beijing	40,000*
2012	London	13,500**

Figure 1.1 Cost of staging selected Summer Olympic Games, 1948–2012.

Figures not adjusted for inflation. *Estimate based on projected infrastructure investment in roads, railways, power and environmental projects. **Projected budget.

Source: CNBC European Business, March 2009.

apparent costs by ensuring that some of the expenditure is hidden in general government budgets. It is clear, though, that there has been a steady rise, above inflation, since the Second World War, with some aberrations in this general pattern.

It is widely agreed that spending in Montreal in 1976 spiralled out of control and that the main stadium cost far too much. In the case of Los Angeles (1984), once the citizens voted not to allow any public finance by the city, the private committee charged with running the Games were under great pressure to limit expenditure. As a result, very little was invested in new facilities. There appears to have been some significant city support in the form of transport, security and other services that were not accounted for in the Olympic costs, which may therefore have been kept artificially low. The estimate for Beijing, by contrast, appears to include significant general infrastructural costs, such as transport projects, which in previous Games have not been included. So the figures need to be treated with caution.

How did London come to be awarded the Games?

The Olympic Games are awarded by the IOC, in a secret ballot of its 100+ members. Candidate cities have to announce their intention around nine years in advance of the proposed year of staging the Games. There follows a period of developing and submitting detailed proposals, official inspections and assessments, lobbying and campaigning, culminating in a presentation at an IOC session, seven years before the proposed Games, at which the vote is taken. London last staged the Games in 1948 and, since 1980, there have been several attempts to bring the Olympic Games to the UK again. Indeed the UK is only the second nation to be awarded a third Olympic Games, and London is the first city to stage a third Games. Over the years, 16 of the 28 Games awarded have been in Europe, and as yet Africa has not staged an Olympic Games, although in the wake of the successful World Cup of 2010, a South African Olympic bid will have a strong chance.

5

Europe	Americas	Asia	Oceania
Athens 1896	St Louis 1904	Tokyo 1964	Melbourne 1956
Paris 1900	Los Angeles 1932	Seoul 1988	Sydney 2000
London 1908	Mexico City 1968	Beijing 2008	
Stockholm 1912	Montreal 1976		
Antwerp 1920	Los Angeles 1984		
Paris 1924	Atlanta 1996		
Amsterdam 1928	Rio de Janeiro 2016		
Berlin 1936			
London 1948			
Helsinki 1952			
Rome 1960			
Munich 1972			
Moscow 1980			
Barcelona 1992			
Athens 2004			
London 2012			

Figure 1.2 Cities staging the Summer Olympic Games, by continent.

Olympics bids do not just happen – nor these days are they simply the product of the desire of the NOC to stage the Games, important a catalyst though that is. Running an Olympic bid is a lengthy and expensive operation, which requires the cooperation and active support of both national and city governments. Obtaining such support requires delicate diplomacy and extensive lobbying. In the process, typically, a variety of separate interest groups with divergent agendas are drawn together. Staging an Olympic Games requires extensive public investment in infrastructure. It is increasingly hard to justify this expenditure simply on the grounds of hosting a 15-day event, however global its appeal. So claims for long-term legacy have to be developed.

Governments and political parties may be attracted to the grandeur and high visibility, and to the potential positive impact on the unity and enthusiasm of the people as a whole. Urban planners may perceive an Olympic project, even if the bid is ultimately unsuccessful, as a means of uncorking funding for strategic projects – new road and rail links, industrial development and housing developments. Architects will be attracted by the possibility of commissions for iconic stadiums and other buildings. Builders and associated contractors will see the potential for large contracts. Local politicians will sense an opportunity for new parks and sporting facilities and for local employment. Most significantly, the establishment of new transport infrastructure and the high profile of the Olympic project attract associated development – speculative housing, industrial development and shopping malls. A well-managed Olympic bid will endeavour to bring together, sometimes in teeth-gritting harmony, all these elements.

It was not always thus. After Athens in 1896, the next three Olympics were staged as adjuncts to international exhibitions and trade fairs. It was not until the 1920s that the profile of the event began to grow. Governments began to perceive the Games as a display of national prowess – most notoriously in the 'Nazi' Olympics in 1936, a public display of Aryan supremacy and German power. In the Cold War era the Olympics became a symbolic battleground. The spread of television from the 1960s onwards escalated the public visibility of the Games and produced an ever-rising revenue stream. However, the costs of the Games too began growing. The Montreal Games in 1976 went so far over budget that the citizens were paying off the costs until the end of the century. Cities became reluctant to mount bids, and in the late 1970s the only bidders to stage the 1984 Games were Los Angeles and Tehran. The overthrow of the Shah of Iran in 1979 in an Islamic revolution brought an end to Iran's bid, leaving Los Angeles as the only bidder. The citizens of Los Angeles were so concerned about potential costs that they voted to deny the Games public money. Faced with no alternative bidder, the IOC was forced to accept the supposedly private Games, to be run by a private not-for-profit organising committee. It became vital for this committee, who would be personally liable for any losses, to minimise expenditure and tap new forms of revenue.

Los Angeles produced a myth – that the Olympic Games could break even, and even make a small 'surplus' (the IOC disapprove of the word 'profit'). In fact, there was extensive hidden public support in the form of transport infrastructure, policing and security. No Games since 1984 has successfully broken even, if the full costs are properly accounted for. The presentation of Olympic Games accounts systematically separates the cost of running the Games and the infrastructural costs involved in preparing for the Games. The accounts can show that the share of television rights payments, sponsorship revenue, ticket sales and other marketing received by the organising committee covers the cost of staging the Games. It does not, however, cover the costs, generally much larger, of building stadiums and associated facilities, which must be borne by the hosting city and country. It is this consideration that has prompted careful thought and debate in countries proposing to bid to stage an Olympic Games. Decisions have to be taken as to whether such expenditure can be justified.

BRITISH OLYMPIC BIDS

London staged the 1908 Games, stepping in at relatively short notice after Italy withdrew. After the Second World War, London once again took up the challenge of staging a Games at short notice. In the context of war devastation, rationing and general shortages, the 1948 Olympics were staged as economically as possible, and have subsequently been dubbed the 'austerity Games'. The UK did not again contemplate campaigning to stage the Games until the late 1970s. An abortive London bid to stage the 1988 Games presaged a series of failed bids, before eventual success in 2005. Horace Cutler became Conservative leader of the Greater London Council (GLC) in 1977 and was a precursor of the shift rightwards that culminated in the General Election victory of the Conservative Party led by Margaret Thatcher in 1979. It was reported in 1978 that London might bid for the Games and that a £60,000 feasibility study was to be commissioned. Meanwhile, several members of the athletics club Ranelagh Harriers had competed in the 1978 New York City Marathon and were amazed at its large scale. Ex-athletes Chris Brasher and John Disley decided to see the New York Marathon for themselves. They did some training and entered the 1979 race. Impressed, Brasher wondered 'whether London could stage such a festival'.[1]

By October 1979 Cutler had presented his feasibility study. The cheap option, costed at £545 million, was based on using Wembley as the main stadium, whilst the more expensive £1.2 billion (£4.5 billion at 2009 prices) proposal involved a new stadium in docklands. In the event a formal bid was never made, probably because Cutler discovered he would not obtain government support. It did, however, prompt him to support the London Marathon.[2] In early 1980 the *Observer* editor Donald Trelford got Brasher and Disley together with the relevant authorities – the GLC, the police, the City of London, the Amateur Athletics Association and the London Tourist Board. GLC leader Sir Horace Cutler insisted, 'You should never ask the ratepayers to bail you out. Not a penny from the GLC.' So the organisers needed sponsorship for the projected £75,000 budget, and agency West Nally signed up Gillette as title sponsors for three years.[3] In 1981 Labour won the GLC elections, and the left-wing Ken Livingstone became the leader, introducing radical policies and using the council as a platform to attack the Conservative government. This infuriated Margaret Thatcher, and after an unsuccessful attempt to block Labour's 'Fares Fair' London Transport policy, and a failure to win the council back in 1985, the Conservative government abolished the GLC. It was a profoundly anti-democratic act, which left London without a single strategic authority, and ill-equipped to manage any centralised planning, far less manage an Olympic Games.

The mythologising of the Los Angeles Games 'surplus' attracted far greater enthusiasm for bidding around the world. In the mid-1980s, six cities (Paris, Birmingham, Belgrade, Brisbane, Barcelona and Amsterdam) entered the race to stage the 1992 Olympic Games. Birmingham won the UK right to bid in competition with Manchester and London. The Birmingham bid was led by the Labour MP and former Minister for Sport, Denis Howell – probably the best Minister for Sport the UK has had and certainly one of the few British political figures with some credibility in the world of international sport governance. The central appeal of Birmingham's bid was the compact main site at the National Exhibition Centre, with excellent transport connections, easy access between venues and the Village, and straightforward security. Olympic insiders, though, were convinced that Barcelona would win, recognising the power and influence of IOC President Juan Antonio Samaranch, who was from Barcelona.

The intense competition meant that budgets for bidding rose dramatically, with the cities spending an average of $10 million each. Lavish receptions were hosted, IOC members were showered with expensive gifts and free travel, and the culture that later led to IOC members being expelled for accepting inducements and bribes for votes began to take hold. In the event, the Games, as widely predicted, were awarded to Barcelona. The Paris bid had some technical shortcomings, but it was well prepared and brilliantly presented – utilising a well-made video and an impressive speech by Jacques Chirac, Mayor of Paris. Birmingham's presentation, by contrast, was over-elaborate, with too many voices speaking as numerous people stood to say one line and then sat down again.[4]

In the sophisticated aristocratic world of the IOC, where utilising bid team members who speak a range of languages is a distinct advantage, Birmingham's bid appeared provincial, with its members rather out of their depth at times. In the competition to wine, dine and shower gifts on IOC members, other cities were more profligate. The rather lukewarm support from the British government (the official letter authorising the bid was signed not by Prime Minister Margaret Thatcher but by Environment Minister Kenneth Baker) did not help Birmingham. At the IOC vote, the government was represented by Minister for Sport, Richard Tracey. The British Minister for Sport has always been a low-status role, and Tracey had not been in the post long enough to have become familiar in IOC circles. Thatcher herself was unpopular with many people because of her support for maintaining sporting links with South

Africa, and 21 of the 47 Commonwealth countries boycotted the 1986 Commonwealth Games in Edinburgh in protest at such links (see Bateman and Douglas 1986; Hill 1992: 101). British logistical support for an American bombing raid on Libya put an end to any hope Birmingham had of picking up any votes from Middle Eastern IOC members (Howell 1990: 326). Amsterdam's chances were undermined by a well-organised Dutch-based anti-Olympic Games protest movement, whose systematic demonstrations targeting IOC members had considerable impact.

Birmingham had developed a strategy of attracting trade fairs, conventions and sporting events, but by 1993, under a new left-wing leadership, had become sceptical and cynical, with one councillor commenting that she 'wouldn't spend ten pounds on the Olympics'.[5] The IOC, concerned at the negative publicity given to the lavish gifts, and the persistent rumours of corruption, instituted a set of regulations to govern the campaigning process, but they were neither rigorous in style nor effectively policed, as the Salt Lake City corruption scandal subsequently illustrated.

The British candidate to host the 1996 and 2000 Games was Manchester, whose bidding team was led by Bob Scott. Scott was a flamboyant theatre entrepreneur who had been head of the 69 Theatre Company and established the Royal Exchange Theatre in Manchester. In 1985 he set up the Manchester Olympic Bid Committee, losing out to Birmingham as the British bid for 1992. Scott had huge enthusiasm and commitment, a broad cultural hinterland and a gift for salesmanship, and for almost a decade devoted his life to the bids. In contrast to the municipal council orientation of the Birmingham bid, Scott built a bid around strong support from the business community, concentrating on those with roots in the north-west. He was also successful at winning the support of the relevant Urban Development Corporation. Privately, Scott expected the first bid to be unsuccessful, but felt that a good attempt would provide a platform for a serious chance second time around. Manchester ran a well-researched and well-targeted lobbying campaign, and Scott's own energy and charisma helped give the team a focus and a sense of purpose.[6] He was able to develop a good rapport with Sir Arthur Gold of the BOA; and also secured a much stronger commitment from the government, with Mrs Thatcher writing a long letter to IOC President Samaranch in support (Hill 1992: 113–14). The bid cost a modest £3 million and may well have been worth it in promoting the image of Manchester on the world stage. Indeed some cities may nowadays take the view that the best value to be obtained from the Olympic Games lies in bidding but not winning – thus gaining some promotional value without taking on the enormous costs of major developments.

Manchester had to compete with two dramatically different but strongly supported bids in the approach to the IOC Session of 1990. The traditionalists favoured Athens, with the emotion and romance of marking the centenary of the first modern Olympic Games by returning to Greece. The modernisers supported Atlanta, the home of Coca-Cola and Ted Turner's CNN, which seemed to epitomise the way that the Games had become dependent on corporate capitalism sponsorship and television revenue. Athens should have won, of course, but the strong conviction of the Athens bidding team that they were the only logical choice antagonised some IOC members, who perceived this as arrogance. A whispering campaign, casting doubts on Greek efficiency, combined with powerful but shadowy forces behind the scenes to win the day for Atlanta. Subsequent disappointment with the Atlanta Games then combined with guilt to ensure that Athens got its Games in 2004.

9

Soon after the awarding of the Games to Atlanta, it emerged that a London bid for 2000, led by Seb Coe, was planned. However, a rival London group emerged, and only under pressure from the British Olympic Association could they agree to merge; too late, however, for the BOA, who elected to stick with Manchester for a second time. The second Manchester bid was launched in March 1992, with a budget of £5 million. The new Conservative Prime Minister, John Major, offered more enthusiastic support than Mrs Thatcher had done, and central government contributed £2 million to the campaign, whilst 24 companies contributed another £2 million. The local council took a clearer line in stressing that the bid had to be linked to regeneration, especially in the eastern part of Manchester, and this in turn helped win the support of Environment Minister Michael Heseltine. Manchester's proposed budget for the Games themselves was £973 million, of which 40% would be spent on the Olympic Village (Hill 1994).

But even Scott knew he was fighting with a handicap, as he subsequently acknowledged:

> I was aware that I was not leading the first XI . . . The international world thinks London when they think Great Britain. If you put up Manchester or any other city other than London, however sound the bid, you cannot get over the fact that you are not London. The world then comes to the conclusion that Britain has decided to send out its second XI and is not taking the competition seriously. I found myself between a rock and a hard place.
>
> (*Daily Telegraph* 26 May 2003)

Once again, Manchester found itself trailing behind two front runners, Beijing and Sydney, who fought a very close battle. Sydney won by the odd vote, after most experts pronounced it too close to call. The experience gained during these two Olympic bids fed into Manchester's successful bid to stage the 2002 Commonwealth Games, headed by Scott. It had become very clear during the 1990s that the IOC could only be attracted to the UK by a London bid.

A LONDON BID?

The London bid for 2012 had its roots in the 1990s. The failure of Birmingham and Manchester to attract significant support had forced the sports community to recognise that it was London or nothing. It was becoming recognised in the UK that, of British cities, only London was likely to be favoured by the IOC, yet the BOA had three times chosen other British cities to bid. The emergence of the bid and its success have to be seen in a political context. The issue of a London-wide authority, development strategies for East London and the Thames estuary region, and the development of the Channel Tunnel rail link were all relevant factors.

The eastern inner-city boroughs of London were socially deprived areas, with poor transport links and extensive derelict sites which formerly housed industry, docks and railway sidings. The government began redeveloping the docklands during the 1980s, establishing the Docklands Development Corporation, a mechanism for eliminating local authority planning processes in order to speed development. In the early 1990s, the then Environment Minister Michael Heseltine launched the 'Thames Gateway' scheme, one of the most ambitious regional regeneration programmes in Europe. From 1997 the Labour government continued to support the Thames Gateway scheme.[7] One of the biggest sites in the area, in Stratford, contained a railway yard, largely disused, a range of light industry, much of it derelict, and a complex network of canals, streams, sewer pipes and other waterways. The Channel Tunnel had opened in 1994, and three years earlier it had been announced that a Channel Tunnel rail link, a high-speed line from St Pancras in London to the tunnel, would be built – running through Stratford. The sheer scale of this project encouraged confidence in the ability of the UK to deliver major engineering projects and the fact that it could include a station on the Olympic site itself was subsequently to prove an asset to the London bid.[8] According to Gavin Poynter, the rail link provided an important catalyst for other improvements in road and rail infrastructure. By 1995 the Thames Gateway Task Force had drawn up plans for 30,000 new homes and 50,000 new jobs to be established in the 'Thames Corridor' by 2021 (Poynter 2005).

A major obstacle to producing a convincing London bid was the absence of a strategic city-wide authority, since Thatcher abolished the GLC in 1986.[9] But it soon became clear that a major world city like London could not be run effectively by 32 local boroughs (plus the City of London), and that some form of central strategic authority was needed. The question could only be raised meaningfully in Parliament once Thatcher had resigned as Conservative Party leader. In a parliamentary debate on the governance of London, in 1991, Labour MP Bryan Gould proclaimed that:

> Londoners know that it is nonsense that our city, uniquely, has no city-wide voice, no one capable of taking a strategic view of the needs and interests that we share as Londoners or of the future that should be ours . . . They know, for example, that London's ill-fated Olympic bid could not be taken seriously as long as there was no one to speak for London.

Labour MP Kate Hoey argued that London had been unable to compete equally with Manchester and Birmingham to get BOA support because of the absence of a 'person or group who could sign the contract with the British Olympic Association' and asserted that the Labour Party's proposal to recreate a streamlined Greater London Authority was the way forward to that. Even the high Tory MP Rhodes Boyson insisted that 'there must be a voice for London. Whether that is achieved by bringing together the various boroughs or in some other way, we need a voice for London . . . Perhaps there should be an elected mayor working with the boroughs.'[10] Despite these views, the Conservative Party remained hostile to anything resembling a revived GLC and it was not until the Labour Party regained power in 1997 that the policy of encouraging the establishment of city mayors with real authority put the re-introduction of a London authority back on the agenda. London finally regained a form of central strategic body in 2000 with the creation of the Greater London Authority.[11]

In 2000, despite being the candidate favoured by Labour Party members, Ken Livingstone was denied the right to run as Labour candidate for Mayor by an ad hoc voting system designed by Labour Party managers to prevent him winning. Livingstone announced he would run as an independent, and despite expulsion from the Labour Party, was duly elected Mayor. With a new authority and Mayor in place, many of the objections to a London bid had been addressed.

Meanwhile, following unsuccessful bids by Birmingham and Manchester for the 1992, 1996 and 2000 Olympic Games the BOA spent time with the voting constituency of the IOC and received the very clear message that 'only when you return to the table with London will we believe that you are serious about hosting a future Olympic Games'. The British Olympic Association decided in 1997 that if there was to be another UK bid, it would have to come from London (*Daily Telegraph*_26 May 2003). The BOA commissioned a feasibility study, developed a strategy, and mounted a lobbying campaign. The feasibility study, conducted by David Luckes, did not appear until 2001, but was a comprehensive analysis, running to 165,000 words and 395 pages.[12] In early 2001 the BOA team presented the feasibility study to the then Secretary of State (Chris Smith), Minister for Sport (Kate Hoey) and London Mayor Ken Livingstone. At that stage the BOA had proposed sites in the west and east of London as options for the Olympic site. But the Mayor insisted that the East London option was the most viable because of the regeneration opportunity that it created. *The Times* (12 March 2001) declared that East End regeneration would be central to a London bid for 2012.

The government, however, was yet to be convinced of the merits of the bid, and the possibility that it could be successful. But in May 2001 they agreed to come together with the BOA and the Mayor to form a stakeholder group that would explore the concept further. In late 2001 the group commissioned the real estate company Insignia Richard Ellis to confirm land availability and Arup to undertake a cost benefit analysis of the bid itself and the staging of the Olympic Games.[13] Later that year the whole project almost collapsed after a government decision not to proceed with the Pickett's Lock athletics stadium forced UK Athletics to withdraw from its commitment to stage the 2005 World Athletics Championships (*The Times* 10/10/01). The British reputation was badly damaged in international sporting circles. By late 2001 the BOA and Livingstone agreed that a Wembley site was impractical and that, in Stratford, a stadium and village could be built close together and near good transport links (*Daily Telegraph* 9 October 2003).

From the outset, the media were heavily involved in attempts to shape public opinion around the bid process. It was the *Daily Telegraph*'s then sports editor David Welch who brought the BOA's decision to bid for the Games with London to wider public attention ('London Must Bid', *Daily Telegraph* 18 July 2003). He launched a sustained and partisan campaign through the *Daily Telegraph* to back the London bid. Welch and his sports team, including the former BBC Sports Editor Mihir Bose, were relentless in selling the merits of a London Games to a largely apathetic public and lobbying politicians to get onside by backing the London proposal.

Indeed such was the link between the paper and the bid team that as the process evolved the Director of Communications for the London 2012 bid, Mike Lee, recognised that steps needed to be taken to cultivate other newspapers, as the links with the *Telegraph* were leading to some disquiet among sections of the print media (Lee 2006: 28). By way of contrast, another sports journalist, Oliver Holt – the award-winning sportswriter of the *Daily Mirror* – had penned an extended essay on why London would not win the bid systematically identifying the misplaced political and economic myths that were surrounding the London bid in 2005 (Holt 2005).

Arup presented its findings in May 2002, based upon a specimen bid in East London. Their conclusions were encouraging but the government continued to worry about the vast scale of the project. A decision was delayed until after the Commonwealth Games in Manchester,

1991		The plan to build a Channel Tunnel rail link, a high-speed line from London to the tunnel, is announced
1994		Channel Tunnel opens
1995		Thames Gateway Task Force plans for 30,000 new homes and 50,000 new jobs in the Thames Corridor by 2021
1997		BOA commissions feasibility study
	May	Labour government elected, new Prime Minister Tony Blair
2000	July	Greater London Authority established
	May	Ken Livingstone elected Mayor of London, as an independent
2001		BOA feasibility study published
	May	Government, BOA and the Mayor form group to consider London bid
	Sept	Olympic group commission Insignia Richard Ellis to confirm land availability and Arup to undertake a cost benefit analysis
	Oct	Government decision not to proceed with the Pickett's Lock athletics stadium forces UK Athletics to withdraw from its commitment to stage the 2005 World Athletics Championships
	Nov	Wembley site seen as impractical. Stratford is preferred
2002	May	Arup presented its findings based upon a specimen bid in East London
2003	Feb	Cabinet delay Olympic bid decision until after the war in Iraq had commenced
	15 May	Government agree to back the London bid
	20 June	Livingstone appoints Barbara Cassani as Chair of the Bidding Committee
2004	15 Jan	The full bid proposal is submitted to IOC
	18 May	IOC includes London on shortlist
	19 May	Cassani resigns; replaced by Sebastian Coe
	10 June	Livingstone re-elected London Mayor, as Labour Party candidate
	15 Nov	Final bidding document presented to the IOC
2005		IOC Evaluation Committee visits all the remaining bidding cities
	6 July	London is awarded the Games
	7 July	London bombing: bombs explode in three tube trains and a bus

Figure 1.3 London Olympic bid timeline, 1991–2005.

Source: various, including LOCOG website, media announcements from LOCOG, BOA, *Evening Standard*, *Guardian*, *The Times*, *Daily Telegraph* and Lee 2006.

where concerns about financing (particularly the huge drain on the public purse) and organisation continued right up until the Opening Ceremony. Manchester was, however, seen as a success, both abroad and at home, and once again demonstrated the UK's ability to deliver major events. The resultant feel-good factor made an impact, and media interest in a London bid increased.

The *Daily Telegraph* became a committed lobbyist for a London bid. The attitude of the *Evening Standard* towards the Games has oscillated during the last eight years. In 2002 an *Evening Standard* editorial (7 August 2002) commented that an Olympic bid would need 'whole-hearted Government backing' and that the 'Government must not be penny-pinching if it genuinely intends to support a serious bid for the Olympics'. It declared that, 'A city of London's size and confidence should not shirk the challenge of attempting to host the biggest sporting event in the world'.

13

Despite extensive lobbying from the BOA and the media, the government remained split on the subject, and unwilling to commit. In the wake of the destruction of the World Trade Center in September 2001, and the invasion of Afghanistan, hawks in the USA were pressing hard for an invasion of Iraq, a plan in which the British Prime Minister acquiesced. In February 2003, the British Cabinet agreed to delay a decision on the Olympic bid until after the war in Iraq had commenced. The final agreement and submission of the bid were delayed by six months by the build-up to the Iraq War.

Finally, on 15 May 2003, the Minister for Culture, Tessa Jowell, announced that the government would back the London bid. A sum of £2.375 billion was allocated to pay for the staging of the 2012 Games in London. These costs would be met by business, the London Development Agency (LDA) and the government. London Mayor Ken Livingstone agreed with Tessa Jowell that each London household would pay an average £20 a year Olympic tax from 2006–07 for a maximum of ten years (*Daily Telegraph* 9 October 2003). The *Evening Standard* editorial (15 May 2004) proclaimed that this was 'a vote of confidence in London as a world city' whilst referring to 'reservations' amongst Londoners. The eventual budget rose to around £10 billion and it has become clear that the initial calculations were inadequately worked out – omitting to take into account, for example, the large sums of VAT that would be due. There is always political pressure to scale down initial budgets in order to secure approval, and this would certainly appear to have occurred in the case of London.

BIDDING FOR 2012

On 20 June 2003 Livingstone appointed Barbara Cassani as Chair of the 'Bidding Committee' (*Daily Telegraph* 9 October 2003). Cassani, an American, was former chief executive of the low-cost airline, Go, but had little experience of the world of international sport organisation – which remains doggedly male, clubbish and rooted in late-night conviviality. Eyebrows were also raised at the choice of an American, especially given the political reactions around the world to the US-led invasion of Iraq. Although Cassani was praised for her team-building work, she proved not to be adept at or enthusiastic about the necessary lobbying work. The full bid proposal was submitted on 15 January 2004. On 18 May the IOC announced the shortlist of bidding cities – London, Paris, New York, Madrid and Moscow – eliminating Rio de Janeiro, Leipzig, Istanbul and Havana. Cassani had already resolved to resign, but those few people in the know kept the secret and it was only on 19 May that it was announced that Cassani would be replaced by ex-Olympic medallist Sebastian Coe, now Lord Coe. Although this was a dramatic and abrupt change, which, despite some adept media management, was met with less than full enthusiasm, it proved to be a key turning point. Coe's knowledge of the world of sport organisation in general and the IOC in particular was a considerable asset, and having been one of the world's greatest athletes made him popular in IOC circles. As an ex-Conservative MP, he also knew how to operate in Westminster circles. The fact that IOC ex-President Samaranch had great affection for him was also an advantage. For the last year before the vote, the London bid was steered and managed with confidence and shrewdness.

At the start of 2004, a deal had enabled Ken Livingstone to rejoin the Labour Party, and in May he won re-election as Mayor, this time as the official Labour Party candidate. The political

14

context of the London bid made for potential tensions between political parties, between city and country, and between sport organisations and political organisations. These tensions were best embodied in the three figures of Seb Coe (an ex-Conservative MP), Tessa Jowell (a Labour MP and Blair loyalist) and Ken Livingstone (a left-wing maverick). It speaks volumes about the enormous symbolic power of an Olympic bid that this frail coalition was able to hold together.

A concerted campaign began to win public support, as any suggestion of an ambivalent or hostile public can damage the chances of success. The final bidding document was presented to the IOC on 15 November 2004. The London Bidding Committee announced that 250,000 people had signed up to support the bid, and the Mayor used the subsequent New Year's Eve firework display to promote the bid. Although there were many individuals and small groups that were suspicious of, or hostile to, the London bid, especially in East London, they never succeeded in finding common cause, devising a united front or mounting a concerted and coherent campaign. The bid gathered significant momentum in the last six months, and by the time the Games were awarded to London in June 2005 it was of course too late for any practical opposition.

The British media, often very critical of the planning of major projects, were, it appears, very well managed by the bidding team. Even the *Evening Standard* (15 February 2005) was now referring to 'massive public backing' and confidently asserting that 'the city will deliver on its promises'. The *Evening Standard*, though, was throughout the decade the site of struggle between the various stakeholders to define Olympic issues, but one antagonism underpinned the story – that between the newspaper (and Associated Newspapers generally) and London Mayor Ken Livingstone.

BOX 1.1 KEN LIVINGSTONE, THE *DAILY MAIL* AND THE *EVENING STANDARD*

This mutual antagonism dates back to the period of the Livingstone-led GLC of the early 1980s (see Curran *et al.* 2005). It was fuelled during Livingstone's first mayoral campaign, and gathered momentum in 2002 when the *Evening Standard* alleged that Livingstone had pushed another man over a wall during an argument at a party. The tension escalated in 2005, in an exchange between Livingstone and *Evening Standard* reporter Oliver Finegold, resulting in allegations, hotly disputed, that Livingstone had made an anti-Semitic remark. As the *Independent* (16 February 2005) described it, the 'now infamous 30-second exchange . . . mutated into a career-threatening war of attrition with Jewish leaders and one of Britain's most powerful newspaper dynasties'.

Livingstone admitted his remarks could be regarded as offensive but not anti-Semitic, and counter-attacked by criticising the *Daily Mail's* flirtation with fascism during the 1930s and subsequent coverage of minorities from Irish immigrants to asylum-seekers. Condemning the *Daily Mail* group as among the 'most reprehensibly managed, edited and owned newspapers in the world', the Mayor suggested that its wartime owner, the 1st Viscount Rothermere, the great-grandfather of the paper's present owner, would have been 'at the front of the queue of collaborators' had Britain been defeated by Hitler (*Independent* 16 February 2005).

The row triggered debate in all parts of the political spectrum. The *World Socialist Website* (4 March 2006)) condemned the 'patently anti-democratic decision' to suspend Livingstone from office for four weeks. The then Conservative MP Boris Johnson used his website to deride the story as 'a non-story, a media spat' and went on to say 'Well, I do not normally side with Red Ken, but on this occasion I say, Ken, whatever you do, don't apologise. Tell the papers to take a running jump . . . any apology, as Ken has made clear, would be completely insincere; and it would be a surrender to media bullying.' Johnson concluded that the remarks were crass but not anti-Semitic. Boris Johnson subsequently defeated Livingstone in the mayoral election of 2008.

Livingstone won considerable respect for his speech in response to the London bombings. The speech was widely praised for voicing sentiments that represented the feelings of many Londoners. The *Sun*, long one of Livingstone's harshest critics, said he had 'captured London's resolve'. The *Times* praised his 'extremely personal and uncompromising words'. Jay Rayner (*Observer* 10 July 2005) described Livingstone as a subtle and gifted orator, and said all those involved with the bid agreed that London would not have won had it not been for the Mayor's efforts. The success of the London Olympic bid and the Congestion Charge, coupled with the positive reaction to the July bombing speech, gave Livingstone a period of favourable press. Jonathon Freedland said that 'A man who, by his own admission, loves power, is poised to get a whole lot more' (*Evening Standard* 27 October 2005). However, just three years later, in May 2008, Livingstone was voted out of office to be replaced by Conservative Boris Johnson. In 2010, Livingstone made clear his intention to run again and he has since been selected as the Labour candidate for Mayor in 2012, with the election just 12 weeks before the London Games.

During the first half of 2005, the IOC Evaluation Committee visited all the remaining bidding cities. Despite concerns over London's traffic, and a transport system in urgent need of renewal, the bidding team were able to impress the visiting committee by taking them along the newly completed Channel Tunnel rail link, demonstrating that trains could get from central London to the Olympic site in around six minutes. The IOC has a small electorate of just over a hundred who vote secretly and do not need to report back to anyone. Individual lobbying is vital, and inevitably, despite tougher IOC rules introduced since the corruption scandals of the late 1990s (see Chapter 2), all sorts of deals and offers, implicit or explicit, are likely to be made. On 23 April 2005 the London bid team were forced to remove an incentives package, including free flights for athletes and financial aid for Olympic teams, after claims that it contravened the bidding regulations. The competition becomes very intense during this final period. By 6 June 2005, it was clear that London and Paris were ahead of Madrid and New York, but not by much. Moscow had withdrawn after suffering trenchant criticism in the evaluation report. The race was widely regarded as too close to call.

The 2005 IOC Session at which the cities had to make their presentations, and at which the voting would take place, was in Singapore. Although Prime Minister Tony Blair was scheduled to host the G8 meeting in Gleneagles in the same week as the IOC Session, the London team managed to persuade him to fly to Singapore first to meet individual IOC members. French

the Olympics and London

President Jacques Chirac made a rather shorter visit and it is believed that IOC members noted the different levels of commitment. Footballer celebrity David Beckham was also utilised as a means of seizing media attention. The IOC members are predominately ageing, affluent and worldly wise, but even the most eminent of them are always flattered by the chance to meet world leaders and the world's most charismatic sport stars. On 6 July, London was awarded the Games and the bid leaders signed the contract.

So why did London win?

It is always hard to interpret IOC votes, given the small unrepresentative electorate, and the secret ballot. Candidate cities have just 100+ delegates to lobby. There have been allegations of corruption since the 1980s, when banquets, lavish gifts, free air travel and other perks were showered on IOC members. Eventually, associated with the Salt Lake City bid for the Winter Games, bribery allegations were substantiated and several IOC members were expelled. Faced with such a public humiliation, the IOC had to introduce more stringent regulations to try and curb the excesses. Nevertheless, it is clear that a lot can happen behind the scenes that does not become public. The line at which hard-nosed political dealing becomes corrupt can be a blurred one, not least because of the non-representative and secret nature of the decision-making process, which, in theory at least, would allow an IOC member to offer his vote to several candidate cities.

All that said, London produced a very credible plan, submitted a thorough and convincing bid (apart from the questionable financial plan), and by all accounts staged an impressive presentation. The bid has to be of a high technical standard, the IOC has to be assured of a high level of enthusiasm in a bidding city, and the presentation should impress. These things, however, can avoid failure but not in themselves assure success. Members and their wives (for the vast majority of members, still, are male) are likely to favour spending two weeks (in highly pampered circumstances, in the finest hotels, with luxury travel) in an attractive city. London has become an attractive city – but so is Paris, and simply being attractive will not win a bid, as Atlanta's victory over Athens to stage 1996 suggested.

The IOC likes a gesture – going to Beijing or awarding the Games to a South American country (Brazil 2016) for the first time, and probably seeking to stage the first African Games soon. The race to stage 2012 did not, though, offer such an option. The very well-planned use of Tony Blair may have had a last-minute influence. The Olympic Session came at a very awkward time for world leaders, coinciding as it did with the G8 Conference in Scotland. But, whereas Chirac paid only a fleeting visit to Singapore, Blair devoted a whole day to an exhausting series of 15-minute meetings with key IOC members. He was meticulously briefed by the London team, who were full of praise for his efforts. It was strangely like a Sebastian Coe race – a few problems at the beginning, then gradually becoming well positioned and putting in a devastating late sprint. By contrast, Paris peaked too early, and once you are a front runner you can become both complacent (taking it too easy) and nervous (afraid to try anything adventurous for fear of losing a vote or two). Beyond this, it is often very difficult to know how IOC members decide which way to vote. All politics involves deals, implicit or explicit, and the politics of sport is no exception.

17

PLANNING FOR THE 2012 GAMES

All Olympic Games organisers face the same problem: when the bid is won they begin their work in the bright sunshine of great publicity, but then for the next six years they have to face a blizzard of critical coverage. Partly this is because of the old principle that bad news makes bigger headlines. For much of the build-up there are generally only two storylines – that facilities will not be ready on time, and that everything will cost too much. So far, the first one has generally proved wrong, but the second one is almost always correct.

News coverage of the Olympic Games is a site of contestation between competing groups struggling for the power to define reality. Newspapers of course are not simply holding the ring, but by their news selection, agenda setting, frames of reference, choice of language, order of priorities, use of photographs, perspectives, and commentary, always impose a positionality on this struggle. Newspaper news stories draw heavily on quotes from sources who are usually implicitly ranked in terms of power. 'Primary definers' are granted a privileged ability to define the issue precisely; 'secondary definers' are able to register competing definitions; and other voices are marginalised (see Hall *et al.* 1978). The structure of such stories, though, is dependent on various factors such as the political perspective of the newspaper, the configuration of public opinion, and the fluctuating political fortunes of particular positions. The challenge for the organising committee is to organise and manage impressions, combating negative stories and promoting positive ones. Once the Games commence, this is much easier because there is a deluge of sport to report. In the build-up, however, media management presents a greater challenge. The situation is complicated by changes of government since 1995 at both national and city levels. Boris Johnson became the Conservative Mayor of London in 2008 and his old fellow Bullingdon Club member, David Cameron, became Prime Minister at the head of a Conservative–Liberal Democrat coalition in 2010. While both will support the Olympic project, neither was implicated in its genesis, and both will feel greater freedom to adopt a judicious critical distance on occasion.

Staging the Games is of course a huge project, for which structures and processes have to be derived from scratch. The London project got off to a quick start, with heads of LOCOG and ODA appointed, and compulsory purchasing and land clearance commenced. Political monitoring posed its own problems. Derek Wyatt MP estimated that five different Select Committees could spend up to £5 million by 2012 on overseeing Olympic-related issues, and proposed a single Select Committee for the Olympics. His proposal has not been adopted.[14]

Simply preparing the infrastructure for the Games is itself an enormous undertaking. In the case of London, land had to be acquired, including purchase of existing homes and businesses on the site. Land clearance and demolition were necessary. For the past two hundred years the East London site had been used by a range of industries, many leaving a toxic legacy, so the soil has had to be cleaned in a purpose-built 'soil hospital'. Despite this, it may well be that parts of the site will never be suitable for permanent residency. Dozens of electricity pylons were removed and replaced by underground cabling. Part of the potential of the London site is that it is riddled with waterways, including the River Lea. This, though, has required extensive works, including 22 bridges, the construction of Three Mile Lock, and dredging of the Waterworks River. The site also required extensive work on roads, security

18

Figure 1.4 Welcome to the Olympic Park. Site clearance and construction commence, and the site disappears from public view behind the blue fence.

centres, fencing and landscaping. The major construction work includes stadiums (main stadium, aquatic centre, velodrome, handball arena), the Media Centre and International Broadcasting Centre, and the Olympic Village. Transport improvements (North London Line platform improvements, new Docklands Light Rail extension, widening of platforms, new lifts) have also been necessary (*Guardian* 3 July 2009).

Olympic design, construction and servicing expertise has now become a mini-industry in its own right and can be an exportable asset. During the preparations for the Olympic Games in Sydney in 2000, the Australian federal government and the New South Wales state government encouraged the promotion of Australian expertise. At least six major Beijing Olympic arenas were Australian-designed and many Australians acted as design consultants. The Australian Company PTW Architects designed the Aquatic Centre for the Sydney Olympic Games, and this helped them win the contract for the Water Cube aquatic centre in Beijing for 2008. Australian architects designed the sailing base in Qiangdao, a stadium in Tianjin and the Hong Kong Equestrian Centre. Australian companies also supplied materials for Beijing – BHP Billiton provided the ores in the medals, Bluescope provided materials for the Olympic torch, and the torch relay was organised by the Australian company, Maxxam International. The lighting control systems in the hotels and Olympic venues were manufactured by the Sydney company Dynalite, the smoke alarm systems by Xtralis, the artificial turf for hockey was made by Sports Technology International, and Argus provided mobile phone antennas for the main stadium. The promotion of the Sydney Games was intimately linked to the promotion of Australia by the Australian Tourism Commission (ATC). The ATC established a sophisticated strategy for using the Games to rebrand Australia as a young, vibrant country. Extensive efforts have been made to promote Australian expertise to London. In Beijing 2008, Austrade (the trade commission of the Australian federal government) hosted a dinner for the London organisers. Australian companies involved in London include Westfield, Lend-Lease, HOK Sport Architecture, Sinclair Knight Merz, Intelligent Risks, PTW Architects, Bligh Voller Nield, Cleanevent, and Denton Corker Marshall. The London Olympics are also seen as a platform for Australian companies to bid for future northern hemisphere projects, such as the Euro 2012 soccer tournament in Poland and the Ukraine, and the Winter Olympics in 2014

19

Figure 1.5 Constructing the main stadium. The first dramatic signs of the Olympic Park, as the stadium rises up next to the River Lea.

in Russia (*The Age* 30 August 2008). Behind the public face of the Games, with its star performers and golden moments, a whole globalised industry has developed.

Towards the end of 2006 the press had begun to pursue the issue of escalating funds. In November the London Mayor's office issued a press release complaining about distortions in the *Evening Standard*. In November the *Evening Standard* (21 November 2006) had claimed that 'the publicly-funded budget for the London Olympics was drawn up in an hour-long meeting between Ken Livingstone and Tessa Jowell in 2003'. The story was hotly denied by Mike Lee of LOCOG and the Mayor's office.[15] In 2007, though, the *Evening Standard* continued to pursue the issue of escalating costs with renewed vigour, culminating in a dramatic front page which proclaimed 'OLYMPICS BILL SOARS TO £10bn' (28 February 2007). Although unsourced, the paper had clear confidence in the figures. Simon Jenkins penned a trenchant attack 'Jowell and Coe have been duped by the biggest overselling scam in history' (*Guardian* 2 March 2007) to which Livingstone responded a week later (*Guardian* 9 March 2007), deriding inaccuracies and condemning the *Evening Standard*'s 'latest invention of a £10bn bill' as 'just false'. Unfortunately for Livingstone, though, just two days later the government confirmed that the costs had indeed risen to £9.3 billion. As the resultant public storm about rising costs gathered momentum, the competing tensions were caught most

2005	Sept	London Development Agency, landowner of the proposed site, commences compulsory purchase of businesses
		Olympic Delivery Authority formed and begins demolition work
	Dec	LOCOG Chief Executive (Paul Deighton) appointed
	Dec	ODA Chief Executive (David Higgins) appointed
2006	Mar	London Olympic Games Act (formally establishes ODA, provides legal sanctions against ticket touts and unlawful use of Olympic words, signs and symbols)
	Oct	Contract for main stadium awarded
	Oct	ODA Chair Jack Lemley resigns, warning of political interference and cost increases. His temporary replacement, Sir Roy McNulty, gives way in 2007 to John Armitt (from Network Rail)
	Nov	Aquatic Centre design, by Zaha Hadid, is unveiled
2007	15 Feb	*Evening Standard* front page: OLYMPICS BILL SOARS TO £10bn
	10 Mar	Government confirms that the costs have risen to £9.3bn
	Mar	Lloyds TSB become first London Olympic Sponsor (at national level).
	June	London Olympic logo launched, to a largely hostile response
	July	LDA hand control of park to ODA; 193 businesses, 425 residents and 35 traveller families have been relocated
	14 Nov	High-speed Eurostar line into St Pancras opens
2008	May	Construction of main stadium starts
	May	Boris Johnson defeats Ken Livingstone in London mayoral election
	July	Lend Lease, intended developer of Olympic Village, encounter funding problems requiring £95m from the contingency fund
	August	Beijing Olympics includes a 15-minute promotion of London in the Closing Ceremony. The presentation, featuring a London bus, David Beckham, Jimmy Page and Leona Lewis, is criticised in the British media
2009	23 Apr	IOC inspection team visits London, and say the project is on time and to budget
	13 May	Olympic Village cannot be built by private sector, and project requires extra government funding as well as £587m from contingency fund
	30 Oct	Recession will reduce value of wider Olympic economic dividend by £3bn, city analysts claim
	2 Nov	LOCOG stage series of events to publicise that there are 1,000 days to go
	11 Nov	Board of the Olympic Park Legacy Company are appointed
	18 Dec	80% of Londoners and 75% of UK in favour of Olympics according to attitudes survey
2010	Mar	Public Accounts Committee say building for the Games is on track, but unforeseen problems were putting pressure on contingency funds
	24 Mar	West Ham and Newham Council bid to use main stadium after Games
	31 Mar	Volunteer recruitment programme launched
	21 Apr	Former IOC President Juan Antonio Samaranch dies
	May	UK General Election: Labour Party defeated and Conservative coalition with Liberal Democrats forms new government
	19 May	Olympic mascots, Wenlock and Mandeville, are launched, to a mixed response
	18 Jun	Ceremonies will be organised by Stephen Daldry, with Danny Boyle artistic director of the Opening Ceremony
	9 Jul	120 world leaders may attend Games, IOC sources reveal. This has major additional security and accommodation implications
	20 Oct	Government's Comprehensive Spending Review: substantial cuts in public spending

Figure 1.6 Timeline of preparations for London Olympic Games since July 2005.

Source: various, including LOCOG website, media announcements from LOCOG, BOA, *Evening Standard*, *Guardian*, *The Times*, *Daily Telegraph* and Lee 2006.

effectively in the *Evening Standard* front page featuring three pictures of then Chancellor Gordon Brown, Culture Minister Tessa Jowell and Mayor Ken Livingstone, faces etched with anxiety as the behind-the-scenes manoeuvres over the budget continued.

A significant number of aspiring definers had begun competing to seize the agenda. LOCOG and the ODA sought to reassure fears and dampen speculation. Once the new official estimates were released on 10 March, LOCOG began subtly to distance itself from the controversy, by pointing out that the finances for construction were now a matter for the ODA. The government, which ideally speaks with one voice and sings from one hymn sheet, was, as pressure to reveal the new inflated budget grew, clearly arguing in private about where the money was to come from. The Treasury was digging its heels in over refund of VAT, the Department of Communities and Local Government was being lumbered with extra costs, and the DCMS was being forced to contemplate raiding the Lottery funds and incurring the wrath of the arts establishment.

The public sessions of parliamentary scrutineers such as the Commons Public Accounts Committee and the Commons Transport Select Committee made it harder to keep such machinations entirely secret. Professional organisations such as the Royal Institute of British Architects were involved in lobbying on behalf of their members' interests. The support offered by Mayor Ken Livingstone has been vocal and enthusiastic but, with no great personal record

Figure 1.7 The main stadium nears completion. With two years to go, the site reaches a peak level of employment and activity.

as a keen sports advocate, is also deeply pragmatic. Livingstone's own interest was in the regeneration and continuing development of London.

Later in the year, the *Daily Mail* criticised 'fat cat' salaries in the project, revealing that Lord Coe earned £285,000 as LOCOG Chair, and Chief Executive Paul Deighton, who it estimated had a personal fortune of more than £100 million, earned £536,000 in the previous year, including a £100,000 bonus (*Daily Mail* 10 September 2007). Fortunately for LOCOG, the row began to abate, as during 2008 the worldwide financial crisis and subsequent recession, triggered by toxic debt and the Lehman Brothers collapse, became a far bigger concern.

Better news for the organisers came in November 2007 with the opening of the new high-speed Eurostar line into St Pancras. Featuring a station on the Olympic site, the line was not established as an Olympic-linked project, but its successful opening helped boost IOC confidence that Olympic development was also on track.

Meanwhile, the ODA had been busy awarding contracts. By mid-2008, £400 million had been allocated to commission Carillion to build the broadcast and press centres. Edmund

Figure 1.8 The bridge to the Westfield 'Stratford City' shopping mall. The construction of this giant bridge reveals the strategic position of the Westfield mall, between the two Stratford stations and the Olympic Park.

23

Nuttall and Skanska were awarded four contracts each, worth a total of £302 million and £200 million respectively, while Dutch company VolkerWessels won three contracts worth £29 million. The Olympic project was also triggering linked projects, to the benefit of the construction industry, such as a £363 million improvement of the Northern Line, being carried out by Carillion and Balfour Beatty, and the £2 billion Stratford City shopping mall being built by Westfield.[16]

The ODA has had to grapple with a range of problems. Jack Lemley, the former ODA chair, left with a £388,000 payoff, just 11 months into his job, amid reports of clashes with staff. Decontaminating the land caused a 12-week delay to the timetable. Nine months was spent changing the design of the stadium and aquatics centre to bring their budgets down, although at £303 million, the aquatics centre is still more than triple its original budget. Declining property values prompted a projected shortfall of £400 million in the value of the Olympic Village, which forced the ODA to reduce the number of apartments from the planned 4,200 to around 3,000, the minimum needed to give every athlete a bed.[17]

CONCLUSION

At the Closing Ceremony of the 2008 Beijing Olympic Games in August the Olympic Flag was passed from the Mayor of Beijing to the Mayor of London, Boris Johnson, and London moved into the spotlight. The world financial crisis began to unfold, and the impact of incalculable levels of toxic debt forced governments around the world to allocate unprecedented sums to prop up the banking system. Although the recession clearly created additional problems for the London Games, it also had some positive aspects in presentational terms. The recession presented a scapegoat. Any further cost over-runs or cuts in the scope of plans could be blamed on the unpredicted financial crisis. In 2007 £10 billion appeared to the public a huge sum, but once the governments of the world had found it necessary to commit hundreds of times as much to bail out the banks, £10 billion seemed a rather trivial sum by comparison. The major negative impact was associated with private sector involvement in the Games. The last remaining hope that Lend Lease would fund the costs of constructing the Olympic Village collapsed, as did the original optimism regarding viable tenants for the media centres after the Games. The government had to intervene, allowing the contingency fund to be utilised.

Since then, however, the news has been largely good. The Olympic Park and its facilities are taking visible shape, and are still on time and to budget. The volunteer recruitment programme has been launched, the online ticketing system is registering people, and leaders have been recruited to direct the ceremonies. In 2010, the General Election resulted in the defeat of the Labour Party and establishment of a Conservative-led coalition with the Liberal Democratic Party. The coalition immediately implemented a programme of massive cuts in public expenditure, but of course it is largely too late for any significant sums to be saved by cutting the Olympic programme. The cuts to local authority expenditure and to sport budgets will inevitably have an impact on support for the legacy of the 2012 Games. However, if the economies of the world are emerging from recession, the London Olympic Games may be perfectly timed to contribute to a feel-good factor – possibly to the benefit of the current British government.

Miejsce na zasadzenie wlasnego jedzenia

WOULD YOU LIKE A SPACE
Nij khaddo utpadoner shothik sthan
TO GROW YOUR OWN FOOD?
Kendi Yiyeceklerinizi Yetiştirebilece iniz Bir Alan

An allotment is a small piece of local land where you can grow food for yourself and your family. It is also a place to relax and meet people.

Charlie Cobb

More allotments will be available after the Olympics. To take advantage of this opportunity you can put your name down for a plot. We are interested in your views on how these allotments could be designed. We invite you to give your ideas to us at the Manor Gardening Society

Open Day on 21st June from 1pm.

If you would like to join the
waiting list for a Legacy Park plot
please provide contact details:

_____

_____

_____

Thank you from all at
Manor Gardening Society
temporarily located at
Marsh Lane Fields, Off Marsh Lane, Leyton E15
www.lifeisland.org

The Manor Gardening Society is very grateful to Villiers Park Educational Trust for its support towards this survey

 Villiers Park Educational Trust

Figure 1.9 Allotment offer. Offered limited space on a section of the Olympic Park after the Games are over, the evicted and relocated Manor Gardens Society allotment holders attempt to gauge future demand.

FURTHER READING

Howell, D. (1990) *Made in Birmingham: The Memoirs of Denis Howell*, London: Queen Anne Press.

Lee, M. (2006) *The Race for the 2012 Olympics: The Inside Story of How London Won the Bid*, London: Virgin.

Poynter, G. and MacRury, I. (eds) (2009) *Olympic Cities: 2012 and the Remaking of London*, London: Ashgate.

Preuss, H. (2004) *The Economics of Staging the Olympic Games: A Comparison of the Games 1972–2008*, Cheltenham: Edward Elgar.

CHAPTER 2

THE IOC AND THE BIDDING PROCESS

A broad division exists between, on the one hand, those one might refer to as 'romantic idealists' – who believe that the Olympic Games can bring about greater internationalism, peace and fraternity, who refer to it as a movement, or a 'family', and treat Olympism as a quasi-religion or civil religion, and those on the other hand who are scathing critics of Olympism because they believe it encourages organisations and individuals – whom they see as corrupt chancers on the make to line their own pockets – inducing potential hosts to spend millions of dollars to bid and persuade just over a hundred people to vote for them, all amidst a prevailing lack of transparency. For the past 20 years the IOC has enjoyed a no-cost promotion strategy, constantly in the glare of the world's mass media – every year at least three hosts and another host to be decided are known about. In the odd years when there is not an Olympic Games taking place a decision will be made at an IOC Session or Congress about where either a Winter or a Summer Olympics will be held in seven years' time (see the Timeline, pp. xv–xvi).

This chapter examines: the nature of the IOC and its relationship to the other components of international sport; the political economy of the Olympic movement and the sports business; and the nature of the bidding process. It seeks to place London's Games, dealt with in the Chapter 1, in relation to the structure of the Olympic movement and the various institutions of international sport. It provides a schematic economic overview of the finances of the Olympic movement. And it analyses the peculiarly contradictory nature of the IOC in terms of its historical formation, its awkward adjustments to modernity and enterprise, and its extraordinary commercial success with the world's strongest brand. This chapter seeks to explore and explain the Olympic Games – and the IOC in particular – by positioning them in their social, cultural, economic and political contexts. The minutiae of the Olympics and the Olympic movement are dealt with in detail elsewhere (see for example Chappelet and Kubler-Mabbott 2008; Girginov and Parry 2005; Girginov 2010; Toohey and Veal 2007).

The chapter is in four parts. First, we consider the relationship of the IOC to other components of international sport, the nature of the IOC and its origins, and argue that it experienced a contradictory formation – having to adjust to both capitalist modernity and enterprise culture. In the past 25 years this involvement with more commercial stakeholders – sponsors and media corporations especially – has raised issues of 'governance' that will continue to influence the future of the IOC and the Olympic movement more generally. We seek to establish the kind of organisation that the IOC is, and how it is similar to and different from other sporting organisations – including how its members are chosen and how Olympic cities are chosen. We offer a balanced assessment of the pros and cons of the IOC.

Second, we look at the changing political economy of the Olympic Games. Some of this is covered in Chapter 3 – especially the 1980s and the relationships between Joao Havelange (President of FIFA), Horst Dassler (CEO of Adidas) and Juan Antonio Samaranch (President of the IOC) – but we will discuss the origins of the arrangements that have come to dominate the Olympics in the past three decades. We also consider the position of the Winter Olympic Games in this changing political economy.

Third, we discuss various issues confronting the IOC and how they have been dealt with – especially candidate cities and the bidding process, and relationships between National Olympic Committees (NOCs), International Federations (IFs) and individual members of the IOC. We offer consideration of the politics of IOC members, especially the presidents, many of whom seem to have been largely right-wing, with some fascist sympathisers. Avery Brundage (IOC President, 1952–1972) has been rightly criticised by many, mostly for his hard line on amateurism rather than his anti-communism, and this has made the others appear rather apolitical and saintly by comparison – but whether this is accurate needs exploring.

Fourth and finally, we consider some of the challenges confronting the IOC in the early twenty-first century – especially contemporary forms and cultures of cheating in sport that pose particular issues for the IOC – doping, violence (both psychological and physical) and corruption (including illegal gambling). This part therefore also offers a provisional assessment of the 'Rogge years'.

WHAT IS THE IOC?

The IOC was and remains an extraordinary association; not representative of nations, but with a membership that chooses its own members by the rules and within limits set by the organisation itself. The IOC remains a club based on the eighteenth-century aristocratic notions of membership associated with a gentlemen's club. This involves procedures such as the self-selection of members, the potential blackballing of applicants who wish to become members (that is, non-selection on the basis of objections by a few rather than by a majority), and clubbability (that is, new members have to fit in socially). In all these ways the cohesion of the group, club or association was forged. Occurring at the end of the nineteenth century 'The universalism and humanism of the concepts and ideology of de Coubertin and the Olympic movement . . . made the movement's interests and institution building appear compatible and convergent with broader processes of international institution building' (Roche 2000: 108). In many ways the IOC helped in the process of the invention of traditions, nation building and the imagining of communities that authors such as Anderson and Hobsbawm and Ranger have written about (see Chapter 6). The IOC, for example, was interested in associating itself with the League of Nations formed after the end of the First World War.

The organisation was not a disinterested party in the formation of nations, however. Hoberman (1995: 16ff.) suggests that the fact that the Scouting and the Olympic movements (in contrast with the Esperanto movement and the Red Cross) sought aristocratic affiliations and royal patronage indicates the degree to which they were ideologically interested in reconciling

28

social classes. In 1908 'European nobility made up 68 per cent of the membership of the IOC, a figure which had declined to 41 per cent by 1924' (Hoberman 1995: 16). He argues that during the 1930s the Olympic movement was essentially 'a right-wing internationalism effectively co-opted by the Nazis and their French and German sympathisers' (Hoberman 1995: 17).

There are currently 111 members (although at the time of writing 112 members are actually listed on the IOC website, but this includes former President Juan Antonio Samaranch who died in April 2010).[1] The IOC appoints its own members, and members represent the IOC in their countries, and are not their country's delegates in the IOC ('Members of the IOC represent and promote the interests of the IOC and of the Olympic movement in their countries and in the organisations of the Olympic movement in which they serve' – IOC 2004: 28). Of the current 111 members, 19 are women; 8 were elected 30 or more years ago; 12 have royal or aristocratic titles; 40 have participated in at least one Olympic Games; and 25 have won Olympic medals. The geographical distribution of the IOC membership reflects the European origins of the organisation: Europe 44%, Asia 20%, Africa 15%, America 15%, and Oceania 5%. There are also 28 'honorary members' of whom four are women and one 'honour' member (the former US Secretary of State, Henry Kissinger). Age limits have often been the subject of debates amongst IOC members. The average age in 1894 was just over 38 years, with the eldest member being 59 years old. The age limit was fixed at 72 years in 1966 and raised to 75 in 1975. By 1980 the average age of the 81 members was over 67 years, with the eldest member 94 years. The age limit was raised again to 80 in 1995, although the average age fell to nearly 62 years. From the 110th Session of the IOC in 1999 the age limit was reduced to 70 for all newly appointed members.

Since formation there have been just eight IOC presidents. Initially, Coubertin had sought to alternate the Presidency according to host city, but after the Paris Olympic Games in 1900 he

Name	Member	President	Country
Pierre de Coubertin	1894–1925	1896–1925	France
Ernest Callot	1894–1913		France
Demetrios Bikelas*	1894–1897	1894–1896	Greece
Alexander Butowsky	1894–1900		Russia
Viktor Balck	1894–1921		Sweden
William M. Sloane	1894–1925		USA
Jiri Guth-Jarkovsky	1894–1943		Bohemia
Arthur Russell, Lord Ampthill	1894–1898		UK
Charles Herbert	1894–1906		UK
Jose Benjamin Zubiaur	1894–1907		Argentina
Leonard Cuff	1894–1905		New Zealand
Comte Lucchesi Palli	1894–1895		Italy
Comte Maxime de Bousies	1894–1901		Belgium
Riccardo Carafa, Duke d'Andria	1894–1898		Italy

Figure 2.1 Members of the IOC in 1894.

*Sometimes rendered in English as Vikelas

Source: adapted from Guttmann 1984: 263; Toohey and Veal 2007.

was elected for a longer term and retained the Presidency until 1925. The latest rules recommend a maximum of eight years (two terms) of office, with the possibility of one extra term. Hence the present incumbent, in office since 2001, Jacques Rogge, will step down in 2013 – unless there is another rule change.

The IOC took its basic organisational shape during the inter-war period. The Executive Board of the IOC, originally founded in 1921, currently consists of the President, four Vice-Presidents and ten other members. All the members of the Executive Board are elected at an IOC Session, by secret ballot, by a majority of votes cast, for a four-year term. Among many responsibilities today, the IOC Executive Board oversees and approves the marketing policy developed and proposed by the IOC Marketing Commission at the IOC Session. The IOC has always been self-recruiting, and views members as diplomatic representatives of the Olympic movement in their home countries, rather than as representatives of their countries at the IOC. Meanwhile National Olympic Committees (NOCs) organise national teams for games events, and where hosts, take a leading role in organising events, although they are not formally represented on the IOC.

An Olympic Foundation is chaired by the IOC President (currently Jacques Rogge) whilst an IOC Olympic Museum in Lausanne, which former President Juan Antonio Samaranch established, acts as a universal repository of the written, visual and graphic memory of the Olympic Games. It cost $70 million to build but over 80% of the funds came from donors or sponsors. As the Olympic Games are a multi-sport event it also required an international level of organisation in the constituent sports. International Federations (IFs) that connected 'nationally powerful national level governing bodies of sport and permitted internationally standardised rules and regulations for international events to be developed, recognised and diffused' (Roche 2000: 109) were required. These networks began to emerge after 1896 but especially following the 1908 games held in London when the organisers – the British Olympic Committee (now the British Olympic Association) and the Amateur Athlete Association (AAA) – were accused of bias by the Americans. The International Amateur Athletic Federation (IAAF) was established the year after the Stockholm Olympics in 1913.

During the 1918–1939 period the IOC 'established itself as the primary authority and actor concerned with international sport, its games event became the preeminent sport event and

Name	Period	Country
Demetrios Vikelas	1894–1896	Greece
De Coubertin, Baron	1896–1925	France
Henri de Baillet-Latour, Count	1925–1942	France
J. Sigfrid Edstrom	1942–1952	Sweden
Avery Brundage	1952–1972	USA
Michael Morris, Lord Killanin	1972–1980	Ireland
Juan Antonio Samaranch, Marquess	1980–2001	Spain
Jacques Rogge, Count	2001–2013*	Belgium

Figure 2.2 Presidents of the IOC, 1894–2013.

* re-elected for a third four-year term, Rogge will have to stand down in 2013.

Source: adapted from Toohey and Veal, 2007: 49; Chappelet and Kubler-Mabbott 2008: 23.

its four-year calendar structured world sport' (Roche 2000: 109). Roche acknowledges that it also 'retained class-ist, sexist and racist attitudes from its late nineteenth century origins' (Roche 2000: 110). Roche asserts that, since the Second World War, the Olympic movement has 'on balance, been a significant force in the promotion of a genuine universalist humanistic ideology', showing a great deal of adaptation to 'pressures generated in its international political environment' (2000: 110–111).

The first version of the Olympic Charter appeared in 1908. The latest version was published at the beginning of 2010.[2] The charter sets out the 'fundamental principles and values of Olympism' and defines the 'rights and obligations of Olympic organisations' which are 'required to comply with the Olympic Charter'.

BOX 2.1 THE FUNDAMENTAL PRINCIPLES (AS STATED IN THE OLYMPIC CHARTER)

Pierre de Coubertin, on whose initiative the International Athletic Congress of Paris was held in June 1894, conceived modern Olympism. The International Olympic Committee (IOC) constituted itself on 23 June 1894. The Olympic Charter is the codification of the Fundamental Principles, Rules and Byelaws adopted by the IOC. It governs the organisation and operation of the Olympic movement and stipulates *the* conditions for the celebration of the Olympic Games. The following are Fundamental Principles of the Olympic movement, as stated in the Olympic Charter, in force as from 1 September 2004:

■ Olympism is a philosophy of life, exalting and combining in a balanced whole the qualities of body, will and mind.

■ The goal of Olympism is to place everywhere sport at the service of the harmonious development of man, with a view to encouraging the establishment of a peaceful society concerned with the preservation of human dignity.

■ The Olympic movement is the concerted, organized, universal permanent action, carried out under the supreme authority of the IOC, of all individuals and entities that are inspired by the values of Olympism. It covers the five continents. It reaches its peak with the bringing together of the world's athletes at the great sport festival, the Olympic Games. Its symbol is five interlaced rings.

■ The practice of sport is a human right. Every individual must have the possibility of practising sport, without discrimination of any kind and in the Olympic spirit, which requires mutual understanding with a spirit of friendship, solidarity and fair play. The organisation, administration and management of sport must be controlled by independent sports organisations.

■ Any form of discrimination with regard to a country or person on grounds of race, religion, politics, gender or otherwise is incompatible with belonging to the Olympic Movement.

■ Belonging to the Olympic movement requires compliance with the Olympic Charter and recognition by the IOC.

(IOC 2009: 44)

Olympism is the 'philosophy' and movement devised by Coubertin. It refers to 'a philosophy of life, exalting and combining in a balanced whole the qualities of body, will and mind'. It attempts to blend 'sport with culture and education' and promote a way of life based on 'the joy found in effort, the educational value of good example and respect for universal fundamental ethical principles'. Such a combination of humanistic ideals with the celebration of physical activity was unusual in the Western philosophical tradition until the English public school developed athleticism. It also has the implication that since the Olympic movement has a *moral* stance based on its ideals/standards, it is open to criticism when it deviates from its own standards. As sport historian and Olympic scholar Bruce Kidd (2010: 158) writes more generally, 'the moral claims of sport legitimize it as a site of struggle'. This is very true of the Olympic movement, Olympism and the International Olympic Committee (IOC).

The Olympic movement is unique in sport, comprising a philosophy and a *movement* that encompasses organisations, athletes and other persons who agree to be guided by the Olympic Charter. The criterion for membership is recognition by the IOC. 'The goal of the Olympic movement is to contribute to building a peaceful and better world by educating youth through sport practised in accordance with Olympism and its values'. The Olympic movement therefore seeks to transcend sport and contribute to world peace and human rights:

> The practice of sport is a human right. Every individual must have the possibility of practising sport without discrimination of any kind and in the Olympic spirit, which requires mutual understanding with a spirit of friendship, solidarity and fair play.
>
> (IOC 2004: 9)

The Olympic Games involves around 36 different sports: 26–28 in the Summer Games and 7–8 in the Winter Games. The IOC, comprising up to 115 members, sits in the middle of a complex network or system. On one side there are the International Federations (IFs) of individual sports, representing about 200 national governing bodies. On the other there are another 200 or so National Olympic Committees (NOCs). Formal negotiations between the IFs and the NOCs and the IOC take place through bilateral meetings. IOC members are just that – members of the IOC; they are not representatives or delegates of a particular sport or country *to* the IOC.

Cultural non-governmental organisations (NGOs) first developed in the last third of the nineteenth century. The international cultural NGOs that developed then were fragile international networks and associations. As Roche (2000: 97) remarks, the creation of specialised governing bodies or International Federations for different sports occurred 'in tandem with the development in the 1890s of a generalist and pluralist international sport movement, namely the Olympic movement, led by Coubertin and the IOC and oriented to the promotion of its sport ideology and the development of its multi-sport games event'. In the period between the two world wars (1918–1939) the Olympic 'model' was important in generating alternative visions of international sport ideology, multi-sport movements and events. These included the Workers' Olympics, Women's Olympics and the British Empire Games (since 1978 called the 'Commonwealth Games').

Many IFs allied with the Olympic movement and organised world championships within the Olympic Games event. The Fédération Internationale de Football Association (FIFA), formed in 1904 in Paris, helped the Olympic Games organisers (the Olympic Games host NOC and the host city) to stage international football world championships in each Olympic Games until the 1920s. Conflicts between the size and professionalism of the sport led to FIFA's decision to stage its own 'world cup' from 1930, 'intermediate to the Olympic four-year cycle' (Roche 2000: 97).

Unlike the international expositions from which the Olympic Games event had emerged, the processes of formalisation, rationalisation and bureaucratisation occurred much more rapidly. Rituals also became a feature of Olympic events during the inter-war period. The main stadium, according to Roche,

> effectively becomes 'diplomatic territory' and a de facto 'sacred site' for the duration of the games. The stadium contains the Olympic flame, the Olympic flag, the flags of the other nations and . . . no advertising or commercial imagery to detract from the impact of the Olympic symbols.
>
> (Roche 2000: 98)

As we noted above, the IOC has only had eight presidents since its inception, and four of them account for 90 years in office. Most have come from small European countries (Brundage is the exceptional non-European). Five of the eight have belonged to nobility, although Samaranch and Rogge received their titles after taking up office. In an IOC handbook produced for sponsors of the Olympic Games in the 1990s the many different forms of address for the then 89 IOC members were listed. Indicative of the unrepresentative nature of the IOC membership, these included: 'Monsieur le President / Dear Mr President' (Samaranch), 'Dear General', 'Dear Colonel', 'Your Excellency', 'Professeur', 'Your Royal Highness', 'Your Serene Highness', 'Altesse', 'Monseigneur', as well as 'Dear Mr', 'Madame', and one 'Dear Ms' (Anita Defrantz, former Olympic athlete and IOC Executive Board member).

Founded by Coubertin in 1894, the IOC is the 'supreme authority' of the Olympic movement with the mission: 'To promote Olympism throughout the world and to lead the Olympic movement'. With its headquarters in Lausanne, Switzerland, the IOC as an organisation has expanded considerably since the 1980s to more than 400 staff (Chappelet and Kubler-Mabbott 2008: 27–34). The IOC benefits from the low taxation regulations in Switzerland which enable it to keep more of its income than it would in any comparable country. (The headquarters of FIFA and UEFA are also in Switzerland for similar reasons.) The IOC has adopted several roles relating to various aspects of sport: ethics in sport, the education of youth through sport, encouraging the spirit of fair play, encouraging/supporting sport and sports competitions, the promotion of women in sport, the fight against doping in sport, protecting the health of athletes, placing sport at the service of humanity to promote peace, ending any form of discrimination affecting the Olympic movement, promoting the social and professional future of athletes, sport for all, sustainable development in sport, and a positive legacy for host cities and countries, blending sport with culture and education, and supporting the International Olympic Academy (IOA) in Olympia, Greece and other Olympic education projects. A year after Coubertin's death (1938) and following his own wish, his heart was placed inside a commemorative stele in Olympia. This rekindled the idea for the establishment of a centre for the Olympic Games in Olympia, and the International Olympic Academy was officially inaugurated on 14 June 1961. Today, some 40 different events take place every year on the premises of the IOA in Olympia.[3]

33

To oversee these roles the IOC operates several 'Commissions' (Toohey and Veal 2007: 54), including the Athletes' Commission (which represents the views of athletes to the IOC, and is composed of retired and active Olympic athletes), the Culture and Olympic Education Commission (which seeks the development of links between sport and culture and education, works with the NOCs, and is responsible for the International Olympic Academy), and the Coordination Commissions for the Olympic Games (which provides the link between the IOC and host city OCOGs, IFs and NOCs).

The Ethics Commission, which establishes ethical rules for IOC and Olympic activities, including a 'Code of Ethics', was established in 1999 following corruption allegations. In addition, the Finance Commission oversees accounting and finance of the IOC, the International Relations Commission promotes relationships between the Olympic movement and governments and public authorities, and the Marketing Commission advises the IOC on sources of 'financing and revenue' as well as on marketing. The Medical Commission assisted in the implementation of the Olympic Medical Code regarding the policing of prohibited drug use, a Nominations Commission organises the nomination of new IOC members, and the Olympic Programme Commission reviews the programme of sports, disciplines, events, and number of athletes, in each Olympic sport. The Olympic Solidarity Commission distributes IOC funds to NOCs, particularly those in less wealthy countries, the Sport and Environment Commission is concerned with promoting a 'green Games', whilst the Sport For All Commission seeks the promotion of general sport participation, adopting the European campaign phrase 'Sport for All'. The TV Rights and New Media Commission is responsible for the overall IOC strategy for future broadcast rights negotiations, the Women and Sport Commission focuses on women's involvement in the Olympics, and the Olympic Games Study Commission studies the 'current scale and cost of staging the Olympic Games' (Toohey and Veal 2007: 54).

THE POLITICAL ECONOMY OF THE IOC

There have been three main phases in the development of the Olympic Games according to Alan Tomlinson (2005a: 60):

1   1896–1928: 'a grand socio-political project with a modest economic profile';
2   1932–1984: 'a markedly political intensification of the event at the heart of international political developments';
3   1984 onward: 'fuelled by the global reach of capital . . . in the international economy of a global culture'.

It is this last phase that we focus on in this chapter, when funding of the Olympics and the Olympic movement have derived mainly from the sale of broadcasting rights and worldwide exclusive sponsorship arrangements.

Over the course of the nearly 120 years since the IOC was formed various symbols and ceremonial features have been developed. These include the five rings symbol (the Olympic Symbol), arguably the most widely recognised logo in the world, which dates from 1913. These rings may represent the five continents, but they have no ancient Olympic Games connection. The Olympic Flag was created in 1914 and first used at Antwerp in 1920. There is some speculation about how the flag, generally handed from host city to host city, got from Berlin in 1936 to London in 1948.

The Olympic Motto – *citius, altius, fortius* (faster, higher, stronger) – was derived from 1886 and the credo of Pierre Didon, a Dominican priest whom Coubertin knew. The Olympic Anthem derives from a Greek poem: 'Ancient, eternal and immortal spirit', put to music by Spyros Samaras. First performed in 1896, it was only officially adopted in 1958. Olympic emblems and mascots (since 1972) are designed for each Games. The Olympic flame, torch and relay, whilst appearing to have great lineage, only dates from Amsterdam, 1928. From 1936, the flame was lit at Olympia from 'the sun's rays'. The torch relay to the host city became a major event but, following 2008, it is unlikely it will follow such an international route. The Olympic flame burns throughout the Games. Medal ceremonies in their current format were introduced in 1932 at the Summer Games in Los Angeles and Winter Games in Lake Placid. These involved medals awarded at ceremonies 'on site' at the events and the use of the three-level podium. Finally, the Olympic Order mimics national honours systems and is for individuals who have either achieved remarkable merit in the sporting world, or rendered outstanding service to the Olympic movement.

In the past 25 years, protecting the 'brand' and image of these 'properties' has become of paramount importance. As the Olympic Charter states:

> The Olympic Games are the exclusive property of the IOC, which owns all rights relating thereto, in particular, and without limitation the rights relating to their: organisation, exploitation, broadcasting, recording, representation, reproduction, access and dissemination, in any form and by any means or mechanism whatsoever, whether now existing or developed in the future.

Hence the symbol, flag, motto, anthem, identifications (including but not limited to 'Olympic Games' and 'Games of the Olympiad'), designations, and emblems, flame and torches are collectively or individually referred to as 'Olympic properties'. All rights to any and all Olympic properties, as well as all rights to the use thereof, belong exclusively to the IOC, including but not limited to the use for any profit-making, commercial or advertising purposes. These rights are protected by law, particularly in Olympic Games host countries.

In addition to broadcasting partnerships the IOC manages the TOP (The Olympic Partner) worldwide sponsorship programme and the IOC official supplier and licensing programme. Since 1985, when the TOP programme started, the financial health of the IOC has been secured by the first two sources – television rights payments and global sponsorship deals. As an article in *The Economist* put it, ahead of the Atlanta Summer Olympics in 1996, 'The zillion dollar games' have developed because 'the power of corporate hype linked with global television is a marvellous machine for promoting sports'. Television rights account for slightly less than 50% of IOC revenue and it is likely that television income will continue to increase. Television income for the 2010 and 2012 Games is already assured at $3.8 billion, an increase of 40% on the $2.6 billion the IOC received for the 2006 and 2008 Games. At the time of writing, negotiations are being conducted for the 2014 and 2016 events, and with such large viewing figures from Beijing the fees are likely to increase substantially, irrespective of the location of the Games.

The IOC refers to its financial operations in terms of an 'Olympic quadrennium' – a four-year period (from 1 January – 31 December). The latest one for which accounts have been made available (2001–2004) generated a total of more than $4 billion in revenue. The IOC distributes approximately 92% of Olympic marketing revenue to organisations throughout the Olympic movement to support the staging of the Olympic Games and to promote the worldwide development of sport, and it retains the rest to cover the operational and administrative costs of governing the Olympic movement. The IOC provides TOP programme contributions and Olympic broadcast revenue to the OCOGs to support the staging of the Olympic Games and Olympic Winter Games. Long-term broadcast and sponsorship programmes enable the IOC to provide the majority of the OCOG's operational budget well in advance of the Games, with revenues effectively guaranteed prior to the selection of the host city. The two OCOGs of each Olympic quadrennium share approximately 50% of TOP programme revenue and value-in-kind contributions, with approximately 30% provided to the Summer OCOG and 20% provided to the Winter OCOG. During the 2001–2004 Olympic quadrennium, for example, the Salt Lake 2002 Organising Committee received $443 million in broadcast revenue from the IOC, and the Athens 2004 Organising Committee received $732 million. The OCOGs in turn generate substantial revenue from the domestic marketing programmes that they manage within their host country, including domestic sponsorship, ticketing and licensing. NOCs – of which there are over 200 – receive financial support for the training and development of Olympic teams and Olympic athletes. The IOC distributes TOP programme revenue to each of the NOCs throughout the world. The IOC provided approximately $318 million to NOCs for the 2001–2004 quadrennium.

Although there appear to have been many positive developments since the Los Angeles Olympics many academics at the time (see the contributors to Tomlinson and Whannel 1984) and since have been critical of the increasing commercialisation of the Games and the likely impact this has had on the event. Portrayed as 'gloom merchants' and 'naysayers' by those involved with the Olympics and associated sports federations, these criticisms are not simply voiced by people who want to put an end to the Olympics. With the increasing involvement of powerful global brands as Olympic sponsors has come attendant commercial rights legislation – to provide exclusivity to their association with the Olympic symbols (the interlocked rings, the name of the Games, etc.) and to avoid 'ambush marketing' which the corporations pay millions of dollars to obtain. Yet this is seen as overly restrictive by smaller businesses and organisations. The Olympic Games also provide a major attraction to sponsors at a national level and thus drain resources away from other non-Olympic sports and cultural activities during the build-up to the event. Criticisms of the IOC as an organisation have also had some impact on its practices.

THE BIDDING PROCESS AND HOST CITY SELECTION

> In this city, you were either working for the Olympics, or you were dreading them – there was no middle ground.
>
> (Manuel Vázquez Montalbán, *An Olympic Death*, 2004 [1991]: 34)

Following the Salt Lake City bid scandal and subsequent reforms in the late 1990s, technically the procedure for bidding and selecting an Olympic host city now appears quite straightforward. If more than one city within a country wishes to bid to host the Games, the country's

NOC selects one. Cities submit bids to the IOC eight–nine years in advance of the Games. An Evaluation Commission (EC) is appointed that reports to the IOC on the bidding cities and progress (only EC members can visit bid cities). The IOC selects a successful bidder seven years in advance of the Games. So in 2013 the IOC will vote on the Summer Games of 2020, and in 2015 it will vote on the Winter Games of 2022, etc.

Bids must provide information on the following topics: motivation, overall concept and public opinion, political support, finance, venues and programme, accommodation (athlete/media villages, hotel accommodation for IOC members, etc.), transport, security, and other general conditions (demographics, environment, climate) and experience of running large-scale (if not mega-) events. In addition, a cultural programme is a requirement of each Games to help 'promote harmonious relations, mutual understanding and friendship among the participants and others attending the Olympic Games' (Olympic Charter). The 'Host City Contract' – between the IOC, the host city and the NOC – is vitally important. All responsibilities and liabilities are vested in hosts, underpinned by stringent 'Rules of Conduct'.[4]

As we have seen, the IOC remains a private organisation, which only accepts invited members. The voting membership of the IOC currently consists of slightly more than 110 people, including the President Jacques Rogge, but fewer than 20 of these are women or active athletes. The IOC contains several members of royal families and corporate leaders and people holding an executive or senior leadership position within an IF or a NOC. It thus remains subject to accusations of lack of transparency whilst it claims to be a movement and a 'family' based on a philosophy beyond politics. Alongside the myths and ideology of Olympism – with elements such as the creed and the motto borrowed from Christianity (Catholicism and Protestantism) – it is not surprising that quasi-religious claims are often made, such as upholding the 'spirit' of the Games. On the other hand critics prefer to portray the Olympics nowadays as an 'industry', a 'machine' and even a 'disease' that creates a blight on the cities and their populations that act as its hosts. These discursive differences manifest themselves in the politics of hosting – and especially in the public relations wars, to which we now turn.

The costs of preparing a hosting bid – let alone staging an Olympic Games – are considerable (Toohey and Veal 2007: 131–132, after Preuss 2004). Nonetheless Olympic economist Holger Preuss (2004: 275) calculates that every Summer Games since 1972 has made a surplus: 'When investments are eliminated from the final balance sheets of the OCOGs and operational expenditures are set against OCOG revenues, it can be stated that all the OCOGs under review [1972–2008] succeeded in making a financial profit'. He operates with a 'decision model' that differentiates between 'Games-related and non-Games-related costs for facilities used during the Olympics'. On that basis, he argues 'an OCOG *should* only have to cover the costs for temporary facilities, overlay and rent' (Preuss 2004: 275, emphasis added). He can only do this by discounting as an Olympic cost many substantial infrastructure projects that have taken place at the same time as or preceding an Olympics – such as a refurbished airport, transport links and other forms of urban redevelopment. This separation of operational from capital investment costs associated with the Olympic Games results from a conventional economist's approach to modelling. As Toohey and Veal state:

> The arguments concerning apportionment of investment costs can also be raised in relation to sporting venues, since they also will continue to be used for other sporting

events and by local citizens long after the Olympic Games are over. Thus the overall capital costs of sporting infrastructure investments should *ideally* be excluded when estimating the cost of running an Olympic Games event.

(Toohey and Veal 2007: 133, emphasis added)

In this way the $2.2 billion deficit for Montreal is transformed into a $0.64 billion surplus (Preuss 2004: 277). This economic approach makes two further important assumptions: (1) the venues will be used and (2) local citizens will use them. This is 'ideal type' modelling. But what about real-world opportunities, costs and impacts?

Mega-events such as the Olympic Games provide multiple meanings for different groups of people – as they happen, when they have taken place and, perhaps especially, as they are being bid for. Hence we know that advocates of hosting the Olympics will deploy a range of discursive strategies to win over public opinion. The main issues around which the hosting of the Olympics has been debated involve the burden of the costs and the distribution of the benefits. Research points to the uneven impacts of the Olympics. Despite much media acclamation, and the accolade 'the best games ever' being proclaimed at the closing ceremony by the outgoing IOC President Juan Antonio Samaranch, the 2000 Olympics in Sydney generated substantial negative impacts on local residents and the environment – giving evidence to the claim that there is potential for conflict between economic and social benefits realised from hosting sports events. Since the late 1970s (and the Montreal Olympics especially) a major concern in considerations of the Olympics has been this gap between the forecast and the actual impacts on the economy, society and culture. That there is likely to be such a gap is now fairly predictable. Pro-hosting advocates tend to gather and project optimistic estimates, while anti-hosting groups articulate concerns. More generally there has been an overestimation of the benefits and an underestimation of the costs of mega-events.

The positive achievements claimed by Games boosters include increased employment, a boost for tourism, opportunities for civil engagement – through volunteering (unpaid work) – and emulation in terms of increased active involvement in physical activity. In addition there is a 'trickle-down' assumption that suggests that industries and other parts of the host city's nation will benefit from the economic upturn and demand for goods and services stimulated by the hosting of the Olympics. Certainly recent past and selected future Olympic hosts have made these arguments. One of the main problems regarding the assessment of the costs and benefits of mega-events relates to the quality of data obtained from impact analyses. Economic impact studies often claim to show that the investment of public money is worthwhile in the light of the economic activity generated by having professional sports teams or mega-events in cities. Yet here much depends on predictions of expenditure by sports-related tourism. Research shows that many positive studies have often been methodologically flawed and that the real economic benefit of such visitor spending is often well below that specified. According to the European Tour Operators Association (*Olympics and Tourism: Update on Olympics Report 2006*), the Olympic Games are 'an abnormality that is profoundly disruptive' of normal patterns of tourism. Another measure of economic impact – on the creation of new jobs in the local economy – has often been politically driven to justify the expenditure on new facilities, and hence the results are equally questionable.

With respect to social regeneration it has been noted that there is an absence of systematic and robust empirical evidence about the social impacts of sports-related projects. Some research suggests that there may be positive impacts from greater community visibility, enhanced community image, the stimulation of other economic development and increases in 'psychic income' – collective morale, pride and confidence. Most commentators appear to agree that there will be a positive outcome with respect to health promotion, crime reduction, education and employment and general 'social inclusion' but without actually having the evidence to support the view. The problem is that there have not been many research projects carried out into this, nor have the methodologies needed to investigate them been adequately developed yet.

Since the early 1990s, when investigative reporting by journalists and social researchers uncovered details of corruption in the Olympic movement, and such news began to damage the reputation of the IOC, the organisation and OCOGs have engaged public relations (PR) companies and spin doctors to assist in managing media messages and the global and local image of the Olympics. News and image management, spin doctoring and PR have become key features in any major public policy development in the UK and throughout the rest of the world.

Clearly the mass media are centrally important in discussing PR 'wars'. Are the media 'boosters' or 'sceptics'? It depends. The private sector media – in the UK the newspaper press and independent TV for example – could be critical if it suited their interests. The public sector – especially the BBC in the UK – has tended to help to sell the 2012 bid and the associated hosting to an uncertain public. The BBC provided saturation coverage of the 2008 Beijing Olympics, sending over 440 journalists and reporters – an unprecedented number. BBC sports reporting can sometimes be accused of adoration that leans towards idolatry of professional and elite athletes. This in turn creates an expectant audience. Irrespective of occasional critical comments and blogs by journalists, the BBC is and will remain a major booster for the London Games. Contradictory opinion poll findings after the Beijing Games about public confidence in the LOCOG 2012 team, however, suggest that a considerable number of Britons remain to be convinced that the 2012 Games will be a success. Some populations, of course, are resistant to the allure of the Games. In September 2008, some 51% of Norwegians were reported as being against giving state guarantees of 15–20 billion kroner ($4–5 billion) for Tromso to host the 2018 Winter Olympic Games. A month later the city had withdrawn from the bidding process altogether. The IOC expects to see evidence of public support in any country that applies to host the Olympics.

Just as reputation and symbolic power have become increasingly valuable resources for elected politicians, so too are they vital for international sports organisations and IFs. In this environment 'crisis communications', in response to bad publicity during 'spin wars', have become part of the PR role. It has been argued that PR's job is essentially to secure or 'manufacture' the consent of the public, which covers both active support and passive acquiescence for economic and social policies and developments. More broadly, Miller and Dinan (2007: 13) argue that PR's role has become 'to position private interests as being the same as public interests' and in so doing undermine the meaning of a public interest separate from that of private corporations. In this respect PR is concerned with bringing other private businesses and civic leaders 'onside' as well as members of the general public. As it has developed, a PR company's task is often to predict and thus ward off damaging attacks, especially in debates in the public sphere about urban development, such as the hosting of the Olympics. Hence an advertisement in the *Guardian* from the London 2012

Olympic Delivery Authority (ODA) asked for 'Community Relations Executives' who would act as:

> the main link between the ODA project teams, contractors and local residents with special regard to the construction impact and have the ability to win the trust of sceptical local audiences through strong interpersonal, influencing and communi-cations skills.
>
> (*Guardian* 24 March 2007, Work: 12)

Events like the Olympic Games, the Football World Cup and other sports mega-events act as sociocultural reference points, and reveal both the appeal and elusiveness of sport. In the age of global television, moreover, the capacity of major sports events to shape and project images of the host city or nation, both domestically and globally, makes them a highly attractive instrument for political and economic elites. It is in this context that the pursuit of hosting sports mega-events has become an increasingly popular strategy of governments, corporations and civic 'boosters' worldwide, who argue that major economic, developmental, political and sociocultural benefits will flow from them, easily justifying the costs and risks involved (Horne and Manzenreiter 2006). Numerous studies fuel the popular belief that sport has a positive impact on the local community and the regional economy. Sport has been seen as a generator of national and local economic and social development. Economically it has been viewed as an industry around which cities can devise urban regeneration strategies. Socially it has been viewed as a tool for the development of urban communities, and the reduction of social exclusion and crime. Hence the increased participation in the 'Olympic City Bidding Game' (Roche 2000: 150) over the past 25 years (see Figure 2.3).

Compared with this conventional – or dominant – view of the Olympic Games and the Olympic movement here are a series of conclusions derived from a recent book and documentary film about the 2010 Vancouver Winter Olympics (Shaw 2008; Schmidt 2007). The Olympics can be seen as a tool used by business corporations and governments (local, regional and sometimes national) to develop areas of cities or the countryside. They permit corporate land grabs by developers. Five major construction projects took place in association with the 2010 Winter Games: the building of the Canada Line (formerly known as the RAV – Richmond Airport–Vancouver Line) connecting the airport and downtown Vancouver; the athletes' village; a convention centre; developments in the Callaghan Valley west of Whistler (the main skiing area where the Olympic snowsport events would take place); and the building of an extension to the 'Sea to Sky Highway' through Eagleridge Bluffs, in West Vancouver, to enable shorter road times between Vancouver and Whistler. The view of one of the contributors to the film was that it was a disaster for any city on the planet to host the Olympics. Host city populations face increased taxes to pay for the 'party'. The poor and the homeless face criminalisation and/or eviction as downtown areas are gentrified – improved to appeal to more affluent visitors or full-time residents. The hosting of such a mega-event skews all other economic and social priorities and means the loss of the opportunity to do other things with public resources spent on the Games. The IOC markets sport as a product, pays no taxes, and demands full compliance with its exacting terms and conditions, including governmental guarantees about meeting financial shortfalls. The end results are 'fat-cat' projects and media spectacles benefiting mostly the corporations that sponsor the Games, the property developers

40

Summer Games

Year	Host	Other bidders
1976	Montreal	Los Angeles, Moscow
1980	Moscow	Los Angeles
1984	Los Angeles	
1988	Seoul	Nagoya
1992	Barcelona	Amsterdam, Belgrade, Birmingham, Brisbane, Paris
1996	Atlanta	Athens, Belgrade, Manchester, Melbourne, Toronto
2000	Sydney	Beijing, Berlin, Istanbul, Manchester
2004	Athens	Buenos Aires, Cape Town, Istanbul, Lille, Rio de Janeiro, Rome, San Juan, Seville, Stockholm, St Petersburg
2008	Beijing	Istanbul, Osaka, Paris, Toronto
2012	London	Madrid, Moscow, New York, Paris
2016	Rio de Janeiro	Chicago, Madrid, Tokyo

Winter Games

Year	Host	Other bidders
1976	Innsbruck	Denver*, Sion, Tampere/Are, Vancouver
1980	Lake Placid	Vancouver-Garibaldi**
1984	Sarajevo	Sapporo, Falun-Goteborg
1988	Calgary	Falun, Cortina d'Ampezzo
1992	Albertville	Anchorage, Berchtesgaden, Cortina d'Ampezzo, Lillehammer, Falun, Sofia
1994	Lillehammer	Anchorage, Oestersunde/Are, Sofia
1998	Nagano	Aoste, Jacca, Oestersunde, Salt Lake City
2002	Salt Lake City	Oestersunde, Quebec City, Sion
2006	Torino	Helsinki, Klagenfurt, Poprad-Tatry, Sion, Zakopane
2010	Vancouver–Whistler	PyeongChang, Salzburg
2014	Soichi	PyeongChang, Salzburg
2018	To be decided at the IOC Session in Durban, July 2011	Annecy, Munich, PyeongChang

Figure 2.3 'The Olympic City Bidding Game', 1976–2018.

*Awarded to Denver but rejected following citizens' plebiscite. ** Withdrew before final vote.

Source: adapted and updated from Roche 2000: 150–157.

that receive public subsidies, and the IOC – which secures millions of dollars from television corporations and global sponsors.

Similar criticisms have been made about the proposed 2016 Summer Olympics to be staged in Rio de Janeiro in Brazil. In October 2009 when Rio was awarded the right to host the 2016 Summer Olympics, in the face of apparently strong competition from a Chicago bid that had been enthusiastically endorsed by US President Barack Obama, it was heralded by the Brazilian President Lula as a sign that his country had moved from being a second-class to a first-class nation. The decision to stage an Olympic Games in South America for the first time was, according to Dick Pound, a Canadian IOC member, 'not an anti-America thing or

41

an anti-Obama thing. It's a sports competition, not true politics' (*Sunday Morning Post*, 4 October 2009). But the opportunities that the successful bid has created for specific construction industry corporations in Brazil to develop parts of the Rio infrastructure, and the impacts this may have upon local communities, will be significant features of development in South America's biggest country over the next five years (Gaffney 2010; Darnell 2010).

Clearly when considering the politics of the Olympic Games the role and impartiality of the researcher is called into question – as Montalbán suggests in the quotation on p. 36 (he was originally writing just before Barcelona hosted the Olympics in 1992), researchers may find that there is no middle ground. Amongst the questions that this section will attempt to answer are: Why do governments and cities compete for the right to host major international sporting events such as the Olympics? What are the commercial underpinnings of hosting the Olympic Games? What can we learn from recent 'bidding wars' about the contemporary politics of the Olympics? How do Olympic 'boosters' and 'sceptics' portray the 'legacies', economic and otherwise, that are proclaimed for the Games?

The attraction of hosting an Olympic Games (or another sports mega-event) is possibly greater today than ever before. It is widely assumed that hosting an Olympic Games represents an extraordinary economic opportunity for host cities (and nations), justifying the investment of large sums of public money. Yet this view has only developed in the past 30 years. Despite Preuss's economic modelling, hosting the 1976 Summer Olympics resulted in huge losses and debts for the city of Montreal. The debt incurred on the interest for the loans to build what turned out to be largely 'white elephant' sports infrastructure was only finally paid off in November 2006 – costing the Montreal taxpayers well over CA\$2 billion in capital and interest costs, without anything like commensurate benefits. Rather than experiencing a post-Olympic boom the economy of Montreal in the mid-1970s went into a steep decline that would last for almost two decades. No wonder then that when the Los Angeles Olympics took place in 1984 there had been no other city seriously bidding to host the event (Whitson and Horne 2006).

Today, established cities in advanced capitalist societies and cities in developing economies alike weigh up the possibility of hosting the Olympic Games. At the time of writing the hosts for the next three Olympic Games (2012, 2014 and 2016) are known and three cities are about to submit 'bid books' for the Winter Games in 2018. At any one time then, at least three cities are anticipating hosting an Olympics and several others are waiting to discover if it will be their turn. The change in the allure of hosting the Olympics has come about partly because of the success that the LA Games appeared to be – in terms of making a substantial financial surplus or profit of over \$200 million, laying a solid economic foundation for a support system for athletes in the USA, and putting on a television spectacular involving many of the world's athletes. The attraction of hosting has also come about because of changes that the IOC has made to the process of selecting cities following investigative journalists' revelations of insider corruption in the 1980s and 1990s (see Simson and Jennings 1992; www.transparency insport.org).

Two examples illustrate this change in the seriousness with which bidding is treated and the attraction of the Olympics. First, since 2000 the IOC has established an Evaluation Commission (EC) to visit candidate cities bidding to host the Olympic and Paralympic Games – both events now taken as part of the Olympic host 'package'. Composed of representatives from the

42

Olympic movement as well as a number of advisers, the EC analyses the candidature files of cities bidding to host the Olympics after they have been submitted to the IOC. It then makes on-site inspections and publishes an appraisal for IOC members before they meet to elect a host city. An illustration of the importance that governments and politicians make of hosting the Olympics is the increased involvement of leading politicians in the process. Tony Blair, then Prime Minister, although scheduled to host a summit of the G8 leading economic nations in Gleneagles in Scotland, flew to Singapore in July 2005 in order to meet IOC members and representatives ahead of the crucial vote deciding which city would host the 2012 Olympics. When the IOC voted in 2007 at its session in Guatemala that the Winter Olympic Games of 2014 would take place in the Russian resort of Sochi, the then Russian President, Vladimir Putin, performed a similar role. That Putin (by then Prime Minister of Russia) held off attending the decision-making about who hosted the 2018 FIFA Football World Cup in December 2010 can now be read as an equally political show of confidence.

The major inducement to engage in Olympic hosting now, as opposed to in the 1980s, is of course financial. The sponsorship and television rights money that the IOC has negotiated covers most of the *operating* costs of the Olympic Games – $2–2.5 billion for the Summer 'edition'. The Games attract vast television audiences – the 2008 Beijing Olympics, for example, drew an estimated cumulative global television audience of 4.7 billion over the 17 days of competition, according to market research firm Nielsen. Such estimated audience figures have to be treated with caution, but Nielson's estimate surpassed the 3.9 billion viewers for the Athens Games in 2004 and the 3.6 billion who watched the 2000 event in Sydney. The 2008 Beijing Olympics was also the most-viewed event in US television history. According to Nielson, 211 million viewers watched the first 16 days of Olympic coverage on the US network NBC.

Large television audiences have meant that television corporations and broadcasting unions have been prepared to pay increasing sums of money for exclusive coverage of the Olympics to the IOC, which has helped them to offset the operational costs of the games. Hence in future, alongside cities such as Paris, London, New York, Chicago, Madrid and Beijing, it is likely that smaller cities, for example Copenhagen (Denmark), and cities in the 'global South', such as Durban (South Africa) and possibly Delhi (India), will consider bidding for the Summer Olympic Games in 2020 and beyond. Acting as host to the IOC's Congress (Copenhagen 2009, Durban 2011) or one of the 'lower-order' sports mega-events (Delhi hosted the Commonwealth Games in 2010) is considered a way of leveraging support for a subsequent Olympics bid. Because of the very late completion of venues and athletes' accommodation which resulted in negative publicity, Delhi may have created more obstacles for itself, although a successful staging of the athletics events themselves may have reassured some that an Olympics could go to India.

CRITICS, CRITIQUES AND CHALLENGES

Since the 1980s, critiques of the Olympics have developed and its contradictions have been exposed by both academic scholars (e.g. see the contributors to Tomlinson and Whannel 1984) and investigative journalists (e.g. see Simson and Jennings 1992; Jennings 1996, 2000) who have sought to promote greater transparency in sport. The credibility and integrity of the

IOC and other international sports organisations (such as FIFA) have been further challenged following proven allegations of doping, physical and psychological violence and corruption. Revelations of doping (perhaps reaching a nadir in 1988 with Ben Johnson and the 100 metres final), bribery and opaque IOC procedures created the environment for serious challenges to the IOC. The romantic idealists (for example Bruce Kidd (1992) and John MacAloon (1981)) faced the scathing critics (such as John Hoberman 1995; Arnd Krüger 1993, and Helen Lenskyj 2000, 2002, 2008).

Different types of criticism have been made about the Olympics. It has been criticised for the rise of excessive commercialism, for hypocrisy and the betrayal of Olympic ideals, and for the promotion of excessive nationalism. Andrew Jennings was an early journalist critic of corruption in the bidding process, the suppression of negative drug test results, bribery in individual contests, the manipulation of press coverage, President Samaranch's links with the fascist Franco regime in his native Spain, the IOC members' acceptance of lavish gifts and the general impact of increased commercialisation. In the academic sphere French Marxist critic Jean-Marie Brohm was joined by Canadian Rick Gruneau, and Alan Tomlinson and Garry Whannel in the 1980s.

Local opposition to the Games has also developed on the basis of concerns over: the huge amount of public expenditure for a very brief athletics and sport festival; persons displaced by development; rent increases; environmental and social impacts; and the lack of public consultation or ability to participate in decisions. The best-known group to date has been the Toronto-based 'Bread not Circuses' (Lenskyj 2000). In Brazil there are already efforts to promote equity of return from the massive investments that are going to be made in light of that country hosting the two largest sports mega-events – the FIFA World Cup in 2014 and the Summer Olympics in 2016.

So the Olympics have shifted from being seen as a movement (Coubertin) to an industry (Lenskyj) and more recently as a system (Chappelet). Based on an idealistic ideology, as a movement the Olympics are seen as an organic, functional, civic religion. Conceived of as an industry – commercial, dysfunctional and corporate – materialist critics consider the ideals of the Olympic movement to be compromised by the growth of involvement with corporate sponsors and media organisations. Viewed more pragmatically as a system – a network of distributed parts, hubs and switches, but also unstable – the Olympics can be viewed as continuing to exhibit contradictory tendencies, whilst enjoying a revival of popularity despite the negative publicity of the 1980s and 1990s.

The so-called 'Olympic Turnaround' (Payne 2005) of the past ten years has been the result of a sustained effort on the part of the IOC to modify its procedures as well as market itself out of a critical corner. It has been a highly political and largely successful shift. As we have seen, the IOC is a self-elected, self-regulating association and, until 1981, it consisted entirely of men. In 1998, Swiss IOC member Marc Hodler announced that there was 'massive corruption' in the IOC and the IOC felt obliged to investigate the claims. This led to what has become known as 'Olympic Reform'. The main reform measures involved: reducing the scope for corruption by amending the procedures for electing candidate cities and abolishing visits by IOC members to candidate cities; the election of 15 active Olympic athletes to the IOC by their peers at the Olympic Games; the creation of a Nominations Commission for IOC membership; the mandate of IOC members to last for only eight years, renewable through

44

re-election; a maximum of 115 members; and the Presidential mandate was limited to eight years, renewable once only for a further four years.

In addition, evaluation and reporting procedures have been further developed. Official reports (from an Organizing Committee of the Olympic Games to the IOC) will include content dealing with:[5]

1 Management and organisation
2 Accommodation
3 Accreditation
4 Broadcasting
5 Olympic Park
6 Communications
7 Construction
8 Creative services
9 Cultural Olympiad
10 Event and guest services
11 External relations
12 Financial services
13 Games services
14 Logistics

15 Marketing
16 Medical services
17 Olympic family and protocol
18 Olympic Villages
19 Opening/Closing Ceremonies
20 Security
21 Sports
22 Staffing of the Games
23 Technology
24 Ticket sales
25 Torch relay
26 Transportation
27 Venue management
28 Youth and education

A new, additional, reporting system was introduced – the Olympic Games Global Impact (OGGI, now OGI) – requiring data to be collected over 11 years by host cities, on 150 indicators, including environmental, social and economic dimensions. No results are yet available from Beijing 2008, the first Games to be included in this system of reporting. For the past 20 years therefore the IOC has enjoyed a no-cost promotion strategy, constantly in the glare of the world's mass media – every year at least three hosts and another host to be decided are known about. In the odd years when there is not an Olympic Games taking place a decision will be made at an IOC Session or Congress about where either a Winter or Summer Olympics will be held in seven years' time.

Talk about legacies across various dimensions has become an established part of Olympic hosting – economic benefits (direct and indirect), the built environment (non-sporting, e.g. transport infrastructure), information and education (concerning sport and culture), public life, politics and culture, sport, elite performance, mass participation, the 'trickle-down' effect, financial support, the built sporting infrastructure, and sporting symbols, memory and history (Cashman 2006). Yet critics still ask if the response of the IOC and the Olympic movement was to treat the problems of the 1980s and 1990s as a crisis of communication rather than as crisis of ethics and morals (Jennings 2000). That is, to what extent has the Olympic movement lost its integrity and distinctive role in world sport?

Undoubtedly there are continuing contradictions of Olympism around various binaries, several of which are dealt with in later chapters:

- equity, equipment and material supply chains and fair trade, corporate social responsibility (CSR) as a strategic device rather than as a real alteration in procedures and processes;
- the extent to which environmental and other forms of sustainability are inevitably compromised despite the attraction of a greening/sustainability agenda;

45

- the launch of new initiatives such as the Youth Olympic Games and policies on doping/health as potentially misguided;
- the infringement of athletes' rights and self-expression in the midst of other changes relating to their status as Olympic athletes;
- the relationship between new global regulatory bodies of sport – such as CAS and WADA – and the Ethics Commission of the IOC.

As Gruneau (2002) suggests with respect to sports mega-events, three important questions are sometimes overlooked: Who benefits? Who is excluded? What scope is there for contestation? We attempt to identify some answers to these questions elsewhere in this book.

CONCLUSION

The IOC claims that the Games offer inspiration as a movement, a family and a philosophy, derived in many respects from Pierre de Coubertin's Christian beliefs and his relationship to organised religion of the late nineteenth and early twentieth centuries. Being critical of the Olympic Games can therefore be likened to 'farting loudly during High Mass in the Vatican' (Shaw 2008: 154). Yet the Olympic movement creates attention for itself by inviting criticism when it deviates from its own proclaimed ethical standards. Hence in the first part of this chapter we considered the IOC as a contradictory formation – having to adjust to both capitalist modernity and enterprise culture. The contradictions led to charges of hypocrisy by critics, and concerns about issues of 'governance' by those seeking to influence the future of the IOC. Developments in capitalism over the past 25 years provide the background against which the allure of hosting the Olympic Games has grown. They also shape the changing political economy of the Olympic Games and these also create the conditions in which criticism of the events develops. As Shaw (2008: 168) states, 'In our consumer culture, mega events, Olympics included, use sports as a platform to sell stuff'. The negative 'legacies' associated with the Games include social polarisation, eviction and displacement of marginal populations, public resources being used for private benefit, global rather than local benefit and the creation of playgrounds for the affluent. When normal political routes and legal processes are short-circuited by governments and local organisers anxious to get work completed on time it is not surprising that critics consider tactics that they hope may create the biggest public relations impact.

FURTHER READING

Chappelet, J.-L. and Kubler-Mabbott, B. (2008) *The International Olympic Committee and the Olympic System: The Governance of World Sport*, London: Routledge.

Lenskyj, H. (2008) *Olympic Industry Resistance*, Albany, NY: SUNY Press.

Toohey, K. and Veal, A. (2007) *The Olympic Games: A Social Science Perspective* (2nd edition), Oxford: CABI.

Vázquez Montalbán, M. (2004 [1991]) *An Olympic Death*, London: Serpent's Tail.

CHAPTER 3

TELEVISION AND THE COMMERCIALISATION OF THE OLYMPICS

The Olympic Games could not have grown to have global impact without television. The Games, as they now exist, are a product of television's power to produce and distribute live global spectacle. Indeed the Games are perhaps *better* understood as a television event than as a sporting one. Of the Olympic sports, only athletics, tennis, football, basketball and boxing have any significantly large spectator following outside the Olympic Games – and in the case of tennis, football, basketball and boxing, the Olympics is only a minor part of their sporting calendar and competitive formats. In our estimate, the other 22 sports combined typically account for less than 3% of television sport on terrestrial television in the UK.[1] The Olympics aside, athletics cannot compete for popularity or financial strength with the major commercialised sports such as football, basketball, golf, tennis, motor racing and American football. The majority of people who watch the Olympic Games do not otherwise follow regularly even the sports that are most prominently featured on Olympic television – athletics, swimming and gymnastics.

Nor can the Olympic sports, for the most part, claim a broad base of participants. Although a fair proportion of Olympic sports can claim a degree of participation, in the UK at least, only football, running, swimming and cycling would count as mass participation activities, and then only if one includes swimming, running or cycling for leisure rather than competition. For example, UK figures suggest that while 12% of men and 15% of women regularly swim, 12% of men and 6% of women regularly cycle, and 10% of men play football, less than 2% of the population regularly play tennis and less than 1% ride horses.[2] So the Olympics does not appear to be popular because of the regular following of its major sports either as spectator or as participant. Rather, it is because it is a spectacular television show, with the badge of being the world's best. Indeed, football's World Cup has a far stronger claim to have a non-television basis to its popularity, with millions around the world involved both as spectators and participants. So, we would argue, it is partly as a spectacular television event that the Olympic Games can be productively understood. As such, it has been shaped by the forces of commodification, globalisation and digitalisation; and it is increasingly shaped by the convergence of the once distinct technologies of television, computers and the internet.

OLYMPIC FINANCES

Capital demands its own reproduction. Money left in a tin is losing the opportunity to gain interest or to accrue profit. The logic of capital is reinvestment. But, as Marx argued, and

47

indeed demonstrated, there is a systematic tendency for the rate of profit to decline. This has two consequences. First, it produces a considerable pressure to rectify the situation, by forcing wage rates down (e.g. by casualisation, unemployment or de-unionisation), by sourcing cheaper materials, and by promoting the product in new markets, or more vigorously in existing markets. The second effect is that capital is constantly seeking new areas to colonise, seeking to monetise areas of human endeavour hitherto not based around profit generation. The development of spectator sport and professional sport can be interpreted in part as instances of capital penetrating and colonising new areas.

The Olympic Games have become an enormous event, not least in terms of their global reach via television, their massive revenues from commercial sources and their huge costs. The Games produce four main sources of revenue – ticket sales, sale of television rights, sponsorship, and licensing and merchandising. The IOC collects television rights payments and international sponsorships and redistributes these funds to the organising committee, the National Olympic Committees and the International Federations. The IOC retains a little under 10% of commercial revenue to cover its own running costs, which include the lavish travel and accommodation available to IOC members. Local sponsorship and merchandising revenue goes to the organising committee. In the four-year quadrennium 2005–2008 the total Olympic revenue was over $5 billion, of which 47% came from television rights, 45% from sponsorship, and only 5% from ticketing. The IOC figures illustrate a steady growth in revenues over the last decade. The one exception is ticketing, where fluctuations are probably accounted for by local factors, as the price of tickets, the numbers available and the percentage sold, vary from Games to Games.

Until recently, when the revenue from sponsorship has grown rapidly, television rights payments have provided the dominant share of Olympic revenue, and the bulk of the money has come from the major American networks. Television revenue for 2010/12 is expected to be over $3 billion, of which two-thirds comes from NBC for the US rights. Of television revenue, 88% comes from the Americas and Europe. Despite the massive growth in the reach and usage of the internet, 'new media' rights payments account for less than half of 1% of this revenue.

A significant portion of these large television revenues are used to contribute to the costs of the organising committees.

Source	2005–2008	percentage
Broadcast	2,570	47.16
TOP Sponsorship programme	866	15.89
Domestic sponsorship	1,555	28.53
Ticketing	274	5.03
Licensing	185	3.39
Total	**5,450**	

Figure 3.1 Olympic revenue, 2005–2008 ($m).

All figures in the chart have been rounded to the nearest $m. Does not include domestic commercial programme revenues. (As with subsequent figures, the source of the statistics is as cited, but the presentation, juxtaposition and calculation based on these statistics is that of the authors.)

Source: IOC (2010) *Olympic Marketing Fact File* (Lausanne: IOC).

Source	1993–96	1997–2000	2001–04	2005–08
Broadcast	1,251	1,845	2,232	2,570
TOP program	279	579	663	866
Domestic sponsorship	534	655	796	1,555
Ticketing	451	625	411	274
Licensing	115	66	87	185
Total	**2,630**	**3,770**	**4,189**	**5,450**
Percentage increase		43	11	30

Figure 3.2 Olympic marketing revenue in the last four quadrenniums ($m).

All figures in the chart have been rounded to the nearest $m. Does not include domestic commercial programme revenues.

Source: IOC (2010) *Olympic Marketing Fact File* (Lausanne: IOC).

Area	Payment	Percentage of total
Americas	2,231.25	67.41
Europe	672.00	20.30
Asia	217.22	6.56
Middle East/Africa	39.20	1.18
Oceania	136.50	4.12
Other (digital, new media, etc.)	14.00	0.42
Total	**3,310.17**	**100.00**

Figure 3.3 Revenue from television rights payments, 2010/2012 ($m).

Source: figures derived from IOC (2010) *Olympic Marketing Fact File* (Lausanne: IOC).

Summer Olympic Games	Broadcast revenue to OCOG
1992 Barcelona	441
1996 Atlanta	546
2000 Sydney	797
2004 Athens	733
2008 Beijing	851

Winter Olympic Games	Broadcast revenue to OCOG
1994 Lillehammer	229
1998 Nagano	308
2002 Salt Lake	443
2006 Turin	406

Figure 3.4 Broadcasting revenue contribution to OCOGs ($m).

Source: IOC (2010) *Olympic Marketing Fact File* (Lausanne: IOC).

Ever since the first proper rights payments from US sources, in 1960, the competition between the major America television networks has driven revenues upwards at a rapid rate. Even when, during the mid-1980s, television executives and IOC members alike doubted that the rises could continue, their pessimism was unwarranted. Only in the last decade can signs be detected that the rises are no longer enormous. The reach of Olympic television is now close to saturation – most people who wish to watch are able to, and television is being challenged by new media for its audiences and hence advertising revenue. However, in an era when broadcast television may be losing a little of its absolute primacy, the Olympic Games are still able to offer live and unpredictable drama, which only sport can provide and hitherto only broadcast television can adequately deliver.

THE GAMES AND THE MEDIA

How did this global spectacle develop? All periodisations have a contingent tendency and we propose here four periods: the pre-television era between 1896 and 1935; the emergence of television as a new technology between 1936 and 1967; the technological perfecting and globalisation of television between 1968 and 1987; and the era of digital transformation from 1988 to the present.

Mediating the Games: 1896–1935

The modern Olympic Games were established in the period of the late nineteenth century in which a modern mass communication system also began to develop. The combination of photography, wireless telegraphy, a reading public and entrepreneurial investment gave birth to the modern popular press. The first cinemas emerged in the closing years of the century, and until television, cinema newsreels were the only way, other than presence at the event, that people could observe sport performance. Not entirely coincidentally, the last decade of the nineteenth century is also a period in which the growth of branded goods and chain stores triggered a substantial growth in advertising. By the end of the twentieth century, of course, global corporations would be providing a substantial revenue stream for the Olympic Games in the form of sponsorship. During the early years of the twentieth century, cinema spread rapidly around the world, and in the 1920s, the first radio broadcasts were made (see Whannel 2002). Photographs of the 1912 Olympic Games were traded commercially. The 1924 Games were the first to be broadcast by radio. In 1932, newsreel cameras were used to determine the winner of the 100 metres. Despite the emergence of television from the 1930s, radio remained an important medium for the Olympic Games for many years.

In 1932, around 1,500 amateur radio operators offered to help broadcast news of the Games internationally.[3] Broadcasts of the Berlin Games of 1936 were sent by short wave to over 40 countries, 105 radio reporters from 41 foreign broadcasting companies transmitted 2,328 reports to all parts of the world.[4] In 1948 the BBC broadcast radio coverage around the world in 40 languages.[5] Radio continued to be an important means of dissemination during the 1950s, but by the 1960s television was on its way to becoming the dominant medium for the Olympic Games.

50

The emergence of television technology: 1936–1967

Before the Second World War, only four countries (USA, UK, France and Germany) had developed viable television technologies. For the Olympic Games, the television era began in Berlin in 1936. Pictures were not broadcast direct to the public, but relayed to around 28 local halls, attracting an audience of around 150,000. The image quality was described variously as 'excellent' to 'unsatisfactory'.[6] Three months after the 1936 Games, the BBC introduced the world's first regular television service, in the London area. But the first real broadcasting of an Olympic Games did not occur until the London Olympics of 1948. Pictures could only be received in the London area. There were just 35,000 households with television licences at the start of 1948, but, possibly fuelled by the Olympic Games, this figure tripled during the year. Around 70 hours were broadcast, with one day alone having seven and a half hours' coverage.[7]

Despite this, television technology spread much more slowly than did the technologies of film and cinema. Before 1960 fewer than 25 countries had launched regular television services and so the patterns of international sport broadcasting had yet to develop. The 1952 Olympic Games in Helsinki were only televised in two countries. In the build-up to the Melbourne Games of 1956, the US networks resisted paying rights for the event, and negotiations with American and European broadcasters were unsuccessful. As a result, only six pre-recorded, half-hour programmes were accessible on a few independent channels in the USA. At the 1956 Melbourne Games, television was installed in the Press Centre for the first time, enabling journalists to watch events happening in the stadium. Six television screens linked by closed circuit, with a camera directed on the scoreboard, brought events and results to the press centre (Yalin 2007).

Year	City	TV rights	Per cent increase	Year	City	TV rights	Per cent increase
1960	Rome	1.2		1960	Squaw Valley	0.05	
1964	Tokyo	1.6	33	1964	Innsbruck	0.93	1,760
1968	Mexico City	10	525	1968	Grenoble	2.6	180
1972	Munich	18	80	1972	Sapporo	8.5	226
1976	Montreal	35	94	1976	Innsbruck	11.6	37
1980	Moscow	88	151	1980	Lake Placid	20.7	78
1984	Los Angeles	287	226	1984	Sarajevo	102.7	396
1988	Seoul	403	40	1988	Calgary	324.9	216
1992	Barcelona	636	58	1992	Albertville	291.9	−10
1996	Atlanta	898	41	1994	Lillehammer	352.9	21
2000	Sydney	1,332	48	1998	Nagano	514	46
2004	Athens	1,494	12	2002	Salt Lake City	738	44
2008	Beijing	1,739	16	2006	Turin	831	13

Figure 3.5 Revenue from television rights payments ($m).

Figures over $10m rounded up to nearest million.

Source: figures derived from IOC (2010) *Olympic Marketing Fact File* (Lausanne: IOC).

By contrast, the 1960 Olympic Games in Rome were relayed to 12 countries on the Eurovision link. The American network CBS paid around $380,000 for the rights, and daily recordings were flown across the Atlantic for retransmission. A total of 21 countries saw some Olympic material on television. The audience potential of the Games was clear when CBS reported a 36% audience share, heralding the start of competitive bidding that would push rights payments rapidly up over the next few decades. New communication satellites (e.g. Telstar, Syncom 3) enabled the first intercontinental live broadcasts for 1964 and 1968, and the Olympics were seen in colour for the first time. Television was coming of age, and it was about to transform sport in general and the Olympic Games in particular.

Perfecting the picture: 1968–1987

The rise of television sport was most closely associated with the BBC in the UK and ABC in the USA. ABC in particular developed a commitment to focusing on the drama, and the stars, epitomised by their two best-known slogans, 'Up close and personal' and 'The thrill of victory, the agony of defeat'. ABC's style featured close-ups, graphics, and microphones placed to pick up the sound of the action. In 1968 ABC scheduled 48 hours of coverage (live and recorded), a threefold increase on 1964.[8] Communication satellites and the spread of television around the world were making the Games a global television event. This, in turn, gave it enormous potential as a platform for symbolic political acts. The Black Power salutes at Mexico 1968, the seizing of Israeli athletes as hostages by a militant Palestinian group at Munich 1972, and

Summer Games			Winter Games		
Year	Site	Countries	Year	Site	Countries
1936	Berlin	1			
1948	London	1			
1952	Helsinki	2			
1956	Melbourne	1	1956	Cortina	22
1960	Rome	21	1960	Squaw Valley	27
1964	Tokyo	40	1964	Innsbruck	30
1968	Mexico City	n/a	1968	Grenoble	32
1972	Munich	98	1972	Sapporo	41
1976	Montreal	124	1976	Innsbruck	38
1980	Moscow	111	1980	Lake Placid	40
1984	Los Angeles	156	1984	Sarajevo	100
1988	Seoul	160	1998	Calgary	64
1992	Barcelona	193	1992	Albertville	86
			1994	Lillehammer	120
1996	Atlanta	214	1998	Nagano	160
2000	Sydney	220	2002	Salt Lake City	60
2004	Athens	220	2006	Torino	200
2008	Beijing	220			

Figure 3.6 Countries broadcasting the Summer and Winter Olympic Games, 1936–2008.

Source: adapted from IOC (2009).

52

the sequence of boycotts that marked the Games between 1976 and 1984 provide three very different instances of exploitation of this opportunity.

The establishment of the Olympic Games as a global television event made it a site of symbolic importance in the Cold War. As soon as the 1980 Games were awarded to Moscow, lobby groups in Western countries began urging boycotts. However, it was not until 1979, and the Soviet invasion of Afghanistan, that a pretext great enough to cause government action arose. US President Jimmy Carter announced a boycott and went to great lengths to pressure other Western countries into supporting it. However, neither this boycott nor the less effective retaliatory one organised by the Eastern bloc in 1984 appeared to diminish the popularity of the Games on television. Indeed the Olympic Games were well established as a ratings winner, and provided a valuable basis around which the networks could announce and promote their autumn schedules. The pattern of US rights payments from 1960 to 1988 was one of continuing and spectacular growth.

During this period, the Olympic Games became the stake in an intense battle between the US networks. The potential for big audiences, even during the day and late at night, and usually during the slack summer season, helped attract additional advertising revenue. By the 1980s the escalation in rights payments was in danger of outstripping the level of advertising revenue. The 1988 Winter Olympics were scheduled for Calgary, an almost perfect site from the point of view of American television, as a large proportion of events could be transmitted live in either late afternoon or peak time on both coasts – the majority of the American television audience is in the east coast (Eastern) and west coast (Pacific) time zones. Consequently the bidding was especially intense. When ABC's determination to retain their 'Olympic Network' tag led them to bid $309 million for the 1988 Winter Olympics, it was widely felt in the television industry and not least at ABC that the payment was too high and could not be recouped in advertising revenue (see Billings et al. 1998). The pessimism was heightened when the American economy slumped in the mid- to late 1980s. The American networks began pressuring the IOC to extract higher rights payments from the rest of the world, with top television executives arguing that the EBU was getting a free lunch. It is notable that the 1992 Winter Olympics, uniquely, brought in less television revenue than its predecessor. However, in the years since, the US payments have continued their upward trajectory. The ever-growing numbers of countries who wished to have their own broadcasters on site prompted the introduction in 1988 of a separate International Broadcasting Centre, distinct from the Press Centre, with commentary, production and editing facilities.[9]

	Summer	Winter	Both combined
1960	0.39	0.05	0.44
1964	1.50	0.59	2.09
1968	4.50	2.50	7.00
1972	7.50	6.40	13.90
1976	25.00	10.00	35.00
1980	87.00	15.50	102.50
1984	225.00	91.50	316.50
1988	300.00	309.00	609.00

Figure 3.7 US network payments for Olympic television rights ($m).

The IOC was indeed to embark on an effort to ensure that countries other than the USA also paid greater sums for the rights. The bidding wars, which had forced the price for the 1988 Winter Olympic Games up to $309 million, precipitated a series of changes that led to ABC Television being acquired by Capital Cities, and the imposition of new budgetary restraints on the acquisition of sporting rights. It was the end of an era for ABC, which had dubbed itself the 'Olympic Network', but was now to lose its prime position to rival network NBC. The economic recession of the early 1980s and the declining power of ABC led to IOC fears (misplaced as it turned out) that the income from US rights payments would drop. At the 1986 IOC Session, prompted by ABC, the IOC introduced a new scheduling – the Barcelona Olympics of 1992 would be followed by the Winter Olympics in Lillehammer in 1994, putting Summer and Winter Games in separate years for the first time. This was designed to protect the American networks from the need to cover the cost of two Olympic events in the same year. The global reach of the Olympic Games grew throughout the 1980s. Claims of audiences of between one and two billion were characteristically made, but although the audiences undoubtedly are large, and the reach great, there are some reasons to doubt the accuracy of global audience figures.

BOX 3.1 DO WE REALLY KNOW HOW MANY PEOPLE WATCH THE OLYMPIC GAMES?

Television audience figures are gathered by a combination of meters on sets and diaries maintained by households. Typically, a panel of a few thousand sample households will have the meters and complete diaries over a period of months. The meters register when a television is on, and which channel it is tuned to, broken down into three-minute segments. Such methods are not universal but variations on them are utilised in 54 countries. These countries contain 75% of the world's population, and 90% of the world's TV households.

Sport organisations quote audience statistics as part of their case for television rights payments and in order to attract sponsors. The relatively reliable statistics for some countries are augmented by estimates for the rest of the world, for public viewing and new media viewing. There are no accurate means of assessing the numbers who watch in bars and other public places, or watch via computers or mobile phones. Apart from the 54 countries for which verifiable data are available, another 166 provided some television coverage of the 2008 Olympic Games. In some countries diary data alone are used. This is a method which, it has been established, is not accurate. For many countries any attempt to estimate an audience can be little more than guesswork.

Whereas the standard unit of television audience statistics is the *average programme audience* (based on those who watched the whole game/match/event), sport organisations have tended to utilise other means. They will quote the *peak figure* (the maximum size of the audience at some point during the event), which is generally around 1.5 times greater, or they will quote the *reach*, which includes anyone who watched for at least three minutes, generally twice the size of the average audience.

In addition, to provide an audience figure for a whole competition, they will aggregate the reach to obtain a *cumulative audience*, resulting in the claim that, for example, 26.29 billion viewers watched the 2006 World Cup competition. A different form of aggregation is provided in the form of *total viewer hours*. This is derived by multiplying the duration of the programme by the number of viewers in the audience. Such figures, especially where based partly on estimates, are demonstrably of little statistical value or accuracy. An investigation by *The Independent* established a consistent pattern in which the audiences claimed by sport organisations were many times greater than the verifiable portion (which is based on 90% of the available audience). Examples quoted from 2006 included:

Event	*Claim*	*Verifiable*
Italy v France (World Cup final)	715.1 million	260 million
American Super Bowl	750m–1 billion	98 million
Winter Olympics opening ceremony	2 billion	87 million
Champions League (Arsenal v Barcelona)	120 million	86 million
Formula One: Brazilian Grand Prix	354 million	83 million
Golf: Ryder Cup (final day)	up to 1 billion	6 million
Commonwealth Games opening ceremony	1.5 billion	5 million

There is clear evidence that the claims of audience size made for major sporting events, including the Olympic Games, warrant closer scrutiny. The Olympic Games claimed global audiences as follows:

1988	Seoul	10.4 billion
1992	Barcelona	16.6 billion
1996	Atlanta	19.6 billion

The above figures are based on the 'cumulative audience'. In 2000 the IOC switched to the use of figures based on 'total viewer hours', resulting in the following claimed audiences:

2000	Sydney	36.1 billion
2004	Athens	34.4 billion

From the early 1980s, aware of the danger of dependence on a single revenue stream from television revenue, the IOC, in conjunction with Horst Dassler of Adidas, had already begun to develop the blueprint for a globalised sponsorship scheme (detailed below). Since the 1990s, the growth of the internet has come to constitute an opportunity for the Olympic movement – but also a challenge. It can, potentially, enable live access to all events, 24 hours a day. However, to date there are no indications that it can produce a revenue stream to rival that from broadcast television.

Digital transformations: 1988–the present

Ever since 1988, the digitalised, computerised and globalised internet dissemination of the Games has begun to emerge. However, Olympic-related use of computers has a long history. At the 1964 Tokyo Games, an electronic computing system was designed by the organising committee and IBM, to report, record and transmit text data of the sports events.[10] At the 1976 Montreal Games, television was linked to the central computerised results system.[11] The growth of the internet and the emergence of the world wide web provided the IOC with both an opportunity and a threat. The net offered a radical new means to promote the Games, the sponsors and Olympism; but also threatened to become a new means of dissemination that could potentially steal television's audience whilst not replacing its revenues.

By 1988, Eastern communism was falling apart, and the IOC was able to move into a boycott-free and image-conscious era. In 1988, Seoul had superb facilities, but the IOC had to prevail on the organising committee to bus in large numbers of schoolchildren to provide the full stadiums that television favours. The story illustrates how central the needs of television had become. Between 1984 and 2008 broadcasting revenues were more than $10 billion.[12] But from the end of the 1980s, deregulation, multichannel television, the internet and digitalisation began to pose new challenges to the cosy relationship between the IOC and television.

US television was struggling to recoup the enormous rights payments. Even after the Summer and Winter Games were separated into different years, it was hard to sell enough advertising to meet the costs. In 1992, NBC tried pay-per-view subscriptions for an enhanced advert-free package on cable, but the scheme failed to appeal to viewers, who of course could still see the bulk of the Games for free. CBS, allied with Ted Turner's TNT, traded 50 hours of their coverage to Turner, who put up $50 million towards the rights.[13]

Just as the IOC had, in the 1980s, assumed greater central control of the negotiation of rights and sponsorship deals, during the 1990s it determined to take greater control of the international feed, the television pictures provided by the host broadcaster to the rest of the world. By 2001 it had established OBS (Olympic Broadcasting Services) to organise the televising of the Games. The OBS is a committee that commissions established broadcasters and production companies from around the world to provide aspects of the coverage. In Beijing 2008, for example, a cooperative joint venture between the OBS and the Local Organising Committee (BOCOG) created Beijing Olympic Broadcasting (BOB), the on-site host broadcaster for the 2008 Games.[14] After International Sport and Leisure (see below) collapsed in 2001, the IOC assumed more central control of both television and marketing. In 2005 it established a separate company, IOC Television and Marketing Services SA.[15]

The rapid growth of the internet has continued to trouble the IOC to this day. In 1996 in Atlanta the first Olympic Games website received 189 million hits. It was introduced in April 1995, and attracted around 10,000 visits per day, growing to 400,000 per day by the time of the Games. In addition, 12–15% of all tickets were purchased online.[16] Just two years later, the Nagano website got 634 million hits, while in 2000 the Sydney website got a staggering 11.3 billion hits. For NBC and the IOC, the internet is a threat in that, without tight content controls, it could potentially cause a significant audience migration from television without producing the revenue flows to compensate. One symptom of these fears was a dramatic shift in the sale of television rights, allowing NBC to acquire the rights to several Games in advance. In addition, television and sponsorship rights became bundled together, with NBC's parent company,

General Electric, agreeing to become a TOP sponsor. For a total commitment of around $5.7 billion, NBC eventually secured rights for 1996, 2000, 2008 and 2012. In one deal struck in June 2003, NBC concluded a deal for the Winter Olympics of 2010 and the Summer Games of 2012 worth in total over $2 billion. This included General Electric paying a minimum of $160m and a maximum of $200 million in sponsorship. The willingness of NBC to conclude deals for the 2012 Olympic Games two years in advance of the choice of site would seem to suggest that the choice of site is no longer seen as a crucial element in determining the value of the rights.[17]

Given the many uncertainties about the future of television as a medium of delivery, as Wi-Fi and high-speed broadband hasten the convergence of television and the internet, it is not surprising that the major US networks were keen to secure television rights for future Olympic Games; nor that the IOC was keen to arrange such a deal. The *Washington Post* said the bid was a 'risky but potentially rewarding go-for-broke attempt by a network to hold on to mass viewership events in an era when cable broadcasters are eroding network clout' but also pointed out that NBC would utilise its own cable networks – MSNBC, CNBC and Bravo – to broadcast Olympic events, reaching as wide an audience as possible and maximising advertising dollars. After the IOC announced that they were expecting a sponsorship dimension to the deal, it was the commitment of General Electric that helped secure the deal for NBC (*Washington Post* 7 June 2003).

The deals that have been struck underline the enormous commercial value of the Games and the power of the IOC. How many other organisations can successfully sell, for around $1 billion, a product not due to be delivered for nine years, when even the host city is unknown? Indeed, the closing of the deals highlights the manner in which the Games have become a recognisable, routinised and ritualised form of spectacle, in which stars, narratives and national identities are all delivered up for audience identification.[18] Despite the caution over the speed of internet developments, gradual controlled use of the internet and pay-for channels has allowed American viewers a greater range and depth of coverage.

Developments in the technology of digital 'geo-blocking' have made it possible for digital rights management systems to prevent digital streams being accessed from other countries or duplicated on other websites. A joint internet monitoring project run by the Chinese and the IOC discovered over 4,000 cases of illegal broadcasting during the 2008 Games (Marshall *et al.* 2010). Generally these broadcasts were rapidly shut down once detected. But peer-to-peer streaming using BitTorrent proved a bit more problematic. A major torrent website, Pirate Bay, had millions of downloads of the Opening Ceremony, and although the IOC requested Swedish government assistance, Pirate Bay remained defiant and the Swedish were unwilling to enforce IOC demands. The IOC were more successful in preventing unauthorised recycling of Olympic material on YouTube, but did also authorise YouTube to establish an Olympic channel available in countries outside the major regional television contracts (Marshall *et al.* 2010).

NBC had reintroduced extra coverage on cable and satellite channels in 2000, expanded the number of outlets for 2004 to allow coverage of all 28 sports, and introduced basketball and soccer channels in 2008. For the Beijing Olympic Games of 2008, for the first time, NBC also utilised its own internet site, nbcolympics.com, to stream events. Possibly as a result of this new, more comprehensive coverage, NBC attained its highest ever Olympic Games ratings and largest advertising sales.[19]

57

In 2008, which Andy Miah (Miah *et al.* 2008) has referred to as 'the first Web 2.0 Games', internet use and video streaming rose dramatically. The NBC website recorded an estimated 1.3 billion page views, 53 million unique users, 75.5 million video streams and 10 million hours of video consumption during the Games. The European Broadcasting Union delivered 180 million broadband video streams. In Latin America, Terra's Olympic site reported 29 million video streams and 10 million video-on-demand downloads (Hutchins and Mikosza 2010). According to BBC Olympics Director Roger Mosey, there was more video streaming in the first day of the 2008 Beijing Olympics than in the whole of the 2004 Athens Olympics. In total the BBC had 2.6 million video streams in Athens and 38 million video streams in Beijing.[20] In China, live streaming was offered online, with viewing audiences of 53 million watching the Olympics on personal computers (Marshall *et al.* 2010).

This substantial and rapid rise in digital video streaming is a strong indicator that the dominance of the Olympic Games by broadcast television could come under increasing challenge. There are no technological reasons why a centralised internet provider (the IOC itself, for example) could not provide comprehensive coverage. Two factors militate against this. First, television advertising, organised on national lines, is still the most effective business model when it comes to generating income. As long as this is the case, the internet is likely to be used as an adjunct, allowing fuller coverage of those events with less viewer appeal. Marshall *et al.* (2010) point out that the need to ensure primacy of broadcast television meant that NBC's website offered heavily mediated highlights packages rather than live streaming of major events. Second, it may be that audiences tend to prefer Olympics coverage geared to their own national belongingness, focusing on their own favoured sports, competitors and medal prospects, framed within a narrative of national specificity. In 2008, Whannel watched Olympic television coverage in China, France and the UK and the different focuses were striking. In France, for example, the handball (a sport barely visible on the BBC) became more and more prominent as the French team progressed towards triumph.

The UK will have completed the switchover to digital broadcasting by 2012, and the BBC's coverage of the London Games will be the first to be entirely digital. The ability of viewers to watch events they have missed by streaming video via the broadcaster's website will become far more heavily used. However, the BBC website will become central to this process. The digital television red button system is constrained by capacity limits and typically carries six streams. In the 2012 Olympics there could be up to 21 events at any one time, and all of these can be sustained in stream form on the website. While the BBC will also use and publicise message boards and blogs, interactivity through social networking will remain relatively marginal to its core coverage.[21] High definition television will also be established although the precise broadcast pattern is yet to be established. Despite the current enthusiasm for 3D cinema, it is unlikely that 3D Olympic coverage will be utilised on any large scale, although there may conceivably be live relays to cinemas.

GLOBALISATION, SPONSORSHIP AND THE DEVELOPMENT OF 'SPORTSBIZ'

Such is the power of live images of nations competing that huge television audiences are mobilised, helping to underpin and justify the expensive bidding races to win the right to stage the Games and the ever more exorbitant costs to host cities. It is the convergence of star, narrative, national identity, live-ness and uncertainty that gives the Olympic Games this unique power as a cultural event. Television has brought a huge income stream, initially dependent on the USA, but since 1988 sponsorship and television income from the rest of the world have become significant too.

Yet the very dominance of television has also transformed the Games in other ways. It has brought commercialism, an end to amateurism, and a heightened intensity of focus, which has encouraged massive investment to prove and display national prowess – and fostered the use of performance-enhancing drugs. It has made the Games part of the global promotion of cities for industry, trade and tourism. This heightened visibility has forced the Games to be staged inside rings of fortified security. Television has robbed the Games of much of their festive potential.

The explosive growth of television sport from the mid-1960s has inevitably had a transformative impact on the culture of Olympism, in three main forms. First, competitive bidding for the television rights between the major networks of the USA moved the IOC from genteel poverty to grand luxury. Second, the heightened visibility of the Olympic Games, the fitness boom of the 1970s, and the ruthless competitiveness of the sport and leisure-goods industry combined to make the Olympic Games an attractive proposition for sponsorship. Third, in becoming the global event par excellence, not to say *sans pareil*, the Olympic Games offered one of the first and still one of the few opportunities for global marketing and global visibility.

There is, in fact, a major paradox at the heart of Olympic marketing. Normally, advertisers and sponsors are primarily interested in gaining television exposure. But the Olympic Games allow no arena advertising (apart from the trademarks of equipment suppliers). Ironically, the ban was introduced in 1928 as a response to fears that the Games were becoming too commercial! The only other major event to bar advertising is the Wimbledon Tennis Championships. So sponsors do not get television space, and are instead buying into association with the world's most recognisable symbol, the five rings, a symbol that connotes world excellence. The only way they can gain television exposure is to buy advertising separately. The paradox is that it is the impression of being 'above' commerce produced by a 'clean' stadium that contributes significantly to the aura of uniqueness of the Games and hence enhances their marketability. Indeed so important is this aura of being above commerce, that the legislation that a country must introduce if it is hosting the Games specifically prevents any advertising within range of the cameras at the Olympic sites.

The World Cup, the Olympic Games and a few other events had by the 1990s become global television events. As such, they had enormous potential to raise more revenue from advertising and from sponsorship, given the right structures. Up till this point the major commercial activity associated with sport was the sports goods business. Two firms, Adidas and Puma, run by two rival members of the Dassler family, had been fighting each other for the Olympic business since 1956. Horst Dassler of Adidas became very adept at making deals, first with individual athletes and then with national teams. He recognised the commercial value of ensuring that whole teams would be seen at the Olympic Games, on television around the world, wearing the Adidas kit. So he offered very good deals to poorer nations, ensuring an Adidas dominance. He was also an inveterate networker, keeping track of dozens of rising sports officials around the world and nurturing their friendship, knowing that they would be the decision-makers of tomorrow. In particular he developed close links with João Havelange, who became head of FIFA in 1974. Two events, the World Cup of 1982 and the Olympic Games of 1984, helped transform the sponsorship business. Working with Patrick Nally, Dassler pursued much greater sums in sponsorship for the 1982 World Cup.

59

Figure 3.8 Sponsorship: the Visa flag at the torch relay, London 2008. Sponsors do not get their name in the stadium, but the torch relay provides opportunities to link the brand name with the five rings, the flag of the host country and the visual background of the host city.

The IOC, partly as result of its aristocratic basis, and partly due to its commitment (up until the 1980s) to amateurism, has always been rather cautious about commercialisation. One early attempt to raise money came in Tokyo in 1964. A new 'Olympia' cigarette brand generated more than $1 million in revenue for the OCOG, but the IOC intervened to ban tobacco sponsorship. Until 1985, all sponsorship revenue was raised locally by the organising committees. However, by 1981, the IOC had for some time been concerned at the dangers of being over-dependent on US television money and established, in 1981, a committee to explore new sources of funding. Meanwhile, the organisers of the 1984 Los Angeles Games, forced by a public vote to rely only on private finance, had had to pursue sponsorship more vigorously, developing the principle of limited product categories with a monopoly sponsor in each one (see Ueberroth 1985). As this forced rival companies (Coke and Pepsi, Kodak and Fuji, etc.), into an auction it proved a very successful means of maximising sponsorship revenue (see Reich 1986; Ueberroth 1985). The alliance of Adidas boss Horst Dassler and FIFA President João Havelange had already reshaped the World Cup using similar principles (see Wilson 1988; Aris 1990; Whannel 1992; Sugden and Tomlinson 1998).

Meanwhile Dassler had gone into partnership with the Japanese advertising agency Dentsu to establish International Sport and Leisure (ISL). ISL was set up as a broker to negotiate television and sponsorship deals. It was hired by the IOC, controversially, without public tender, to establish the TOP programme, which involved persuading the NOCs to relinquish their own local rights in the key product areas, in order that the IOC could market the Games to sponsors centrally. Thanks to the Dassler link, by 1986 its executives were able to boast, with false modesty, 'we are a small company – we only have three clients – the Olympic Games, the World Cup and the World Athletics Championship'.[22] With Dassler as a major influence, the IOC developed its global Olympic sponsorship system TOP, first used in 1988.

After the 1988 Olympic Games the IOC also assumed a much greater degree of central control over the key negotiations on television revenue and sponsorship (see Larsen and Park 1993). The introduction of limited product categories with sponsor exclusivity meant that by 1992 there were just 12 TOP sponsors, but they brought in $10–20 million each (see Barney et al. 2002). Dassler, who is widely believed to have used his influence to aid the election of both Havelange and Samaranch, was now reaping his reward in power, influence and money. He was the central figure in a web of mutually linked interests, and his power was considerable. In the event he died in 1987, but the transformation he had wrought defined the sporting environment as the 1990s began.

Almost half of the total revenue of the Olympic movement still comes from television, but now 45% comes from sponsorship, while a mere 5% comes from ticket sales, giving a clue to the importance of the spectator in the scheme of things. It is worth noting that at the Olympic Games, as at other major events, a large proportion of tickets go to the Olympic 'Family' – sponsors, corporate hospitality and the media. For some major sport events less than 60% of tickets have been available to the general public. In general terms, the IOC retains 8% of this revenue, and the rest is shared out between the NOCs, the IFs and the OCOGs.

The TOP programme, established in 1985, has now become a permanent feature, even if it has not grown as dramatically as its promoters might have hoped. Both Adidas and ISL lost their way after Dassler died in 1987, and ISL drastically over-extended itself and went into bankruptcy in 2001. The TOP programme is now in its seventh round (TOP 7), and currently involves nine corporations (Coca-Cola, Acer, Atos, GE, McDonald's, Omega, Panasonic, Samsung and Visa). In IOC speak, these corporations are part of the 'Olympic Family' and are referred to as partners – 'Worldwide Partners of the Olympic Games, Partners of the International Olympic Committee, Partners of the Vancouver 2010 and London 2012 Olympic Games, Partners of all National Olympic Committees, and Partners of all Olympic teams competing in Vancouver 2010 and London 2012'. One big happy family.

The introduction of limited product categories with exclusivity in each has proved to be a very effective mechanism for increasing revenue. Sponsors are hoping that the expenditure will produce a yield in terms of sales and brand awareness. These benefits are notoriously hard to assess.

The 11 companies in TOP 5 were Coca-Cola, John Hancock, Kodak, McDonald's, Panasonic, Samsung, Atos Origin, Sports Illustrated/Time, Swatch, Visa International and Xerox. The TOP

	Year	Companies
TOP 1	1985–1988	9
TOP 2	1989–1992	12
TOP 3	1993–1996	10
TOP 4	1997–2000	11
TOP 5	2001–2004	11

Figure 3.9 Development of the TOP sponsorship programme.

sponsors are given a range of privileges including substantial numbers of tickets. On the Olympic sites in 2012, it is likely that the only soft drinks on offer will be Coca-Cola products, and McDonald's will be the only fast food available. Ambush marketing laws will allow Olympic stewards to confiscate from spectators the products of their competitors. Purchasers of tickets may find that only the Visa card is acceptable. The TOP Programme is global and is organised centrally. Each organising committee may also sell local sponsorships, but cannot make deals with competitors of the TOP sponsors and so must generally avoid the main product categories of the TOP programme.

The sponsors also benefit from extraordinary legal protection against their competitors. The IOC insists that a victorious host city signs – immediately after the vote result is announced – a contract which requires the organising committee to ensure that its government provides a legislative tool to enforce strict brand protection. The host city, the NOC and the OCOG have to ensure that no unauthorised marketing, advertising or promotion can refer to 'the Games, any Olympic team or the year of the Games or imply any connection with the Games, any Olympic team or the year of the Games'.[23] In the UK legislation already existed, in the form of the Olympic Symbol (Protection) Act 1995 which prevents unauthorised use of the Olympic symbol, the word Olympic, and 'Citius Altius Fortius' or similar words.[24] After the award of the Games to London, this Act was updated and augmented by the London Olympic Games and Paralympic Games (Protection) Act 2006 which provides the power to combat ambush marketing (Ewing 2006: 14).

This Act effectively requires anyone, not just Olympic organisers, to do what the IOC wants them to do. The Act states that 'Advertising regulations . . . shall aim to secure compliance with

Figure 3.10 Merchandising: the Olympic pins. Official merchandising, in shops and online, provides a valuable additional revenue stream for the organising committee, while customised legislation provides legal protection against 'unauthorised' goods and vendors.

obligations imposed on any person by the Host City Contract'.[25] The draconian powers provided by this Act to prevent unauthorised attempts to suggest an association with the Games by use of words like Olympic, London, Summer and 2012 are of course open to abuse. This Act is part of a broader tendency, more evident in the USA, for corporations to seek to control the very language we speak. It is bizarre that the use of the words London and Summer might be subject to legal restriction. The Act uses a word-based definition of 'intention to suggest a relationship between a company and the Games' (see Figure 3.11). It is forbidden to use a combination of words in Group 1 with words in Group 2, or a combination of words in Group 2.

One legal commentary has even asserted that 'The laws relating to the 2012 Olympics are probably the most restrictive ever in their scope . . . even simple messages of support such as "X supports the London Olympics" or "come to our bar and watch the 2012 Games on the big screen" would probably infringe the London Olympic Association Right'. The Act allows existing well-established users (e.g. The Olympic Café) to continue and it makes provisions for news and journalism and 'honest statements of fact'.[26] However, at least one university has already declined to label a seminar series with the word 'Olympic' for fear of infringing the Act. Fortunately, there are signs that common sense may prevail and these heinous powers will be restricted to their more appropriate, if debatable, function.

However, Ewing states that 'the protection applies not only to commercial sponsorship but to political opposition, and is underpinned in some cases by the criminal rather than the civil law'. People carrying anti-Olympic slogans could be charged with criminal offences. Ewing argues that companies given such privileges and protection by the state should be required to demonstrate a commitment to the highest ethical standards throughout their corporate operations. In particular it ought not to be the business of the state to protect companies that operate – in this country or elsewhere – in breach of international human rights standards (Ewing 2006: 16).

Ewing singles out McDonald's and Coca-Cola as two companies with questionable records. McDonald's 'appears to make no commitment to human rights on its website' and Ewing cites instances of anti-union conduct in Canada, Russia, Germany and Indonesia. Ewing declares that 'there are few human rights activists who will be impressed by the celebration of McDonald's in particular on the IOC website'. Ewing says it is remarkable that these allegations appear not to have been fully investigated by the IOC, and if the allegations are true, 'it is even more remarkable that these companies enjoy extraordinary legal privileges as a result of contractual obligations imposed by the IOC on London and other host cities' (Ewing 2006: 21–31).

Group 1	Group 2
Games	Gold
Two Thousand and Twelve	Silver
2012	Bronze
Twenty Twelve	London
	Medals
	Sponsor
	Summer

Figure 3.11 Restricted word combinations.

Source: Ewing (2006: 15) quoting the London Olympic Games and Paralympics Act 2006, Schedule 4.

CONCLUSION

The dilemma for the IOC is that it wishes to utilise all the new media resources of the internet and social networking sites to promote the Olympics brand while remaining in control. But as Hutchins and Mikosza argue, there is a shift in the 'media sport content economy' from the comparative scarcity of television channels to the 'digital plenitude' of the new media environment in which online media challenge both market-driven logic and central control. As they graphically put it, 'the carefully designed and fertile "media garden" tended by the Olympic Movement over the past 25 years was sporadically beset by weeds – uninvited, unpredictable, socially driven, participatory digital media' (Hutchins and Mikosza 2010).

Top sport stars now are the point of intersection between the global spectacle of the Olympic Games and the celebrity-dominated media culture, and star image has become a promotional tool. The issue of sport actuality as intellectual property poses a contradiction – the IOC is selling the images of performance, but the performers receive nothing for this – how long will they be content with this situation? In an era in which top sport stars have agents to oversee their interests, their intellectual property and image rights could become the site of a legal challenge to the current structure of Olympic finance. The great paradox at the heart of the Olympic Games is that this commodified and hugely lucrative global spectacle is owned and run, not by a private corporation with shareholders, but by what is in effect a combination of trust and an eighteenth-century gentlemen's club. So far this situation, combining the archaic and the entrepreneurial, has survived, and arguably thrived despite – indeed perhaps partly because of – its internal contradictions. Its evolution will serve as a fascinating barometer for the future of public spectacle, which we examine further in Part III. In Part II, though, we examine the roots of the modern Olympic Games and their development into a mega-event.

FURTHER READING

On television and the Games

Billings, A. (2008) *Olympic Media: Inside the Biggest Show on Television*, London: Routledge.

Moragas, M. de, Rivenburgh, N. K. and Larson, J. F. (eds) (1996) *Television in the Olympics*, London: John Libbey.

Puijk, R. (1997) *Global Spotlights on Lillehammer*, Luton: University of Luton Press.

Real, M. (1986) *Global Ritual: Olympic Media Coverage and International Understanding*, Paris, France: UNESCO.

On commercialisation

Barney, R. K., Wenn, S. R. and Martyn, S. G. (2002) *Selling the Games: The IOC and the Rise of Olympic Commercialism*, Salt Lake City: University of Utah Press.

Simson, V. and Jennings, A. (1992) *The Lords of the Rings*, London: Stoddart.

Smit, B. (2006) *Pitch Invasion: Adidas, Puma and the Making of Modern Sport*, London: Allen Lane.

PART II
FROM OUT OF THE PAST

CHAPTER 4

REVIVING THE OLYMPICS

The establishment of the modern Olympic Games in 1896 involved a classic instance of the invention of tradition, in which elements of the ancient Greek Games, English public school education, nineteenth-century sport festivals, emerging cultures of physical education, and a contemporary French perspective were grafted together. This took place in the context of late nineteenth-century European politics, and particularly the attempts of France to cope with the humiliation of its defeat by German forces in 1870, the year before a united Germany became a nation-state.

The ancient Olympic Games were held every four years for more than 1,000 years (between 776BC and AD260) in Olympia in the state of Elis. They continued to be held with some interruptions until AD393 when the Christian emperor Theodosius banned pagan festivals, including the Games. They were not the only such events in ancient Greece – there were Pythian, Nemean and Isthmian games, and many smaller-scale events, but the Olympic Games were the most important and longest lasting (Finley and Pleket 1976: 13). All these games were sacred and religious in character, staged to please the gods such as Apollo and Poseidon, and the Olympic Games were dedicated to the God Zeus. They were held at the religious shrine of Olympia, the site of a Temple to Zeus with a 40-foot-tall gold, silver and ivory statue, which was one of the Wonders of the Ancient World. Competitors, trainers and judges all took an oath before the statue that they would obey the rules. Oxen were sacrificed and victors crowned in front of the statue (Kidd 1984).

The Games were attended by many thousands of spectators. Initially only a single sprint of 190 metres was staged, but the programme gradually expanded to include more foot races, boxing, wrestling, pankration (unarmed combat) and the pentathlon (discus, javelin, jumping, running and wrestling). There were no team events. Contrary to their mythologising in the nineteenth century, the Games were not amateur in character – the ancient Greeks knew no such concept (see Young 1984, 2004: xi). Rewards for victory could be great. Money, pensions and gifts were common, and an Olympic victory could form a platform to launch a career in politics (Kidd 1984). Experts differ on the issue of material rewards for success at the Games. It is generally agreed that while the immediate rewards were limited to the olive wreath of victory, winners received rich rewards, both in cash and in privileges, when they returned home. Some, such as Young, believe this was always the case, others, such as Pleket, maintain that this only became the case in the later era of the ancient Games. Others again attribute growing professionalism to the Roman influence. Evidence is limited and inconclusive (Hill 1992: 7).

Some of the events would appear extremely violent to us. Combat often continued till death. The events grew out of military training in the context of the warlike and combative culture of Greek life. The Games lasted as long as they did in part because of the principle of the Olympic truce. This required safe passage to be given to all competitors and spectators. It also forbade other states from attacking Elis during the Games, and barred Elis from attacking its neighbouring states. The truce did not prevent wars but it did protect the Olympic Games from disruption by them (Kidd 1984).

The economic and political system of Greek city states was rooted in slavery and patriarchy. They were ruled by small elite male groups, whose power and wealth were sustained by a slave-based economy. Women, many of whom were slaves, had no political rights. Even when more elaborate forms of 'democracy' began to evolve, most notably in Athens, the dependency on slave labour remained. In the Games, only free males could enter, and women were barred as spectators (Kidd 1984). There were, though, also female sporting contests, such as those honouring the Goddess Hera.

It is important, of course, to be wary of generalisation about events which lasted over such a long period of time. The most striking and consistent feature which marks the ancient Games as distinct from their modern revival was their pagan religious character, as opposed to the secular form of the modern Olympic Games. The modern Olympics too, though, do feature

Figure 4.1 The start line at the ancient stadium in Olympia, Greece. Since the excavations of the site of the ancient Games at Olympia during the nineteenth and twentieth centuries, the ancient stadium has become a site of 'pilgrimage', an appropriate term for a movement so committed to ritual and religiosity. (Photograph courtesy of Annette Hofmann).

elements of reworked neo-pagan ritual, most notably the lighting of the 'sacred' flame from the rays of the sun, the conveying of this flame, by means of a torch relay, to the Olympic site, and the burning of the flame throughout the 15 days of the Games.

EMERGENCE AND REVIVAL

The collapse of the Roman Empire meant that, in the Western world, knowledge and understanding of the classical world of Greece and Rome declined for many centuries. During the Renaissance there was a period of rediscovery and reappropriation of Roman and Greek cultures that placed the Latin language and Greek philosophy at the heart of humanist education. Once inscribed at the core of Western education and philosophy, the classical influence remained strong through the Enlightenment and into the nineteenth century. In particular, the reformed English public schools of the mid-nineteenth century placed emphasis on the need to develop mind and body in harmony, inspired by ancient Greek philosophy. It was out of this that the cult of athleticism developed.

The ancient Olympic Games were certainly not lost from memory until the nineteenth century. A multi-volume book on the Olympic Games was published in 1419. Shakespeare and Milton both mention the Olympic Games in their work, as later do Goethe, Rousseau and Byron.[1] Voltaire referred to the *jeux olympiques* and Flaubert and Gide both used the word *olympique*, although not referring to sport (Mandell 1976: 29). But it was with the emergence and development of organised sport in its modern forms, from the eighteenth century onwards, that the term 'Olympic' began to enter into wider usage. Festivals involving sporting activity had been common across Europe from medieval times. Indeed multi-sport festivity, far from dying out in the fourth century, had continued to thrive in medieval fairs and festivals.

In the seventeenth century, Robert Dover established the Cotswold 'Olympick Games', which were staged with some gaps for the next 250 years. Robert Dover staged the events, in part, in order to combat the 'joyless moralism of the Puritans, whom he loathed' (Kidd 1984). Robert Dover was born in Norfolk, sometime between 1575 and 1582, and died in c.1652. He was a barrister, and may have been Catholic, but there appear to be few firm facts about his life. It is not clear whether Robert Dover founded or revived the Cotswold Games, but his involvement dates from 1612. The games owed more to the festive traditions of medieval England than they did to any knowledge of the Greek Games. They included singlestick combat, wrestling, cudgelling, dancing, jumping in sacks and shin-kicking (Williams 2009).

In staging such an annual event, Dover was provoking a puritan backlash, but was able to draw on the support of *The Book of Sports*, an official proclamation, which defended the right of respectable leisure after worship. It was first issued in May 1618 by James 1, and reaffirmed in 1633 by Charles I (Williams 2009). The games were terminated during the Civil War, but reinstated after the Restoration. They were certainly staged in 1725, and carried on into the nineteenth century. In later years they apparently became quite rowdy and were again terminated, this time by Act of Parliament, in 1851. They were revived once more in 1951 in conjunction with the Festival of Britain, and by 1972 were being invoked in discussion as part of a case for the importance of England in reviving the concept of the Olympic Games (Williams 2009: 150–170).

However successful Coubertin's establishment of the IOC and the modern Olympic Games at the end of the nineteenth century was, it has to be considered in context. From the late eighteenth century and throughout the nineteenth century, various forms of multi-sport festival were developed – in Greece, Scandinavia, North America and not least in the UK. The Highland game tradition of Scotland was revived during the 1820s and spread to North America by the 1850s. Circus-style entertainment incorporating elements of the Roman circus were developed in Paris from the 1820s and in New York in the 1850s. Use of the terms 'Olympic' and 'Olympian' occurs in Scandinavia in the 1830s, and in Liverpool in the 1860s. More significantly, the Much Wenlock Games were established in Shropshire in 1849 by Dr William Penny Brookes, a significant influence on Coubertin. The Greeks made several attempts to revive Olympic Games from 1859 onwards. So Coubertin's own project did not develop in a vacuum.

European sporting cultures

The process by which sport took on organisational forms only developed through struggle and contestation between competing notions of 'sport'. In eighteenth-century English dictionaries, 'sport' meant the field sports of hunting, shooting and fishing. By 1900, in Europe, the term typically denoted organised sporting contests, with the team games of football, rugby and cricket prominent. Yet in Asia, Africa and Latin America, the term would either have had no social currency or very different connotations. In the twentieth century, international sport governing bodies, including the IOC, would play a key role in establishing a new dominant understanding of 'sport'.

Two of the most influential sporting cultures, based partly on different conceptions of gymnastic exercise, were to emerge in Germany and Sweden during the nineteenth century. In Germany, this occurred around the Turnen Societies, and their pioneering figure Friedrich Jahn, and involved apparatus-based exercises. Johannes C. F. Guts-Muths, the father of German gymnastics, who was a formative influence on Friedrich Jahn, wrote about the ancient Games in his *Gymnastik für Jugend* (1793). In Sweden, the key figure, Ling, favoured free-standing exercise performed in disciplined unison. These two variants of gymnastics, along with the culture of athleticism and team games developed in English public schools from the 1840s, constituted, by the mid-century, three major European traditions of sporting exercise. When Coubertin began his own investigations into the subject of physical education, deeply influenced by his childhood reading of *Tom Brown's Schooldays*, he favoured, right from the start, the English model.

One of the earliest instances of the explicit use of an imagined and idealised ancient Olympism as a model was in Drehberg, outside Wörlitz in eastern Germany. Between 1777 and 1799, Prince Franz staged a festive competition supposedly based on the Olympic Games of antiquity. The games included horse races and gymnastic contests. The contestants were boys and girls from the surrounding schools, which were based on a model of progressive, child-oriented education, Das Philanthropin, devised by the prince. The event was not restricted to athletics, and also included celebration of Saturnalia, the Roman festival of wild joy, even debauchery. It was a day when class differences were ignored and rulers could fraternise, as Franz did, with their subjects. Marriageable girls were encouraged to dance with potential

70

mates until deep into the night.[2] According to Gary Schwartz, the games were part of a pedagogic and social ideal, played by schoolchildren to give 'a competitive edge to the physical training that was part of their humanistic education'. Schwartz says that the Drehberg fair became famous, drawing thousands of visitors and serving as propaganda for Wörlitz as a model for the world. Goethe attended and recommended it to the entire court of Weimar.[3]

In France in 1796, during the Revolution, 'Jeux Olympiques' were staged on the Champ de Mars in Paris (Kidd 1984). In Sweden, in 1834 and 1836, Gustav Johan Schartau organised sporting events, which he referred to as 'Olympic Games', in Ramlosa. Schartau was a disciple of the Swedish gymnastics pioneer Ling and was Professor at the Royal Charles Academy in Lund. There was also an 'Olympic'-styled event in Hungary. Vermes Lajos from Subotica, a landowner, a sport enthusiast and an athlete, organised sports competitions in which the best sportsmen took part at Lake Palić between 1880 and 1914, and several sports grounds were especially built.[4] In France, 'Olympic' games were organised for the students of a Dominican seminary near Grenoble in 1832, and continued to be held every two years until the twentieth century. An early winner, in 1846, was Henri Didon, who subsequently became a priest and, many years later, gave Coubertin the Olympic Motto 'Citius, Altius, Fortius – Faster, Higher, Stronger' (Durry undated).

In popular entertainment, as well as in education, the term Olympic was in circulation. In the early nineteenth century, the Cirque des Champs-Élysées, also known as the Cirque Olympique, was an enclosed hippodrome off the Champs-Élysées. The Cirque Olympique subsequently established itself in a building near Temple in 1827. The manager, Louis Dejean (1797–1879), then acquired a new permanent building, the Cirque d'Hiver, to provide a winter base for his touring circus, selling the old Cirque Olympique building in 1847. Located near the Place de la République, the Cirque d'Hiver is the world's oldest functioning extant circus building, and the company is also the world's oldest circus still active.[5] Franconi's Hippodrome, established in New York in 1853, staged Roman chariot races and Roman circus events. The arena, which held 6,000, was built by American showmen and named after the Italian horseman Antonio Franconi, who, with family members, performed in the Cirque Olympique in Paris. It included an indoor auditorium and an open-air course, around 300 metres long. As well as horse and chariot races, it featured gymnastics, ostrich races and monkeys, deer, camels and elephants. Although quite successful, it was demolished in 1859 to make way for the Fifth Avenue Hotel.[6] An Olympic Club was created in Montreal in 1842. It staged a two-day 'Olympic' Games in 1844, which included the first public lacrosse match, featuring aboriginals versus non-aboriginals. However, during the nineteenth century the Scottish 'Highland Games' and 'pedestrianism' (professional athletics) may have been more influential and popular forms of multi-sport festivity.[7]

In Ireland and Scotland there was a long history of staging multi-sport festivities, which still exists today in the form of the Highland Games (see Jarvie 1991). These were based on earlier Irish festivals, the Tailteann Games, which are known to date back to the twelfth century. After the years of oppression following the final defeat of the Jacobite rebellion in 1745, in which manifestations of 'Scottishness' such as the wearing of the plaid and the speaking of Gaelic were outlawed, the Victorian aristocracy embarked on a reinvention of Scottish tradition, in tartan-drenched form. This was given great impetus by the enthusiasm of Queen Victoria for Scotland, her acquisition of Balmoral, and the subsequent emergence of a culture

Jarvie calls 'Balmorality'. However, the reinvention and re-emergence of Gaelic traditions was already under way when the Celtic Highland Games were revived in the early nineteenth century. The thousands of Irish and Scots who emigrated to North America took these traditions with them, as marked by the staging of 'Caledonian Games' in Boston (1853) and New York (1856).

The Much Wenlock Games and the National Olympian Association

By the mid-nineteenth century then, there are plenty of examples of the use of the term Olympic or Olympian. At this point, three social themes begin to converge in the work of a few sporting pioneers. The first is the revival of interest in ancient Greek culture and in particular the concept of the development of mind and body in harmony. The second is the resultant cult of athleticism developed in the English public schools. The third is the growing concern within the Victorian bourgeoisie with social reform and rational recreation. The Much Wenlock Games, established in 1850 by William Penny Brookes, constituted a more organised and concerted attempt to establish a regular event. Brookes was probably the first person in this period to bring together the idea of the sport-based festivity, the term Olympic, and a revival of Greek philosophical principles. Historian David Young argues that he, rather than Coubertin, might be seen as the founder of the modern Olympics, although it is true, as MacAloon reminds us, that only Coubertin had the international breadth of vision crucial to the project (Young 1996: 12; MacAloon 1981). Hill, more cautiously, regards him as an 'intriguing footnote to world sports history in his own brand of rational recreationist intervention' (Hill 1992: 9–15).

Brookes, born in Much Wenlock in 1809, was the son of a doctor, became a doctor himself, and also, in 1841, became a JP. Like many middle-class gentlemen in this period, he became concerned with social reform and with encouraging rational recreation among the working classes. He founded the Agricultural Reading Society to promote 'useful information' and the 'Olympian Class' (renamed in 1860 the 'Wenlock Olympian Society') to 'promote the moral, physical and intellectual improvement of the inhabitants of the Town and neighbourhood of Wenlock'. Brookes set up the Agricultural Reading Society to encourage people to read as a way of informing their voting, after the 1832 Reform Act extended the franchise. He also wanted to discourage the local population from drinking (Hill 1992: 9). In 1850, he organised the first Much Wenlock Olympic Games. They included athletics, quoits, football and cricket. Brookes had an interest in Greek culture, but was also possibly also aware of and influenced by the Cotswold Games of Robert Dover (see Williams 2009). The Olympian Society organised annual games, which gradually came to be more athleticist and national in profile. Brookes, as a doctor, sports enthusiast and rational recreationist, had strong views on the necessity of providing physical education in state schools, and welcomed the 1871 Act in which instruction in drill for up to two hours a week and no more than 20 weeks a year could count as part of school attendance. In the late 1870s Brookes argued for the introduction of Swiss-style gymnastics in schools, and was a vigorous advocate of the values of athletics for the masses:

> The encouragement of outdoor exercise contributes to manliness of character. I say contributes, for true manliness shows itself not merely in skill in athletic and field

sports, but in the exercise of those moral virtues which it is one of the objects of religion to inculcate.

(cited in Hill 1992: 10)

In 1862, a Liverpool Olympic Festival had been held on the military parade ground, Mount Vernon, the first of six such annual events. The festival was promoted by John Hulley (1832–1875), a gymnasium owner and physical fitness expert, and Charles Melly (1829–1888), a Victorian philanthropist (and an ancestor of jazz singer George Melly). Hulley had been co-founder of the Liverpool Athletic Club. Melly was involved in the National Association for the Promotion of Social Science, the Working Men's Improvement Society, 'ragged schools', the Unitarian Mission, and the provision of infirmaries, public parks, playgrounds and drinking fountains for all.[8] Melly, as an ex-pupil of Rugby School, was a product of the muscular Christianity ethos. Hulley and Melly proposed to revive ideas of physical perfection, drawing on what they knew of the ancient Olympic Games, and, it was claimed, the Liverpool Olympic Festivals 'were organised on the lines of the ancient Greek ones'.[9]

Around 10,000 people turned up to watch running (120 yards and 300 yards), walking (1.5 miles and four miles), high jump, long jump, pole leap, throwing the disc (discus) and the cricket ball, boxing, wrestling and gymnastics. The following year the crowds grew to 15,000.

Figure 4.2 The German Gymnasium. Built by the German Gymnastic Society in 1864, this was the first purpose-built gymnasium in the United Kingdom. Ernst Revenstein, an organiser of the first National Olympian Games in London in 1866, was a president of the society.

A third event, in 1864, was marred by gambling and prostitution, prompting the organisers to move the 1865 event to Llandudno. That same year they were involved in establishing the National Olympian Association. After one more year at Llandudno the Olympic Festival returned to Liverpool for a final year in 1867, which featured over 300 competitors. After this point financial problems meant that no more were staged.[10] Meanwhile, Brookes had organised the third Shropshire Olympics which were combined with the thirteenth Much Wenlock Games (Matthews 2005: 56).

Brookes and the National Olympian Association were able to stage the First National Olympian Festival in London in 1866. The first National Olympian Games were organised by William Penny Brookes, John Hulley and Ernest Ravenstein of the German Gymnastic Society (GGS) in London. Ravenstein managed the Games, and many of the several nationals belonging to the GGS took part in the Games, as did cricketer W. G. Grace (Anthony 1986). A second National Olympian Games were held in Birmingham in 1867, with a third in Wellington, Shropshire the following year. But the embryonic Olympic movement in Britain was crushed by the rise of the Amateur Athletic Club (AAC), which, concerned to exclude the lower orders, introduced the famous clause excluding 'mechanics, artisans and labourers'. The AAC opposed the National Olympics and after 1868 only the Wenlock Olympic Games continued in England (Matthews 2005: 58). After a long drawn out struggle between various aspirants to control and define both athletics and amateurism, a compromise was engineered by a group from Oxford and Cambridge who persuaded the supporters of the AAC to drop the commitment to the exclusion of the working class, but to retain the concept of amateur sportsmen, excluding any form of professionalism (see Lovesey 1979). The resultant formation of the Amateur Athletic Association (AAA) produced a template for the distinction between amateur and professionalism that was copied by many other sports, and came to constitute a taken-for-granted reality amongst the bourgeois gentlemen who formed subsequent organisations. Brookes worked hard to promote the Olympic idea from 1850 until his death, which was, ironically enough, in 1895, one year before the first modern Olympic Games were staged (Matthews 2005: 57). A fourth National Olympian Games took place in 1874 in Much Wenlock, followed by a fifth in 1877 in Shrewsbury, and a final one in Hadley in 1883.

Morpeth also appropriated the Olympic name in 1883 for its annual Morpeth Games. The Morpeth Olympic Games involved Cumberland and Westmorland and featured wrestling and professional athletics. They took place regularly between 1881 and 1959, originally as a one-day event, but by 1912 popularity prompted their extension to a second day.[11] The area in which they were staged has been marked by street names – Olympia Hill and Olympia Gardens – and a local shop called Olympia Stores (which was recently closed and converted into flats).[12] Unlike the Olympic festivals in which Brookes was involved, this cannot be regarded as a significant forerunner of the Olympic Games. It does, however, contribute to the accumulating instances from the late eighteenth to late nineteenth centuries of the common use of the term Olympic to denote a multi-sport festival.

Greece, Soutsos and Zappas

The politics of the soil alone would seem to give the Greeks a privileged claim to 'ownership' of the concept of the Olympic Games. Coubertin was alert enough to this to recognise the

74

symbolic importance of staging the first Games in Greece, but the relationship of Coubertin, and the IOC to Graecian proprietorial claims was always an uncomfortable one. Coubertin, who in the end wished to be the father of the event, paid more credit to Dr Brookes than to Zappas and the other Greek pioneers. Later, when the second and third Olympic Games were shambolic, Coubertin was grateful to the Greeks for staging an interim or 'intercalated' games, but had no desire to encourage a regular Greece-based event. For the hundredth anniversary year of 1996, the IOC, in the view of many, chose mammon over tradition in awarding the Games to Atlanta; subsequent guilt, Greek righteous anger and strong lobbying prompted them to make amends by awarding the 2004 Games to Athens. So the Greek attempts at revival during the nineteenth century have been the subject of contestation and debate by historians ever since.

The growing interest in ancient Greece in general, and the Olympic Games in particular, was fuelled by archaeology and excavation of some of the key sites, including Troy, Mycenae and Olympia. The idea of excavating to unearth the site of the ancient Olympics was mooted in the eighteenth century, and the site was discovered by excavations in 1766, with additional early excavations in 1787. There were further excavations by the French in 1829, and a real breakthrough by German archaeologists in 1852. The first excavations on a major scale, though, did not take place until 1875 and, after a decade of extensive work, an Archaeological Museum was opened on the site in 1886. The 1889 'Exposition Universelle' in Paris included models of the excavations.

Young considers the idea of a Greek revival to have been commenced by Panagiotis Soutsos, a poet, publisher and patriot. From 1833 onward, his poems alluded to the Olympic Games. In 1835 he contacted the government to propose that 25 March be made a national holiday in celebration of the War of Independence, and that the celebration should include a revival of the Olympic Games. His proposal envisaged a four-year cycle, with the Games staged in four Greek cities. There was no immediate response, but in 1838 the town of Letrini established a committee to revive the Olympics, although no such event took place. Soutsos continued his campaign through the 1840s, but further developments were due to the work of Evangelos Zappas (see Young 1996).

Evangelos Zappas (1800–1865) was a wealthy landowner and businessman of Greek ancestry. In early 1856, he proposed a permanent revival of the Olympic Games, and offered to finance the project. The first of the Zappas Olympic Games was held in 1859. He also provided funds for the eventual restoration of the ancient Panathenaic Stadium, although this was not completed until after his death. Zappas-inspired Olympic Games were staged in Athens in 1859, 1870, 1875 and 1889, with varying degrees of success. In 1859 Dr William Penny Brookes was in contact with Greece, sending £10 to be presented to the winner of an event in the Olympian Games. Brookes, corresponding via the British Ambassador, also urged the Greek government to revive the ancient Games.

The 1870 Games in the restored stadium were the most successful of the Zappas Olympics, with over 30,000 spectators, and enthusiastic reviews in the newspapers. Members of Athens's elite then suggested that the Games should be restricted only to athletes from the upper class and that the general public be banned. This social exclusion damaged the 1875 Games, which attracted only 24 athletes and small crowds. Young (1996) called the 1875 Zappas Olympics a 'disaster'. The next event in 1889 was a badly run event in a gymnasium, and in 1891 and

1893 the Panhellenic Gymnastic Society took up the baton. The Zappas Olympic Games and the Much Wenlock Olympian Games were more important staging posts on the road to full revival than many of the other events which merely utilised the Olympic word.

COUBERTIN, THE FRENCH AND THE ENGLISH

So, during the nineteenth century, the term 'Olympic' was coming into more common usage, and multi-sport events were being staged, not least in the UK and Greece. That Coubertin's model was ultimately the one that became dominant was due to a combination of circumstances. Coubertin's own determination, his organisational and diplomatic skills, and his social contacts were central. His early exposure to and romantic obsession with the world of English school sport, as portrayed by Thomas Hughes in *Tom Brown's Schooldays* – which Coubertin first read in 1875, when he was 12 – was significant. All this, though, must be set in the context of social and political factors. The Olympic Games were only one manifestation of the emergence of modern organised spectator sport that had been growing for a hundred years, but was by the late nineteenth century becoming a more significant form of leisure activity. Sport and the modern media began their fateful interaction around the time that the first modern Olympic Games were staged. In this sense the emergence and the success of the modern Olympic Games were in part the outcome of social processes beyond the ability even of as striking a figure as Coubertin to manage. Sport acquired national and then international governance between 1860 and 1920. Regular international competitions (such as football's World Cup) were established. It seems inevitable that some form of international multi-sport event would have evolved. Coubertin's distinctive contribution consists of the construction of this in the form of Olympism, which combined ritual, festival and spectacle, ethical principles and a particular, if not peculiar, organisational form.

BOX 4.1 **BARON PIERRE DE COUBERTIN**

Pierre de Coubertin (1863–1937) was born in Paris in 1863, the fourth child of an aristocratic Catholic family. Educated at Jesuit schools and colleges, he completed a Bachelor of Science degree in 1881. His interest in education and sport led him to his life's project, reviving the Olympic Games. He was married in 1895 to Marie Rothan, from a Protestant family (who lived until 1963 when she was 102). Their first son, born in 1896, was afflicted by sunstroke at the age of two and never recovered, leading a vegetative existence. Their daughter, Renée, was born in 1902. In later years Coubertin suffered financial problems and the family home had to be sold. He died in 1937 at the age of 74.

One needs to understand the emergence of media sport in relation to modernity and capitalism, and particularly in relation to the period from 1880 to 1914. What was going on in this time? It marked the pinnacle and final moment of grandeur for the British Empire, before its challenge by new rising powers such as Germany and the USA and its ultimate eclipse and demise. It marked the rise of Germany, formed in 1871, and the rise of German power, provoking new alliances and rivalries in Europe. It marked the rise of American power towards its dominance of the world economy. The British historian Asa Briggs (1991) identified it as the period of the birth of mass entertainment. The spread of literacy, wireless telegraphy, development of a mass circulation popular press and the emergence of cinema from the mid-1890s were all factors. Branded goods had become more common, distributed more effectively by the new chain stores. A revolution in advertising was bringing brand names to the domestic vocabulary.

This period fostered the birth of modern sport – the establishment of governing bodies, agreed rules, competitions, stadiums and spectatorship. To an extent this can be seen as a process of a rationalising modernity – bureaucratised, systematised, institutionalised, rule-governed, and subject to quantification (Guttman 1978). In its routine separation of performer and spectator, it also established the structural bases for the commercialisation and commodification of sport that become such a central part of the Olympic story from the 1970s onwards. From the late nineteenth century, sport was also in the forefront of globalising processes – some of the first international bodies were sport-related ones such as the IOC, the IAAF and the ILTF. National and international competitions grew in scope and ambition, most notably with the establishment of the modern Olympic Games in 1896.

But if it was a world that was becoming more globalised it was certainly not a flat world and this process was not a neutral one. The very technologies and infrastructures of communication inscribed the dominance of the major imperial powers. Telegraph lines linked the peripheries of empires to their core centres in Paris and London – so it was, for example, easier for Ghana to contact London than neighbouring Upper Volta (now Burkina Faso).

Sport diffusion was strongly linked to the structure of empires (cricket and rugby spread to British Empire countries and almost nowhere else). By comparison, soccer – increasingly rejected by the British bourgeoisie in favour of rugby, was spread by skilled tradesmen, engineers, etc. to South America and elsewhere but not to the British Empire countries. The old imperial rivalries between Britain and France were replayed in sport as each country sought to be a dominant organising force, with greater success going to the French. Despite American economic power, its own sports, lacking the support of an established imperial network, did not export successfully. Indeed the cultures of sport in the USA were characterised by the establishment of a distance from Europe, and the construction of a distinctive American-ness. The myths of origin around baseball and American football minimised and marginalised their European sources. International sporting organisation was largely forged by English and French elites. So it was in this period that the modern world – the world of the twentieth century – was largely forged and, with it, modern spectator sport and the roots of media sport.

Coubertin's own youthful world was one in which a mood of national shame prevailed. The impact of the defeat of France on 1 September 1870 at the battle of Sedan, less than eight weeks after Napoleon III had declared war on Prussia, was considerable. On 4 September 1870 France became a republic again, and the following year France lost Alsace and Lorraine, as Germany became a united nation and a threat of growing significance to France. Coubertin was greatly concerned at what he regarded as the physical degeneracy of French youth, especially when compared to the well-trained and disciplined German youth. His lifelong concern for education and in particular physical education was shaped by this formative moment.

The novel *Tom Brown's Schooldays* was to have a great influence on the growing cult of athleticism, and on the thinking of Coubertin, who read it as a boy and reread it as an adult. According to Mangan, Coubertin was inspired not so much by the actual headmaster, Dr Arnold, as by the version of him that existed only in the imagination of Thomas Hughes. In *L'Education en Angleterre* (1888), Coubertin testified to an absolute belief in the English boarding school system (Mangan 1981: 130). The association of sport and moral education became a significant element in Coubertin's rearticulation of Olympism. It was not just an obsessive admiration for the Hughes version of Arnold, though – more generally, Coubertin was something of an anglophile, who was also heavily influenced by Hippolyte Taine's *Notes sur Angleterre* (1872).

BOX 4.2 *TOM BROWN'S SCHOOLDAYS*, BY THOMAS HUGHES

The novel *Tom Brown's Schooldays*, by Thomas Hughes, is identified in many British sport histories as an emblematic text, representing the emergence of the cult of athleticism and the ethos of muscular Christianity. The popularity of the book led to an over-emphasis on the importance of Rugby School and of its headmaster, Thomas Arnold. The new Victorian bourgeoisie were preoccupied by the ever-present danger of lower-class unrest. Arnold was haunted by visions of mob violence, chaos and revolution, and lay awake at night contemplating the ever-growing crowds of workers demanding parliamentary reform (Gathorne-Hardy 1977: 80–81).

Thomas Hughes (1822–1896) was the son of a paternalistic Tory who sent him to Rugby School. He became an active Christian Socialist and muscular Christian, organising gymnastics, boxing, rowing and cricket at the Working Men's College (Lowerson 1993: 158). His one successful novel, *Tom Brown's Schooldays*, was hugely popular with the middle-class families who were being attracted by the new reformed public schools and it had a significant influence on the subsequent growth of the cult of athleticism. In the book, Tom, reduced on his first day to a 'motionless body' by a rugby scrum, is nonetheless transformed by the end of the tale into an active and rounded person – thus boys were turned into men through the process of schooling.

Hughes's fictionalised version of Dr Arnold differs significantly from Arnold himself. There is little evidence that Arnold directly and deliberately promoted cricket and football for their educational value (McIntosh 1952: 30). He had only a mild interest in the games themselves, but encouraged them as part of his new regime of power, based on a reformed prefect and fagging system, with Christian morality and social responsibility at its core. Hughes's rather humanised and jolly portrayal of Arnold's regime was 'made rosy by nostalgia' (Birley 1993: 209–210). However, the masters and prefects under his influence took to athleticism with a growing enthusiasm (Holt 1989: 80), although Mangan establishes clearly that the real seed-bed of athleticism was at other public schools, such as Uppingham (Mangan 1981). By the 1860s, Birley suggests,

---

sport was seen as 'the great character-builder on which the nation depended to train its leaders' (Birley 1993: 286). The 1860s saw the introduction of games masters, professional coaches, and inter-house and inter-school competitions. Mangan suggests that parents and masters alike subscribed to the ethical value of games as a source of good sense, noble traits, manly feelings, generous dispositions, gentlemanly deportment and comradely loyalty (Mangan 1981: 132).

Many accounts of the period emphasise the commitment to developing sound minds and healthy bodies, and its roots in classical Greece. Yet in Tom Brown we also see the traces of an English philistinism – a lack of interest in the cultivation of the intellect. Social Darwinism – in which life is conflict, strength comes through struggle, and success is the prerogative of the strong – became more influential in the second half of the nineteenth century. There was a gulf between the constructed image of the schools and the brutality of existence within them (Mangan 1987: 139–142).

(Extracted from Garry Whannel (1999) 'From "motionless bodies" to acting moral subjects: Tom Brown, a transformative romance for the production of manliness', *Diegesis: Journal for the Association for Research in Popular Fictions* 4.)

Coubertin combined, sometimes uneasily, a very real commitment to internationalism with a deep concern for France and its education system. He also had pacifist sympathies (see Quanz 1993). He was influenced by social theorist Frédéric LePlay who, concerned at the impact of class division, sought means to restore peace and harmony (see Guttmann 1992: 7). He believed that sporting competition between all the nations of the world could lead to mutual understanding and respect between individuals of different nations, races and social positions (Charpentier and Boissonnade 1999: 32).[13]

Coubertin believed that the classic gymnasia of ancient Greece (basically sports fields rather than modern enclosed buildings) enabled a triple unity: between different sporting disciplines, between young and old, and between practical and theoretical approaches (Hill 1992: 6). In turn, this last point relates to the Greek notion of developing mind and body in harmony, which also underpinned the development of athleticism in the English public schools of the nineteenth century. For Coubertin, this did not involve a unity of men and women; whilst in favour of greater social equality, Coubertin did not extend this to gender, and to the end he was hostile to the involvement of women as competitors.

Coubertin visited England several times during the 1880s, to study the educational system. In 1883 he visited Oxford and Cambridge and also the public schools of Rugby, Harrow and Eton.[14] By 1887 he had also gained knowledge of Winchester, Wellington, Marlborough, Charterhouse, Coopers Hill, Westminster and Christ's Hospital. He contrasted the lack of physical education in French schools with active physical activity in English schools. He became an ardent campaigner and lobbyist, visiting the UK and USA to produce reports for the French government on physical education. His report on the USA represented America as a place where the gymnastic systems of Jahn and Ling were being rejected in favour of British team games.[15]

Coubertin knew and understood diplomacy, and made elaborate manoeuvres to build political allies. A keen rower, Coubertin visited Henley Royal Regatta. He was impressed by the Henley organisation, which he described as 'three concentric circles' – the nucleus, the nursery and the façade. This distinguished those who were deeply committed, those who could be educated to the cause, and those whose position and influence could be useful. This model was used as the basis of the IOC constitution (Anthony 1997) and indeed still serves as a characterisation of the way the IOC operates today. When planning the Paris Congress that established the IOC, Coubertin was politically astute enough to include dignitaries from Scotland, Wales and Ireland as well as England.

In 1881 Brookes visited France and was so taken aback by the physical degeneracy of the population that he wrote to the French government on the subject (Hill 1992: 11). In January 1890, Brookes wrote to Coubertin, they commenced a correspondence and in October Coubertin visited Brookes in Much Wenlock (Hill 1992: 11–13). Brookes was then aged 80, whilst Coubertin was only 26. Brookes and Coubertin continued to correspond, Brookes lending his support to the Olympic project. In 1890, Coubertin wrote in *La Revue Athlétique* that 'If the Olympic Games that Modern Greece has not yet been able to revive still survives today, it is due, not to a Greek, but to Dr W. P. Brookes'.[16] Coubertin invited Brookes to the 1894 Congress but he was too ill to attend and died the following year, missing his dreamed-of Olympic revival by just one year. It is also clear that Coubertin knew of the work of Zappas. According to some assessments, Coubertin subsequently tended to gloss over and minimise the role of his predecessors, Zappas and Brookes. He did, though, write an obituary of Brookes for the *New York Review of Books*, in which Brookes is described as his 'oldest friend' (Anthony 1986).

In England, the fears of the bourgeoisie at the threat from the 'lower orders' and their desire to maintain social distinction had led to the development of a sharp division between amateur and professional sport. In governing bodies for sport, professionals were either excluded altogether, as was the case with athletics, rowing and tennis, or had their inferiority marked, as was the case with golf and cricket. Only the Football Association, faced with the huge popularity of professional football and the threat of a breakaway, had been forced to compromise and admit professionalism. Rugby, by contrast, ended by splitting into two distinct sports, one professional and one amateur. Coubertin was certainly concerned about the commercialisation of sport, which he saw as a threat, and he shared the values and orientations of the world of aristocratic links and gentlemen's clubs in which amateurism was a taken-for-granted feature of sporting contestation. However, he never regarded amateurism as the most vital issue. Nevertheless, the modern Olympic Games inherited and enshrined for the next 90 years a concept of 'amateur' born of class discrimination. It was during the Presidency (1952–72) of Avery Brundage that the issue came to a head, and only in the 1980s, when the widespread payment of athletes could no longer be ignored, did the IOC move to neutralise the issue by making it a concern of the individual sport federations rather than of the IOC.

At the same time that Coubertin's plans for the IOC and the first Olympic Games were beginning to crystallise, so were plans for a multi-sport event linking British Empire countries. This scheme, with roots in imperial power and racism, was developed by John Astley Cooper, who began proposing a Pan-Britannic Festival in print in 1891. This idea was overtaken by the modern Olympic Games, but it laid the seeds of the idea that resurfaced as the Empire

Games. Indeed Cooper and Coubertin met in the early 1890s to discuss these matters, but Cooper's essentially racist and imperialist vision cannot have appealed to Coubertin. Cooper's ideas combined

> several important aspects of life – culture, industry and athletics in a grandiose festival celebrating the British race. The concept implied, but did not explicitly state, that the race was superior; Cooper asked if Britons were ready to undertake 'actions for the benefit of mankind which may make the name of England to be sung for all time as an example to races yet to come'.
>
> (Moore 1987: 146)

It is clear, according to Moore, that Cooper's idea was intended to include 'only adult males from the so-called white Dominions – Australia, New Zealand, Canada and South Africa as well as those subjects eligible in Great Britain' (Moore 1987: 148). In the event, the Empire Games were first staged in 1930 in Hamilton, Ontario, at a moment when the relationship between the UK and the old 'white' empire countries was being reshaped. Historian Richard Holt commented that 'the loosening bonds of Empire came at the same time as new economic pressures were being placed upon the relationships between the Dominions and Britain' (quoted in Phillips 2000: 5).

The subsequent trajectory of the Empire Games makes an interesting contrast with the Olympic Games – the very title of the event, unlike that of the World Cup or the Olympic Games, had to keep changing to match contemporary political realities. Until 1950 it was the 'British Empire Games', after which it became the 'British Empire and Commonwealth Games'. In 1970 the embarrassment of 'empire' was dropped, and the games became the 'British Commonwealth Games'. Four years later, in a symbolic deterritorialisation, 'British' was dropped and the event became the 'Commonwealth Games'.[17] The huge success of the Olympic Games and subsequently both the World Cup and football's continental championships has reduced the status of the Commonwealth Games immensely – but none of this could be foreseen in 1890.

THE 1894 CONGRESS AND THE 1896 GAMES

During the 1880s, Coubertin's commitment to educational reform, his research into physical education and his interest in the concept of reviving the Olympic Games were converging. At the Exposition Universelle in 1889, he organised the first Congress of Physical Exercise and school competitions. In the last decade of the nineteenth century the long gestation of Coubertin's thinking came to fruition. At a conference at the Sorbonne in 1892, he spoke with eloquence about the project of re-establishing the Olympic Games (Charpentier and Boissonnade 1999: 29–33). Coubertin utilised the fifth anniversary of the Union des Sociétés Françaises de Sports Athlétiques (USFSA) in 1892 to propose the project of reviving the Games. He ensured that at the 1893 General Assembly, the Society would stage a Congress to discuss the project further (Hill 1992: 18). He then discovered a general lack of enthusiasm for the revival of the Games and was forced to recast the proposed Congress as being primarily about amateurism, with the Olympics as a side issue. He was, however, able to recruit two strong

Figure 4.3
The De Coubertin monument. The heart of De Coubertin was entombed in this monument in Olympia which has become another site of Olympic pilgrimage. Students and their professors from all over the world attend the annual International Olympic Academy, and a visit to the De Coubertin memorial is obligatory. (Photograph courtesy of Annette Hofmann).

supporters, Charles Herbert, the secretary of the English AAA, and Professor William Sloane, of Princeton University (Hill 1992: 19–20). In the event, the 1894 Congress established the IOC and instigated the planning of the first modern Olympic Games, to be staged in Athens in 1896. The choice of Athens is the subject of considerable confusion. Evidence from the minutes suggests that delegates favoured London. Young suggests that Coubertin, having himself determined in advance upon Athens, manoeuvred to ensure this outcome (Young 1996: 100–105).

The 1894 Congress was attended by 79 delegates, representing 49 organisations from 12 countries (Mandell 1976: 86). The meeting was, not surprisingly, heavily European, with Australia and the USA the only non-European countries represented. In the event, the first IOC had 13 members, all male. There were two each from Great Britain and France, and one each from Italy, Greece, the Russian Empire, Austria-Hungary, Norway-Sweden and Bohemia.

There were three non-European members, from the United States, New Zealand and Argentina. The IOC was established as a body whose members did not represent any external body, nor were they answerable to any external institution. The IOC alone was the owner of the Olympic Games, and the custodian of 'Olympism'. It determined to have regular Congresses every few years, along with annual meetings referred to as 'Sessions'. The IOC's rules call on it to guide modern sport into desirable channels, and promote the development of those fine physical and moral qualities which are the basis of sports.

CONCLUSION

In the establishment of a new regular event, symbols, myths, narratives and an imagined history are all important. From the start, certain traditions were invented. There was an Opening Ceremony, with a key ritualised opening phrase. Winners got a silver medal and an olive wreath, and runners up a copper medal and a laurel wreath. National flags were hoisted at victory ceremonies. Coubertin derived the 'Faster, Higher, Stronger' motto from a 1891 speech by the Dominican priest, Father Henri Didon. The Olympic Oath taken by competitors, was first written by Coubertin in 1906, but was not utilised until 1920. The Olympic Village, the Olympic Flame and the Olympic torch relay did not appear until much later.

That there was a substantial mythologising of the ancient Greek Games has long been clear. Where blemishes in Olympic 'purity' are acknowledged this is often ascribed to the malign and decadent influence of the Romans in the later period of the ancient Games. An English Olympian, Theodore Cook, manages, with patrician grandeur, to link the supposed commercialism of the Romans with late nineteenth-century sporting professionalism:

> But we may at least remember that the ancient Games of Greece were only ruined by the professionals of the late Roman Empire, that there was once a time when athletic energy did not imply limited liability companies, when first-rate games did not depend on gate money for their existence.
>
> (Cook 1908: x)

In Athens in 1896, there were 81 athletes from 12 countries, and another 230 athletes from Greece, in 9 disciplines and 43 events. The Games also included the marathon, devised by the French philosopher Michel Breal shortly after the Congress of 1894 (Durry, undated). There were nine sports: cycling, fencing, gymnastics, lawn tennis, shooting, swimming, athletics, weightlifting and wrestling. So both the organisation and the Games were almost entirely European, but Coubertin was keen to get his show on the road. Coubertin did not expect the Greeks to be capable of staging the Games but was convinced by Dimetrias Bikelas that it could be done. In the event, once the Greeks secured the Games, they tended to sideline Coubertin, who was upset not to be more involved. He was further put out when the official account only mentioned him once, although he retaliated by proclaiming of the Olympics, in his own introduction to the report, 'I claim its paternity with raised voice'. The King of Greece wanted to have the Games permanently sited in Greece and Coubertin had to utilise his diplomatic skills in proposing a separate Pan-Hellenic Games, spaced between the Olympics. In the event this only happened in 1906 (Hill 1992: 20–25).

The question of whether Coubertin, Brookes, Zappas or indeed others have the best claim to be the key figure is in the end not crucial, although clearly Coubertin has by far the strongest claim to have formed and shaped modern Olympism. The modern Olympics came into being because of the energetic work of all these figures, but the project was successful because the combination of circumstances was favourable. Indeed it seems inevitable that some form of international sporting event would have been created. What is of greater interest is the particular manner in which this happened, allowing the IOC, itself a very peculiar organisational form, ownership over such a powerful symbolic cultural event.

FURTHER READING

Coubertin, P. de (2000) *Olympism: Selected Writings*, Lausanne: International Olympic Committee.
Finley, M. I. and Pleket, H. W. (1976) *The Olympic Games: The First Thousand Years*, London: Chatto & Windus.
MacAloon, John (1981) *This Great Symbol: Pierre de Coubertin and the Origins of the Modern Olympic Games*, Chicago: University of Chicago Press.
Mandell, R. (1976) *The First Modern Olympics*, Berkeley: University of California Press.
Young, D. C. (1996) *The Modern Olympics: A Struggle for Revival*, Baltimore, MD: Johns Hopkins University Press.

CHAPTER 5

FROM WORLD'S FAIRS TO MEGA-EVENTS

Whilst this book is concerned with the Olympic Games, we consider it essential that the modern Olympics are understood in relation to other developments of their time. The early Olympic Games as a cultural form were closely linked to international or universal expositions (expos) or world's fairs. Although they achieved some independence from 1912 onwards it was only in the post-Second World War television era that the Olympics were able to become a fully fledged stand-alone sports 'mega-event'. This chapter traces that development, examining how the Olympic Games retained elements of its origins whilst it altered in relation to other significant political, economic and cultural processes. Historically the sport genre of mega-event can be seen as the cuckoo's egg in the world's fairs' nest. Whilst world's fairs drew and continue to draw many more people to their locations and last much longer temporally than an Olympic Games or football World Cup, they are nowhere near as highly mediated or as TV-dependent as sports mega-events. The Olympic Games, however, became the 'world championship of world championships' (Donnelly 1996: 35) and a mass-mediated global spectacle (as we have seen in Chapter 3). This potentially vast global audience is one of the major dimensions in any claims to be a mega-event.

In this chapter we look first at alternative views of the growth of the Olympic Games, in the context of Empire and capitalist modernity. Next we briefly describe the development of the first three Olympic Games (1896, 1900 and 1904) in relation to world's fairs and expos. Then we shed particular light on London's experience of hosting the 1908 and 1948 Olympics and, finally, we consider alternative sports and physical culture events and the growth of the reach of the Olympics in the twentieth century.

WORLD'S FAIRS, EMPIRE AND TECHNOLOGY

In this section we contrast two broad approaches to the Olympics – what might be called the structural and the phenomenological. Maurice Roche (2000, 2003) suggests that the transition from world's fairs to sports mega-events reflects a broader differentiation in stages of modernity – from early, through mature to late periods of modernity. From the mid-nineteenth century (and the 'Great Exhibition' held in London in 1851) until 1914 and the start of the First World War these mega-events reflected an ambitious and optimistic view of progress. From the end of that war in 1918 until the early 1970s, despite the major wars, economic and political crises and other social and cultural events of the twentieth century, there was an assumption of qualified progress underpinning the expos. From the mid-1970s onward there has been

85

greater uncertainty about the future attached to the mega-events. Over this period mega-events have moved from being 'timekeepers of progress' to 'media events'. In fact Roche (2003: 107) contends that late modernity is an 'event-oriented culture' providing people with 'important cultural resources for the organization of time and identity at both a personal and a societal level'. In this culture, sports mega-events

> provide people with enduring motivations and special opportunities to participate in collective projects which have the characteristics of, among other things, structuring social space and time, displaying the dramatic and symbolic possibilities of organized and effective social action, and reaffirming the embodied agency of people as individual actors, even if the latter is only displayed in the activity of spectatorship.
>
> (Roche 2003: 109)

To unpick this statement a little it is worth considering the extent to which world's fairs in the nineteenth and early twentieth centuries were linked to the emergence of 'a system of international politics undergirded by a liberal capitalist world order' (Keys 2006: 184). In these emerging conditions technology, trade and imperialism played a part in the struggles between the French and British empires and the rising new US power. The international sport 'system' that developed in the first half of the twentieth century (discussed in Chapter 2) with the IOC, NOCs and IFs 'run primarily by men in Western democracies' (Keys 2006: 185) can be seen to be dependent on this context.

The first significant 'expo' was held in the 'Crystal Palace' in Hyde Park, London, in 1851 under the title 'The Great Exhibition of the Works of Industry of All Nations'. This British exhibition was an attempt to make clear to the world its role as industrial leader. As the 'Great Exhibition' was the first international exhibition of manufactured products, it influenced the development of several aspects of society, including art and design education and international trade and relations, and it set the precedent for many subsequent international exhibitions, also referred to as 'world's fairs', which have been staged to the present day.

The main attractions at expos are the national pavilions, created by participating countries, at which innovations in science, technology, manufacturing and the arts can be displayed. This remains the case today where the current (2010) expo in Shanghai has been receiving millions of visitors to marvel at new designs and technologies. A particular attraction for the burgeoning Chinese middle class is the Japan Pavilion, featuring the latest in toilet technology with high-efficiency flushing systems, heated seats and built-in bidets (Pierson 2010).

As Figure 5.1 illustrates, between 1851 and the 1970 expos or world's fairs presented various novel types of industrial machinery, manufacturing processes (steel making), materials and energy sources (petroleum, gasoline engine, the peaceful use of atomic energy), modes of transport (the elevator, monorail, moving sidewalk, mass production cars and airplanes), media and communication (mechanical typesetting, which underpinned the newspaper industry, the telephone, telegraph, cinematography and television) and buildings (Eiffel Tower). Since the signing of the 1928 Convention on International Exhibitions, the Bureau International des Expositions (BIE) has served as the international sanctioning body for expos. BIE-approved fairs are divided into a number of types: universal, international or specialised. They usually last between three and six months. Unlike the Olympic Games, however, they do not follow a

from out of the past

Year	City	Visitors (millions)	Technology
1851	London	6.0	Industrial machinery
1853	New York		Elevator
1862	London	6.2	Steel making, mechanical typesetting
1867	Paris	6.8	Aluminium, petroleum, gasoline engine
1873	Vienna	7.2	
1876	Philadelphia	9.9	Monorail, large steam engine, telephone, telegraph, typewriter
1878	Paris	6.0	Internal combustion engine, rubber tyres, refrigeration, phonograph
1889	Paris	32.0	Electric light, Eiffel's Tower
1893	Chicago	27.5	Alternating electric current, electric light bulb, electric train, kinetoscope
1900	Paris (including 2nd Olympic Games)	48.0	Moving sidewalk, military technology, large screen cinematography
1904	St Louis (including 3rd Olympic Games)	19.7	Flying machines, long-distance wireless telegraph, radio tube
1908	London (including 4th Olympic Games)	8.4	
1911	Glasgow	11.5	
1915	San Francisco	18.8	Mass production cars
1924/5	London	27.0	
1933/4	Chicago	48.7	Deco architecture and design, experimental television
1939/40	New York	45.0	Rocketry, nylon, plastics, domestic air conditioning, mass television
1958	Brussels	41.5	Nuclear reactor, atomic clock, atomic energy
1967	Montreal	51.0	Lasers, split-screen film technology
1970	Osaka	64.2	

Figure 5.1 Selected world's fairs and expos and new technologies, 1851–1970.

Source: adapted from Roche (2000: 43, 46, 160).

regular four-year cycle. The Olympic Games have been associated with breakthroughs in new technology, but this is more tangential to their main purpose. New developments in design and the use of materials for constructing venues and facilities have been a feature of the Olympic Games since at least the Tokyo Summer Games in 1964. Arguably in recent years also the Olympics have served as a test-bed for new technologies in the media and in terms of security and surveillance. We discuss this more in Chapter 8.

As we noted in Chapter 2, John Hoberman (1995: 6 ff.) argues that the International Olympic Committee (IOC) formed in 1894 bears comparison with other idealist international organisations developed at the end of the nineteenth century and beginning of the twentieth century, such as the Red Cross (1863), Esperanto (1887) and the Scouting Movement (1908). He argues that such groups 'belong to a genre of international organizations' based on anxieties about war and peace, and comprising bourgeois and socialist factions (Hoberman 1995: 11). All four organisations were ideologically distinct from Marxist internationalism and the First International founded in 1864. They share elements in common with cultural movements such as Wagnerism (developing from 1872) and the Salzburg music festival that began in 1920.

Hoberman (1995: 15–17) suggests that a comparison between Coubertin and Baden-Powell (founder of the Scouts) and the approach of the IOC to nobility reveals the autocratic politics of the founder of the modern Olympics. As we have seen in Chapter 2, the IOC was not founded as an 'association' of democratically elected members, but as a 'club' derived from the model of the Henley Royal Regatta, in England.

In contrast with this view of the growth of the Olympics, tied very much into the development of international political systems and capitalist modernity, anthropologist John MacAloon (1984, 2006) argues that the event or international exposition genre – of which world's fairs and the Olympics were a part – derived from a cultural movement that shared affinities with the spirit of modern sport. The 'MacAloon thesis', as Roche (2000: 91–94) calls it, is expounded in several other places (MacAloon 1981, 1996, 1999) and discussed more fully in Chapter 8 of this book. He essentially sees the Olympic Games as a 'modern secular ritual' (MacAloon 1999) and (referring to the Barcelona Games in 1992) a highly complex operation (MacAloon 1996: 75–76). For MacAloon, spectacle as a distinct genre is 'neither good nor bad, neither liberating nor alienating' (1996: 272). Hence there is a need to evaluate 'particular spectacles' because spectacle is a new genre of cultural performance which offers the chance to gain control over the difference between image and reality (as discussed by Boorstin (1961) and Debord (1967/1970), amongst others). He argues that 'the Olympic Games create a sort of *hyper-structure* in which categories and stereotypes are condensed, exaggerated and dramatized, rescued from the "taken for granted" and made objects of explicit and lively awareness for a brief period every four years' (1996: 274–275). He concludes that the Games have become a 'sort of collective divination about the fate and condition of the world . . . a nervous dramatization of our hopes that the ensuing divination will be reassuring and that the Games will go on forever' (1996: 280 n. 71). In the next section we comment briefly on the 1896, 1900 and 1904 Olympic Games in the light of this discussion. In particular we identify the lack of prominence of the Olympics and sport in general amongst the public at this time.

THE EARLY MODERN OLYMPIC GAMES: 1896–1904

MacAloon (1981: 198–203, 244–247) notes how the first modern Olympic Games held in 1896 in Athens can best be described as haphazard and unremarkable. They were poorly advertised, attracted few athletes and gained little coverage in the European press. Representatives of 13 nations attended the inaugural Olympic Congress in 1894 and another 21 sent their written support, but only 12 nations were represented in Athens (USA, Germany, UK, Australia, France, Denmark, Greece, Sweden, Switzerland, Bulgaria, Hungary and Chile). There were nine sports: cycling, fencing, gymnastics, lawn tennis, shooting, swimming, athletics, weightlifting and wrestling. The athletes were almost entirely European, but Coubertin was keen to get the Olympic show on the road.

In 1900 in Paris the Olympic Games were overshadowed by the world's fair. Originally the Games were advertised as the 'Competition of the Exhibition', as a sideshow. It is impossible to find traces of the main stadium because there was no main stadium – the track and field events appear to have been held mostly in fields in the Bois de Boulogne, and the swimming in the Seine. Young (2004: 154) says that athletes did compete sporadically on the outskirts of Paris, but 'there were no crowds of spectators and apparently most athletes did not even know

they were in the Olympics. It was a total failure.' Coubertin called the 1900 Olympics a 'humiliated vassal' to the world's fair (Keys 2006: 207 n. 22). Nonetheless the Paris 1900 poster features a woman holding fencing épées and a helmet, and French Olympic historians Charpentier and Boissonade (1999: 54) write 'this intrusion of women in the sporting domain, till now reserved for men, provoked arguments involving some talented writers'. French intellectuals such as Emile Zola, Sully Prudhomme and Léon Bloy were disdainful of sport, Bloy commenting that sport was the best way to produce 'a generation of cripples and dangerous cretins'.

If Paris was a humiliation for Coubertin in his own backyard, although somewhat understandable in the context of the French disdain for team games at the beginning of the twentieth century, he must have been very demoralised by the 1904 edition of the Olympics, held in St Louis. In fact he did not attend, stating that it was 'completely lacking in attraction' (cited in Keys 2006: 207 n. 22). Originally awarded to Chicago in 1901, the Third Olympics was staged as part of the 1904 World's Fair in St Louis, which is also known as the Louisiana Purchase Exhibition. It was scheduled to commemorate the acquisition by the United States of America of 828,800 square miles of France's claim to the territory of Louisiana in 1803, but was delayed by a year. The Louisiana Purchase doubled the size of the United States at the time and comprises 23% of the US landmass today. The St Louis World's Fair therefore staged the third modern Olympic Games, although very much as a sideshow. In addition various 'Anthropology Days' were scheduled as part of the Olympic Games – with the scientific goal of measuring the performances of 'savages' against 'civilised' men. As John Bale puts it: 'members of ethnic groups from the "living displays" on the grounds of the Louisiana Purchase Exposition . . . were presented to the public as athletes and put through tests (i.e., modern sports events) designed for the trained athletes of Europe and North America' (2008: 325). Needless to say, the performances of the 'natives' were rated as inferior.

In a collection of essays, Susan Brownell (2008) and contributors – including Gems (2008) and Knott (2008) – consider these events and the ideas of 'race', imperialism and the West that underpinned them, and their continuing ramifications over a hundred years later. Brownell poses the questions 'Why do Olympic Games now attract much greater global attention than world's fairs, when a century ago they were only a minor side event? and what does this tell us about the world in which we now live?' (2008: 1). We have explored our answers to these questions in connection with the globally mediated nature of the Olympic Games in Chapter 3. As Brownell and her contributors underline, the disciplinary impact on anthropology of the associated International Congress of Art and Science held in conjunction with the world's fair was highly significant as evolutionary racial models started to give way to the cultural relativist paradigm (associated with Franz Boas). Held in 1904, the Scientific Congress was actually more international than the Olympic Games, with 96 foreign participants – including sociologists Max Weber and Ferdinand Tonnies, Henri Poincaré and many others – and it also helped to consolidate physical education as a discipline.

As Brownell (2008: 29) notes, the association of the Olympic Games with world's fairs made sense at the time. It continued the association of sports with market fairs and linked the demonstration of (physical) progress to that of technological development. Modern sport was clearly a subservient cultural form. Nonetheless official sports events during the 1904 World's Fair actually took place between 14 May and 19 November, and 9,000 athletes competed in 400 events. The Olympic Games, however, only lasted from 29 August to 3 September, with

80 competitions and 687 entrants who were mostly American – and all were men apart from six women in the archery competition. There were only eight nations involved, four of them European, and some confusion about the true nationality of the athletes remains to this day. Typically, crowds were no more than 4–5,000. As Knott states (2008: 297 n. 5), 'In 1904 the Olympics did not yet represent the pinnacle of sporting events: to many, they were still considered an oddity'. The chaos of the Olympics in St Louis can be illustrated with reference to the experiences of the 'German' delegation which German Olympic historian Karl Lennartz (1983) has noted. First, although it was hoped to send more, 20 athletes travelled, but only 17 participated – '10 Turnern, 2 Leichathleten, 7 Schwimmern, und einem Fechter' ('10 gymnasts, 2 track and field athletes, 7 swimmers and one fencer') (Lennartz 1983: 131). Second, the absence of any accommodation specifically for athletes attending the St Louis Olympic Games meant that the wealthy brewer Adolphus Busch of the Anheuser-Busch company provided German gymnasts housing. Third, not all of the athletes in the German delegation were German. Adolf Spinnler, from Switzerland, competed for the Germans because he was a member of the Esslinger Turnverein (gymnastic club) near Stuttgart in Germany. Another athlete, Otto Wahle, a member of the Austria Wien Club in Vienna emigrated to the USA in 1900 and retained his Austrian citizenship, but also competed as part of the German delegation in 1904 (Knott 2008: 281–282). Yet another athlete, Julius Lenhart who won a gold medal, this time representing the USA, was also Austrian. Olympic historians from his country have since tried to claim Lenhart as an Austrian Olympic champion (Lennartz 1983: 116). As Knott (2008: 281–282) suggests, this imprecision about nationality and representativeness at the Olympics illustrates well the shift in meaning that sport and the Olympics have undergone since 1904.

St Louis was marked by another distinctive attraction. World's fairs had begun to display peoples of the world from 1889 as a central feature of ethnological displays. At the 1904 World's Fair and Olympic Games, 3,000 'native peoples' were on display. Whilst the Anthropology Days section can be perceived as an odd, naïve and racist practice today, in this way sport has played an important role in the encounters of the West with its Others. International expos had operated according to various cultural themes since the 1870s – peace, brotherly love, and understanding among nations. Before the Olympics, games events had been developed to promote national unity; Pierre de Coubertin sought to promote peace through internationalism. As Brownell states, his was 'the idea of combining in the medium of sport the lofty aspirations and educational goals of the world's fairs with popular ethnography and the neoclassical revival' (2008: 50). From the first London Olympics of 1908 onward, when the Parade of Athletes was established as a part of the opening ceremony, nation-states were recognised as the only legitimate global units in the Olympic Games. It was on the basis of cultural rather than 'racial' differences that Otherness would be represented. 'World's Fairs . . . are still important global events, but are not the important purveyors of novel intercultural experiences that they once were' (Brownell 2008: 51). They have been eclipsed by the Olympic Games, which allow 'records', seemingly objective quantifications of national difference, to be kept. As Charpentier and Boissonnade note:

> At Saint Louis, where the aftermath of the Civil War is still visible, although equality between blacks and whites is proclaimed, racial discrimination still persists. The Organisers mounted shameful 'Anthropological Days', special competitions reserved for those who the Americans considered to be sub-human.
>
> (Charpentier and Boissonnade 1999: 64)

St Louis was an opportunity for the Anglo-American to claim superiority over the 'primitive' nature of others. These included Ainus from Japan, Yehuelche Indians from Patagonia, pygmies from Central Africa, a variety of ethnic groups originating in the Philippines and many others representing tribes of indigenous Americans. To publicise these days, anthropologists persuaded the legendary Apache chief Geronimo to put in an appearance (Charpentier and Boissonnade 1999: 64). These 'natives' competed in standard running events and also in novelty events like mud wrestling and climbing the greasy pole. Len Tau and Jan Mashiani, two black students at Orange Free State University, were South Africa's first Olympians. However, they were billed as 'Zulu savages' and were participants only in the Anthropology Days segment of the competition. (http://www.historyhouse.com/in_history/olympics/ accessed 19 October 2010). The World's Fair village from which participants were taken was organised with what popular prejudice regarded as the most advanced tribes at the centre, where there stood a 'model Indian school'. In this human zoo, the so-called least civilised peoples were exhibited at the fringes. W. J. McGee, head of the Anthropology Department at the World's Fair, stated: 'the aim of the Department of Anthropology at the World's Fair will be to represent human progress from the dark prime to the human enlightenment, from savagery to civic organization, from egoism to altruism' (quoted in Gems 2008: 200). The crown jewel was a 47-acre site organised by the US government to display the conquered peoples of the Philippines, the newest American possession acquired during the recently concluded Spanish–American War. A homage to imperialism, the exhibit was designed to show how America would bring progress to savage peoples. The participants in the Anthropology Days events included Crow, Sioux, Pawnee, Navajo and Chippewa people from the United States; Ainu from Japan; Cocopa from Baja California in Mexico; two 'Syrians from Beyrout', Patagonians from South America, Zulus and pygmies from Africa and, from the Philippines, Moros, Negritos and Igorots. Teobang, another African, was described simply as a cannibal.

(http://www.antropologi.info/anthropology/copy/anthropological_days.html
accessed 19 October 2010)

Matthews (2005) offers an attempt to defend the Games as more successful than other accounts recall, blaming Coubertin's own 1933 memoir for elevating the Anthropological Days to greater significance than they warrant. Matthews himself, in contrast to other historians, seems curiously reluctant to acknowledge the Anthropological Days, not mentioning them until late in his book and then only in the context of criticising Coubertin for offering a misleading account of the events. Matthews claims the 1904 Games were seen as a success at the time and blames Coubertin's memoirs for changing the climate of assessment. He says Coubertin also misrepresented developments in claiming it was Roosevelt who decided that the Games should be moved to St Louis from Chicago, and not the IOC or Coubertin. Matthews charges that Bill Henry's *An Approved History of the Olympic Games*, published in 1948, drawing on Coubertin, was even more condemnatory. Matthews accuses Henry of fabrication, but frustratingly does not cite clear sources supporting his alternative versions of events (Matthews 2005: 209–210). In contrast, Young's curt summary (2004: 154) is that the 'games were not truly international; almost all the athletes were North American. Attendance was poor, organization abysmal, and sometimes even perverse'.

Analytically, the focus of the 2008 Brownell collection is on the 'framing' of behaviour that leads to a plurality of interpretations of experiences. Frames of spectacle, festival, ritual and game are the main interpretative frameworks for understanding the 'performance system' of the Olympic Games (using MacAloon's development of Erving Goffman's 'frame' concept; Goffman 1974; MacAloon 1981, 1984). The general 'MacAloon thesis', that the exposition genre of mega-event was crucial to the genesis of the Olympic Movement, and thus that a cultural movement had a shared affinity with the spirit of modern sport, is generally sustained rather than subjected to a critique by most of the contributors. A few, including Brownell, indicate they have some differences with MacAloon's thesis, but all are interested in the Olympic Games and world's fairs as performances in process.

The relative insignificance of the early Olympic Games was a reflection of the marginal status of sport in much of Europe, where according to Keys (2006: 48) it was still often regarded 'with suspicion as the "English disease"'. Additionally at this time, as Brownell notes, 'With the exception of the special situation in Greece, the Olympic Games were simply not strong enough to stand on their own financially' (2008: 30). For the first three editions of the twentieth century (1900, 1904 and 1908) the Olympic Games were a sideshow to world's fairs and international expositions. However, in 1908 the Games began to be taken more seriously in their own right. In the next section we turn to London and the 1908 Olympics where, although held in conjunction with a world's fair, the Games were not upstaged by it (Keys 2006: 207 n. 22). The next section offers a more detailed account of the first and second London Olympic Games that seeks to illustrate the relationships and agencies involved in their construction.

LONDON, EXHIBITIONS AND THE OLYMPIC GAMES

We want to commence this section by highlighting two themes in Roche (2000). First, he is concerned with the ways in which expos reflect the development of capitalism, nationalism and imperialism. Second, he regards them as important focal points in the emergence of an international dimension in modern public culture. Clearly there is a potential contradiction here, indeed a contradiction manifest in the person of Baron Pierre de Coubertin, whose life project was the establishment of the modern Olympic Games. As we discuss in more detail in the next chapter, Coubertin was a committed internationalist who inscribed internationalism into the founding documents, practices and rituals of the Olympic Games. But he was also a patriot who was concerned about the poor physical state and indiscipline of French youth, and worried about the decline of his country and its eclipse by the rising power of Germany. The tension between nationalism and internationalism continues to be a significant feature of the Olympic Games.

Whatever Coubertin was, he was no economist, and the lack of a clear financial strategy for supporting the nascent Olympic Games, as we have seen, forced Coubertin to attach the Games of 1900 and 1904 to the world's fairs in, respectively Paris and St Louis. Such events have tended to draw on a combination of public and private organisation and finance, have

92

had to balance short-term intentions with the question of legacy, and have been caught between idealism and pragmatism. Mega-events are rarely simply the realisation of a clear blueprint from a commanding designer; rather they are the outcome of competing intentions, interests, preoccupations and strategies. Where mega-events are concerned, a study of the relationships between national politicians, local politicians, sports administrators, builders, architects and town planners is often instructive.

We focus in this section therefore on aspects of the three London Olympic Games of 1908, 1948 and 2012, but we have also included the 1924/25 British Empire Exhibition, the stadium of which was subsequently used for the 1948 Olympic Games. One of the most striking features of mega-events is how rarely they utilise the sites of previous events, almost as if they wanted to avoid taking on the ideological detritus of a former conjuncture. In 1908 the London Olympics had close links – and shared a site (the 'White City') – with the Franco-British Exhibition near Shepherd's Bush. The 1924/25 British Empire Exhibition shunned the option of the White City site from 1908, and established itself at Wembley Park. In 1934 the Empire Games used the newly constructed Empire Pool at Wembley, yet used White City for the athletics. In 1948 the hastily arranged and financially pressed London Olympic Games did utilise the Wembley site originally constructed for the Empire Exhibition of 1924/25 but just three years later, in 1951, the Festival of Britain rejected both Wembley and White City and based its major attractions in Battersea Park and on the South Bank in central London. The Millennium Dome, rejecting all other available options, was built on a derelict industrial site in North Greenwich. In many cases the sites subsequently suffered years of decline, neglect and decay. The White City stadium was demolished in 1985 and there is no visible memorial proclaiming its moment of glory as the 'Great Stadium' of the 1908 Olympics. Wembley stadium has been demolished but reborn in rebuilt form, and the Empire Pool survives, renamed the 'Wembley Arena' and recently renovated. The rest of the site has been crumbling for years, and is only now undergoing substantial redevelopment. Very few traces of the Festival of Britain remain, aside from the Festival Hall. But, after the 2012 Olympic Games, a vast privately owned shopping mall at Stratford in East London will become the beneficiary of the massive public investment in infrastructure. This section therefore explores the significances that we can read into these events, crossing as they do concepts of nation and internationalism; past and future, heritage and tradition, public and private, production and consumption, festival and spectacle.

The Franco-British Exhibition of 1908

The Franco-British Exhibition had its roots in late nineteenth-century diplomacy. The decline of France after Napoleon, the end of the period of Franco-British wars, the French defeat by the Prussians in 1870, the formation of Germany in 1871, and the growing power and ambition of Germany meant that France had to forge alliances with Britain. The Entente Cordiale was signed in 1904, and the Franco-British Exhibition in 1908 was planned to celebrate it. It attracted 8 million visitors, and only included goods and produce of Britain, France and their respective colonies. The British Empire at this point still commanded one-quarter of the world's land, and one-quarter of the world's population. The British navy was twice the size of the next largest (Mallon and Buchanan 2000). Founded on the imperatives of trade and diplomacy, the Franco-British Exhibition was structured around an imperial ideology of civilisation, brought to savage peoples, for their betterment. Like previous such events, it combined displays of technological mastery, educative rational recreation and popular amusement.

London only acquired the Olympic Games of 1908 after Rome pulled out. The 1904 IOC Session in London awarded the Games of 1908 to Rome. In 1906 Rome withdrew. This was attributed to the impact of the Vesuvius eruption, but in fact the Italian prime minister was opposed to the project and prevented funding, which he wanted to spend on other projects like the Simplon tunnel (Mallon and Buchanan 2000). It was clear that no government funding would be available for building a main stadium, but the Franco-British Exhibition organisers agreed to build the stadium complete with running and cycling tracks and a swimming pool, in return for 75% of the gate receipts. The stadium was projected to cost £44,000[1] but some estimates suggest it may have been a lot higher (e.g., Zarnowski 1992). The Exhibition organisers also agreed to give £2,000 to the BOA, but this was later increased to £20,000 (Mallon and Buchanan 2000: 4). It appears that the Exhibition organisers were prepared to accept a loss on the stadium in return for the benefits of bringing extra visitors to the exhibition, and of course they retained the use of the stadium after the Games. The BOA made £6,000 and the Franco-British exhibition £18,000 from gate receipts (Mallon and Buchanan 2000: 5). Although the Exhibition was prompted by diplomacy, its key organising figure was a showman and promoter, Imre Kiralfy.

BOX 5.2 IMRE KIRALFY

Hungarian and Jewish, Imre Kiralfy was born in 1845, and soon showed a precocious talent for music, art and especially dance. He toured Europe, performing with his siblings, and saw the 1867 International Exhibition, and in the USA the Kiralfy brothers became producers of spectacles such as Jules Verne's 'Around the World in 80 Days'. Kiralfy also worked with and no doubt learned from Barnum and Bailey. Returning to London, he rebuilt the Earl's Court exhibition grounds as a small-scale version of Chicago's White City in 1893, complete with Ferris wheel, amusement park and exhibition halls in an Indian style. At night the grounds were electrically illuminated. As a member of the British Empire League and a senior Freemason, Kiralfy was undoubtedly well connected.

The first initiative towards the Exhibition came from the French Chamber of Commerce and the Lord Mayor of London, the objective being for France and England to display their industrial achievements. Kiralfy was commissioned to create it. Initial costs were raised through donations, and any profits were intended to go to 'some public purpose' (Knight 1978: 1). The 140-acre site was eight times larger than the Great Exhibition. 123,000 people visited on the opening day and the caterers, J. Lyons & Co., planned for 100,000 per day (Knight 1978: 4).

Before work started, a company called the International and Colonial Commercial Co. Ltd was established. Subsequently eight directors resigned, and this appeared to leave the Kiralfy brothers in effective control. The name of the company was changed to Shepherd's Bush Exhibitions Ltd, and I. and C. Kiralfy and associates took up over 16,000 shares. A public

94

company, the 'Great White City Ltd', was established and acquired significant shares in Shepherd's Bush Exhibitions Ltd (Knight 1978: 5).

The site benefited from investment in transport infrastructure. The Central London Railway was extended from Shepherd's Bush to Wood Lane Station in 1908 to serve the Franco-British Exhibition. There was also a separate station on the Metropolitan Line, also called Wood Lane. Following the success of the exhibition, the temporary station became a permanent fixture, with passenger demand buoyed by the creation of a number of new entertainment venues in the area, notably the White City Stadium.

The site featured elaborate white-walled palaces and waterways. The central court had a lake and illuminated fountains. There were 20 palaces and 120 exhibition halls.[2] Orientalism was a dominant stylistic motif. Rickshaw drivers were brought to London from Asia to work on the site.[3] There was a distinct contrast between the elements of rational recreation and hedonism. At one pole was the London County Council exhibit of municipal works and at the other the showmanship of Kiralfy. The latter is illustrated by the general attractions on the site, which by the time of the Japan–British Exhibition held two years later included: Brennan's Monorail, the Flip Flap, the Great Mountain Railway, the Wiggle Woggle (a form of slide), Witching Waves, the Motor Racing Track, the Submarine, Webb's Glassworks, Whirling Waters, the Canadian Toboggan, the Spiral Railway, and the Hall of Laughter.[4] In 1908 the stadium contained running and cycling tracks, an open-air swimming pool and a pitch for football, hockey, rugby and lacrosse, and held 93,000 spectators.[5] It is clear that, despite the large investment in the site, it must have been lucrative. The attractions alone generated much revenue, as Figure 5.2 illustrates. Combined, these attractions alone brought in around £200,000 – close to £20 million in 2010 terms.[6]

The site continued to be a viable exhibition venue for some years. In 1909, the Imperial International exhibited the imperial achievements of the Triple Entente powers: France, Russia, and Britain. In 1910 the Japan–British Exhibition emphasised the suitability of Japan as a worthy ally of Britain. The 1911 Coronation Exhibition, the 1912 Latin–British Exhibition and the 1914 Anglo-American Exhibition followed these. During the First World War, the army used the site. From 1921 to 1929, it became the venue for the British Industries Fair.[7] In 1927 the Greyhound Racing Association leased the stadium for greyhound racing. The Amateur

	Passengers	Revenue (£)
The lake in the Court of Honour	1,108,700	27,000
The Flip Flap	1,110,800	27,000
The Mountain Scenic railway	2,800,000	70,000
The Spiral	653,600	16,340
Canadian toboggan	807,000	20,175
Old London	500,000	12,500
Mountain Slide	250,000	6,250
The Johnstown Flood	715,000	17,875
The Stereomatos	425,000	17,875

Figure 5.2 Selected attendances at the 1908 Franco-British Exhibition.

Source: Knight (1978: 38–42).

95

Athletic Association (AAA) Championships were first held there in 1932. The BBC bought part of the site in 1949 and built the Television Centre, which opened in 1960. Athletics moved to Crystal Place in 1971, the last greyhound racing took place in 1984 and the Great Stadium was demolished a year later (Mallon and Buchanan 2000: 6).

As for the owners, one resigned as director of Shepherd's Bush Exhibitions Ltd in 1918, whilst Imre Kiralfy died in 1919. Bits of the site were sold off during the 1920s and 1930s (to the BBC, and to Hammersmith Council for the White City housing estate). The stadium was leased to the Greyhound Racing Association. Shepherd's Bush Exhibitions Ltd began its voluntary wind-up in 1950, but was not dissolved until the 1960s, its assets of £550,000 being used to pay surtax, solicitors' fees and liquidators' fees with the remainder being divided amongst shareholders (Knight 1978: 6). It is not clear what happened to the 'public purpose', referred to by the organisers. The stadium disappeared with no trace and no proper commemoration of its historic role. The White City was not simply demolished, but virtually obliterated from history. Apart from a small marker and a display inside the BBC building, there is no visible sign, memorial or plaque to indicate that an Olympic Games was ever staged here.

Exhibitions and Empire Games: 1924/25 and 1934

The idea of a great exhibition to celebrate Empire trade had been discussed in 1913, when it was planned to stage it at White City. By the 1920s the British economy, damaged by the impact of the First World War, was already beginning to feel the impact of the rise to dominance of the USA. The idea of a British Empire Exhibition was revived, and Lloyd George and the Prince of Wales actively supported the project (Roche 2000: 61). The government committed half the £2.2 million needed, the rest coming from pubic subscriptions. The government acted as co-guarantor of the expo and it intervened to have its appointees on the organising committee. Parliament supported the project in 1920 on the grounds that the expo would 'benefit trade, provide employment and be a token of goodwill towards the dominions' (Roche, quoting Stallard 1996: 7). In 1922, the government provided the funding for it to go ahead. The White City site was still intact but was rejected as a suitable location, in favour of Wembley Park in north-west London.

BOX 5.3 WEMBLEY PARK

The Wembley site itself has an interesting history. Wembley Park had belonged to the Page family since the sixteenth century. In the 1870s the estate was landscaped and at the end of the nineteenth century it was purchased by the Metropolitan Railway to create a pleasure grounds. The Park opened in 1894 and it was only 12 minutes from Baker Street, thanks to the Metropolitan Railway station at Wembley Park (Brent Heritage 2002). In 1895 Metropolitan's Chairman, Sir Edward Watkin, seeing the need to attract people to the railway, decided to construct a major tourist attraction close to the station. During a visit to Paris in 1889, Watkin had seen the newly constructed Eiffel Tower, and set up the Metropolitan Tower Construction Company. The tower was going

---

to be 1,200 feet high (compared to the 849 feet of the Eiffel Tower) but building difficulties, marshy ground and financial problems curtailed full completion. The first stage of the tower was eventually opened to members of the public in 1896, by which time pleasure gardens had been created around it. In 1899 the Tower Construction Company went into liquidation, and in 1904 'Watkin's Folly' was demolished.[8]

Construction of the site began in January 1922 with the Wembley Stadium finished in time for the 1923 FA Cup Final. When it took office in 1924, the Labour Party actively supported the expo project (Roche 2000: 61). The project was framed by imperialism throughout – made explicit on the first page of the *British Empire Exhibition Handbook*:

> I welcome the opportunity that will be afforded by the British Empire Exhibition to increase the knowledge of the varied resources of my empire and to stimulate inter-imperial trade . . .
> (HM The King, quoted in *The British Empire Exhibition: Handbook of General Information*, 1924)

> we must unite to make the British Empire Exhibition a success worthy of our race . . .
> (HRH The Prince of Wales, quoted in *The British Empire Exhibition: Handbook of General Information*, 1924)

Apparently, contractors made 'huge profits', whilst the government made a loss. The Board of Trade produced a report suggesting the government 'might minimise involvement in future world's fairs and suggesting some form of international regulation minimising the frequency with which fairs could occur' (Stallard 1996: 10).

At the exhibition's heart were 16 buildings representing the Empire countries. These ranged in size from the Australian 'palace' to the smaller West Indies/British Guiana pavilion, which sold cocktails and displayed exhibits on sugar. The West African building was a miniature reproduction of the walled city of Zaria in Nigeria; Ceylon's was modelled on the Temple of the Tooth in Kandy; Burma reproduced in Burmese teak one of the gates of a famous pagoda at Mandalay. A street of Chinese shops represented Hong Kong, and East Africa was represented by a white-walled Arab building. Inside, the countries themselves had organised displays of their goods and products. The Australian pavilion sold 7 million apples. The Canadian pavilion promoted butter with a life-size sculpture of Edward, the Prince of Wales, in the setting of his cattle ranch at Pekisko, Alberta. The 1924 tableau included the prince, a horse and several outbuildings set against the distant foothills of the Rocky Mountains, all carved entirely out of Canadian butter – 3,000 pounds of it (Clendinning 2006). The butter tableau was an advertisement for Canada's dairy industry, the Department of Agriculture, and the wonders of modern refrigeration since the entire scene was preserved behind glass and kept at a cold storage temperature a few degrees below freezing. The following year, and possibly to reuse the enormous cold storage display case, a refrigerated butter sculpture of the Prince of Wales in the costume of a First Nations chief (Chief Morning Star) alongside several

97

Native women, a tepee, a dog and a small child, was produced. According to the British newspapers, Edward in 'full feathers as an Indian chief' was one of the new wonders of Wembley (Clendinning 2006).

As well as several train stations, the exhibition benefited from what it claimed was 'the world's first bus station'. Car transport was only just beginning to impact. No new roads were constructed specifically for the Exhibition, but the origins of the North Circular Road are contemporary with it.

The 1908 Franco-British Exhibition – extravagant, a visual feast, exotic – had shown the flair of a promoter who had worked with Barnum. The 1924 British Empire Exhibition by contrast seemed more official, pompous, worthy – and dull. Ulick Wintour, an ex-civil servant who had worked at the Ministry of Food and the Stationery Office was picked as a man who could get things done – he introduced his engineer friend Owen Williams to Maxwell Ayrton, who was to be the architect of the Exhibition's main buildings – but he did not seem to have the P. T. Barnum spirit.[9]

The rational educative impulse of the Exhibition was clear. The official guide said of the potential visitor, 'In a single day he [sic] will learn more geography than a year of hard study would teach him' (quoted in Roche 2000: 63). And not just geography – the General Post Office exhibited a working model of an automatic telephone exchange, and the Ministry of Health had a model of sewage disposal. But, as Maurice Roche argues, whatever messages about empire were intended would have been filtered through the strong entertainment, fairground and leisure character of the expo (Roche 2000: 63). There is an apologetic note sounded for 'amusement' in the handbook:

> No matter how attractive or interesting an exhibition may be, a certain degree of fatigue is always involved. In order to obviate this, Wembley will be equipped with what will certainly be the finest Amusements Park in the world.
> *(The British Empire Exhibition: Handbook of General Information*: 35)

The site staged a daily 'Pageant of Empire' featuring 15,000 performers and hundreds of animals. There was an amusement park and fairground rides – dodgems, river caves, water chutes and a rollercoaster and a number of dance halls. Roche says that 'dancing and popular music were strongly associated with the experience of visiting the expo' (Roche 2000: 63).

After the Exhibition, the buildings were sold and many demolished. The stadium was saved. Before the Second World War some large engineering and luxury goods manufacturers took over the empty buildings of the Empire Exhibition. Unlike most previous expos, which used temporary architecture, many of the buildings at Wembley were built as permanent structures, with 'after use' in mind (Roche 2000: 63). Despite this they didn't seem to get any significant after use. Just as the 1924/25 Empire Exhibition had eschewed the earlier White City site, so the 1951 Festival of Britain did not utilise Wembley. Newness and novelty constantly win out over economy and legacy!

In 1934, the second Empire Games (since 1978 renamed the Commonwealth Games) came to London. The original idea for a multi-sport event linking Empire countries had its origins in imperial power and racism. As noted in the previous chapter, John Astley Cooper began proposing a Pan-Britannic Festival in print in 1891. This idea was overtaken by the modern

98

Olympic Games, first held in 1896, but it laid the seeds of the idea that resurfaced as the Empire Games. As we have noted, Cooper asked if Britons were ready to undertake 'actions for the benefit of mankind which may make the name of England to be sung for all time as an example to races yet to come' (Moore 1987: 146).

It is clear, according to Moore, that Cooper's idea was intended to include 'only adult males from the so-called white Dominions – Australia, New Zealand, Canada and South Africa as well as those subjects eligible in Great Britain' (Moore 1987: 148). The Empire Games were first staged in 1930 in Hamilton, Ontario, at a moment when the relationship between the UK and the old 'white' empire countries was being reshaped.

The Empire Pool (now known as Wembley Arena) was built for the Empire Games of 1934. The building was built by private enterprise as a commercial project and is still owned by a private company. It is a unique building, not only for its structural form with long cantilevers meeting in the middle as a three-pinned arch, but also because it was designed entirely by an engineer, with no involvement by an architect. This fact is clearly demonstrated in the style.[10] It was built on part of the site of the lakes which had been laid out for the British Empire Exhibition ten years earlier. The design did not attempt to blend with the adjacent Palaces of Art and of Industry that had survived from the Empire Exhibition. It was designed as an adaptable, all-purpose performance space. The swimming pool was closed at the outbreak of war (1939) and was subsequently only used as a pool for the Olympic Games (1948). The Wembley Arena building was listed Grade II in 1976.

Two years after the Empire Games of 1934, one of London's earliest exhibition buildings – the Crystal Palace – burned down. The building, built for the Great Exhibition of 1851, had been moved in 1854 from Hyde Park to Sydenham Hill, forming the dominant feature of what became known as Crystal Palace Park. The site remained derelict for the next 60 years, and is still largely derelict, with only the brick arches of the lower level still visible.

The 1948 Olympics

If 1908 was a time when the Empire was still just dominant, and 1924 a time when it was under threat, the 1948 Olympic Games were staged by a country whose Empire was being dismantled. The USA was now the dominant force. The old Empire Exhibition site at Wembley had already fallen into decline, and must have served as a poignant visual metaphor that Britain's economy was seriously weakened by the impact of the war. Post-war reconstruction was only just beginning to make an impact. The relaunch of television after the war, however, enabled the 1948 Games to be the first ones to be broadcast live by television.

As was the case with the 1908 Games, the 1948 Games had to be organised very rapidly, in less than two years. But, unlike the 1908 Games, this had to be done in a context of a country still recovering from the impact of the war, with shortages, rationing and a severe fuel crisis in the run-up to the Games. There is a striking emphasis on economy in the Olympic report, the authors pointing out ways in which they attempted to control costs – no new facilities were built, for example. So the Games were not, unlike Games of more recent years, to produce any architectural symbols of modernity, although they did utilise the rather hefty-looking halls of the Empire Exhibition constructed in the era of Art Deco.

99

A concern with how to mark Britishness drew on the past, tradition and heritage in its use of Big Ben and Kipling. The arts competitions, added as official events at the 1912 Stockholm Olympics, by contrast, being restricted to works in architecture, sculpture, painting, literature and music and inspired by sport and produced during the Olympiad (the preceding four years), were predominantly modernist in tone and style. The organising committee chose as a symbol the clock tower of the Houses of Parliament, with the hands of Big Ben pointing to 4.00 p.m., the hour at which the Games were declared open (Official Report 1948: 22).

Pragmatic concerns seem to have marked the organisation of the torch relay and the opening ceremony. There is a map of the route in the 'Illustrations from the XIVth Olympiad Sport in Art Exhibition'. To keep the cost down, the route was almost as direct as could be – from Olympia across the sea to Italy, straight up the east coast and then across the Alps, north through France and then along the Rhine valley, and then by ferry to Dover. According to the Official Report, 'the Committee decided after careful consideration, that the torch relay, first held in 1936, had a great symbolic value to the Olympic Games and that, although considerable expense would be involved, it should be included in the plans for the Games' (Official Report 1948: 22).

Led by bastions of the establishment, the organising committee was clearly concerned to do things properly and not to tamper unduly with tradition – there was little innovation in the staging of the Games. There was, however, an excitement around the engagement with emergent technologies – particularly television, still only two years into its post-war relaunch. If post-war austerity made for a pragmatic approach, the Olympic movement itself would seem ill-equipped for both modernity and austerity. The IOC was then – and to a degree remains – dominated by European aristocracy. In 1948 only 41 countries were represented on the IOC, 24 of them European. The 66 members, all male, included three princes, five counts, two barons, a marquis, a duke, two his excellency's, two lords, two generals, and a colonel. As for the London Organising Committee, the President of the Games was the Rt Hon. The Viscount Portal, DSO, MVG; and the chairman of the organising committee was the Rt Hon. The Lord Burghley, KCMG.

By the early 1980s, this aristocratic IOC body had become firmly wedded to commercialisation, but in 1948 the Official Report stated that because the IOC had to ensure that the Games were promoted 'not so much as a commercial venture but in the best interests of sport', many means of raising money were not permissible, such as the inclusion of advertisements in the brochures and programmes. In the balance sheet, receipts were £761,688 and expenditure was slightly less, leaving a small surplus (£29,420) which presumably went to the British Olympic Association. The IOC received £5,000. Wembley Stadium was paid £92,500, around 12% of the total revenue of the Games, so was also one of the beneficiaries.

In some ways this Olympic Games was on the cusp of the transformation from a pre-media event to a global spectacle. From today's perspective, the media-management strategy has a fascinating quaintness about it. The Press Department policy in the build-up to the Games was as follows:

> The Press Officer decided to tackle every individual critic and follower on his own ground and persuade him by specialist treatment, of the rightness of the course.

100

Those with influence on the sports side of the newspapers were encouraged and those hoping to intrude with political opinions avoided or completely ignored.

(Official Report 1948: 105)

The arts competitions, on which Coubertin was so keen, were staged for the last time in 1948 (Girginov and Parry 2005: 206). Since 1948 there have been art *exhibitions* linked to the Games, but not competitions.

As far as legacy is concerned, £1,000 was to be allocated for the establishment of a permanent record of winners at the main stadium (Official Report 1948: 29). There is a picture of two plaques on the external wall of the stadium – they seemed to be either side of the circular entrance gate between the two towers. Wembley subsequently established itself as the home of England international football, the twin towers were mythicised and the stadium was the venue for the 1966 World Cup Final. The Olympics appeared to retreat from view. The lack of any real commemoration at either the White City or Wembley stadiums is striking, and the London 2012 bid chose not to make a lot of the 1908 and 1948 Games.

The shopping mall: 2012

Considering the 2012 bid, and the possibilities of drawing on England's traditions and heritage, especially in terms of sport, the inspiration of Coubertin, Penny Brookes, Robert Dover and all of that, it is somewhat surprising that there is such an absence of memorial to 1908 and to 1948. As we have discussed already in Chapter 1, the organisational separation between a delivery authority (which organises venues and facilities) and the organising committee (which organises and markets the Games), adopted by London, was also utilised by Sydney in 2000 (see Preuss 2004: 17). The great merit of this separation is that it removes some infrastructural expenditure from the official budget. Although, combined, the official figure for London 2012 is £11.3 billion, because of a distinction between 'Games-related' and 'non-Games-related' costs it is possible to suggest that the organising committee actually cover their costs from revenue and make a surplus, whilst the 'non-Games-related costs', in our terms the hidden subsidy, means the host city picks up a large tab.

As we have argued, the Australian property development company Westfield seems to be the key beneficiary, and is now the key developer of the Stratford site, which is so closely tied to the 2012 Olympic Games. Westfield have established around 124 shopping centres in Australia, New Zealand, the UK and the USA and, with around £14.3 billion of assets, can lay claim to being the, or at least one of the, world's largest retail property groups. The Stratford City development is one of the largest regeneration projects in Europe. It includes homes, shops and accommodation for athletes in the 2012 Olympics. In the media narration of the major controversy surrounding the soaring cost of the 2012 Olympic Games, there was virtually no reference to the Stratford City Development, although it looks likely to be one of the most tangible, long-lasting and profitable legacies of the Olympic Games.

ALTERNATIVE SPORTS EVENTS AND THE OLYMPIC GAMES

As Barbara Keys (2006: 49) writes, by the 1920s a division of labour had been established in international sport that has persisted more or less until today. The IOC – an undemocratic as well as Eurocentric 'club' dominated by rich European men – determined the programme, location and general philosophy governing the Olympic Games, while the national Olympic committees (NOCs) oversaw participation and the IFs set the technical regulations and made final judgements on the eligibility of athletes to take part. Along with other international sports organisations – such as FIFA – the IOC helped to establish sport as an international regime – a form of governance without government, based on the rules and norms not of localities but of sport. Sport developed increasingly popular festivals that provided a physical and temporal locus for the sporting 'imagined world' (Keys 2006: 184). Rites and symbols have been constructed which in turn provide a sense of sport as a global force. It is this that has given sport a feeling of autonomy from 'ordinary' life and social contexts. That this had been accomplished is one of the major contributions of the Olympic movement to world history.

Of course, as we have shown in this book, sport is not really so distinct from its social, political, economic and cultural contexts. The development of the Olympics as a major, if not the premier, sports mega-event was accomplished through accommodations and struggles. Before the Second World War, Olympic or 'bourgeois' sport had powerful rivals – in Europe, workers' sport and gymnastics; in the rest of the world, traditional games and contests, as Eichberg (1998) amongst others has shown. Workers' Olympics, women's sports events and the professional football World Cup all developed and waned in particular socio-historical conditions. Sport's central position in contemporary conceptions of 'physical culture' is a historically contingent outcome, not the product of some natural evolution. We look at this in more detail in the next chapter.

Before the Second World War, the Left critiqued sport on the grounds that it was 'bourgeois sport'. From this perspective, it was seen as a form of bread and circuses, devised to distract workers from their real interests. Workers' sport promoted instead collectivism, mass participation, gender equality and internationalism. Strongest in Germany, workers' sports organisations existed in most European countries. Tens of thousands of participants and hundreds of thousands of spectators were involved in the events in Vienna in 1931, for example (Riordan 1984). In addition to workers' events there were the Soviet Games and women's Olympics (Hoberman 1995: 7). Figure 5. 3 outlines a few of the alternative events in existence between 1920 and 1938.

Gradually, however, policy changed in the Soviet Union. Engagement with, rather than the establishment of alternatives to, bourgeois sport became the means by which it was thought internal and external legitimacy could be secured for the alternative economic system. In the same manner, although alternatives to sport existed – such as the Turnen movement in Germany, which highlighted processes rather than products or results – they gradually became co-opted by sport. From being an alternative to sport they became an alternative sport amongst many (Keys 2006: 182–183). International competitive sport became the playing field – and the surrogate battlefield between ideological systems – as we discuss in the next chapter.

From the 1904 Olympics – which were small and feeble, piggy-backed on to the St Louis exhibition, and included athletes who did not know they were in the Olympics (just as in

Year	Olympic Games	Worker's Olympics	Women's Olympics	Football World Cup	Empire Games	Soviet Games
1920	Antwerp					
1921		Prague				
1922			Paris			
1924	Paris					
1925		Frankfurt				
1926			Gothenburg			
1927		Prague				
1928	Amsterdam					Moscow
1930			Prague	Uruguay	Hamilton	
1931		Vienna				
1932	Los Angeles					Moscow
1934			Prague	Italy	London	
1936	Berlin	(Barcelona)				
1938			(Vienna)	France	Sydney	

Figure 5.3 Selected major international sports events, 1920–1938.

Source: adapted from Roche (2000: 101).

Paris four years earlier) – to 2008 and the Beijing Summer Olympic Games (with over 10,000 athletes competing from 204 NOCs, watched by 24,562 accredited media personnel representing 159 countries) there has been a major change in the social and global significance of sport, and Olympic sport especially. Sport as an exciting, entertaining and economically and politically exploitable resource has become the cultural form that can create the mega-events which unite the globe through televised coverage (see Figure 3.6, p. 52). The growth in television coverage is echoed by the growth in numbers of nations, NOCs and athletes (including women) involved in the Olympic Games.

In 1908 the Olympic Games in London were subordinate to the World's Fair, and simply one part of a celebration of imperial might and power. The UK grasp of science and technology had yet to be seriously challenged. By 1948 the Empire was in its final decline. Britain was just starting to get to grips with its post-war subordinate political role. The 1948 Games were in part a heroic gesture, born out of the wartime 'make do and mend', 'Britain can take it', working together, collectivist spirit. The Games were on the cusp of the television era, although it was to be another 20 years before the Games began to be transformed culturally and economically by television. Developments in TV from 1936 onward have made major sports mega-events such as the Olympic Games and the FIFA World Cup more important than world's fairs and expositions because they are more likely to be widely – and, since the 1960s, globally – mediated.

As interest in architectural design and the construction of forms suitable for Olympic cities developed (Munoz 2006), there has been a fascinating and consistent denial of the past. The British Empire Exhibition of 1924 did not use the White City site; the 1934 Empire Games did not use Wembley as its main stadium; the 1948 London Olympics didn't utilise the 1908 site; the Festival of Britain didn't use Wembley Park either; the legacy of the Festival of Britain was ignored or marginalised by the Millennium presentations in the Dome; the 2012 Olympic bid made little of tradition, choosing not to foreground the two previous occasions when London

Olympics	Year	City	Nations/ National Olympic Committees (NOCs)	Female athletes	Total athletes
I	1896	Athens	13	0	311
II	1900	Paris	22	12	1,330
III	1904	St Louis	13	6	687
*	1906	Athens	20	7	884
IV	1908	London	22	36	2,035
VIII**	1924	Paris	44	136	3,092
IX	1928	Amsterdam	46	290	3,014
X	1932	Los Angeles	37	127	1,408
XI	1936	Berlin	49	328	4,066
XIV***	1948	London	59	385	4,099
XV	1952	Helsinki	69	518	4,925
XVIII	1964	Tokyo	93	683	5,140
XXIII	1984	Los Angeles	140	1,567	7,078
XXVII	2000	Sydney	199	4,069	10,651
XXIX	2008	Beijing	204	4,637	10,942§

Figure 5.4 Growth in participation at selected Summer Olympic Games.

* This event celebrated the 10th anniversary of the first modern Games; whilst officially intercalated by the IOC it is not numbered as an Olympic Games. **The VI Games (scheduled for Berlin) were not held due to the First World War, but it is officially counted by the IOC. ***The XII and XIII Games (scheduled respectively for Tokyo, then Helsinki and London) were not held due to the Second World War, but are officially counted by the IOC. § The IOC also records 24,562 accredited media representing 159 countries.

Source: adapted from Toohey and Veal (2007: 199); Greenberg (1987: 9); IOC (2010) http://www.olympic.org/en/content/Olympic-Games/All-Past-Olympic-Games/Summer/Beijing-2008/ (accessed 19 August 2010).

staged the Olympics. Indeed when the circus leaves town, there is rarely a viable economic strategy for the abandoned buildings – which decay until eventually they are obliterated. It is as if all these iconic buildings and sites are so firmly attached to the configuration which gave birth to them that there is a form of ideological contamination in which they cannot be used or even referred to until they have been rased, purged or otherwise sanitised and rendered ideologically neutral again.

CONCLUSION

Today, not only are the Olympic Games an enormous lever for moving public policy and uncorking infrastructural investment – public investment, private gain – they are also a major contributor to the conception of the world as one place. Sports mega-events, especially (but not only) in their mediated form, provide one of the means by which identity is constituted and reconstituted in the modern world. They enable 'temporal and spatial distance to be reconstructed and re-experienced, in memory and anticipation, in the telemediated lifeworld that characterizes the contemporary period' (Roche 2003: 109). In this chapter we considered the development of the Olympics as a stand-alone sports event. We also considered alternative sports and physical culture events and the growth of the reach of the Olympics in the twentieth century.

The key economic dynamics of the Olympic Games today are associated with globalising processes, transnational corporations, urban renewal, consumption and the new urbanism. Just as the major legacy of the 2012 Olympic Games will be the construction of Stratford City, a major development with a shopping mall at its heart, so a shopping mall opened in White City/Shepherd's Bush in West London in 2008, built on the site of and obliterating the last traces of the series of eight glass palaces that constituted the main entrance to the Franco-British Exhibition of 1908. The White City shopping mall and Stratford City have one other thing in common: they are both owned by Westfield, a company that was also associated for a while with Multiplex, which built the new Wembley Stadium on the site of the 1948 Olympic Games. If in 1908 the focus was on trade and production, by 2012 the focus is very much on spectacle and consumption – courtesy of the shopping mall. The third part of the book, which starts with the next chapter, explores the development of the Olympics as part of the spectacle of modernity.

FURTHER READING

Brownell, S. (ed.) (2008) *The 1904 Anthropology Days and Olympic Games: Sport, Race, and American Imperialism*, Lincoln, NE, and London: University of Nebraska Press.
Keys, B. (2006) *Globalizing Sport: National Rivalry and International Community in the 1930s*, Cambridge, MA, and London: Harvard University Press.
Roche, M. (2000) *Mega-Events and Modernity: Olympics and Expos in the Growth of Global Culture*, London: Routledge.

PART III

THE SPECTACLE OF MODERNITY: TOWARDS A POSTMODERN WORLD?

CHAPTER 6

THE INTERNATIONALIST SPIRIT AND NATIONAL CONTESTATION

The Olympic Games were conceived partly as an international meeting ground, and the first International Olympic Committee contained several figures who also played an active role in international peace organisations. Yet, from the start, tensions and rivalries between nations disrupted the internationalist aspirations of Olympism. Indeed from the earliest years, for a combination of pragmatic, political and cultural reasons, national-based structures, practices and rituals began to develop. National flags, teams, uniforms, anthems at the victory ceremonies, and the 'unofficial' medal tables in the media – all contribute to an image of the Olympic Games as a symbolic contest between nations. During the 1908 Games there were several acrimonious disputes between British and American officials. The 1936 Games became notorious as the 'Nazi Olympics', and in the Cold War era the Games became a symbolic battleground between East and West, communism and capitalism. The IOC also had to manage divided societies in Germany, Korea and China; Middle East tensions associated with the establishment of Israel and displacement of the Palestinians; the impact of decolonisation and establishment of emergent independent nations; and the demands for the isolation of South Africa over apartheid. This chapter examines the inherent contradictions between internationalism and national organisation, outlining the development and management of political tensions by the Olympic movement.

Since the end of the Second World War, being a *nation* in the modern world has come to be signified by two things: belonging to the United Nations and marching in the Opening Ceremony of the Olympic Games. However, it is clear around the world that the status of nations and states is subject to contestation. Ireland, Catalonia, the Basque country, Taiwan, Hong Kong, the two Koreas, Palestine and Belgium provide diverse examples of the disputed nature of national boundaries and state authority.

What constitutes a 'nation'? In different contexts (the League of Nations, the UN, the IOC) different criteria and definitions of nation have been applied. Interestingly, the IOC has a longer list than the UN: 12 'nations' are included in the IOC but not the UN. Many of these can be seen as unresolved issues in decolonisation. The 12 include three British territories (Bermuda, British Virgin Islands, the Cayman Islands); four US territories (American Samoa, Puerto Rico, Guam, American Virgin Islands); and two Dutch territories (Aruba, Netherlands Antilles). Of the remaining, two are linked to China (Chinese Taipei, Hong Kong) and the other one is Palestine. A nation, Benedict Anderson famously argued, is an imagined community – not a natural product of geographical boundary, or linguistic unity, but a construction by practices of mapping, naming, identifying and narrativising (Anderson 1983).

Although the nation-state is now generally taken for granted as the primary legal entity into which the world is divided, the primacy of the nation-state is a comparatively recent phenomenon. Over the last few centuries, empires controlling multiple nations have been a significant element in geopolitical organisation and before that city-states had considerable power in many parts of the world. The rise of the nation-state took place during the nineteenth century and is neither permanent nor unchallenged.

The apparent fixity of nation-states is an illusion. Many nations that now exist did not have national status in 1896, and some that existed then, do not now. Even in supposedly stable Europe the pace of change has been dramatic. Germany and Italy are less than 150 years old, and Germany was a divided nation between 1945 and 1990. The Soviet Union welded a set of diverse nations together between 1922 and 1991. After both world wars in the twentieth century the boundaries of Europe and the Middle East were redrawn by the victorious powers. Some nations disappeared, others came into being. The collapse of empires (the Austro-Hungarian, the Ottoman and the British) produced new independent nations. Some nations (Czechoslovakia, Yugoslavia) have been created and ceased to exist since 1918. The re-Balkanisation of the last two decades has seen the return to statehood of Croatia, Bosnia and Serbia. Around the world, national boundaries are under challenge, from regional and local forces, from competing national, linguistic, ethnic or religious forces. In countries such as South and North Korea, Ireland and Belgium, separate and competing visions of nation remain unreconciled. By contrast, some nations once divided by war (North and South Vietnam) have become reunified. In some countries, regional demands for independence are strongly asserted, such as in Spain (Catalonia, Basque) and China (Tibet). In some countries there are strong antagonisms between the main nation-state and a former part of it that has become independent (China and Taiwan). Some 'nations', such as Kosovo, have declared their status as nation-states, but have yet to achieve wider recognition or legitimacy.

It could be argued that the IOC has been not simply reflecting this process, but playing an active role as constructor – not least because appearance as a nation on the Olympic stage helps advertise an identity and confer a legitimacy. The German Democratic Republic and Cuba, for example, had explicit policies to utilise the Olympic Games to buttress their visibility and legitimacy on the world stage. The battle to isolate South Africa focused on the Olympic Games because of the event's global prominence and symbolic power. The presence of Palestine as an Olympic 'nation' carries a powerful message to the world. The IOC, however, has from the start been caught within tensions of its own making, between its internationalist aspirations and its nation-based structures and rituals. Indeed despite his internationalism, Coubertin's own ambitions were also shaped by the humiliation inflicted on France by Germany in 1870–71, when Alsace Lorraine was annexed. Coubertin's interest in physical education was not unconnected to the need to rebuild French power. Yet Coubertin's vision was also internationalist. The IOC was one of the earlier organisations with global aspirations. Once the IOC was established, many other sports acquired governing bodies during the subsequent two decades (for example IAAF, FIFA, ILTS). The IOC has always been opposed to, and has never endorsed, the concept of medal tables, ranking nations by success. However, the media have always offered such tables and seek to dramatise the Games as a context of prowess between nations. Indeed national belonging-ness and national identity constitute prime means by which audiences around the world engage with the Games.

110

Conceptions of the world do not exist independently of power relations. From the fifteenth century, voyages of exploration by the dominant nations of Europe enabled a Eurocentric mapping of the world, which contributed to Western constructions of the global imaginary. The aspiring colonial powers conceived of the rest of the world as territory to plunder, and peoples to exploit and enslave. Closely linked to the expansion of territory through empire-building, the religions – especially Christianity and Islam – had always sought to expand their base of adherents, and developed visions of a global reach, built through evangelical activity. The Catholic Church could be seen in this context as an early internationalised organisational structure, and the Freemasons, too, developed an international ambition. During the eighteenth century, new and challenging ideas developed: about the rights of man and rights of woman, universal brotherhood, and republicanism, symbolised in the French revolutionary slogan 'Liberty, Equality and Fraternity'. So while trade and colonisation had already recognised and demarcated the world, it is not altogether surprising that some of the first impulses to develop internationalist links were associated with the development of socialism. The International Workingmen's Association, founded in 1864, became known as the 'First International'. Its founders, recognising that capitalism was an international system, sought to build international links between trade unionists and other organised workers around the world.

During the second half of the nineteenth century other early international organisations were those associated with the establishment of conventions and practices that might assist trade, such as the Universal Postal Union, the International Bureau of Weights and Measures, and the International Sanitary Conference. In 1851, the Great Exhibition in the UK preceded a whole series of international exhibitions, later dubbed 'world's fairs' – one of the first cultural forms to specifically name the 'world' as its scope. The rise of the nation-state in the nineteenth century had in turn produced new forms of contestation, in which the great empires of Europe negotiated a complex set of secret treaties, whilst fighting for colonial dominance of the rest of the world. The culmination of this process in the First World War persuaded powerful nations of the need to impose some international order by means of an international organisation – the League of Nations was established in 1919, and, following its collapse and the Second World War, the United Nations was formed in 1945.

So the establishment of the IOC needs to be seen in the context of the emergence of a diverse set of international organisational forms between 1850 and 1950. We have become familiar with a range of global organisations – the Boy Scouts, the Red Cross, Médecins Sans Frontières, the World Bank, UNESCO, the International Monetary Fund. Many are not really global but have global aspirations. In this context, four features of the IOC are striking: first, that it was founded relatively early in the context of international organisations; second, that it was almost the first real sporting international body; third, that it has succeeded, perhaps more than any other organisation, in being genuinely global in its reach; and fourth, that it has survived for over one hundred years without significant split, schism or challenge to its authority.

It is salutary to remember that in 1896, Germany was only 25 years old as a nation-state, and Italy only 35. Given the extent to which the IOC was a club dominated by European aristocracy and nobility, and the relative difficulty of international travel, it was predictable that the first Olympic Games were a largely European affair – only a dozen nations were represented, all but three European (they were USA, Germany, UK, Australia, France,

General organisations		Sport organisations
1851	International Sanitary Conference	
1861		First English cricket side to tour Australia
1863	International Committee of the Red Cross	
1864	First Geneva Convention	
1864	International Workingmen's Association	
1872		First international football match
1874	Universal Postal Union	
1875	International Bureau of Weights and Measures	
1881		International Federation of Gymnastics
1886		International Rugby Football Board
1892		International Rowing Federation
1894		International Olympic Committee formed
1896		First modern Olympic Games
1899	First Hague Convention	
1900		Union Cycliste Internationale formed
1904		FIFA, world governing body of football
1906		FINA: International Swimming Federation
1912		IAAF (athletics) formed
1913		ITLF (tennis) formed
1919	League of Nations	
1919	International Federation of Red Cross and Red Crescent Societies	
1920	World Organisation of the Scout Movement	
1930		First Football World Cup staged
1945	World Bank	
1945	International Monetary Fund	
1945	United Nations	

Figure 6.1 Development of international organisations.

Denmark, Greece, Sweden, Switzerland, Bulgaria, Hungary, Chile). From the start, the Games featured the symbols and rituals of nation – national flags were hoisted during the victory ceremonies. The first Games could not be said to be a genuine competition between nations as many of the teams had an ad hoc character – being made up of friends and acquaintances of the organisers, tourists who happened to be in Athens (see McFee 1990) and in one case, students of a member of the NOC. Whilst the first Games were neither national nor international, the stage was set for this key tension around which the Games developed. During the next 12 years the Games struggled to survive, being staged as a sideshow to international trade fairs (the Exposition Universelle in Paris in 1900, the World's Fair in St Louis in 1904 and the Franco-British Exhibition in 1908. In one contemporary description, the Franco-British Exhibition was at Shepherd's Bush and the Olympics 'took place alongside the enormous site' (Cook 1908:14).

There were significant tensions in 1908 between the USA and the UK. The cause of Irish Home Rule was important to many Irish Americans, including those in the American Olympic squad, and the American team refused to dip their flag as they passed the Royal Box at the Opening Ceremony. The officials were all British, and after they had disqualified an American runner, the Americans were quick to accuse them of bias. The ensuing bitterness continued

112

1896	12
1900	22
1904	9
1908	26
1912	28

Figure 6.2 Nations competing in the Olympic Games, 1896–1912.

after the Games, and before the 1912 Games the IOC decided that in future there would be an international team of officials and judges.

The Swedish team returned home in 1912 after a disputed decision in a wrestling match. It was already becoming abundantly clear that the spectacle of the Games constituted a site for symbolic contestation around concepts of national belongingness. In 1912 Finland was under the control of Russia, but the Finnish team refused to march under the Russian flag and the IOC allowed them to march behind the Finnish flag, to the huge delight of the crowd. At first the growth pattern of the Games appears erratic, with an especially low turnout in St Louis in 1904, largely for geographic reasons, but by 1912 it was clear that the Olympic Games had become established as a recurrent ritual practice of growing significance.

BETWEEN THE WARS: COMMUNISM AND FASCISM

The growing tension between Germany, Russia, Britain and France during the build-up to 1914 had its impact on the IOC, especially as Berlin was awarded the 1916 Games. When the First World War broke out, Theodore Cook, a British IOC member, demanded the expulsion of German members, and when this was rejected, he resigned. By contrast, Coubertin opted to protect the IOC by moving its headquarters to neutral Switzerland, where it has remained ever since (Guttmann 1992: 37). The 1920 Games were awarded, rather pointedly, given that Belgium was the first victim of the war, to Antwerp. The IOC maintained its own policy of inclusion by leaving the invitations to the organising committee, and Germany was not invited to the Games of 1920 and 1924.

Its finely tuned sense of international diplomacy meant that the IOC was prone to mark the claims of rising powers by awarding them Games. The cancelled 1940 Games would have been in Tokyo; China's economic dynamism and growing political significance was finally rewarded with a Games in 2008; the Olympics will be going to Rio in 2016; and one could reasonably expect a South African and an Indian Olympics in the next 30 years. It is also worth noting that neither Berlin 1916 nor Tokyo 1940 happened, due to world conflicts in which the proposed host nations were deeply involved. After both major wars, organising committees responded to anger and political sensitivities by withholding invitations to the defeated nations.

The early years of the Olympic Games constitute an interesting case study in the invention of tradition, in which both the internationalist and nationalist aspects of the Games were buttressed by ritual. The Olympic oath-taking ceremony and the Olympic flag were introduced in 1920. An Olympic hymn, different each time, was used until the Rome Olympics, after which the 1960 version became the permanent Olympic Hymn. The first Olympic Village was constructed for the 1924 Games in Paris. When Paris was awarded the 1924 Games, the

113

architect imagined 'the most beautiful stadium in the world' (Gravelaine 1997: 13). The village was conceptualised as an innovative construction that would be built to last and used after the Games, and one commentator at the time described it as 'a beautiful village, with all modern comforts installed' (see Charpentier and Boissonnade 1999: 118). On a research visit to the area in 2001, we could find no remaining traces of the village.

The Olympic flame was first lit in the stadium in 1928 and the torch relay was introduced in 1936. The Olympic oath illustrates the tensions neatly – taken on behalf of all the competitors as an international group, it nevertheless commits them to competing 'for the honour of our country and the glory of sport'. The nationalist dimension was ritualised by the establishment of medal ceremonies, the raising of national flags, the playing of national anthems and the parading in national teams in the Opening Ceremony.

The impulse to internationalism has led to a continuous recruitment of new nations, yet national rivalries and political tensions have also meant exclusion for some nations. The newly communist Russia was not invited to the 1920 Games. Countries held responsible for the 'Great War' were excluded from participating, so athletes from Germany, Austria, Bulgaria, Hungary and Turkey were relegated to bystander status. Indeed, Germany was not readmitted until 1928. The scope of the Games continued to grow in the inter-war era, despite a dip in numbers of nations for Los Angeles in 1932.

The inter-war years in Europe were characterised by political instability, stemming from the poorly conceived settlements imposed by the victors of the First World War, the rise of fascism, and the establishment of Soviet communism. Financial crises contributed to instability, from the rampant inflation that wrecked the Weimar Republic, through the Wall Street Crash of 1929 into the Depression of the 1930s. There was a social revolution in manners and morality, less deference to the aristocracy and greater emancipation of women. During this period, the Olympic movement faced its most significant challenge to date, in the workers' sport movement, and the first real tarnishing of its image in the 1936 Games.

The workers' sport movements

In the aftermath of the First World War (1914–1918) and the Russian Revolution (1917) the workers' sports movement developed rapidly, and a whole series of workers' sports events or 'workers' Olympics' were staged during the 1920s and 1930s as an alternative to the official 'nationalistic' and 'bourgeois' Olympics (Krüger and Riordan 1996). The workers' sports movement grew out of the foundation, in Germany in the 1890s, of the Workers' Gymnastic Association. This was established to provide an alternative, and opposition, to the German Gymnastic Society, which had become an intensely nationalistic organisation. Similar groups developed all over Europe, varying in type, but with a shared intention to provide working-

1920	29
1924	44
1928	46
1932	37
1936	49

Figure 6.3 Nations competing in the Olympic Games, 1920–1936.

114

class people with healthy exercise in a socialist context (Riordan 1984: 99). At first the focus was on less competitive, exercise-based activity, but after the First World War the orientation shifted towards competitive sports. The movement was split by the divergence, following the successful Russian Revolution, between socialist and communist organisations. The socialists remained with the Lucerne Sports International (LSI), whilst communists broke away to associate with the Red Sports International (RSI), sponsored by Russia.

Riordan singles out four ways in which these movements challenged the IOC Olympics. First, while the bourgeois Olympics encouraged participation in national teams, the workers' Olympics stressed internationalism. Second, unlike the IOC Olympics, which imposed minimum standards of performance and limits on numbers per event, the workers' games emphasised mass participation. Third, the IOC Games were seen as largely confined to the sons of the rich and privileged (amateurs, almost entirely male) and the IOC itself was seen as an aristocratic body whilst the workers' games opposed chauvinism, elitism, racism and discrimination. Fourth, the workers' movement did not believe the Olympic spirit of true amateurism and international understanding could be achieved in a bourgeois-dominated movement (Riordan 1984: 103). The opening ceremonies at the workers' games dispensed with 'nationalist' flags and anthems, and competitors and spectators sang revolutionary hymns such as 'The Internationale'. The movement climaxed in 1936, when, with thousands of would-be participants already in Barcelona, the Spanish fascists staged a putsch, triggering the start of the Civil War. Many of those who had come to compete ended up enlisting in the International Brigade (see Murray 1987; Steinberg 1978; Wheeler 1978).

The period of the Popular Front, uniting communist and socialist parties across Europe during the late 1930s, was unable to halt the rise of fascism and Nazism, and just a year after the Antwerp Workers' Olympics of 1937, Hitler's German troops marched into Austria. The staging of the official Olympic Games in Germany had already provided Hitler with a huge public canvas on which to paint a disturbing image of Nazi power. The 1936 Games proved to be the last for 12 years.

Berlin 1936: the 'Nazi Games'

Although nationalism was already written into Olympic ritual, the 1936 Games, which became notorious as the 'Nazi Olympics', elevated the foregrounding of national power to a dramatic new level. The 1936 Games constituted the moment when the aspirations of Olympism for internationalism and peace were forced, dramatically, to confront the realities of national power and its associated symbolism. The rise to power of the Nazis came amidst growing concern around the world over the treatment of German Jews. Hart-Davis (1986) argues that Germany attempted to produce the appearance of a normal society during the Games, although the concentration camps established from 1933 were known about, and that US and British ambassadors relayed critical information back to their governments, but it was not taken seriously enough. He outlines the ways in which, from 1933, Jews were gradually excluded from organised sport. The IOC endeavoured to extract a promise that this would not be so, and the Germans agreed to a statement that they would abide by Olympic principles, but had no intention of reversing the anti-Jewish sport policies.

Year	Venue	Event	Organisers	Participants	Spectators	Countries
1921	Prague	Unofficial 'Workers' Olympics'	Czechoslovak Workers' Gymnastic Association			13
1925	Frankfurt	1st Workers' Olympics	Lucerne Sports International		150,000	19
1928	Moscow	First Workers' Spartakiad	Communist Sports Organisation	4,000		14
1931	Vienna	2nd Workers' Olympics	Lucerne Sports International	80,000	100,000	23
1932	Berlin	2nd Workers' Spartakiad	Communist workers	Banned by German authorities		
1936	Barcelona	3rd Workers' Olympics	Joint socialist and communist organisers	Spanish fascists stage putsch on morning of Opening Ceremony	Many would-be competitors remain to fight in International Brigade	
1937	Antwerp	Rescheduled 3rd Workers' Olympics	As above	27,000	50,000	17
1943	Helsinki	Planned 4th Workers' Olympics	As above	Not staged due to outbreak of war in 1939		

Figure 6.4 Mass-participation workers' sports events, 1918–1939.

Source: Riordan (1984: 98–112), information included on numbers where available.

During the three years before the 1936 Games there were extensive efforts to promote a boycott, especially in the UK, USA and France. In 1934 in New York, there was a mock trial of Hitler that attracted 20,000 people to Madison Square Gardens (Hart-Davis 1986). In 1935, Supreme Court Judge Jeremiah T. Mahoney published a pamphlet entitled 'Germany has Violated the Olympic Code', which contained specific and detailed instances of discrimination against German Jews in the context of sport. By 1935, according to one opinion poll, 43% of Americans were in favour of a boycott (Guttmann 1984: 72). IOC leaders, however, were inclined to accept reassurances from the German organisers at face value, and showed little willingness to investigate more carefully. There was also, demonstrably, a degree of anti-Semitism within Olympic circles.

Avery Brundage[1] privately referred to the 'Jewish proposal' to boycott the Games, and claimed that every boycott call was 'obviously written by a Jew or someone who has succumbed to Jewish propaganda'. In fact, Guttmann suggests, although many American Jews did play an active role, Catholic organisations and individuals were prominent in leading the boycott campaign (Guttmann 2006). Sigfrid Edstrom[2] wrote, in a letter to Avery Brundage, 'they [Jews] are intelligent and unscrupulous. Many of my friends are Jews, so you must not think that I am against them, but they must be kept within certain limits'; and Baillet-Latour[3] also in a letter to Brundage, wrote that he was not personally fond of Jews. But Baillet-Latour at least made some attempts to get the Germans to honour their pre-Games pledges of no discrimination against Jewish athletes in German team selection (Guttmann 1992: 53–71). Brundage, by contrast, for the rest of his life insisted, against all the evidence, that there had been no such discrimination. Guttmann argues that it was his fight against the boycott that turned him anti-Semitic.[4] The one IOC member who opposed the Games and supported the boycott, American Ernest Lee Jahncke, was expelled from the IOC to be replaced by Brundage (Guttmann 1992: 53–71). Baillet-Latour, IOC President from 1925 to 1942, was succeeded by Edstrom (1946–52) after which Brundage became President and served from 1952 to 1972. The fact that three consecutive presidents, over a period of almost 50 years, can at the least be regarded as somewhat anti-Semitic, prompts speculation about the cultural climate within the IOC during this period.

The Berlin Games were not simply used as a propaganda platform, as is sometimes asserted; indeed the Nazi authorities went to some lengths during the Games to mask the true nature of the ideological transformation they had brought about. Nevertheless, the general desire to celebrate Aryan might inflected the presentation of the Games, not least in the innovation of the torch relay. Berlin Olympic organiser Carl Diem had a scholarly interest in ancient Greece and found support from Hitler, who admired Doric architecture (Hart-Davis 1986: 52). The torch relay, mythologised as a return to ancient Greek roots, was utilised by the Nazis as a symbol of Aryan power. The ancient Greeks did have relays carrying torches but there is no evidence that they ever did so in connection with the Olympic Games. Diem suggested a relay, referring to ancient vases for authority. Hitler was persuaded that the Third Reich ought to sponsor the current excavations at Olympia. Coubertin supported the idea as it seemed to help legitimate the link between the ancient and modern Games. Krupp, the German arms producer, created and sponsored the torches. The Nazi anthem, the 'Horst Wessel Lied', was played in ancient Olympia when the flame was lit. The song contains the line 'Already millions are looking to the swastika, full of hope'. It was also sung at the Opening Ceremony. 'Altars were set up along the way for semi-religious ceremonies in the tradition of the ancient fire cults, which had been prevalent in ancient Greece as in ancient Germany' (Krüger and Murray 2003). Arguably, this was the point at which the embryonic neo-paganism underpinning some Olympic rituals was consolidated.

In Vienna, 10,000 Austrian Nazis greeted the torch with cries of 'Heil Hitler' and demonstrated against the Jewish members of the Austrian Olympic team, shouting 'Perish Judah'. Five hundred had to be arrested (Walters 2006:193). The ceremony in Vienna was used by the Austrian Nazis as a demonstration of their power, whereas the one in Prague resulted in street fighting between Sudeten Germans and Czechs. Hart-Davis says of the events in Vienna surrounding the torch relay, 'The message of the evening was clear. In a place as politically volatile as Vienna, the Olympic Games were an explosive subject' (Hart-Davis 1986: 137). As the torch relay was under German jurisdiction rather than that of the IOC it could be used for unabashed Nazi ceremonies (Krüger 2003: 32–33). The ritual of the relay, and its version in the Leni Riefenstahl film of the Games, was to make explicit the supposed link between Germany and ancient Greece. The Reich was portrayed as the repository for ancient Greek virtues. The president of the organising committee, Lewald, said that the Olympic torch created 'a real and spiritual bond between our German fatherland and the sacred places of Greece founded nearly 4,000 years ago by Nordic immigrants' (Walters 2006: 193). The whole ceremony in Olympia was of course an invention, but the version in the Riefenstahl film was a further reconstruction of an invented tradition – she fabricated it in take after take, eventually insisting on a naked male runner (with whom she subsequently had an affair) rather than the man in modern gym shorts who was the original choice (Graham 1986: 61).

When the flame was finally lit in the stadium, the BBC commentator gasped in shock before pronouncing, 'I don't think anyone expected such a big flame', inadvertently producing in the process a rather chilling metaphor for the rise of the Nazis.[5] Hart-Davis says that in the lighting ceremony in Olympia in 1936 a 'ridiculously long' message from Coubertin was read out (Hart-Davis 1986: 133). Walters suggests that Coubertin was, in effect, blackmailed by the Nazis, after he stupidly accepted a secret donation from them. The last public statement from the ageing Coubertin praised the 'grandiose games' which, he asserted, magnificently served the Olympic ideal (Guttmann 1992: 70). Although the Games were, on a technical level, a great success it was not a proud moment for the Olympic movement, with its aspirations for peaceful internationalism. Having been established as a routinised and cyclical ritual by this time, the cancellation of any Olympic Games marks the dramatic disruption of diplomatic relations by global conflict. The 1940 Olympic Games, scheduled for Tokyo, and the 1944 Games, scheduled for Helsinki, did not take place.

THE NEW WORLD AND THE COLD WAR

After the Second World War the Olympic Games resumed their growth trajectory, despite a small drop for the Melbourne Games of 1956, which were affected by boycotts. However, the end of the war did not mean a return to peace or to the world of the 1930s. Rather a profound new geopolitical environment came into being as the European map was redrawn by the USA and the Soviet Union. The next few decades were dominated by the economic, political and cultural contestations between capitalist America and communist Russia. While

1948	59
1952	69
1956	67
1960	84
1964	94
1968	113

Figure 6.5 Nations competing in the Olympic Games, 1948–1968.

the possession by both of nuclear weapons prevented direct military confrontation, nevertheless, around the world the struggles of peoples and nations were strongly influenced by the respective regional influences of the dominant superpowers.

In 1979, Richard Espy (1979: vii) wrote 'The Modern Olympic Games symbolize the struggle between man's ideals and the reality within which he must live'. The notion is suggestive of the era of Cold War and the symbolic contestation which framed the Olympic movement from 1945 to 1989. In the first Olympic Games after the war, the defeated nations Germany and Japan were not invited, although Italy was, and the Soviet Union did not compete. During the 1930s the Soviet Union, after the Revolution, had largely abstained from international sport, not being part of IFs or the IOC, and instead fostered the development of the RSI.[6] After the Second World War, however, they adopted the strategy of entering international competitions in order to demonstrate the superiority of the communist system. In 1948, though, the USSR had not sought recognition from the IOC and did not have an NOC. The American vice-president of the IOC, Avery Brundage, a strong anti-communist, was opposed to accepting communist individuals as members of the IOC, but did not favour excluding countries from the Olympic movement on the grounds of their political system (Espy 1979: 28). China had intended to compete, but the successful culmination of the communist revolution in 1947 put an end to the plans. In 1948, the Opening Ceremony in London took little more than an hour and consisted of presentation of VIPs and the teams marching in. The elaborate spectacle of the ceremony, as we now know it, has evolved since largely for television.

Germany, East and West

In 1952 the Soviet Union entered the Games for the first time since Russia competed in 1912. Developments in post-war reconciliation allowed Germany and Japan to compete. After the conclusion of the Second World War, Europe was, effectively, divided into two spheres of influence, the western half dominated by the USA, and the eastern half by the Soviet Union. Germany was divided into Soviet, American, British and French zones, and Berlin itself, lying in the eastern (Soviet) part of Germany, was also divided. The continued Western occupation of half of Berlin was to prove a provocation to the Soviet Union for the next 35 years. A Soviet-inspired blockade of Berlin during the late 1940s was broken by a massive airlift of goods from the West. In 1962, the East Germans constructed the Berlin Wall, which succeeded as a physical barrier, but provided the West with an enormous symbolic victory in propaganda terms.

In 1950 the IOC gave provisional recognition to the West German Olympic Committee. However, a parallel East German NOC began seeking affiliation to international sport federations. An intense debate developed within the IOC, commencing at the Vienna session

119

of 1951. Some members argued that an NOC had to be part of a legitimate state (and East Germany was yet to seek or gain recognition). Some members wanted to emphasise the remit in the charter to bring the youth of the world together, recognise both NOCs and hope for future reunification, whilst others believed this would merely emphasise the division. The IOC tried without initial success to promote the idea of two NOCs but a joint German team (see Hill 1992: 34). In 1952 a German team comprising only West German competitors featured in the Games, with the East Germans withdrawing (see Espy 1979: 35–36). Deteriorating relations between the IOC and the East German NOC led to a vote against recognition. In 1955, the Soviet Union released East Germany from its status as the 'Soviet zone' of Germany, and recognised it as an independent state. The East German NOC was then formally recognised but only on condition that it cooperated in forming a single team (see Hill 1992: 34–37).

While the IOC was, as so often, driven by pragmatism, many of the European aristocrats were hostile to the communist cause, as was the American millionaire Avery Brundage (IOC President 1952–1972). Despite West German opposition to the recognition of East Germany, the two NOCs were able to enter a joint team in the Games between 1956 and 1964. The competitors shared a flag, emblem, uniform and lodgings (see Hill 1992: 38). Such rapport was remarkable, given that this was the period of heightened Cold War tension. In the 1960 Games in Rome, as in Melbourne, the two Germanys competed as one team, with victories being marked by Beethoven's 'Ode to Joy' from the Ninth Symphony, rather than the national anthem of either (Charpentier and Boissonnade 1999: 293). In August 1961 the Berlin Wall was constructed and, in retaliation, the Western countries began denying visas to East German sportsmen and women for skiing and hockey tournaments (Espy 1979: 77).

During the 1960s it became clear that the existence of East Germany was an established fact that warranted international recognition. The majority of IFs were accepting East Germany as a separate nation and the IAAF allowed separate East and West German teams in the European Championships of 1966. The IOC agreed to recognise two NOCs although, in the case of the eastern one, the resolution referred to 'the geographical area of East Germany'. In Mexico City in 1968, two Germanys competed for the first time, and the IOC agreed to accept the name 'German Democratic Republic (GDR)' (Hill 1992: 39). By the 1970s the West German government developed its Ostpolitik, which aimed at peaceful coexistence, with the hope of eventual reunification. The GDR had immense Olympic success during the 1970s and 1980s, although suspicions of systematic use of performance-enhancing drugs were amply confirmed after 1991 when the East German archives became accessible to researchers.

China and Taiwan

China had been involved in the Olympic movement since the 1920s. The first Chinese IOC member was elected in 1922 and the IOC had recognised the Chinese NOC (Hill 1992: 40–45). After the communist revolution, many nationalists, including some NOC members fled to Formosa (now Taiwan), but the NOC retained recognition. Avery Brundage later argued, with considerable disingenuousness, that the NOC had simply changed its address! However, Lord Killanin (President 1972–1980) later stated that there was no trace at Lausanne of any such change of address having been recorded (Hill 1992: 40–45). In 1952 the People's

Republic of China (PRC) informed the IOC that it had an established body, the 'All China Athletic Commission', and wished to apply for recognition as an NOC. The Formosans too were seeking recognition and an invite to the 1952 Games. This placed the IOC in a quandary once again. They opted to accept teams from both, in advance of considering recognition for China's NOC (Hill 1992: 42). Despite this diplomatic pragmatism, the Formosans declined to acquiesce and although the China team set off, they reached Helsinki too late to participate (see Espy 1979: 36–37).

In 1954 the IOC recognised the NOC of the PRC whilst maintaining its recognition of Formosa's. The China committee was known as the 'Olympic Committee of the Chinese Republic' (changed in 1958 to 'Olympic Committee of the People's Democratic Republic of China'). The Formosa committee retained the title the 'Chinese Olympic Committee'. The IOC resorted to the rather slippery claim that it was recognising territories under the control of an NOC and not as nations (Hill 1992: 40–45).

By 1956, the IOC had on the one hand successfully persuaded the two German nations to enter one team, but on the other agreed to recognise NOCs from both China and Formosa (see Espy 1979: 44–45). This time a more assertive China objected and did not compete in 1956. At the start of 1956 the third Chinese IOC member Shou Ti-Tung, elected in 1947, requested that the Formosa Olympic Committee be expelled. Brundage was dismissive. Later in the year, the PRC withdrew from Melbourne in protest and in 1958 it withdrew from the Olympic movement and from all IFs (Hill 1992: 42). After a period of relative openness ('Let a hundred flowers blossom') China had entered a period of tougher ideological stance (the 'Great Leap Forward') and isolation from 'imperialist' organisations, denouncing Avery Brundage and withdrawing from the IOC (Espy 1979: 63). Chinese IOC member Shou Ti-Tung resigned, dubbing Brundage a 'faithful menial of US imperialists' (see Hill 1992: 40–45).

The IOC attempted to resolve the issue, by insisting that the Formosa committee could not go on purporting to represent China, but must reapply, choosing a name that reflected the territory that it actually controlled. This fairly moderate proposal led to a storm of controversy in the USA in which Brundage, who was (falsely) represented as having expelled Formosa, was bitterly criticised (Espy 1979: 65). In 1960 the Formosa NOC proposed that it be known as the Republic of China, in accord with its UN recognition. The IOC accepted this but insisted that at Rome they compete as Formosa. The team carried a sign reading 'Formosa', but displayed a placard reading 'Under Protest'. In 1968 the name the 'Olympic Committee of the Republic of China' was reaffirmed by the IOC (Hill 1992: 40–45). In the 1970s, US foreign policy pursued rapprochement with China, and President Nixon visited China in 1972. In 1971 the UN recognised the PRC and expelled Formosa/Taiwan, giving its seat on the Security Council to China. The IOC resolved that China would be welcome back if it accepted Olympic rules and the continued presence of Taiwan (Hill 1992: 40–45).

From the mid-1950s then, the IOC was beginning to experience greater difficulties with managing national contestation, and in 1956, in the evocative words of Charpentier and Boissonnade, 'heavy clouds darkened the Olympic sky' (1999: 259). It was a year of dramatic political events: the escalation of the Algerian war of independence (1954–1962), Russian tanks on the streets of Budapest to crush the local more liberal-minded regime, and the English and French invasion of Egypt in response to Colonel Nasser's nationalisation of the Suez Canal. Spain, Holland, Italy, Switzerland, Iraq and Egypt announced their withdrawal from the

Games. Israel, its troops mobilised, sent only a symbolic delegation of three (Charpentier and Boissonnade 1999: 259). A water polo match between Hungary and the USSR turned into a grudge match with, according to some witnesses, the water turning red with blood. Against this backdrop of national contestation, there was one positive internationalist development – the Closing Ceremony featured, instead of competitors marching in teams, as in the Opening, 500 representatives of the 4,000 competitors who 'marched as a single cavalcade' (Espy 1979: 58). North Korea sought to enter a team for 1964, but the IOC insisted on a joint Korean team. The North agreed but the South refused. The IOC then threatened that in that case it would admit North Korea. The South remained intransigent – so North Korea was admitted as a separate team (Espy 1979: 82–83). It seems clear that the IOC did not merely reflect political decisions taken elsewhere but was actively interventionist. It operated, though, not so much in accord with high principle, or in relation to clear constitutional principle, but rather with pragmatic responses to specific circumstances.

Palestine, Israel and the Middle East

Up until the Second World War, Palestine had an Olympic Committee although, as a 'mandate' territory, it competed under the British flag. So Palestine was invited to compete in 1948. However, the United Nations had recommended the partition of Palestine, and the State of Israel was declared in 1947. The Palestine NOC became the Olympic Committee of Israel, with the intention of competing under the Israeli flag, although some Arab nations objected to the 'Zionist' flag. Under the threat of a boycott, the IOC, once again opting for a short-term pragmatic, if not pedantic, solution, declared Israel ineligible. It argued that as the original Olympic Committee had been given recognition under the national designation of 'Palestine', and as this Palestine committee no longer existed, and since 'Israel' had not applied for recognition, it was ineligible (Espy 1979: 29; and see Trory 1980: 18). Israel's new NOC was subsequently recognised and an Israeli team competed in 1952 in Helsinki. Seven countries boycotted the Melbourne Games: Spain, Switzerland and the Netherlands, to protest the Soviet invasion of Hungary; and Lebanon, Egypt and Iraq, to protest Israel's invasion of the Sinai and the Gaza Strip.

Palestine was accepted as a member of the Olympic Council of Asia in 1986, and the International Olympic Committee recognised Palestine as a nation for Olympic purposes in 1993, both events triggering reactions of outrage in Israel and amongst Zionists worldwide.[7] Fighting a rearguard action, Israel attempted, in 1996, to persuade the IOC to bar the use of the word 'Palestine', suggesting instead 'Palestinian Authority, Palestinian Autonomy or Palestinian Delegation'. Palestine teams have participated in the Olympic Games since 1996. In 1996 a reception hosted by Andrew Young brought together Israel and Palestine Olympic delegates. The Palestine and Israel Olympic Committee delegations were filmed by the world's media exchanging greetings.[8]

In 2004 the PLO leader Yasser Arafat announced that the Palestinians would observe a truce during the 2004 Olympic Games. Since the death of Arafat in November 2004 and the rising power of Hamas in Palestine and the right wing in Israel, attitudes have hardened considerably and it will be a surprise if the Middle East does not become an issue in the run-up to the London Olympic Games of 2012.

Decolonisation and newly emergent nations

In the post-war era, the last great European empire, the British Empire, was dismantled. A UK weakened in the wake of the war was unable to combat movements for independence. While independence for India (1947) was seen as the watershed, the process of decolonisation was to be long drawn out. The Bandung Conference in 1955 organised by the Colombo group of countries (Burma, Ceylon, India, Indonesia and Pakistan) brought together representatives from 24 African and Asian countries to discuss shared economic objectives and the end of colonialism (Espy 1979: 47). In 1962 Indonesia, the host of the Asian Games, refused visas to Taiwan and Israeli competitors. The following year the IOC suspended the Indonesian NOC, which withdrew from the Olympic movement. President Sukarno then took the initiative in establishing the proposed Games of the New Emerging Forces (GANEFO). An initial conference, with delegates from Cambodia, China, Guinea, Indonesia, Iraq, Mali, Pakistan, North Vietnam, the UAR and the Soviet Union, and observers from Ceylon and Yugoslavia, drew inspiration from the 1955 Bandung Conference (Espy 1979: 81). China is believed to have been the driving force behind these proposals.

The first GANEFO was staged in 1963 with a second scheduled for Cairo in 1967. Part of the geopolitical substructure of this, of course, was the impact of the Sino-Soviet split which meant that China and the Soviet bloc were competing with each other as well as with the West for influence in the 'Third World'. A session of the GANEFO council was held in Beijing in 1965 and it was decided to hold an Asian GANEFO at the same time as the Olympic-approved Asian Games (Espy 1979: 109). Cairo pulled out of staging the next GANEFO in 1967 for financial reasons. China during the cultural revolution became more inward looking and, in Espy's words, 'GANEFO died a quiet death' (1979: 110). After this brief episode in separatism, Third World countries became more focused on the Olympic Games, utilising the event as a symbolic opportunity to announce their independent presence on the world stage – and the number of NOCs rose steadily to reflect these aspirations. The numbers of competing nations grew steadily up till 1976, with a dip in 1980 caused by the US-led boycott.

Apartheid and South Africa

A 'cultural boycott' played a significant role in the isolation and stigmatisation of the South African apartheid regime. The sports boycott of South Africa led the way, giving the issue a high profile and encouraging the extension of the boycott into other areas. Although it also required well-directed pressure from campaigning individuals, organisations and countries, it could be argued that the IOC was a leading force in the sporting boycott.

South Africa first competed in 1908 in London and had sent a team to every Games since then. No black competitors were ever chosen by the exclusively white South African Olympic Committee. This appears not to have been an issue for the IOC, which in the 1950s had no African members. It was only in 1959 that campaigning began within the IOC, led by the Soviet Union member, Alexei Romanov (Ramsamy 1984: 45).

In 1961, South Africa became a republic and began to introduce additional laws enforcing segregation. In 1963 the IOC met with the African NOCs who insisted that no invitation be issued to South Africa for the 1964 Games. The IOC asked the South African NOC to make a public statement opposing racial discrimination and when there was no response, the South Africans were excluded from 1964. Fighting back with a diplomatic offensive, which involved rallying its supporters within the IOC and offering some rather vague and meaningless conciliatory statements, South Africa was able to secure an IOC invitation for 1968. However, a campaign to fight back was mounted by the Supreme Council for Sport in South Africa (SCSA) and the South African Non-Racial Olympic Committee (SANROC), with the support of black African states and black activists in the USA, led by Harry Edwards. The threat of a boycott by around 40 countries forced the IOC to make a U-turn and ban South Africa. The arrogant response of South Africa, warning the IOC not to meddle in its domestic affairs, was sufficient to alienate the support that it still had in the IOC, and in 1970 South Africa was expelled from the organisation (Ramsamy 1984: 45–48).

At the start of the 1960s, the IOC had been seeking, in vain, reassurance from the South African NOC that apartheid in sport did not exist, or would be eradicated. The South African National Olympic Committee (SANOC) seemed unable or unwilling to oppose the South African government publicly and so South Africa were not invited to take part in 1964 (Espy 1979: 87). Although many on the IOC were not crusaders against racism, the organisation nonetheless deserves some credit for being one of the organisations to outlaw South Africa. The whole story highlights the growing symbolic power of the Olympic Games, and presages the era of boycotts and political protests. In 1966 the SCSA was formed – largely to campaign against South Africa. Some compromise proposals from SANOC, involving a mixed team at the Olympics, persuaded the IOC to readmit them. This triggered a huge reaction in the NOCs and elsewhere, with many countries and individuals threatening to boycott. The IOC was forced into constructing a face-saving formula for getting the South Africans to withdraw.

CONCLUSION

Given the complex issues that the IOC has had to manage during the twentieth century, it is a considerable achievement that the movement has never split, or suffered any significant defections. Indeed it may be because of the peculiar construction of the IOC – dominated as it has been by European aristocracy – that its very closeness to the dominant classes of powerful nations has enabled it to function, at times as an alternative (if self-serving) form of diplomacy. Nor is this influence limited to Western Europe. After the division of Europe and the emergence of communist nations in the East, the IOC was able to absorb and clasp to its bosom the new apparatchiks of Eastern Europe, who had influence within their countries. By the mid-1970s, though, the apartheid issue and the Cold War were to trigger a wave of boycotts in which, in the television era, the huge symbolic force of the Games became clearer and more dramatic than ever before. It is striking that it was in this period that the appointment of Juan Antonio Samaranch as IOC President was made. Samaranch was the most ambassadorial of presidents, using his own diplomatic background and delicate utilisation of the art of public tact and private pressure to preserve and enhance the power of the IOC. He was also to be responsible for a ruthless IOC revolution, removing the obstacle of the term 'amateur' from the constitution, dispensing with long-serving Secretary Monique Berlioux, and working with Horst Dassler of Adidas to transform the system of selling sponsorships. The new President had doubtless learned about ruthlessness in the pursuit of political ends in his earlier career. In November 1967 he had been on his knees in front of the fascist General Franco, taking the oath of office, prior to becoming a National Councillor (see Boix *et al.* 1994, picture on rear cover). Samaranch, it appears, was a loyal supporter of the Spanish fascists and remained so right up to Franco's death in 1976, just four years before he assumed the presidency of the IOC (see Jennings 1996; Jennings and Sambrook 2000).

FURTHER READING

Allison, L. (ed.) (1993) *The Changing Politics of Sport*, Manchester: Manchester University Press.

Charpentier, H. and Boissonnade, E. (1999) *La Grande Histoire des Jeux Olympiques*, Paris: Editions France-Empire.

Hill, C. (1992) *Olympic Politics*, London: Manchester University Press.

Tomlinson, A. and Young, C. (eds) (2006) *National Identity and Global Sports Events*, Albany, NY: State University of New York Press.

CHAPTER 7

POLITICS AND THE OLYMPICS

It is often thought that the English journalist and author George Orwell condemned sport outright as simply 'war minus the shooting' (see Davison 1998: 442). He certainly did not think it was a great means by which to solve problems in international relations. But he also recognised that it was not the cause of such problems: 'big scale sport is itself, I think, merely another effect of the causes that have produced nationalism' (Davison 1998: 442–443). Orwell was writing just after Moscow Dynamo (a team of Soviet soldiers) had played a series of matches in Britain shortly after the end of the Second World War. His closing point was that 'you do make things worse by sending forth a team of eleven men, labelled as national champions, to do battle against some rival team, and allowing it to be felt on all sides that whichever nation is defeated will "lose face"' (Davison 1998: 443). Whether we entirely accept his analysis or not we can see that Orwell was acutely aware of the *symbolic* politics of sport.

Despite Rule 51 in the Olympic Charter, which states that 'No kind of demonstration or political, religious or racial propaganda is permitted in any Olympic sites, venues or other areas' (IOC (2007a) Olympic Charter: 98), the modern Olympic movement has had to contend with wars, boycotts, protests, walkouts and even a terrorist attack. As the Olympics have become a global televisual event it has become more available for symbolic political action. From the late 1960s onwards the Olympic Games have been caught up in symbolic politics, taking two main forms: the *promotional* opportunities offered by the Games to enhance reputations – by competing, winning medals and hosting them, as well as refusing to participate in them through different forms of boycott – and the opportunity to *protest* about a perceived social injustice by 'seizing the platform' that the Games offer through such a globally mediated mega-event (Price 2008). In addition the Games have developed amidst changes in economic ideologies – from state-led, mixed economies to privatised economic orthodoxies.

As Chapter 6 indicated, in the period between 1968 and 1984 the Olympic Games became the site of more highly focused symbolic political contestation in which the boycott became a significant political weapon.[1] This chapter examines the politics and the mythologising of key moments of the Games by focusing on three main trends in international relations and political economy: the emergence of boycotts and political theatre, particularly between the 1960s and the end of the 1980s; the growth of national and place promotion as a form of reputational politics; and the growth of the Olympics as an economic investment opportunity as neoliberalism increasingly became the 'common sense' of international political economy

the spectacle of modernity

from the 1980s onwards. These trends are in tension and overlap, so that for example the 1984 Summer Olympics in Los Angeles can be seen to illustrate each of them. At the same time, focusing initially on events such as the Black Power salutes in the 1968 Olympic Games in Mexico which triggered a period of boycotts and political theatre (1976, 1980, 1984), we seek to highlight the process whereby that form of politics has largely been marginalised in favour of promotional politics in more recent Games. This chapter thus continues to explore the international political and economic context that shaped the politics of the Games from the 1960s onwards, whilst identifying the development of the politics of legacy and sustainability which are considered in Chapter 10.

POLITICS AT THE GAMES

It is possible to describe the politics at the Olympic Games in terms of a number of different contrasts and features. According to Toohey and Veal (2007: 87–118) for example, there have been several different forms of political *interference* in the Olympic Games: *internal politics* within the nation where the Olympics are being staged; *international rivalries*, based on either different political or different ideological disputes and the use of the Games to advance national agendas; competitors using the Games as a forum for *political demonstrations* against their national governments; non-participants using the Games to *further their political causes*; participating nations trying to equate Olympic success with their *social, economic and political superiority*; and *politics within the IOC* impacting on Olympic policy. It is easy to illustrate these.

As we have seen in the previous chapter, the Games awarded to Berlin in 1916 provided the earliest example of the second type of political situation facing the Olympic Games. When the First World War began in 1914, pressure was exerted by the Allied powers to move the Games. As the Games could not be relocated to an alternative site they were cancelled, for the first time in the history of the modern Games.[2] Berlin in 1936 was the location of the infamous 'Nazi Games'. Problems stemmed from the issue of discrimination against Jews in Germany under the Nazi regime. To compensate for the growing world opposition, the Nazis spared no effort in their preparations.

The 1936 Olympic Games were intentionally awarded to Berlin so that Germany could show that it had regained its status among European countries. With the Nazis in power, however, Adolf Hitler used the event as a platform to demonstrate his theories about racial superiority. Although the 'Nazi Games' were a very powerful propaganda exercise, the attempt to claim Aryan superiority through athletic performance failed, as African-American Jesse Owens became the hero of the Games winning four gold medals. During the long jump competition, Owens's German rival, Luz Long, publicly befriended him in front of the Nazis. Long was killed during the Second World War, but Owens kept in touch with his family for many years after the war.

Following the war, the 1948 Olympics in London took on a greater political significance as participation came to symbolise political recognition and legitimacy. Germany and Japan were not invited to London because of their wartime roles, while the Soviet Union was invited but did not participate. To limit Britain's responsibility to feed the athletes, it was agreed that the participants would bring their own food. No new facilities were built, but Wembley stadium had survived the war and proved adequate. The male athletes were housed in a Royal Air Force camp in Uxbridge and the women were housed at Southlands College (now part of Roehampton University) in dormitories. The 1948 London Games were the first to be shown on television, although very few people in Britain yet owned sets. Though there had been much debate as to whether or not to hold the 1948 Olympic Games, and there was concern about the outcome, they turned out to be a popular success. Approximately 4,000 athletes participated, representing 59 countries.[3]

In 1956, Egypt withdrew from the Melbourne Games due to the Suez Canal conflict. The same year, there were revolts in Poland and Hungary against the regime in Moscow, which led to Soviets troops firing on unarmed crowds in Budapest – and fights breaking out between Hungarian and Soviet athletes in Melbourne.

The first Asian country to host the Olympics, Tokyo in 1964, spent $3 billion rebuilding the city to show off its post-war success. Yoshinori Sakai, who was born on the day that Hiroshima was destroyed by an atomic bomb, was chosen as the final torchbearer.

Sporting success is often tied to nationalistic attempts to promote social, economic and/or political superiority. Here Olympic medal tables take on the role of describing the outcomes of a proxy war. How successful this is in actually convincing populations of national supremacy or developing national pride is subject to some dispute, however (see Hilvoorde *et al.* 2010).

Finally, the internal make-up and politics of the IOC have impacted on Olympic Games outcomes. As we have shown in Chapter 2, the IOC is a self-elected, self-regulating association and, until 1981, it consisted virtually entirely of men. After evidence of corruption, the IOC felt obliged to investigate the claims. The main reform measures that resulted – to do with the organisation, sport and athlete issues, the host city selection process, financial control and transparency and membership – are also discussed in Chapter 2. The political debate then and since is nicely summed up in the titles of two books published in the 2000s: *The Olympic Turnaround* (Payne 2005) and *The Great Olympic Swindle* (Jennings and Sambrook 2000). On the one hand, the IOC is now seen as efficient, reformed and recovered. On the other hand, it is seen as remaining manipulative, promotional and unreconstructed.

THREE TRENDS IN THE POLITICS OF THE GAMES

In this section we attempt to classify the politics of the Olympic Games in the past 50 years. Broadly speaking, we discern three trends: the use of boycotts as a form of political theatre – to abstain, as an individual or group, from engaging with the Olympics or some related organisation – as an expression of protest; the use of the Olympics for reputation promotion (for a cause, a socio-political or economic ideology, or a city host, region or national location); and the development of neoliberalism as the common-sense context for the staging of the Olympic Games. Figure 7.1 outlines recent Olympic Games in terms of their best fit with each of these trends. The rest of this chapter explores the trends and identifies features of each of the Games that illustrate them.

Boycotts and political theatre	Promotional and reputational politics	Neoliberalisation of the Games
1968 Mexico	1972 Munich	1976 Montreal
1980 Moscow	1992 Barcelona	1984 Los Angeles
1984 Los Angeles	2000 Sydney	1996 Atlanta
1988 Seoul	2004 Athens	2012 London
	2008 Beijing	
	2016 Rio de Janeiro	

Figure 7.1 Three trends in the politics of the Olympic Games, 1968–2016.

Boycotts and political theatre at the Olympic Games[4]

> The number of boycotts associated with the Olympics is somewhat ironic as one of the original ideas behind the establishment of the modern Games was to create a free international sporting community that no nation-state would manipulate to its political advantage. Clearly, this aim has not been realized so far.
>
> (Bairner and Molnar 2010: 163)

Boycotts have occurred at the Olympic Games for three main reasons: as part of the Cold War; because of apartheid, 'race' or imperialism; and in terms of nations being divided by political or ideological differences.

As we have seen in Chapter 6, it was the Helsinki Games in 1952 that marked the beginning of Cold War tensions. Capitalist West Germany participated for the first time, and the USSR participated in the Olympics for the first time since the Russian Revolution of 1917. The USSR initially planned to house its athletes in Leningrad and fly them into Finland each day. In the end, separate housing facilities for communist/Eastern bloc athletes were set aside. East Germany was denied its request to be included, and a German team made up entirely of West German athletes attended. From 1956 to 1964 the two Germanys were forced to reach their own Olympic truce and compete as a joint team.

As mentioned above and in Chapter 6, three separate protests affected the Melbourne Games in 1956, each in its way related to differences between capitalist and communist countries. The People's Republic of China (PRC) withdrew after the International Olympic Commission recognised Taiwan, and would not return to the Olympic movement until 1980. Egypt, Iraq and Lebanon protested at Israel's invasion of the Sinai Peninsula, while Spain, Switzerland and the Netherlands boycotted the Games over the Soviet invasion of Hungary. The conflict between the USSR and Hungary erupted during the Games when they faced each other in the water-polo semi-final. The referee abandoned the game after a fierce exchange of kicks and punches. Hungary, leading at the time, was credited with a victory. The match became known as the 'blood in the water' match.

Over 60 nations, including West Germany and Japan, boycotted the Moscow Games in 1980 to protest at the Soviet invasion of Afghanistan. The American-led boycott reduced the number of participating nations from 120 to 81, the lowest number since 1956. Countries such as Britain and France supported the boycott, and the UK government under Margaret Thatcher

129

Olympics	Boycott	Explanation/other issues
London 1948		The two major Axis powers of the Second World War, Germany and Japan, were not invited; the Soviet Union was invited but did not send any athletes.
Helsinki 1952	People's Republic of China (PRC)	The PRC was protesting at the Republic of China (Taiwan) being recognised by the IOC – the PRC did not return to Olympic competition until the 1980 Winter Games. The Soviet Union attended for the first time, but East Germany was denied its request to be included and a Germany team made up entirely of West German athletes attended.
Melbourne 1956	Egypt, Iraq and Lebanon (Suez Crisis); Netherlands, Spain and Switzerland (Soviet Union's invasion of Hungary); People's Republic of China (protesting at the Republic of China (Taiwan) being allowed to compete (under the name 'Formosa').	Egypt was invaded by Israel, the United Kingdom and France after Egypt nationalised the Suez canal; the political frustrations between the Soviet Union and Hungary boiled over during a men's water polo semi-final – the 'blood in the water' match.
Tokyo 1964	Indonesia and North Korea (after the IOC banned teams that took part in the 1963 Games of the New Emerging Forces).	South Africa expelled from IOC due to apartheid. SA would not be invited again until 1992.
Mexico City 1968		'Black Power' salute performed by Tommie Smith and John Carlos, African-American athletes who came first and third in the 200 metres race, during the medal award ceremony. The Tlatelolco massacre, 10 days before the Games began – more protesters were shot by government forces.

Munich 1972	Munich massacre – members of the Israeli Olympic team were taken hostage by the Palestinian terrorist group Black September.
Montreal 1976	Tanzania led boycott of 22 African nations.	IOC refused to bar New Zealand, despite the New Zealand rugby union team's tour of South Africa.
Moscow 1980	US President Jimmy Carter issued a boycott of the Games to protest the Soviet invasion of Afghanistan and a total of 62 eligible countries failed to participate.	A substitute event, titled the Liberty Bell Classic (also known as the 'Olympic Boycott Games'), was held at the University of Pennsylvania in Philadelphia by 29 of the boycotting countries.
Lake Placid 1980	The Republic of China (Taiwan) refused to compete under the name of 'Chinese Taipei'.	To date, the only case of boycotting the Winter Olympic Games.
Los Angeles 1984	The Soviet Union and 14 of its allies; Iran and Libya also boycotted the Games.	The Eastern bloc organised its own multi-sport event, the 'Friendship Games'.
Seoul 1988	North Korea; Albania, Cuba, Ethiopia, Madagascar, Nicaragua and the Seychelles.	North Korea was (and still is) technically at war with South Korea.
Sochi 2014	In August 2008, the government of Georgia called for a boycott of the 2014 Winter Olympics	In response to Russia's participation in the 2008 South Ossetia war. Sochi is within 20 miles of Abkhazia, a disputed territory claimed by Georgia.

Figure 7.2 Boycotts and political issues at selected Olympic Games, 1948–2014.

Sources: Bairner and Molnar (2010); Hill (1996); Toohey and Veal (2007).

placed enormous pressure on British athletes not to take part. Because the British Olympic Association (BOA) had no direct government funding it was able to resist and allow athletes to participate if they wished. Probably due to a lack of competition, the Moscow Games became quite successful for the British athletes, who finished ninth overall. The exact number of boycotting nations is difficult to determine, however, as a total of 62 eligible countries failed to participate, but some of those countries withdrew due to financial hardships, only claiming to join the boycott to avoid embarrassment. A substitute event, titled the Liberty Bell Classic (also known as the Olympic Boycott Games), was held at the University of Pennsylvania in Philadelphia by 29 of the boycotting countries.

Following the Western boycott of the 1980 Games, the USSR led a boycott by 14 socialist nations of the 1984 Games based in Los Angeles. The absentees claimed the Los Angeles Olympic Committee was violating the spirit of the Olympics by using the Games to generate commercial profits. The Eastern bloc organized its own multi-sport event, the Friendship Games, instead. For different reasons, Iran and Libya also boycotted the Games. US media tycoon Ted Turner also launched the Goodwill Games following this period. The first Games, held in Moscow in 1986, featured 182 events and attracted over 3,000 athletes representing 79 countries. The Games were later bought from Turner by Time Warner Australia, who organised the Brisbane 2001 Games, before announcing that it would be the last.

For the first time since the 1972 Munich Games, there was no organised boycott of the 1988 Olympics in Seoul. North Korea stayed away, as it was still technically at war with South Korea, and it was joined by Albania, Cuba, Ethiopia, Madagascar, Nicaragua and the Seychelles. Otherwise the Games went on with little interruption, and their success represented a major milestone on the journey from dictatorship to democracy for South Korea. IOC President Juan Antonio Samaranch seemed to manoeuvre very cleverly to avoid a boycott in 1988 – stringing the North Koreans along with largely empty promises of shared events – for example, the marathon run across the demilitarised zone. With Samaranch appearing as the great conciliator, North Korea appeared to lose most of the support it had.

The 1980s thus saw the second peak of Cold War politics during the Reagan years, and the sudden collapse of the Soviet Union at the end of the decade. The boycotts of 1980 and 1984 required the politicians to struggle quite hard to get support. Hence in 1980 the BOA, not having government funding, was able to resist the pressure of Margaret Thatcher to a certain extent. Similarly in 1984 the Soviets were not able to carry the whole communist bloc with them as they sought to boycott the Los Angeles Games. Arguably this began to discredit the boycott as a weapon – because the Games go on, and no one remembers who was not there.

The Rome Games in 1960 marked the end of South African participation in the Olympic Games for 32 years. The 1960 Olympics also saw the coming to prominence of African-American athletes, such as Wilma Rudolph and Cassius Clay (later to change his name to Muhammad Ali). And marathon-runner Abebe Bikila, running barefoot, became the first black African Olympic champion. Free of other major political disruptions, the Rome Games became a showcase for Italy, attracting a record 5,348 athletes from 83 countries. In the 1960s many countries had curtailed their sporting links with South Africa and Rhodesia because of their apartheid policies. In 1963 South Africa was expelled from the Olympics due to apartheid. It would not be invited again until the 1992 Olympics.[5]

Despite the existence of boycotts prior to it – for example in 1964 Indonesia and North Korea both withdrew from the Tokyo Games after the IOC decision to ban teams that took part in the 1963 Games of the New Emerging Forces – arguably it was the Mexico City Games in 1968, and the Black Power demonstration that took place there, that triggered off a sustained period of boycotts as political theatre at the Olympics for the next two decades (including 1976, 1980 and 1984).

Before the Mexico City Olympics in 1968 many Mexicans believed that spending large amounts of money in the name of sport was unjustified. Many argued that the money should have been spent on housing or welfare resources instead. Then, ten days before the Opening Ceremony, the most violent response to a demonstration by students about government policy occurred. The Tlatelolco Massacre involved more than two hundred protesters shot by government forces. The Mexico student murders, although largely neglected at the time in the mainstream media and since in most books about the Games (certainly compared to the massive prominence given to the Munich hostage story, see below), contributed to the sense that the Olympics was a politically useful platform that could be 'seized' (Price 2008).

BOX 7.1 THE TLATELOLCO MASSACRE, MEXICO CITY, 1968

The Tlatelolco massacre, also known as the 'Night of Tlatelolco', was a government massacre of student and civilian protesters and bystanders that took place during the afternoon and night of 2 October 1968, in the Plaza de las Tres Culturas in the Tlatelolco section of Mexico City. While at the time, government propaganda and the mainstream media in Mexico claimed that government forces had been provoked by protesters shooting at them, government documents that have been made public since 2000 suggest that the snipers had in fact been employed by the government.

New declassified information about the massacre is available thanks to a collaboration between *Proceso* magazine in Mexico and the US National Security Archive. The National Security Archive has investigated the Tlatelolco massacre since 1994 through records obtained under the Freedom of Information Act and archival research in both Mexico and the United States. At the time, Mexico was still ruled by the Institutional Revolutionary Party (PRI) and absolute secrecy continued to surround the tragedy at Tlatelolco.

Although estimates of the death toll range from 30 to 1,000, with eyewitnesses reporting hundreds of dead, the Archive's Mexico Project director Kate Doyle has only been able to find evidence for the death of 44 people. At least information about who died as a result of the ferocious violence unleashed by government forces in the Plaza of the Three Cultures in October 1968 is now available.

(http://www.gwu.edu/~nsarchiv/NSAEBB/NSAEBB201/
index.htm (accessed 17 November 2010))

133

The year 1968 was one of global unrest: Europe was rocked by student protests, the Vietnam War raged on, Martin Luther King and Robert Kennedy were assassinated and the USSR invaded Czechoslovakia. Meanwhile at the Olympics, East Germany competed separately for the first time. Tommie Smith and John Carlos, who finished first and third in the 200 metres, gave the Black Power salute during the US national anthem as a protest against racism in the US. White Australian Peter Norman, who finished second, also wore a badge supporting the same cause as Smith and Carlos, but has mostly been written out of the history of this moment (Osmond 2010).

BOX 7.2 THE BLACK POWER SALUTE

On 16 October 1968 Tommie Smith won the 200 metre race in a world-record time of 19.83 seconds, with Australia's Peter Norman second and John Carlos in third place. The two US athletes received their medals shoeless. Smith wore a black scarf and Carlos had his tracksuit top unzipped. All three athletes wore Olympic Project for Human Rights badges. Both US athletes intended to bring black gloves to the event, but Carlos forgot his. It was Peter Norman who suggested that Carlos wear Smith's left-handed glove, this being the reason for him raising his left hand, as opposed to his right, differing from the traditional Black Power salute. When the US national anthem, 'The Star-Spangled Banner', played, Smith and Carlos delivered the salute with heads bowed, a gesture that became front-page news around the world. That such a relatively small gesture could create such a response paved the way to the Olympics becoming a major platform for the playing out of political theatre for at least the next two decades.

The Olympic Games as promotional opportunity: from boycotts to boosterism

The largest Games staged to date at the time was the 1972 Olympics in Munich, West Germany. Twenty-seven years after the Second World War, the Games were supposed to represent peace. Despite the iconic architecture, and with competitions well under way, the Munich Games are most often remembered for the terrorist attack that resulted in the death of 11 Israeli athletes. With five days of the Games to go, eight Palestinian terrorists belonging to the Black September group broke into the Olympic Village, killing two Israelis and taking nine other members of the Israeli Olympic team hostage. The Palestinians demanded the release of 200 prisoners from Israel. In an ensuing battle, all nine Israeli hostages were killed, as were five of the terrorists and one policeman. IOC President Avery Brundage took the decision to continue the Games after a 34-hour suspension. Seventeen people were killed in total, but it is still unclear what actually happened in the shoot-out. Key questions still remain unanswered satisfactorily, including: Who killed the Israeli hostages? The police or the hostage-takers? IOC President Brundage was pilloried for stating that 'the Games must go on', but could he have done otherwise? What would another IOC president do in similar circumstances?

In Montreal in 1976 around 30 African nations staged a last-minute boycott after the IOC allowed New Zealand to compete. Some of the teams withdrew after the first day. New

Zealand's All Blacks rugby team had recently played in the racially segregated South Africa, which had been banned from the Olympics since 1964. The controversy prevented a much anticipated meeting between Tanzanian Filbert Bayi – the former world record holder in both the 1,500 metres and the mile – and New Zealand's John Walker, who had surpassed both records to become the new world record holder. Walker went on to win the gold medal in the 1,500 metres.

Taiwan also withdrew when communist China pressured Canada (its trading partner) to deny the Taiwanese the right to compete. In Montreal in 1976 the high cost and construction of facilities for the Games attracted criticisms. The event began and concluded with many unfinished facilities. Partly in response to this the internal politics of the Olympics in Canada have been hard fought ever since. In Toronto a group opposing a bid, Bread not Circuses, was formed and became one of the strongest anti-Olympic organisations in the world. It lobbied against Toronto's 1996 and 2008 Olympic Games bids and the Vancouver bid for the 2010 Winter Games. Bread not Circuses argued that the perceived profits from the event were only short-term 'economic steroids'.

The period 1988–1992 was a watershed in the shift from boycott to 'boosterism' at the Olympic Games. Barcelona in 1992 was and continues to be seen as a huge success, especially for urban redevelopment, thus inaugurating the idea of (and emphasis on) the Games as a tool for boosterism – urban promotion, (re-)design and legacy. The 1992 Barcelona Games also marked the first Olympic Summer Games since the end of the Cold War. Latvia, Lithuania and Estonia fielded separate teams, whilst the rest of the former Soviet Union competed as the 'Unified Team'. Germany competed under one flag for the first time since 1964, while post-apartheid South Africa (including Nelson Mandela) was invited, ending a 32-year ban.

The neoliberalisation of the Games

In many ways, the Los Angeles Games of 1984 were the tipping point in the shift to the next phase of the politics of the Olympics. These Games figure in two columns in our Figure 7.1. After Montreal in 1976 a critique of quasi-Keynesian government policy approaches in the advanced capitalist economies, including sports mega-events, began to develop. A new economic orthodoxy began to emerge – referred to in the UK as Thatcherism and in the US as Reaganism – which emphasised the failure of state-produced solutions to social and economic problems (including the staging of Olympic Games) and which instead valorised the hosting of more privatised Games. Explicitly ideological, this approach impacted on the 1984 Games in a way which made popular capitalism and neoliberalism the common sense of the rest of the 1980s and since. The collapse of 'actually existing socialism' and the demise of the USSR by the end of the 1980s complemented this development. Rather than reprise the old Cold War antagonisms, the politics of hosting the Olympics now revolved around boosters and sceptics involved in debates over the branding and promotion of cities as 'world class' destinations, and the politics of environmental sustainability and legacy. Critics and sceptics now had to find different ways of seizing the platform. The Los Angeles Games were not only a pivotal moment in the evolution of the Olympics, they also helped to legitimate a sweeping neoliberal political project in the United States, with influences that have been felt across the globe (Gruneau and Neubauer 2011).

Whilst the bombing of electricity pylons was undertaken in an attempt to interrupt the Barcelona Opening Ceremony, the 1992 Games are always heralded as a success. They presented the idea to the world that the Olympics could be used to channel the aspirations of other cities and regions to redevelop and refashion huge parts of their territory. The age of urban and regional 'boosterism', linked to notions of legacy, environment, and sustainability, was born. Based upon ideas that the collective public interest would best be served by urban entrepreneurialism and wealth creation via trickle-down economics, the politics of redistribution gave way to a politics of recognition, or identity politics. The neoliberalisation of cities was matched by a similar political and economic development in the hosting of the Olympic Games.

The neoliberalisation of the Olympics involves: governance structures bypassing local municipal political structures; indirect public subsidies to the IOC – since national public resources have to be spent in support of and with the promise of showcasing 'world class' events; and other attempts to enhance the reputational status and attractiveness of host locations, whilst cutbacks occur elsewhere in public investment. The IOC retain control of the newly commercialised Games while OCOGs bear the risk, especially the financial and security risks. Cities bid to host the Games as a means of public diplomacy, and national governments use the opportunity to operate forms of soft power.

It was in this way that the Atlanta Games in 1996 were held without any governmental support. This led to a commercialisation of the Games that disappointed many. In addition, a pipe bomb exploded in Atlanta's Centennial Olympic Park on 27 July 1996, during the Games, killing two people and injuring a further 110. Although the incident was referred to as a terrorist bomb, the motive or group responsible was never determined. Approximately 10,000 athletes participated in Atlanta, representing 197 countries (including Hong Kong and the Palestinian Authority). The choice of Atlanta saw the commercially driven modernisers/neoliberalisers win out over tradition. The problems with Atlanta, and then with corruption, appear to have led to a shame-faced IOC voting to give the 2004 Summer Olympics to Greece.

The Sydney Games in 2000 were the largest ever, with 10,651 athletes competing in 300 events. Despite its size, the event was well organised and renewed faith in the Olympic movement after the 1996 Atlanta bombing. The Australians chose Aboriginal athlete and national hero Cathy Freeman to light the Olympic torch. In 2004 the Olympic Games returned to its origins when Athens hosted the XXVIII Olympiad. Greece was the birthplace of the ancient Olympic Games more than 2,000 years ago, and Athens staged the first modern Olympic Games in 1896. However, 2004 was the most guarded Olympic Games in history and the biggest – and most expensive – peacetime security operation ever.

The 2008 Games, staged in Beijing, provoked outrage from human rights groups who said that allowing China to host the Games legitimised its repressive regime. Protesters also claimed that China would use the Games as a propaganda tool. Supporters of the Games argued that the Olympics would accelerate the progress of social liberalisation in China. Taiwan government officials strongly supported the Beijing Games, believing that the event would reduce the risk of China using force against its neighbour. Arguably, the choice of Beijing as host was over-determined by political and economic judgements – Tiananmen Square may have happened in 1989, but by the 2000s China was a very big and growing market.

Ironically it was the attempt to use the Olympic torch relay as a global rallying call – and at the same time as an opportunity for sponsors to be seen to be associated with the Olympics

Figure 7.3 The battle of the flags. The 2008 Summer Games, staged in Beijing, provoked outrage from human rights groups who said that allowing China to host the Games legitimised its repressive regime. Here the flags of Tibet and China vie for position in Central London during the torch relay in April 2008.

Figure 7.4 Tibet and China clash. Protesters and counter-demonstrators make their case during the 2008 torch relay in Central London in April 2008.

– that proved most costly to the image of the Beijing Olympics. The torch relay opened the door for conflict and thus brought back political theatre to the Games (Horne and Whannel 2010). Whilst in Beijing the organisers of the Games were using 'One World One Dream' as one of their key slogans, around the world the torch was followed by protests – about human rights in China and the relationship between China and Tibet – as the photographs taken during the London leg in April 2008 show.

We have already discussed London 2012 at length at the beginning of this book. In 2016, however, Rio de Janeiro will host the Games, barely two years after Brazil has hosted the FIFA

Figure 7.5 'One World One Dream'. With slogans such as these the Games can be used as a propaganda tool.

football World Cup. The final section of this chapter therefore considers the local politics of the Rio decision as an example of neoliberalisation of the politics of the Olympics.

THE LOCAL POLITICS OF RIO 2016: THE VILA AUTÓDROMO STORY [6]

Many 'Cariocas' (Rio de Janeiro locals) glued themselves to their TV screens at 11 a.m. local time on 2 October 2009, awaiting the results of a decision about whether or not Rio de Janeiro would host the 2016 Summer Olympic and Paralympic Games. Chicago was removed in the first round. Then it was Tokyo's turn in the second. Then finally it was down to Madrid and Rio – and with a vote of 66 to Madrid's 32, Rio was chosen to host the 2016 Games. On Copacabana beach (proposed site of the 2016 beach volleyball competition) a huge party had been scheduled – whether or not Rio was selected. A relic of the past with an ageing population, Copacabana still represents the heart of tourism in Rio. One of Rio's best samba schools, Salgueiro, performed live, along with MPB (Brazilian Popular Music) star, Lulu Santos. Tens of thousands of people showed up, skipping work or school, and causing massive traffic jams on a work day, to witness the decision, as Cariocas like to do, collectively, in a party atmosphere (Williamson 2010).

This decision was very much the icing on a decade of steady development. Brazil has been one of the few economies that have remained stable and growing. The World Bank predicts Brazil will go from tenth largest economy in the world to fifth by 2016. Brazil is the fifth largest market in the world, and it has recently discovered (to the detriment of the environment) the largest offshore petroleum deposits in the world. Funds for Olympic development in Rio come from Brazil's federal government: they would have gone elsewhere in the country if Rio had not been selected for the Olympics. So, from Rio's perspective, this is an opportunity for greater investment with little expense by the city. In short, an incredible opportunity for a turnaround in a city that, in a matter of decades, lost its status as the nation's capital to Brasilia and its industry to São Paulo. The State of Rio's largest sources of income in recent years have been offshore oil, which employs few people in the city, and pensions. The economy is starting to grow now for the first time in 30 years.

It is because of its stagnant economy, historically low-quality municipal administration, deteriorating public schools and historic conflicts between local, state and federal officials, that Rio, the size of New York, has a murder rate six times higher – a figure the media enjoy reminding us of without providing any context. Over the last hundred years the number of favelas (slums) in the city has grown from one (Morro da Providência, the first in Brazil) to over a thousand, ranging in size from just hundreds of residents to hundreds of thousands of residents. Some 40% of the city's favelas are controlled by drug gangs. Another 40% are controlled by vigilante militias that are often run by off-duty police officers. Yet, despite their reputation, it is important to note that less than 2% of favela residents are actually involved in illicit activities.

Whilst there were no vocal groups organised in Rio specifically against the Olympic bid, there were several groups on the ground concerned with the legacy these Olympics would bring to Rio.[7] A few miles west of Copacabana is Barra da Tijuca, an area of the city once characterised by endless marshes, that has been entirely developed over the past 30 years. Referred to by some as Rio's 'Miami', Barra da Tijuca is characterized by 5–15-storey buildings, just minutes from the beach, with no mixed use. Moving away from the beach, and the private condominiums, one finds private shopping malls lining the main thoroughfares. Residents drive between apartment blocks, each featuring its own private gym, swimming pool, and often bakery and other facilities. They then drive to the malls. Any planner leaving Copacabana and heading towards Barra can see that planners had little to say when Barra was developed (the area was developed overwhelmingly by private real estate developers), and it was developed so as to guarantee minimal contact with the city's poor, with no concern paid to transport efficiency, a sense of community, or even the effects of raw sewage. In short, Barra was developed with little forethought.

Rio's community organisers complain about the individualism and lack of ethics inherent in local culture. Barra was built in response to this and the city's well-known class division. And, to the proponents of Barra-style development, the seemingly ever-expanding wave of luxury condos spreading across the city's western horizon, without a favela in sight, has been a source of satisfaction. This brand of development is the golden vision of Rio's mayor (since 2009), Eduardo Paes, who himself was raised in Barra. Paes is the first of Rio's mayors to benefit from a combination of a capable technical team, a time of economic prosperity, and good relations with the governor and president. Hence, powerful circumstances have confirmed to see his will prevail.

On the far edge of Barra, next to Jacarepaguá Lagoon, and across the street from five new luxury condominiums, there is an apparent 'stain' on the horizon. Vila Autódromo, settled over 40 years ago by fishermen who lived subsistence lives miles away from the developed part of the city, and later by workers brought to the site to build the city's Formula One racetrack (Autódromo Internacional Nelson Piquet, also known as Jacarepaguá), is today a working-class neighbourhood with some 4,000 residents.

When the first fishermen arrived here long ago the lagoon was immaculate. Today, it receives sewage and garbage from neighbouring apartment blocks. The fishermen who remain complain of times when there are no fish – apart from the occasional tilapia, a fish that feeds on detritus. Yet residents recount what happened in 1992, when the city tried to remove them for the first time. In a judicial action requesting the full removal of the community, it was alleged that Vila Autódromo caused 'aesthetic and environmental damage' to the surrounding area. This came at a time when Barra had been identified as the new destination for commercial, sports and residential facilities, which, as was made clear by the judicial action, meant that a 'new aesthetic' was necessary – one where the poor were excluded.

Community organisers worked effectively on two fronts, through judicial channels, blocking municipal attempts at eviction, and with the State government, to secure their stay. They worked with the State of Rio's government which owned the land to prove that they had been settled there for decades. As a result, in 1994 Vila Autódromo received title from Governor Leonel Brizola, with the right to use the land for 40 years.

Despite having received title from the state, on several occasions – from the widening of a neighbouring road to preparations for the Pan-American Games – municipal officials have threatened the community with removal (including Paes himself when working within previous administrations). The Olympics, however, offered just the opportunity. Days after the announcement that Rio had been chosen to host the 2016 Olympic Games, the city's largest daily newspaper, O Globo, announced plans to remove Vila Autódromo to make way for the Olympics venues.

Community leaders were only invited to speak with the mayor after they led a demonstration with hundreds of protesters representing 20 communities outside City Hall in early March 2010. These 'conversations' are described by organisers as 'one-way dialogues', where the city states its intentions without much room for discussion. It seems clear that, once again, the Olympics had simply provided a rare opportunity to make plans for the city that avoided the obligation for public comment while making evictions publicly acceptable to the middle class and the bulk of neighbourhoods who wouldn't be affected.[8]

While eviction in low-income, informal areas has become a not uncommon consequence of mega-event planning worldwide, violations of housing rights have reached significant proportions during recent Olympics. According to the Centre on Housing Rights and Evictions (COHRE 2007), 1.25 million people were forcibly evicted in Beijing in the lead-up to the 2008 Games. By comparison, the displacement of 4,000 people from Vila Autódromo might seem an insignificant number. But other removals in the name of the Olympics and urban revitalisation are occurring throughout Rio. The Secretary of Housing recently announced the planned demolition of homes in Mangueira and Morro da Providência, two favelas in the vicinity of important Olympic sites. These favelas must make way for urbanisation projects and

140

cable-car lines that will connect tourist attractions with the famous Maracanã soccer stadium and transport hubs. Between the two communities, an expected 1,800 families will be resettled, bringing estimates of the total number of displaced individuals close to 10,000.

The international press has provided positive coverage for several recent Rio city and State initiatives. The community (pacification) policing units or 'UPPs' have been successfully installed thanks to a State programme in nine favelas, driving out drug lords and providing a sense of calm. The federal government's 'Growth Acceleration Programme' has brought heavy investments in infrastructure to a handful of favelas. Attention is being paid to improved public transportation, ranging from expansion of the metro and Bus Rapid Transit, to cable (teleferic) cars providing access to steep favelas. The city is investing heavily in the 150 worst-performing public schools with special science programmes, computers, and more. All of this sounds great to those who are not familiar with the diversity of Rio's favelas. Whilst the large communities are all benefiting from such investments, the smaller communities, even older ones like Vila Autódromo that hold title, are at risk of full removal. They don't hold many votes. They don't 'appear' in the newspapers, and a by-product of being 'safe', ironically, is that Vila Autódromo and its neighbours – the communities most at risk from the Olympics – are all peaceful. Williamson (2010) sums up the attraction of the location to developers:

> What, one might ask, is so critical about this site that makes its removal for the Olympics such a priority? Well, apparently even the Mayor can't handle this question. In October 2009, he announced the site would be used to build the Olympics Media Facility. But months later plans changed. The City has now decided to move several facilities to the Port Area the Mayor seeks to revitalize. When asked if this affects Vila Autódromo, municipal officials say, 'no.' The most recent map shows essentially nothing built in the area. It simply needs to be maintained as part of the 'security perimeter' for the Olympic venues . . . The only explanation for the lack of creativity, transparency, and willingness to dialogue and compromise shown by the City on this issue is its desire to maximize real estate speculation in the area. The community is not only a 'blemish' which in and of itself will reduce values in the vicinity, but it also occupies a very valuable piece of land, which after the Olympics, can be developed. And all this on the edge of Jacarepaguá Lagoon, which will be cleaned up as part of the environmental legacy of the Games. The area will be Rio's 'new Lagoa', in reference to the Rodrigo de Freitas Lagoon, where currently real estate is most valuable. Vila Autódromo is seen as an impediment to this development.
>
> (Williamson 2010)

Likewise in the zona norte in Rio de Janeiro, the Joao Havelange Olympic Stadium (the Engenhão) which will be the venue for the Opening and Closing Ceremonies and the main track and field facility is located in the working-class suburb of Engenho de Dentro, 'a site chosen for its low land values and proximity to major highways' (Gaffney 2008: 187). Additionally, the 2006 renovation of the Maracanã Stadium was a response to FIFA's requirement for stadiums that host World Cup finals matches to be all-seater.

It is in this way that sport, and sports mega-events such as the Olympics especially, may appear superficially as credible tools of development. Yet they do so in ways that do not challenge

141

Figure 7.6 Rio: Maracanã and Engenhão from the air. In 2014 Rio de Janeiro will stage the final match of the FIFA World Cup in the Maracaña Stadium (closest to the camera) and then two years later the eyes of the world will be on the nearby João Havelange Olympic Stadium (Engenhão) as Rio hosts the Summer Olympic Games.

inequalities or neoliberal development. In fact the hosting of sports mega-events may be a most convenient shell for the promotion of neoliberal agendas, since they do not deviate from top-down notions of economic and social development. The apparent shift of the two biggest sports events organisers, FIFA and the IOC, towards holding mega-events in the 'South' (South Africa in 2010, Brazil in 2014, and Rio in 2016) or developing market economies (Russia, to host the football World Cup in 2018) connects with recent attempts to link sport and social development.[9] But mega-events in the South are compromised by the weaker position of the host countries to bear the burden of hosting and the opportunity costs being relatively much higher than in the advanced economies (Darnell 2010). In this way they highlight the neoliberalisation of the politics of the Olympic Games.[10]

Mike Featherstone (2007: xviii) has noted that 'if there is an emergent global culture, consumer culture has to be seen as a central part of this field'. For Featherstone, in these circumstances consumption cannot be seen as an 'innocent act', but rather as 'part of the chains of inter-dependencies and networks which bind people together across the world in terms of production, consumption and the accumulation of risks'. Studying sport under such circumstances focuses on the way sport has become one of the transnational cultural forms

the spectacle of modernity

BOX 7.3 BUILDING BRICS BY BUILDING STADIUMS

The acronym 'BRIC' (standing for Brazil, Russia, India, China) was coined in 2001 by the Goldman Sachs economic consultant Jim O'Neill.[11] It has since become a common umbrella term in business, media, academic and government rhetoric about the future potential of these 'emerging giants', in particular the threat/opportunity that these economies present to the developed world. The regionalised perspective of BRICs encourages a commodified picture of these countries around major risks/opportunities: investment, global hegemony and social transformation. The BRICs can be seen as the West/North's dream of a new East/South with geopolitical status and power to rival the developed world. Indeed, much BRICs discourse echoes Cold War rhetoric.

Consideration of individual BRICs and mega-events, and associated media representations, reveal four main challenges around consumption, construction, containment and communication:

1   *Consumption*: sport (and sports mega-events) becomes a central rather than peripheral cultural form in the growth and spread of capitalist consumer cultures – tourism, consumerisation and global visitor destinations. This creates an issue about the possibility of *under-consumption* – are the Games popular, really?
2   *Construction*: designing, building, engineering, sustaining 'iconic' facilities prompts the traditional questions: Will the facilities be ready on time? At the stated costs? And of adequate standard? Will the facilities be more a form of monumentalism, reflecting wider international political and economic power relationships, than a contribution to the communities where they were built?[12]
3   *Containment*: security and surveillance technologies connected with sports mega-events were a developing market before 9/11. Social control and surveillance may be important, but for whom? And of whom? As with other major sports events in South America, great security will be evident during the two mega-events to be held in Brazil in 2014 and 2016 (McLeod-Roberts 2007).
4   *Communication*: reaching the world audience; managing the message. What happens when things go wrong? The perils of media coverage of countries in the South to the North, and East to the West, have been explored recently by Dimeo and Kay (2004) and Horne and Manzenreiter (2011). Studies have demonstrated that developing countries run several risks when hosting large events, not least of which is being portrayed negatively in the global media. Coverage of events in developing nations is always prone to negative responses when something goes wrong.

in and through which consumer culture is fuelled. Much recent writing on sport has shown how the three main features of contemporary consumer capitalism – globalisation, commodification and inequality – shape and contour contemporary sport and sports mega-events, such as the Olympics.

With sports mega-events, two features of consumer culture can be highlighted: *transformation* and *consumerisation*. Mike Featherstone (2007: xxi) remarks that central to consumer culture is the transformation of 'lifestyle, living space, relationships, identities, and, of course, bodies'. We argue that consumerisation – the process of the construction of people with consumer values and outlooks – has impacted on personal and collective identities and the development of new lifestyles (Horne 2006).

Consumer culture itself has a developmental history of transformations, and as Lee (1993: 135) suggests, the growing importance of cultural and service markets since the 1970s has represented a dematerialisation of the commodity form and the growth of 'experiential commodities' including cultural events, heritage attractions, theme parks, commercialised sport and other public spectacles. Echoing Harvey (1989), Lee concludes that the rapid growth of these experiential commodities represented a 'push to accelerate commodity values and turnovers' (Lee 1993; 20) and 'make more flexible and fluid the various opportunities and moments of consumption' (Lee 1993: 137). Hence the last two decades of the twentieth century saw the restless search for novel ways to expand markets in the advanced capitalist economies and develop new ones elsewhere. Lee (1993: 131) suggests that this explains the spread of consumerism to the rest of the world, the development of a vast children's market, and 'the deeper commercial penetration and commodification of the body, self and identity'. Sport has been part of this transformation and has been transformed in turn.

Consumption for symbolic purposes and status value might be thought to be the preserve of the affluent in the advanced capitalist countries. Indeed substantial numbers of the world's population – including between a third and a quarter of those people who live in the advanced capitalist countries – are mainly interested in consumption for material provision rather than for 'show'. Yet the idea of consuming goods for their symbolic value as much as if not more than for their use value is not restricted to these post-industrial societies. By the end of the twentieth century consumerism had spread as a global 'culture-ideology' mainly for two reasons (Sklair 2002: 108ff.): first, capitalism has entered a globalising phase and, second, the technical and social relations that structure the mass media have 'made it very easy for new consumerist lifestyles to become the dominant motif' (Sklair 2002: 108). Hence '"consumerism" may influence even the symbolic life of the poor' (Bocock 1994: 184) and sport is one means of bringing this about.

Of course, contemporary sport is not simply a set of commercial media spectacles, even if it often seems that way. Sport as an active practice continues to be undertaken and played by millions more participants than the relatively small number of elite athletes whose performances are routinely broadcast on national and, increasingly, international media networks. In addition many more people than actually participate in it *follow* any particular sport. Popular involvement in sport is one of the major accomplishments of the hundred years or so since modern sport was established. But sport is not naturally followed any more than people naturally go shopping. Sport consumers and audiences are *made*, not born.

Sport consumerisation appears initially to have relied upon local and national affiliations. Globalisation has offered the opportunity to expand this process of consumerisation, and the mass media of communications have played a major role in the creative process whereby sport is transformed. In turn, as mediated sport has become an accepted part of everyday life-worlds it has also come to have an influence in consumption choices and aspirations for particular consumer goods and lifestyles. Hence sport today – especially through a focus on large-scale ('mega') mediated events and celebrity accomplishments – plays a major role in the

144

maintenance of consumer culture, through marketing, advertising and other promotional strategies.

The recent crisis of capitalist financial regulation – in which vast sums of public money were used to support banking and other financial institutions floundering after the poor judgements and speculative dealings by private financiers – is a useful reminder that government intervention to support advanced capitalism is not an aberration. Arguably, however, we have moved to another phase in the development of neoliberalism as a hegemonic economic theory – disaster capitalism based on the 'shock doctrine' (Klein 2007). This involves using a crisis to reshape the economy in the interests of business. The Olympic Games surely provide a positive, uplifting, even inspiring diversion during times like these, and there are more serious topics for a social scientist to research. As this chapter (and the book as whole) will make clear to anyone with this view, the Olympic Games are a global spectacle attracting vast audiences, but also a deeply political phenomenon. Researching the costs and benefits of sports mega-events is itself a political activity. It can involve researching the powerful – the elite of business leaders and government officials – as well as leaders of sports organisations who gather together to formulate hosting bids or to stage events after a successful bid has been made. It can also involve research into the ongoing activities of organisations more sceptical of the benefits of the event which are themselves investigating the claims made by mega-event promoters or 'boosters'.

CONCLUSION

It is difficult to accept that the politics of the Olympic Games should be understood as a continuing form of imperial power, as J. M. Brohm (1978) once suggested. Today the politics of the Olympics revolves around such issues as containment – terrorism, security, surveillance and civil rights associated with restrictions on freedom of movement and expression – and human rights and rights to freedom from eviction and adequate housing. Such issues came to prominence during the Beijing Olympiad – for example, the protests surrounding the torch relay in 2008 (Horne and Whannel 2010) affected several thousand people in London associated with the 2012 Games, and will continue into 2016 in Brazil and the Rio Olympics. The tensions between the politics of redistribution and the politics of recognition, including for example the rights of aboriginal and indigenous people, remain a part of these developments.

FURTHER READING

Bairner, A. and Molnar, G. (eds) (2010) *The Politics of the Olympics*, London: Routledge.
Gaffney, C. (2010) 'Mega-events and socio-spatial dynamics in Rio de Janeiro, 1919–2016', *Journal of Latin American Geography* 9 (1): 7–29.
Hayes, G. and Karamichas, J. (eds) (2011) *Olympic Games, Mega-Events, and Civil Societies: Globalisation, Environment, and Resistance*, Basingstoke: Palgrave.

CHAPTER 8

FESTIVAL, SPECTACLE, CARNIVAL AND CONSUMPTION

In 1984 one of us wrote 'the Olympic Games cannot be both a television spectacle and a people's festival' (Whannel 1984: 41). It was a polemical point made by a young man, and clearly the Olympic Games as a cultural practice embrace aspects of both festival and spectacle. Yet the challenge does point to the different visions of the Olympic Games, the tensions between them, and the difficulty of holding on to both festival and spectacle in the same globalised mega-event. The London Olympics will be surrounded by unprecedented security – there will be fences, gates, scanners, sensors, comprehensive databases, hazard profiles and radio-controlled drone aircraft. If previous events are a valid precedent, a large proportion of the tickets for the major events will be parcelled out to the 'Olympic Family', including their corporate friends, sponsors, media organisations, and VIPs and celebrities. It is not promising terrain for a people's party. However, the presence of such a major event in a big city will have a galvanising effect – people will want to celebrate and party. The Olympic Games are not confined to stadiums but will be viewed in homes, bars, malls and parks, where an atmosphere of festivity and jollity can develop. The Olympic Park can become a festive cockpit. The torch relay extends the presence of Olympism more broadly in both space and time. There will be spontaneous events, informal celebrations, casual merry-making and carnivalesque costumes. The extent to which these activities are encouraged and fostered, or scrutinised and policed, will help to set the tone for the Games as the London public will experience them.

The portents for joyous people's festivity are not, so far, especially encouraging. Already the Olympic Park has been the site of symbolic contestation. During construction, the Park has been surrounded by a high blue fence, some miles in length. This fence has been utilised by graffiti artists and by local artist groups who have adorned it with various acts of creativity. In response, the ODA reportedly introduced a daily patrol, in which a man cycled round the perimeter fence, phoning in reports of any outbreaks of art or vandalism, depending on one's perspective. A quad bike would then set off, driven by a man with a pot of blue paint, who would erase the damage and restore the pristine blueness. As the Olympic project developed, the fence began to be decorated with 'official' artwork, some from local schools, and sponsors' banners began to appear. So, in the spirit of maintaining the blueness, some local artists took to painting over the sponsors' banners with their own pot of blue paint.

One of the sites of wider festivity is supposed to be the 'Cultural Olympiad'. In the UK, the Cultural Olympiad has encountered problems. When the Olympic budget was first planned, large National Lottery sums were redirected from the arts to the Olympic project. The impact

146

of this was to produce hostility to the Olympics amongst the arts community, which has since responded in lukewarm fashion to the invitation to contribute to the Cultural Olympiad. Those organisers who have pursued the possibility of Olympic-related projects have found that funding is limited, that they are not able to approach competitors to the existing Olympic sponsors, that most sponsorship opportunities have already been taken up by the Olympic Organising Committee, and that the brief and the mission are ill-defined and uninspired. Two years into the Olympiad, the impact of the Cultural Olympiad has been minimal, and during 2010 a new head was appointed. In the current economic climate, with the arts facing substantial cuts, the exciting new Olympic-related projects are still possible, but the outlook is not especially promising.

The imperatives of security tend to push organising committees towards a suspicion of the general public, who are perceived more as an element that needs to be controlled, channelled and organised, rather than as active participants whose spontaneity can contribute to the festivity. At major sporting events, authorities often provide giant screens for the many people who do not have tickets. This has the merit from the perspective of social control, of encouraging the corralling of people in specific areas that can be more conveniently policed. Even in Beijing, screens were established around the city. In the last few days before the Games, though, there appeared to be a loss of nerve regarding street crowds. Many (although not all) of the live screens reportedly remained blank during the Opening Ceremony. Chinese citizens were urged to stay off the streets and watch the Opening Ceremony at home, on television. On the first days of the Games, the 'live' screens in the centre of Beijing were showing, not live sport, but tedious edited highlights of earlier events, including a long sequence of Chinese leaders greeting foreign dignitaries. The anticipation for London 2012, by contrast, is that live screens will be available around the country, in parks, bars, public

Figure 8.1 The Water Cube, Beijing 2008. Olympic building is increasingly concerned to be 'iconic', but security needs often mean that non-ticket holders are restricted to a distant view.

147

Figure 8.2 The main stadium, Beijing 2008. The new spectacular style of public space: this could be an arts centre, a museum or a shopping mall. Space for festivity or temple of spectacle and consumption, or both?

squares and shopping malls. At least one part of the Stratford site is sure to be warm and welcoming – the Westfield shopping mall, one of the largest in Europe, and due to open in 2011. Cleverly positioned in the space between the Olympic Park and the two stations (Stratford and Stratford International) that serve it, the mall will be, metaphorically and literally, the gateway to the Olympics. We will enter and leave through the temple of consumption, a temple that will still be pulling in the crowds long after the Olympic circus has packed its tents and left.

The emergence of the modern Olympic Games drew on festival – the Much Wenlock Games were and remain festive in character. As the Games developed so did its rituals, including the spectacle of the Opening and Closing Ceremonies. Before television, of course, these forms of spectacle had a very different character – they were designed for the spectators present in the arena and not for the electronic spectators around the world. This chapter considers the relation between the festive and spectacular aspects of the Olympic movement. First, though, the very terms we are utilising here – festival, spectacle, carnival and consumption – need further examination.

THE FESTIVE, THE SPECTACULAR AND THE CARNIVALESQUE

'Festival' is about festivity and therefore fun. It is exceptional – festival is different from, and interrupts, everyday life. It is celebratory. Often, it required religious sanction. It is consequently also cyclical, and recurrent, which gives it a timeless dimension. In this sense the major occasions of sport, cyclical and recurrent, and causes for celebration, are also festive. Festival is collective or communal – the focus is on the shared participatory nature of the experience, more than on any performance. Yet spectacle and festival are hard to separate entirely. When Walter Benjamin discusses nineteenth-century shopping arcades and walking in the city, or when Richard Dyer (1978) discusses entertainment, they are referencing communal and shared pleasures, yet also referencing spectacle – whether the spectacle of window shopping or of film viewing. The terms denote, not so much definable objects, as ways of seeing and ways of being. In the second half of the nineteenth century the emergence of branded goods, chain stores and advertising shifted shopping from the functional to the spectacular mode (see Bowlby 1985), and the present-day mall has become a cathedral in which popular leisure and spectacular consumption interact. Festivities typically involve the provision of enter-tainment, the consumption of food and drink, and the retailing of commodities, as well as spontaneous communality.

One common element of festivity is the firework display. Are fireworks spectacle? Fireworks are interesting in that, at their most spectacular, they are conventionally laid on by the authorities as a show, a spectacle. But fireworks also induce a sense of wonder which never dulls. A firework display is, arguably, a form of spectacular entertainment, but an intriguing one. It is all but impossible to represent or relay fireworks. They are transient – gone as soon as they appear. They cannot be effectively televised, photographed or even painted – they have to be witnessed in person. No mode of representation can adequately capture the experiential dimension of a firework display. A firework display can be free or admission can be charged – although fireworks are not readily confined within the view of people in a stadium. A firework is a commodity but a firework display resists commodification – it cannot be encompassed within a room, a hall or even a stadium – it is a process and not a product, ephemeral in nature, not open to repetition.

The 'digitally enhanced fireworks' featured in the television coverage of the Beijing 2008 Opening Ceremony caused a huge controversy, in which accusations of fakery were bandied about. Part of the firework display was 'real' and live, but other parts appeared to have been pre-recorded and used to enhance the television image. Such accusations, though, only make sense if one is conceptualising the Olympics as an event that is televised, rather than as a television event. Clearly the Opening Ceremony is precisely a constructed artifice in the tradition of show business, and how it is constructed has always involved smoke and mirrors. One of the authors was in Beijing during the evening of the Opening Ceremony, although not inside the stadium. While there clearly were real fireworks, the full display could not be properly seen either from inside the stadium or from immediately outside it. Fireworks covered a large geographical area. (The previous day, batteries of firework mortars could be seen in various parts of the city, including Tiananmen Square, a few miles south of the Olympic Stadium.) Only on television could the whole production, complete with digital augmentation, be properly perceived. Festivity and spectacle are enmeshed on such occasions.

The word 'spectacle' denotes the pleasures involved in watching and to some extent therefore a relation between an event, performance or object and an observer. In this sense it references a less participatory model of pleasure than does the term 'festivity'. Spectacle has been somewhat under-interrogated – in that it comes laden with two readings. The first, derived from the Roman Circus, is that it was a mere distraction with the purpose of political control, and the second, derived from Guy Debord, is that it performs an ideological role in consumer capitalism. So in leftist critical discourse the term is, almost inevitably, weighted down with strong connotations of negativeness and irredeemability. Broudehoux (2007: 389) argues that 'Beijing's spectacular Olympic preparations have in many ways acted as a propaganda tool and an instrument of pacification to divert popular attention from the shortcomings of China's rapid economic transformation, accompanied by rampant land speculation, corruption, and uneven development'. So spectacle becomes associated with oppression and control, and can be utilised to mask poverty and social exclusion.

The term has acquired, in a range of analytic traditions, a negative character. In diverse writing by Theo Adorno, Guy Debord, Daniel Boorstin and Jean Baudrillard, spectacle is regarded as ideological, a mode of commodification, as empty, and as all-pervasive. Machiavelli, as Kellner (2003) has pointed out, advised the productive use of spectacle for political control. Martin Jay argued that Debord's critique of commodity fetishism is similar to the puritan critique of idolatry (see Frow 1997). MacAloon has criticised the tendency for the term 'spectacle' to become a baggy catch-all concept.

The leftist critique of spectacle has certainly been haunted by a tendency to collapse back into one-dimensionalism. Commodification, commercialisation, globalisation and spectacle, even when utilised to analyse complex social contradictions, tend to become merely negative warning signs. There is a need to deconstruct the term 'spectacle'. Kellner in *Media Spectacle* (2003) refers to mega-spectacle (OJ, 9/11, Princess Di) but does not offer a clear definitional statement. Maurice Roche (2000) has drawn attention to the multidimensional character of mega-events – modern and non-modern, national and non-national, mediated and non-mediated. Horne (2011a) also highlights the combination of symbolic and material dimensions, and outlines the way such events function as lightning conductors, accelerating global flows and connections with modernity. However, it is surely hard to understand contemporary popular culture without some sense of spectacle. All forms of entertainment that establish some form of distance separation or boundary between performance and audience can be considered as, in part, forms of spectacle. This does not in itself require a negative or pejorative use of the term 'spectacle'.

The word 'carnival' denotes a special and particular form of festivity. While carnival has an everyday meaning – associated with parades, extravagant costumes and excess – it has been given a more precise meaning in the writing of Bakhtin, especially in *Rabelais and His World* (1965). Carnival in this sense involves inversion, subversion and transgression. Normal power relations are inverted: temporarily, the powerless acquire the trappings of power, while the powerful are mocked or rendered powerless, the established order is subverted, there is a suspension of norms, and conventions and laws are transgressed. Carnival has become associated with masks and costumes that reveal the performative aspect of gender roles and sexual relations. Carnival might imply a degree of temporary licence allowed by authority, but often carries the sense of danger and excitement that such authority might be overturned,

150

disobeyed or defied. In Bakhtin's discussion of Rabelais, the world of the carnivalesque is one of spontaneity, informality and irreverence: 'these images are opposed to all that is finished and polished, to all pomposity, to every ready-made solution in the sphere of thought, and world outlook' (Bakhtin 1965: 3).

A key feature of carnival for Bakhtin is the absence of a clear distinction between performers and spectators: carnival 'does not acknowledge any distinction between actors and spectators. Footlights would destroy a carnival, as the absence of footlights would destroy a theatrical performance'. Participation is essential to carnival, which has to be, temporarily, all-embracing, and 'everyone participates because its very idea embraces all the people. While carnival lasts, there is no other life outside it . . . Such is the essence of carnival, vividly felt by all its participants' (Bakhtin 1965: 7). All these terms present problems of definition and distinction. All are frequently used in a common-sense manner, in rather vague and general ways. (See Manzenreiter's (2006) critical discussion of these terms, especially 'spectacle', and MacAloon's (1999) critique of 'spectacle'.)

As discussed in Chapter 5, MacAloon (1999) sees the Olympic Games as a 'modern secular ritual'. He identifies four genres of Olympism as cultural performance – spectacle, festival, ritual and game (1984: 242). In recent years, though, it can be argued that there have also been manifestations of carnivalesque behaviour at major sporting events – face-painting, joke banners, dressing in elaborate costumes and coordinated costumes, often with a degree of arbitrariness (e.g. Viking hats). The Mexican wave, which does not coordinate with and is not a response to on-field action, often arises when the action is dull, and is a reassertion of the primacy of the spectator (we can make our own amusement). This form of behaviour, while it may be amusing and/or disruptive, is plainly not in any deep sense subversive. By contrast, if, as in the situationist slogan, 'revolution is the festival of the oppressed', it can be argued that the carnivalesque character of recent anti-capitalist and anti-globalisation street demonstrations is a more pertinent instance of the political character of carnival. Boje (2001), for example, refers to the carnival of resistance to globalisation discourse. But the oppressed surely deserve a wider concept of festival. Indeed the informal structure, if not anti-structure, of popular festivities is in itself an assertion, a self-validation, a celebration of the community of the popular.

Official public events, though, often involve a combination of spectacle, displays of political power and demonstrations of technological mastery. The most advanced uses of digital technology in the simulation programmes of military planning and video games and the combination of digital and mechanical technologies in theme parks have converged. In official public leisure the crowd is managed and controlled. There are, though, no clear distinctions that can be made. All forms of festival and carnival involve some element of spectacle. Spectacles are rarely without some dimension of the festive, and some outbreak of the carnivalesque. It cannot be claimed that spectators are ever entirely and simply passive. Equally, the claim that in carnival the distinction between performer and spectator is erased does not stand up to examination – there is a difference between being on the float and off the float, for example. Nevertheless, if one accepts a schematic application in which these terms can help to clarify parameters, their use can then offer some purchase on understanding the Olympic Games and its particular articulation of elements of spectacle, festivity and carnival.

ANALYSING THE SPORTS SPECTACLE

The work of Victor Turner is regarded by Dayan and Katz (1992) as important in this context, and they suggest that 'festive events deserve a theory which takes specific account of their festive dimension: that is what Victor Turner has taught us' (1992: 231). Influenced by Turner, MacAloon (1984) produced a schematic analysis of the relation of rite, drama, festival and spectacle. One interesting interface between spectacle and festival can be seen in the cultural practices which have evolved around the growing use of large screens in city centres and parks, relaying live pictures of major sporting events. Audiences picnic, drink, celebrate. Carnivalesque modes of dress appear. Major sport events cut into the structured regularities of everyday life. They prompt people to stay up into the early hours, or to drink beer at breakfast while watching live broadcasts of sport events in bars. These rituals disrupt the time of work discipline. They are part of a tradition of 'dysfunctional' practices that constitute resistances to the tyranny of work – celebrating St Monday, taking a 'sickie', the three-hour lunch break, doing nothing. They belong to a defiant hedonistic culture, associated with drink, sex and being 'bad'.

Indeed at many major events the organisers have nurtured and encouraged such settings. At the Torino Winter Olympics in 2006, the organisers established an Olympic plaza in which many of the medal ceremonies were staged. Just as the spaces of the city have become more festive at times of major sport events, the stadium experience has become more controlled. This is typified by the giant card stunts, much loved by television and by sponsors and advertisers. They reduce the spectators to a participant in a ritual they cannot perceive or enjoy. They become the serfs of the television production centre, responding to a command by waving an abstraction – a card that is merely one cell of a giant mosaic.

Where and how in this interface of spectacle and festival are politics articulated? If popular culture is conceived as the interface between organised political discourse and popular common sense, then politics lies partly in the process whereby discursive elements are legitimised or delegitimised. So what are the moments of instability, destabilisation, ruptures, breaks and challenges? And what are their conditions of existence? Given that the dominant political configuration is neoliberal, then how can the discursive elements of neoliberalism be disarticulated? How can the truly festive be retrieved from corporate control?

A challenging politics attempts to expose the crimes of the powerful, unmasking details of their wealth and where it comes from. It also endeavours to publicise the conditions of poverty. The key test is political effectivity. Clearly joyous, spontaneous and carnival elements temporarily reinscribe the communal and the social in civil society, suggesting new relations of individual and collective, real space and cyber space. But when the mode of the music changes, do the walls of the city really shake? It is instructive here to pay attention to the physical environment of public space. Just as during the nineteenth century the railway station became the new cathedral – the new grand public architecture – in the twentieth century the sport stadium was the new cathedral. In the London 2012 Games the stadium moves closer to that other modern cathedral of consumption, the shopping mall. The stadium provides and enables the spectacle of perfectly honed bodies in competitive movement. The mall offers the spectacle of the commodity. Sport and leisure wear in the form of the branded goods of Nike and Adidas link the stadium and the mall.

152

Figure 8.3 Beijing shopping mall. Inside an upmarket shopping mall in central Beijing, directly opposite the grand hotel commandeered in its entirety for the duration of the Games by the IOC, this spectacular display reproduces the running track as a catwalk for fitness chic.

VORTEXTUALITY AND THE DISPERSED SPECTACLE

The Olympic Games are a reification of place and time – the elaborate and expensive campaign to be awarded the Games, the subsequent seven-year countdown, the construction of grandiose iconic architecture and the two-week vortextual focus on the host city. The Olympics are a vortextual spectacle – they suck attention in with a considerable intensity, temporarily dominating the news agenda (see Whannel 2010). Around the world, for two brief weeks, television screens, newspaper pages, internet sites, blogs and twitterings focus upon the Olympic Games. The Olympic site is briefly the centre of the world. But the Olympics are also a dispersed spectacle. They can be and are consumed around the world on television, on internet sites, and through the print media. Giant live screens are provided in parks, city squares and shopping malls. (This is all even more true of the football World Cup which is in the end more effective in calling up the patriotic subject.)

Global televised mega-events have both a centrifugal and centripetal character. They are about both convergence and fragmentation. Everything focuses on the host city or host nation, and yet they can be consumed everywhere. Furthermore, they are in some ways more readily consumed at a distance. Being in Beijing in August 2008 felt too close – like trying to watch

153

Cinerama in the front row. Conversely, the embedded, immediate and experiential nature of 'being there', has come to seem a partial and incomplete experience compared to the sense of completion, comprehensiveness and technological mastery bestowed by television. We would suggest here three phases in the development of the sport spectacle. First, pre-television, major events could only be fully experienced at the site, as with a world's fair. Second, television extended the live immediacy of the sport to the domestic sphere around the world. Third, the ubiquity of the electronic image, digitalisation and the new media have rendered this image in two ways – (1) the image has become better, sharper, closer, more analytic (replays) than the live experience can be, and (2) it is available, indeed unavoidable, everywhere in public spaces (at least metropolitan ones) in bars, in malls, in streets.

So the Games, like the football World Cup, have become a dispersed spectacle – the existence of a global audience with their own shared and embedded experiences is as important a part of the event as the spectators at the site. Olympic images are also disseminated across multiple media platforms in a variety of forms – merchandising, mascots, computer games, ring-tones, wallpaper. An interesting dimension of the dispersed spectacle is the massive visibility, during the Opening Ceremony, of officials and athletes capturing the scene on their cameras and mobile phones. The resultant images could travel around the world as readily as broadcast television. So the World Cup and the Olympic Games have spawned forms of dispersed spectacle that could be seen as forms of deterritorialisation, yet in the reification of place, and promotion of cities there is also a reterritorialisation.

But the Games are dispersed not only in space, but also through time. The launching of a bid and the winning of a bid might be celebrated through a series of public events which mobilise the spectacular and the festive and even to a degree the carnivalesque. The torch relay provides a further set of occasions dispersed around the world (although, after the 2008 torch relay was utilised for human rights protests, Olympic insiders are forecasting that this will be the last global torch relay to be staged). Even when the Games conclude, the party can continue. In September 2008, after Beijing, the Australian team were paraded through the centre of Sydney, in an event which also included a trailer for London featuring (you can probably guess) a red London bus, umbrellas and bowler hats, and a band playing the *Dad's Army* theme tune. Global television events such as the Olympic Games and the football World Cup, then, have become dispersed spectacles – they occur not simply at the site but around the world in myriad locations – homes, cafés, bars, malls, squares and parks – framed by a range of national and local hopes and fantasies, consumed in ways which are shaped by gender, class and ethnic formations, assumptions and expectations.

Despite the plans for the 2012 cultural programme, it is by no means certain how much it might contribute to popular festivity. The art competitions on which Coubertin was so keen were first introduced in 1912 and survived until 1948 (Girginov and Parry 2005: 206). More recently, concerted attempts have been made to revivify the cultural dimension, now dubbed the 'Cultural Olympiad'. The success of this enterprise has been uneven (see Stevenson 1977; Garcia 2001; Garcia and Miah 2006). The London 2012 website and the Arts Council national plan for 2008–2011 outline aspirations, but, at the time of writing three years into the Olympiad period, few concrete projects are yet visible. One of the stranger manifestations of the cultural dimension illustrates a rather uncomfortable attempt to manage Olympism in the age of commercial sponsorship: the Coubertin Olympic Awards Competition, run by the International Pierre de Coubertin Committee and the Institute of Business Ethics, offers an

154

annual essay prize. The competition challenges students to write a research essay on how the Olympic ideals of fairness, integrity and openness can help businesses balance commercial success with their social responsibilities.[1] Here, once again, the contradictions and tensions at the heart of the Olympic movement are at work – the address to idealism harnessed to the public relations needs of corporate capitalism and the Olympic sponsors.

SECURITY, RISK AND SURVEILLANCE

Ever since the establishment of payment for admission to enclosed arenas, the interface between inside and outside has required fences and control mechanisms to prevent those not entitled to enter from entering. In the risk society, both actual risk and the heightened sensitivity to risk have dramatically increased surveillance, boundaries and monitoring. In the post 9/11 environment, of course, both risk and fear have become more significant. Corporate architecture has resorted to modern versions of the devices of medieval castles – the moat, the drawbridge and the portcullis – to reduce the threat of unauthorised incursion.

The Olympic Games survived a previous period, between 1968 and 1984, when its very visibility as a global event gave it great power as a platform for symbolic political acts. The perceived threat that, once again, the Olympic Games may be utilised as such a platform has pushed security expenditure to new heights. It is not clear that these expenditures are subject to adequate scrutiny – which politician, after all, wants to be on record as having cut the security budget? Among its many other roles, the London Olympics will function as a giant test-bed for 'state of the art' security technologies.

MacAloon speaks for the vibrant presence of festival outside the stadiums, which goes unwitnessed by those who do not attend and observe. He does, though, acknowledge the impact of security from as early as 1976, commenting that Montreal introduced security measures that 'radically segregated credentialed from un-credentialled participants, and this security effect has been multiplied one-hundredfold since the 1970s' (MacAloon in Tomlinson and Young 2006: 21). Indeed the Games have always provided both a challenge and an opportunity for the cultures of control. The relevant authorities have generally attempted to 'cleanse' the site, the surrounding area, and indeed sometimes much of the city, of its 'undesirables'. American writer Richard Schweid, who spent a year in Barcelona in 1991–1992, recounts that in the build-up to the Games, the municipal government cancelled all licences and permissions to work the Ramblas during the Games. 'Officials did not want the usual horde of beggars, buskers, street musicians, mimes, jugglers, shell-game hustlers and fire-eaters asking tourists for their time and change'. Prostitutes were moved to the Zona Franca, a warehouse district on the edge of Barcelona. However, Schweid observes, the city did allow some regular street entertainers to remain. He also notes that during the Games, the police were not notably in evidence and that the city carried out its role of host to perfection (Schweid 1994: 176).

The heightened atmosphere of fear triggered by 9/11 meant that the organising committee for Athens 2004 came under pressure from the European Union and the USA to increase spending on security. In the event, Greece spent a record $1.5 billion on security, using more than 70,000 security forces. American troops provided a training exercise, practising responses to dirty-bomb attacks and hijackings. Chemical sensors, cctv cameras and hidden microphones were installed, controlled by computer surveillance. Patriot missiles, fighter planes and US

155

battleships were deployed. Brendan O'Neill (2005: 1) argues that the city was 'under US occupation for the duration of the Games (albeit at the invitation of the Greek authorities), as both shorelines and airspace fell under the command of US and Greek troops'. There is of course, a genuine dilemma for any organising committee, as Phil Cohen (2005: 6) points out: 'No one wants a "Fortress Olympics" yet both athletes and spectators need a safe environment. The danger is that risk management drives the whole enterprise and stifles the aleatory principles that alone make the games a joyful occasion worth remembering'.

For London, the original security budget of £337 million has already grown to around £1 billion, but one suspects that a lot of security spending is 'off budget', hidden in general police or security budgets. The UK already makes extensive use of cctv; indeed the BBC reported (2 November 2006) that there were 4.2 million cameras in the UK.[2] Robot drone aircraft have already been deployed in the UK in the Olympic context – at the 2011 Olympics handover party in the Mall. As many as 25 police authorities have or are acquiring drone planes. As has often occurred before, the London Olympics will be used to test new security technologies (*Guardian* 22 February 2010).

In a whole range of ways, the control culture has become a more prominent feature of the Olympic Games. Legislation prevents unauthorised use of Olympic-related words, and allows the London Organising Committee right of entry to homes to search for 'pirated', i.e. unauthorised, Olympic goods, but also banners for protests. The people are seen as a risk that has to be managed. So major sports events utilise the crowd as extras, enabling the card stunts that can only be seen properly on television, and channel spontaneous behaviour into regimented behaviour, such as the rituals of victory ceremonies, cup-giving, the playing of loud music. (Characteristically, at major football events, stadium anthems like 'We are the Champions' are played over the public address system, drowning out and eliminating the possibility of any spontaneous responses to the joy of victory.)

The torch relay is nominally a festive event, allowing people on the streets to 'spontaneously' celebrate Olympism. But in fact the growing scope of the torch relay has largely been driven by the desire of sponsors to maximise their promotional opportunities, given the ban on arena advertising. The London leg of the route of the 2008 torch relay was swamped with the representatives of sponsors giving away flags, banners, giant gloves, posters, anything that could be utilised to display their brand name.

In 2008, though, it became clear that the supporters of a free Tibet would use the torch relay to promote their cause, and that some groups would actively try to disrupt the relay. The torch had to be escorted by a military guard, disguised as athletes in track-suits, whose role was to muscle away any demonstrators. In the UK, the Chinese Embassy mobilised British-based Chinese students to form a counter-demonstration who would cheer and wave Chinese flags. In Trafalgar Square the two groups came close to clashing, in a dramatic face-to-face confrontation involving the waving of giant flags – reminiscent of a medieval battlefield (see Figures 7.3 and 7.4 on p. 137). The various groups responsible for controlling the relay were in disarray as the relay stopped, started, and stopped again. The torch had to be transferred in coaches and buses for sections of the route to avoid the most hostile demonstrations (see Horne and Whannel 2010). In a way, this could be seen as a rare instance of the carnivalesque breaking through despite the attempts at total control.

How are we to employ our terms here? An attempt by the Chinese organisers to stage a spectacle which might have a festive character was disrupted by groups whose interaction produced an alternative political theatre which had a carnivalesque character, and which seized the agenda from the organisers and their sponsors. It was an interesting public example of what happens when the planned spectacle is disrupted. Later that year, an IOC veteran insider confided, through gritted teeth, that he did not imagine that such an international torch relay would be staged again.

A carnival involves the streets being taken over by the people, but the Olympics involve the streets being taken over by the IOC. One of the requirements on the OCOG is to enable rapid transit for IOC members and the Olympic Family between their luxury hotel and the venues. This is accomplished by establishing an Olympic route in which Olympic-related travel gets priority. This can involve dedicated Olympic lanes, priority at traffic lights and intersections and other measures. The ODA requested in 2008 that the government establish the 'Olympic Route Network' and this network of roads on which Olympic traffic will have priority is displayed on the London 2012 website (http://www.london2012.com/olympic-route-network). It will be hard for Londoners not to feel that their city has been invaded and taken over by strangers. The substantial use of Olympic cars to ferry VIPs is probably not good news for London taxi drivers. In 1992, in Barcelona, taxi drivers were encouraged to replace their old vehicles with smarter ones, and to take classes in English and politeness to foreigners. However, the Barcelona Organising Committee provided more than 2,000 courtesy cars for the Olympic Family, buses for the media, and limited venue access to official Olympic traffic. This so upset taxi drivers that ten of their leaders went on hunger strike (Schweid 1994: 199). Despite enthusiastic predictions of visitor numbers, analyses of tourism patterns have consistently documented the tendency of people to stay away from Olympic cities during the Games.

None of this will prevent a festive dimension to the Games, of course, but it seems likely that festivity will be contained and controlled by order and organisation – it will be allowed in delimited spaces, subject to surveillance and policing. A picnic in the Olympic Park could be very pleasant, but only if spectators are allowed to bring in their own food and drink, and not have to rely solely on the questionable delights of official suppliers McDonald's and Coca-Cola. The further from the intense cultures of control that must inevitably dominate the Park, the more chance the festive and even the carnivalesque might have to thrive. If big screens are installed around the city and, within such spaces, a degree of relaxation of policing takes place, then a more people-oriented festivity will be able to develop. However, the gap between the performers and spectators in the arenas and the people in the public spaces of London may be all too clear.

CONSUMPTION: WESTFIELD AND THE STRATFORD CITY MALL

While public focus fell on the Olympic Games, far less attention was paid to the associated development of a large shopping mall. Given the substantial degree of public investment in the Games, the issue of legacy has become a central topic. While the real legacy value of, and future economic support for, many of the sporting venues have been questioned, one aspect of the Olympic project seems likely to produce a successful and highly profitable legacy. The huge shopping mall being built by Westfield is perfectly situated in both space and time. With prestigious anchor tenants such as John Lewis and Marks & Spencer, it neatly spans the space between Stratford International Station and Stratford Station, providing excellent transport links to much of London. The entrances to these stations will provide direct access to the mall, which will also offer one main entrance into the Olympic Park. The mall will benefit from the Olympic publicity and, scheduled to open in 2011, will receive an additional boost within a year, with the procession of up to 100,000 people a day during the Olympic fortnight in summer 2012.

As this is such a key development, the various bodies involved in the Games are being surprisingly coy about it. It is fairly hard to find any references to the Stratford City Development or Westfield on the websites of LOCOG, the ODA, the LDA, the Mayor's Office, the Department of Transport or London and Continental Railways. It is extremely difficult to find any clear financial information about the relation of public and private investment in the site. Even in an otherwise impressive and comprehensive study of Olympic cities from the perspective of urban development (Poynter and MacRury 2009), there were only a few fleeting references to the Westfield Mall.

Like the Games itself, the Stratford City Mall has its origins in government policy for regeneration in the docklands, the Thames Gateway and the lower Lea Valley. In 2002, two developers, Chelsfield and Stanhope, formed Stratford City Developments and proposed a £3.5 billion mixed development at Stratford, in East London, on a 150-acre site on the route of the Channel Tunnel rail link, then under construction. Newham Council granted planning permission in October 2002. At this point the proposed development comprised 5 million ft^2 of office space, 2 million ft^2 of retailing, 4,850 homes and 2,000 hotel rooms, along with schools, libraries and other public facilities. It was planned to begin construction in 2006, completing by 2020(!) (*The Times* 20 October 2002). Just months after Newham granted planning permission, the government was won over to the Olympic idea, considerably enhancing the value of the Stratford development, should London win.

But the Stratford City development plans were making slow progress. Both companies had a record in the field: Chelsfield handled the Paddington basin scheme, whilst Stanhope were responsible for the Broadgate development (*The Times* 10 September 2004). But Chelsfield were already troubled by internal problems when they got planning permission, and their sale of Wentworth Golf Club had triggered a boardroom row. The Chelsfield stake interested three companies (Westfield, Multiplex and Aldersgate). It appears that the three formed a consortium, Duelguide, which acquired the Chelsfield stake, sometime between October and December 2004.[3] However, Multiplex was already in serious financial trouble caused by its involvement in building the new Wembley Stadium, on which by May 2005 it estimated its losses to be around £45 million.[4] Just two months later, on 6 July 2005, the London bid was successful and both land and proposed development suddenly became worth significantly more. In December 2005, Aldersgate, together with associates, acquired the Multiplex share of Duelguide, paying £127.5 million for the Multiplex rights in the Stratford City development site and its stake in Global Switch business.[5]

Those who now had a stake in the development were: London and Continental Railways (LCR) which owned the leasehold of the 170-acre site; Stanhope, and the two partners in Duelguide, Aldersgate and Westfield. But the various companies did not establish an easy rapport, Westfield and Aldersgate in particular having a difficult relationship. Under pressure from an increasingly impatient LCR, the companies agreed to a proposed 'shoot-out' auction

158

in which the highest-bidding partner would buy the others out. But in May 2006, under more pressure from LCR and the various public bodies (ODA, LDA, the Mayor's Office), Stanhope agreed to sell its stake (*Independent on Sunday* 14 May 2006). Aldersgate were reported as being prepared to pay between £50 million and £55 million and seemed the favourite, but Frank Lowy, Westfield Chairman (in Europe with his 244ft yacht for the football World Cup), had not given up.[6] In June it was announced that Westfield had acquired full ownership of Stratford City Developments, buying the Aldersgate stake for around £150 million (*The Age* 13 June 2006). On 2 March 2007, the ODA, LCR and Westfield announced they were now in exclusive talks with the Australian-based property consortium Lend Lease to develop the Olympic Village and Zones 2–7 of Stratford City, which comprised housing, commercial and hotel development. Westfield retained responsibility for Zone 1, comprising the main shopping mall, as well as residential, leisure, hotel and office facilities.[7]

By the start of 2008, Westfield were evidently keen to commence work on Stratford City, although some final contractual details remained unresolved, and they were permitted to establish building contracts under licence.[8] By March Westfield were clear that the mall could be open by 2011, and the ODA had agreed to provide some infrastructure, such as roads and bridges. Westfield also had infrastructural spending commitments under the terms of the S106 Planning Agreement negotiated with the LDA.[9] By April clear physical progress was visible.[10] In May 2008 it was announced that LCR was selling the land to Westfield. This was rather surprising, given that back in March 2007 LCR Managing Director (stations and property) Stephen Jordan had said: 'LCR is pleased to be working with all parties, not only to provide essential infrastructure for a successful Games in 2012, but to provide key elements of legacy – the homes and jobs people need.'[11] It appeared to mean that Westfield now became the sole landowner and sole developer for the Stratford City project.

2001	Nov	Stratford site for Games preferred to Wembley
2002		Chelsfield and Stanhope form Stratford City Developments and propose a £3.5bn mixed development in East London, on a 150-acre site on the Channel Tunnel rail link route then under construction
	Oct	Newham Council granted planning permission
2003	15 May	London bid to go ahead
2004	19 Oct	Westfield, Multiplex and Aldersgate form a consortium, Duelguide
2005	6 Jul	IOC awards Games to London
2005	Dec	Aldersgate acquires the Multiplex share of Duelguide
2006	May	Westfield buys Stanhope stake in the Stratford development
	June	Westfield buys Aldersgate stake in Stratford City Developments
2008	Mar	Westfield mall could be open by 2011. ODA agrees to provide some infrastructure, such as roads and bridges
	May	LCR sells the land to Westfield
	17 Jul	*Guardian* reports that Westfield persuaded government to contribute tens of millions of pounds to ensure the mall will be open for the Games
2011		Westfield's Stratford City mall plans to open

Figure 8.4 The Stratford site and the Westfield mall.

Sources: Company websites, company press announcements, newspaper reports.

It was reported in the *Observer* (24 August 2008) that Westfield's Frank Lowy had persuaded the Olympic Delivery Authority to hand over what was understood to be in excess of £100 million to ensure that the mall would be open in time for the 2012 Games. It is hard to understand quite why Westfield needed an incentive for an outcome very much to their own advantage, and according to the *Observer*, Culture Select Committee members would push ODA officials for an answer. It would seem that this article may well be referring to the infrastructural work that the ODA agreed to undertake in the S106 Planning Agreement. In November 2010, with the main building work complete, major retailers signed up, and with just one year until the official opening Westfield chose to cash in by selling half of their development to a consortium of Dutch and Canadian finance houses for £871 million (*Daily Telegraph* 23 November 2010). In doing so, they retain significant control and a substantial stake in the future of the mall, whilst also recouping a significant amount upfront.

When infrastructural development is carried out by a combination of public and private agencies, it can be difficult to unravel cost and benefit, or public finance and private finance. The Westfield London mall at White City/Shepherd's Bush is a case in point. A new station at Shepherd's Bush on the West London Line has been constructed by Westfield, together with Network Rail, prior to Transport for London (TfL) taking over responsibility for overground services.[12] Westfield gained massively in becoming the focal point of shopping in the area,

Figure 8.5 The Westfield advertisement. The Westfield mall, with its dream location between station and Olympic Park, combines elements of an upmarket shopping, leisure and entertainment location.

boosted by reorganisation of transport, with TfL rerouting many bus routes away from the existing town centre and to the new Westfield shopping mall.[13] It is relevant to ask whether the negotiations leading to the signing of S106 Planning Agreements are adequately transparent and accountable.

CONCLUSION

While the British press made much of the dramatic increase in the London 2012 budget, little focus fell on the disbursement of this budget. In all the public furore about the costs of the Olympic Games which raged from February to May 2007, there was a significant absence. There was very little, if any, discussion of where the £9 billion+ was actually going. Who would receive this money, and to do what? Who was gaining? Aeron Davis has argued that business journalism is 'highly dependent on information and advertising subsidies'; that a 'Financial Elite Discourse Network' has grown up; and that 'in effect, business news has been captured by financial elites' (Davis 2000: 82–89). Our understanding of business and financial issues through journalism is likely to be limited by the shaping and framing work of the public relations operations of powerful corporations.

The Olympic Games has become an enormous lever for moving public policy, uncorking infrastructural investment – public investment, private gain. The key dynamics are associated with globalising processes, transnational corporations, urban renewal, consumption and the new urbanism. In such a context, it could be argued that festivity becomes a side-effect, rather than a partner, of spectacle. One major spectacular legacy of the 2012 Olympic Games will be the Stratford City Mall. Ironically, the London Westfield mall, opened in 2009, was built on the site of the entrance to the Franco-British Exhibition of 1908, which contained the main stadium of the London Olympic Games of 1908. The 2012 Olympic Park itself is currently scheduled to open on time and on budget. Writing two years before the staging of the London Olympics, though, much is uncertain and only a fool would make over-confident predictions. It is planned that, after the Games, the main stadium will be occupied by the London football club West Ham United, with the involvement of Newham Council, which will ensure community availability, but other questions about legacy funding remain to be resolved. We judge, though, that not only will Westfield's Stratford City mall be a huge success and a lasting legacy, but future Olympic bids are likely to include such a development as a part of their strategy.

FURTHER READING

MacAloon, J. J. (ed.) (1984) *Rite Drama Festival Spectacle*, Philadelphia, PA: Institute for the Study of Human Issues.
Moragas, M. de, MacAloon, J. and Llinés, M. (1996) *Olympic Ceremonies: Historical Continuity and Cultural Exchange*, Barcelona and Lausanne: IOC Olympic Museum.
Tomlinson, A. and Young, C. (eds) (2006) *National Identity and Global Sports Events*, Albany, NY: State University of New York Press.

CHAPTER 9

LEVEL PLAYING FIELDS

This chapter examines issues of access and equity at the Olympic Games. It considers: the composition of the IOC; the relationship between affluent and poor countries; social class and the exclusion of professionals; the involvement of women in the Olympics; 'race' and racism; and disability sport and the Paralympic Games. It examines the contrast between the rhetoric and the practice of Olympism. The governance of the Olympics is still dominated by a European male aristocracy. The commitment to amateurism, only abandoned since the early 1980s, gave the Games a distinct social class character. The first black member of the IOC was invited to join in 1963; the first women members were accepted in 1981. Women were excluded entirely from the early Games, and only since the 1980s has the full programme of events begun to be opened to them. Even here there remain areas of contestation and controversy, such as ski jumping. The Paralympic Games, even after a long struggle for inclusion, are still staged as a separate event. Through 'The Olympic Programme' (TOP) major corporations, most notably NBC and its parent company General Electric, are in a position to exercise a shaping influence on the development of the Games. This chapter asks the question: 'Who are the Games for?'

Maurice Roche (2000: 41) outlines four ways in which sports mega-events, such as the Olympic Games, 'provided opportunities and arenas for the display and exercise of "civil society" in addition to "the state" both at national and international levels' at the turn of the nineteenth century. Specifically focusing on the modern Olympic Games and the IOC, established in 1894, he argues that the Games were connected to four developing ideas about global citizenship: *universal citizenship*, and the associated discourse on human rights; *mediatised citizenship*, and the right to participate in the Olympics as a media event; *movement citizenship*, and the right to participate in the Games as a sports organisation and a movement; and *corporate citizenship*, or the position of the IOC as a collective actor in global civil society.

Here we primarily focus on the first and third of these forms of citizenship – the extent to which the Olympics offer a level playing field to those who wish to participate, and thus contribute to the expansion of human rights. As a 'movement', the IOC claims to be quite different from other sports organisations and their mega-events. The problem is that – even if the Olympics were seen by progressives and reactionaries alike as a positive cultural innovation a hundred years ago – this was essentially a dream built upon a particular set of values and relationships (embodied in the ideology of nineteenth-century amateurism, and based on Western, masculine and (upper) social class-based moral conceptions) that simply no longer apply.

Members of the IOC today and many sports people and physical educators still believe that sport has a higher social and moral purpose, but elite sport has also become a more integral part of capitalist consumer culture, and the mega-events such as the Summer Olympic Games are its commercial spectacles. The Olympics use its difference as a 'movement' with an ideology (Olympism) different from other world cups and commercial events (such as the FIFA World Cup, or Cricket or Rugby Union World Cup finals) to provide it with its own distinctive 'brand'. Anti-commercialism can thus enhance its commercial value! However, the IOC faces two main challenges – around democracy and fair play. Under siege since the 1990s about its undemocratic procedures, it remains 'a self-recruiting and secretive elite international club, directly accountable and accessible to nobody but itself' (Roche 2000: 207). Despite the establishment of an ethics commission and various other sub-committees attempting to bring about Olympic reform, since the 1990s the IOC has had difficulty, beyond those people ready to accept its ideology, in convincing others that it is operating according to the highest standards of democratic governance. This situation has not been aided by the increase in revelations of cheating in sport, and especially the use of performance-enhancing drugs, in a context where the chasm between the rewards from success and the anonymity derived from losing has widened considerably.

In order to assess whether there can be a levelling of the playing field through the Olympic Games this chapter will outline the four key social divisions that underpin the world of sport and the Olympics specifically: social class, 'race', gender and disability. Sport, fairness and a level playing field are difficult to achieve since inequalities in material conditions give rise to massive disparities in resources between nations, which tables showing medals per capita or GDP reveal, and which media constructions of valiant but ultimately unsuccessful athletes such as 'Eric the Eel' portray. Media portrayals of Olympic athletes are generally positive, viewing athletes as trying hard despite the odds, but the reality is that over half of participating nations and their athletes do not obtain a medal of any colour.

In the most economically developed countries meanwhile, nationalism spurs on the search for gold medal success via the production of elite athletic bodies and highly specialised athletes. The cost of Olympic gold medals has been growing (Donnelly 2009). The Olympics cannot escape from the social context (including existing beliefs and ideologies) of their formation or of their current manifestation. Olympic change through time tends to reflect, rather more than refract, wider social changes, although it can send out strong messages that help construct certain beliefs about sporting abilities and opportunities. Generally though, the IOC follows social change – economic, political, ideological and cultural – rather than leading or promoting it. But this is not a criticism of the Games alone since sport and sports institutions generally are more of a conservative force than a force for progressive social change. The next sections focus on the four main divisions and areas of political debate in this light.

SOCIAL CLASS: OLYMPIC SPORT AS A VEHICLE FOR OVERCOMING CLASS HOSTILITY AND DIFFERENCES

Social class has played a major role in influencing the construction of, organisation of, consumption of, and participation in modern sport. Class was central to the formation of modern sports culture, and the Olympics were part of that. Class position (of origination) and class of destination are linked through ideas about social mobility. Sport is a powerful symbol of mobility and change in social status. Class has an important influence on sport participation and the character of specific sport cultures. For the first 80 years, the IOC upheld the notion of amateurism and outlawed professionalism in Olympic sport. This partly reflected the social background of Coubertin and his other IOC members who largely viewed their position as one of being social class conciliators. Sport offered a means of 'calming' proletarian 'bitterness' (Coubertin 2000 [1920]: 225). As sociologist Pierre Bourdieu (1978) once noted, sport has been 'an object of struggles between the fractions of the dominant class and also between the social classes'. Nowhere is this more apparent than in inclusion and exclusion at the Olympic Games and in the Olympic movement.

As we have discussed in Chapter 4, Coubertin arrived at his view of sport and physical education from studying the English public school system. This was a highly elitist system based on the wider social class structure. During the nineteenth century the use of organised athletics and 'athleticism' as an educational ideology 'became established as the "essence of school life"' (Simon 1975: 8; Mangan 1981). Key features of this ideology were anti-intellectualism, anti-individuality and conformity. Athleticism was thus a form of character training, developing physical and moral courage, loyalty and cooperation and the ability both to command and to obey (Mangan 1975). Dunning (1975) argues that mid-nineteenth-century public school reforms in Britain, including an emphasis on athleticism and muscular Christianity, represented a compromise between rising industrial bourgeois and declining aristocratic interests. Reform led to the 'incipient modernisation' of team games (especially association football or 'soccer') into modern sports by stimulating the development of codified rules designed to 'civilise' the games and equalise participants. Who played whom in the games fixtures, however, became one of the key indicators in defining not just the status of schools, just as it did in the 'Ivy League' in American universities, but also the structure of the public school network as a whole. As de S. Honey (1975: 27–31) noted, by 1902 there was a relatively close community of 64 boys' schools which interacted with each other in two or more activities, including rowing, athletics, gymnastics, rifle shooting, cricket, rugby, association football, racquets and fencing. Interaction in activities with differential prestige attached to them created different social levels of schools.

Rather than signalling the embourgoisement (or downward cultural mobility) of the aristocratic elite, it can be said that the reformed public schools were thus able to capture middle-class talent (Gruneau 1981: 355). In this way English public schools came to play a formative role in the reproduction and 'promotion of gentry-class power' (Wilkinson 1964: ix) in the nineteenth century. Wilkinson identified public schools as a political system with a political role: 'maintaining order by ethical restraint rather than by law' (1964: ix). The English (and Scottish) public schools selected and reinforced certain values and created a specific public school ethos, as well as a social stratum, that prided itself on public service, amongst other things. The aim was to create a boy who was capable of loyally obeying 'his supervisors and who at the same time could command a regiment or head a government' (Arnstein 1975: 236). According to Bertrand Russell, 'the concept of the gentleman was invented by the aristocracy to keep the middle classes in order' (Arnstein 1975: 235). By 'capturing' the nouveaux riches within the category of gentlemen, the public school 'acted as an "escape-valve" in the social system' (Arnstein 1975: 235). It was this elitist social class context that most influenced Coubertin (for more detail see Chapter 4).

To what extent does social class influence who plays, who competes, and who wins gold medals in elite sport and Olympic sport today? Despite a longstanding sports policy rhetoric about securing 'Sports for All' in the UK and the successful 2005 bid presentation, which placed such a lot of emphasis on inspiring more people to participate in sport, participation rates in recreational sport in the United Kingdom have not significantly altered (for a recent review see Girginov and Hills 2008: 2097–2100). In fact since the implementation of government spending cuts in 2010 there has been a growing concern about the Olympic Games participation legacy. In addition, prior to the London bid, data cited by academics such as Holt and Mason (2000: 6–9), the Office for National Statistics (1998) and sportscotland (2002) all showed the continuance of stratified sports cultures in Britain.

Rowe and Moore (2004) suggest three reasons for the decline in participation since the 1990s: people have competing demands on their time; people have a greater number of leisure choices, many of which promote more sedentary behaviour; and the quality of the sports infrastructure (for participants) has been declining. As a consequence of lack of investment over the past 30 years, some 500 recreational sports centres have closed, and local authorities estimate that they require £500 million to upgrade existing facilities (*Guardian* 21 August 2004). Research conducted in the past 20 years confirms the continuing relationship between independent schools, elite sport performance and social class (Horne 2006: 146–149). A research project on *The Development of Sporting Talent 1997* (English Sports Council 1998) interviewed 924 (approximately 500 men and 420 women) of Great Britain's top sportsmen and women in 11 sports – athletics (track and field), cricket (male and female), cycling, hockey, judo, netball, rowing, Rugby League, Rugby Union (male and female), sailing and swimming. Athletics produced the 'most typical elite sports people' – someone educationally well qualified, from a higher socio-economic group, who had had a family member involved in sport. Of participants, 29% were from the professional and managerial social class (AB), 32% were from the clerical and non-manual class (C1), 28% were from the skilled manual (C2) and 12% were from semi-skilled and unskilled manual classes (DE). This compared with 19% AB, 34% C1, 21% C2 and 25% DE in Great Britain's population as a whole. In rowing, over 50% of elite rowers were educated at independent schools, compared to only 5% of the GB population as a whole. Rugby League had the most manual/working class profile (67% were C2, D or E), whilst in Rugby Union 41% of elite male players and 24% of elite female players were educated at independent schools. Of elite sailing athletes, 24% were educated at independent schools; 61% were from AB, 22% were from C1, 17% were from C2, and none came from D or E social class backgrounds. Swimming contained the most 'upper-class' profile of all the sports – 21% had attended independent schools, 69% were from AB, 24% were from C1, and only 6% were from C2, D or E social classes.

The authors of the report that summarised the data noted that the opportunity to realise sporting potential was still significantly influenced by an individual's social background. They concluded that:

> a precociously talented youngster born in an affluent family with sport-loving parents, one of whom has (probably) achieved high levels of sporting success, and attending an independent/private school, has a 'first-class ticket' to the sporting podium. His or her counterpart, equally talented but born in less favoured circumstances, at best has a third-class ticket and at worst no ticket at all.
>
> (English Sports Council 1998: 13)

This conclusion was underscored following the Sydney Summer Olympic Games in 2000, when a survey suggested that 80% of British medal winners at the Games went to independent schools (*Guardian* 21 August 2004).

More recently at the Beijing Games in 2008 'Team GB' secured 47 medals across 12 sports disciplines – athletics (track and field), boxing, cycling, equestrianism, gymnastics, kayaking, pentathlon, rowing, sailing, swimming, taekwondo and windsurfing. As many were team events, there were 70 individual athletes in total who were medal holders. Five athletes won more than one medal: Chris Hoy (cycling, three gold); Rebecca Adlington (swimming, two gold); Jason Kenny (cycling, one gold, one silver); Tim Brabant (kayaking, one gold, one bronze); and Tina Cook (equestrianism, two bronze). Of these, 41% (28 athletes) were educated at independent schools, 13% (nine) were from religious or faith (voluntary-aided) schools and 46% (32) were from state comprehensive schools (also referred to as 'maintained schools'). This compares nationally with between about 7% of school pupils in the independent sector and 93% in the state 'maintained' sector. Former independent school students were clearly overrepresented amongst the medal winners in Team GB: they took 31% of the gold medals, 44% of the silver medals and 45% of the bronze medals.

We know that models of the potential for behaviour to change resulting from people's exposure to sports mega-events, such as the Olympic Games, need to be improved to properly understand the complexity of motivations to participate in sport and physical activity (Coalter 2004). Rather than 'trickle-down' or 'role model' speculation, Coalter suggests that participation change agents may need to be 'embedded' and/or be involved at the grassroots level. Shilling (2007) poses questions about the existence of multiple social capitals (especially cultural, symbolic and physical capital; that is embodied cultural capital) operating in and through schools that may impact on the propensity of individuals to participate in sport. Related to these capitals, or resources, are the body pedagogics (Shilling 2004) that frame and shape physical capital. Future research will be needed to explore these in order to investigate the participation legacy of future Olympic Games. Gender dynamics complicate the picture, but generally sport assists in the reproduction of the social order – sport and social class are 'mutually reinforcing categories' (Jarvie 2006: 302).

'RACE' AND THE IOC: OLYMPIC SPORT AS A VEHICLE FOR TESTING 'RACIAL' DIFFERENCES

Bairner and Molnar (2010: 3–4) identified three main forms of the politics of 'race' associated with the Olympics. First, there is institutional racism amongst member nations, which was particularly evident in the Games of 1904 (St Louis and the Anthropology Days) and 1936 (Berlin and the attempt to assert the superiority of the Aryan 'race' and the Nazi regime). Second is the opportunity to protest/demonstrate overcoming racism – 1968 (Mexico City) stands out here, as we have mentioned in Chapter 7. Third is the relationship between ethnicity, 'race' and sports performance. The 1904 Anthropology Days, for example, were essentially racial contests set up to measure and demonstrate 'race' as an explanation of performance. But this 'science' of differences has not disappeared despite declarations since the Second World War about the imprecision in using the concept of 'race', and within sport it remains a debating point to this day (see for example Entine 2000 and Hoberman 1997).

166

In his recent book, Carrington (2010: 15) consciously avoids discussing what he calls the 'rather obvious markers that readers might have expected to encounter' in a book about 'race' and sport: for example Muhammad Ali, the failed boycott of the 1968 Olympics and the political protests staged at them. In attempting to think about 'race' and sport 'beyond *Beyond a Boundary*' (the widely acclaimed book written by C. L. R. James (1963)) Carrington argues that analysis of sport in 'an age still marked by the historical scars of Empire and racial exclusion' remains an essential task, especially to consider the 'importance of sporting spectacles' in shaping national identities (2010: 163–165). He suggests that the London Olympics in 2012 may provide 'an important public space within which to re-imagine the national story'. Rather than ignoring it, acknowledging the history of racism and 'race' in Britain in all its complexity in shaping the present could be valuable. The 2012 Olympics 'might just signal the revival of a truly multicultural nation finally at ease with itself' (Carrington 2010: 165).

Evidence gathered in the past 20 years by public agencies and academic researchers in the UK points to some of the issues and challenges ahead. UK Sport estimated that 10.3% of its funded athletes were from black and minority ethnic (BME) groups, which compared favourably with the 7.9% of the 2001 UK population from such communities. Analysis of the GB Team which represented Great Britain at the 2008 Beijing Olympic and Paralympic Games, showed that 7% of the athletes in the GB Olympic squad and 3.6% of athletes in the GB Paralympic squad were from BME groups. UK Sport estimated that 16% of the coaches who were part of the GB Olympic Team for the Beijing Olympic 2008 Games were from BME groups (Long *et al.* 2009). Yet research into the relationship between black and Asian people and sport since the 1990s has demonstrated the historical and contemporary extent of racism in various British sports – athletics, basketball, cricket, rugby league and rugby union, football, hockey, boxing and others (for example, see the collections edited by Carrington and McDonald 2001 and Jarvie 1991).

Few systematic studies into non-white people's participation in sport at grassroots level have been undertaken. It is apparent that levels of participation in sport are not equal for all ethnic groups. In 1996, 46% of white adults had participated in one activity (excluding walking) during the previous four weeks, compared with 41% of black people, 37% of Indians and 25% of Pakistanis and Bangladeshis (Sport England 1999a). Ethnic minorities are also under-represented in their use of local authority swimming pools (Sport England 1999b).

Analysis of sports-specific participation by ethnic minorities has not been possible due to the small sample sizes, but in 2000 Sport England published *Sports Participation and Ethnicity in England National Survey 1999/2000*. This was the first large-scale survey (with 3,000 non-white adult respondents) focusing on England. It found that 49% of ethnic minority men compared with 54% of white men had participated in sport in the previous four weeks. Of ethnic minority women, 32% compared with 39% of white women, had participated in sport in the previous four weeks. The survey found that 39% of black Caribbean and Indian people, 31% of Pakistani people and 30% of Bangladeshi people participated in sport. Compared with the general population, few ethnic minorities declared walking as a physical activity (e.g. only 19% of Bangladeshi women compared to 44% of the total population). The findings showed differences between the participation of men and women. Swimming had a low priority – whereas football involvement amongst men was about the national average (10%).

Such research into the physical activity of black and minority ethnic people – in Britain as elsewhere – has tended to focus on two main themes. On the one hand are *equity issues* – to do with what Coakley (2003) calls the 'sports opportunity structure', the preserving of prejudices despite black excellence in sport, and 'stacking' – the over-representation of black athletes in certain positions in team sports deemed to require less intelligence. Various anti-racism campaigns (for example 'Let's Kick Racism Out of Football' in 1993/1994, 'Hit Racism for Six!' in cricket in 1995 and 'Football against Racism in Europe' in 2002) have developed in response to these issues. On the other hand, research has begun to look at *resistance to* or *accommodation with* racism through the consumption of sport. Whilst some black people have used sport as a route of black cultural resistance to racism and positive identity formation (Carrington and McDonald 2001), others, especially male youth in the USA, have been enticed into following their 'hoop dreams' (Brooks-Buck and Anderson 2001).

The mass media play a major role in the creation of such aspirations. According to Brookes (2002: 107ff.), research into media representation has developed to challenge the conceptual notion of stereotyping. The increasing commodification of sport has affected the way black people are represented in the sports media and targeted as consumers. These ideas relate to developments in the theoretical conception of personal and social identity which have emerged in the past 15 years, especially the idea that identity is an ongoing process. This last idea questions the value of the concept of stereotype and suggests instead that 'racial identity is not stable, essential or consistent; it is dynamic, complex and contradictory' (Brookes 2002).

Relatedly, Carrington (2010) argues that it is useful to 'read the politics of sport and race diasporically'. Cassius Clay's performance in boxing at the 1960 Olympic Games in Rome placed the African-American at the centre of attention (Hylton 2009: 18–19). When in the 1960s the civil rights movement in the United States was at its height, John Carlos and Tommie Smith promoted the Black Power movement to a global audience in Mexico City in 1968 (Hylton 2009: 11). In this way, 'black' national stars have acquired global significance through involvement in sports events that have been mass mediated. Several other of the most 'iconic moments in African-American sporting history occurred *outside* of the United States' – Jesse Owens in Berlin in 1936 and Wilma Rudolph in Rome in 1960. Hence Carrington argues, 'African-American athletes are associated more with international geographical markers than with American ones' (Carrington 2010: 58).

Yet these accomplishments also promote an expectation of performance by black athletes. Hylton (2009: 81–82) relates that he showed a photograph of Kostas Kenderis winning the 200 metres sprint final at the 2000 Sydney Olympic Games to students. He asked them what was wrong with the photograph. The consensus of his classes was that a white sprinter had actually finished ahead of black athletes. If black achievement in track and field has become the conventional wisdom, so too has underperformance in other Olympic events. Hence Eric Moussambani's swim in Sydney made him a universal representative of Black Africans in water in the British media (as 'Eric the Eel'). By contrast Eddie Edwards's ski jumping performance in Calgary in 1988 (nicknamed 'Eddie the Eagle') did not get reduced to deficiencies in his biology or make him a representative of an entire continent (Carrington 2004: 89).

Media coverage of the 2012 Olympics, and all Olympic Games subsequently, needs to be examined in terms of the racialised construction of potential and previous Olympic champions. As Carrington (2010: 137–140) notes, media discussion after both the decision to award London the hosting of the 2012 Olympics (on 6 July 2005) and the bombing of London Underground trains and a bus the following day (on 7 July 2005, often referred to as '7/7')

168

raised the issue of multiculturalism in Europe. If 6 July involved a positive and strong celebration of multiculturalism and the development of a tolerant, open and diverse city, media reaction to the events of the following day suggested that multiculturalism had fanned the flames of intolerance, segregation and ethnic tension. Both reactions also demonstrated the potential power of sport to influence, aid in, or even thwart the creation of ethnically diverse communities in the UK.

GENDER: OLYMPIC SPORT AS A VEHICLE FOR THE DEMONSTRATION OF GENDER DIFFERENCES

Coubertin's views about the role and place of women in sport, and those of many of his fellow members of the IOC, have thrown a shadow over the Olympic movement since its inception. Struggles over women's right to participate, equality in the number of events available to them and the organisation of the Olympic movement more generally have taken place (Hargreaves 1984, 1994, 2000; Bandy 2010). Despite this, as Hargreaves (1994) also demonstrated, some men have supported the inclusion of women in sport and the Olympics in particular. Inclusion has involved debates about the number of female participants, the number of events and the leadership opportunities open to women.

The IOC had no women members until as recently as 1981, when it appointed two; it has been making attempts to catch up since. By 1995 still only seven out of 107 IOC members were women. It established a 20% threshold goal for the inclusion of women in National Olympic Committees (NOCs), National Governing Bodies (NGBs) and International Federations (IFs). In 2009 only 16 of the 107 members of the IOC were women (14.9%) and only one member of the 15-member IOC Executive Committee was female (WSF 2009: 2).

Women's sporting participation at the Olympic Games has, however, shown greater improvement, as Figure 9.1 shows.

Year	Host	Women	Men	Women's sports/events
1900	Paris	22	975	4/2
1904	St Louis	6	645	1/1
1908	London	37	1,971	1/2
1912	Stockholm	48	2,359	3/6
1920	Antwerp	65	2,561	2/6
1924	Paris	135	2,954	5/11
1952	Helsinki	519	4,436	6/25
1960	Rome	610	4,736	6/29
1972	Munich	1,059	6,075	8/43
1980	Moscow	1,125	4,238	12/50
1988	Seoul	2,194	6,197	17/86
1996	Atlanta	3,512	6,806	21/108
2000	Sydney	4,069	6,582	25/132
2008	Beijing	4,637	6,305	26/137

Figure 9.1 Gender and participation at selected Summer Olympic Games.

Sources: IOC (2010a); Toohey and Veal (2007: 199).

Women were first included in the 1900 Olympic Games in Paris. According to the IOC, at those Games there were 22 female participants, or 2.3% of the total number of competitors (IOC 2010a). In Beijing in 2008 the 42% participation rate for women was a record, up from less than 12% in 1960 (Rome), 22% in 1980 (Moscow) and 38% in 2000 (Sydney). Women competed in 26 out of the 28 Olympic Sports and in 137 events. This compared with 175 events for men, and so this imbalance is one area that continues to attract critical attention.

Despite Coubertin's view that 'If some women want to play football or box, let them, provided the event takes place without spectators, because the spectators who flock to such competitions are not there to watch as sport' (Coubertin 2000 [1928]: 189), in August 2009 the IOC agreed to the request from the International Amateur Boxing Association (IABA) to allow women to take part in boxing. Hence in London in 2012 women's boxing will take place for the first time at the Summer Olympics. In April 2011, the IOC announced that for the first time women's ski jumping would be permitted to take place at the next Winter Olympic Games to be held in Sochi (Russia) in 2014. An IOC Executive Board held in October 2010 had postponed its decision. The International Ski Federation, the world governing body, supported the inclusion of this event, whilst the IOC appeared to resist (see *Box 9.1*). What is also noteworthy about this attempt to gain approval for another (women's) event at the Olympics is that a Canadian judge ruled in 2009, ahead of the 2010 Winter Olympics in Vancouver, that although the women were being discriminated against, the issue was an International Olympic Committee responsibility and thus not governed by Canadian laws. The court further ruled that the Canadian Charter of Rights and Freedoms did not apply to VANOC, the organising committee of the 2010 Winter Olympic Games.

BOX 9.1 WOMEN'S SKI JUMPING: THE STRUGGLE TO BECOME AN OLYMPIC EVENT

Ski jumping (for men) has been part of the Winter Olympics since the first Games in Chamonix Mont-Blanc in 1924. The existence of a men's competition without a women's competition has become a major bone of contention as the field of elite female competitors has grown. In May 2006, the International Ski Federation (FIS) decided to allow women to ski jump at the 2009 Nordic World Ski Championships in Liberec, Czech Republic (won by Lindsey Van of the United States), and then to have a team event for women at the 2011 world championships in Oslo. FIS also plans to start a women's ski jumping World Cup circuit in the 2011–2012 season. Women have competed on the Continental Cup circuit since 2005.

In 2006, FIS also decided to submit a proposal to the International Olympic Committee to allow women to compete at the 2010 Winter Olympics in Vancouver. In November that year the Executive Board of the IOC rejected the proposal for a women's ski jumping event in 2010. The reason given was the low number of athletes as well as few participating countries in the sport. The Executive Board noted that women's ski jumping had yet to be fully established internationally. Jacques Rogge stated that women's ski jumping will not be an Olympic event because 'we do not want the medals to be diluted and watered down', referring to the relatively small number of potential competitors in women's ski jumping. It has been noted that while the number of women in ski jumping is not insignificant, the field has a much wider spread in terms of talent, in that the top men are all of a similar level of strength competitively, while the women are more varied, even in the top tiers. Supporters of women's ski jumping argue on the other hand that there are 135 top-level female ski jumpers in 16 countries, saying that is more than the number of women competing at that level in some other sports that are already in the Winter Games.

A group of 15 competitive female ski jumpers filed a suit against the Vancouver Organizing Committee (VANOC), claiming that conducting a men's ski jumping event without a women's event in the Vancouver Winter Olympics in 2010 would be in direct violation of Section 15 of the Canadian Charter of Rights and Freedoms. The ski jumpers wanted a court declaration that VANOC must either hold women's ski jumping in 2010 or cancel all ski jumping events. VANOC argued that the IOC decides which sports are allowed in the Games and that the Charter doesn't apply to it. For its part, the IOC had insisted that its decision to keep women's ski jumping out of the Vancouver Games was based on technical merit, not discrimination. The arguments associated with this suit were heard in court in April 2009 and a judgment was made in June 2009 against the ski jumpers. The judge ruled that although the women were being discriminated against, the issue was an International Olympic Committee responsibility and thus not governed by the Canadian Charter. The court further ruled that the Canadian Charter of Rights and Freedoms did not apply to VANOC. Subsequently three British Columbia judges unanimously denied an appeal on 13 November 2009.

In 2006, the IOC had said that past world championships were one of several criteria used to determine which of several possible new events would be included in the 2010 Winter Olympics. 'Events must have a recognized international standing both numerically and geographically, and have been included at least twice in world and continental championships.' The statement said the decision not to include curling mixed doubles and women's ski jumping in the 2010 Winter Games 'was made as their development is still in the early stage thus lacking the international spread of participation and technical standard required for an event to be included in the programme'. But advocates for the inclusion of women's ski jumping say the IOC formally dropped that requirement in 2007.

In October 2010 the International Olympic Committee's ruling Executive Board chaired by President Jacques Rogge held a joint meeting with the National Olympic Committees. The Executive Board considered whether to include women's ski jumping for a third time. Gian-Franco Kasper, President of FIS, reported that he was 'very optimistic' that all five proposed ski events would win approval, if not immediately then in the coming months. 'They don't need additional courses or anything built,' he said. 'And there is enough space in the programme.' However the IOC delayed the decision until April 2011. The IOC's Executive Board claimed that they needed more time before making a final decision and this has now been made by IOC President Jacques Rogge after the events had staged their World Championships. The IOC had said that it believed including the events would increase universality, gender equality and youth appeal, and in general add value to the Games, but it wanted more time to study them. After the World Championships held in Oslo in February 2011 President of the FIS Gian-Franco Kasper said he was very optimistic that ski jumping for women would be in the Olympics in 2014. Final approval from the IOC, however, had to wait until the meeting in April 2011.

(Sources: Hofmann 2011; Vertinsky et al. 2009)

Women's participation in sport in general still attracts debate. Some writers suggest that over a hundred years after its formation, modern sport is a 'rather less reliable ally of hegemonic masculinity' (Rowe 1995: 130). Others argue that sport, via its links with consumer culture, continues to play a part in the assertion and affirmation of specific hegemonic ideals of masculinity (Day 1990). Fischer and Gainer (1994), for example, analysed a range of research studies investigating the relationship between gender and sport and concluded that:

> the consumption of sports is deeply associated with defining what is masculine and, concurrently, what is not feminine. It has been noted that participating in and watching sports lead to a range of masculinities, and each of them relies for its definition on being distinct from femininity.
>
> (Fischer and Gainer 1994: 101)

Their conclusion is shared by historical studies that have emphasised how sport was a gender-distinguishing activity, related to a changing gender order – for example, in the USA between the 1840s and 1890s, and in the UK between the 1820s and 1880s (Burstyn 1999; Whitson 1994). The 'gendering' of sport by men involved various techniques, including: definition; direct control; ignoring and/or trivialising women's sport or their involvement in sport. For men, sport was a primary socialising experience – into masculine identities, hierarchical social bonding and various forms of masculinity. Hence women faced marginalisation in their consumption of sport. The macho (or 'fratriarchal') culture of sport is repeatedly reinforced with every media report of the sexual misbehaviour of young male elite athletes or men associated with the administration of the sport. Only analysis of the social meanings and interactions of specific subcultural groups, the media portrayal of women as athletes and the gendered consumption of sport (for example, Wellard 2002 and Fleming 1995) can reveal the nature of women's and men's practices and settle these kinds of questions with respect to the Olympic Games.

Vertinsky et al. (2009) use a framework developed by McDonagh and Pappano (2008) to examine the history of women's ski jumping, and document the modes of regulation which have developed around female participation in ski jumping competitions and women's historical exclusion from the Olympic Games. Vertinsky et al. approach sport as a socially constructed space and system, which over one hundred years since its establishment still privileges the male body as superior. Sport therefore is viewed as not simply reflecting social and gender realities but as helping to play a key role in constructing them. Hence in their view,

> a central problem with organized sport has been the way that sport-related policies – especially those enforcing sex segregation – have codified historical myths about female physical inferiority, fostering a system which, while offering women more opportunities than ever before, has kept them from being perceived as equal athletes to men.
>
> (Vertinsky *et al.* 2009: 44)

From this approach, sex segregation in sport does not reflect actual sex differences in athletic ability, but instead helps to construct and enforce the premise that males are inherently athletically superior to females. This premise has been built on three assumptions (which Vertinsky *et al.* call the 'three I's'), which have their origins in nineteenth-century beliefs about the female sporting body and women's proper role in society: female *inferiority* compared to males; the need to protect females from *injury* in competition; and the *immorality* of females who compete directly with males.

Challenging these assumptions, they suggest – following McDonagh and Pappano (2008) – requires moving through a four-stage process: (1) challenging the prohibition of women from participating in certain sports activities; (2) allowing women to participate in sports activities on a sex-segregated basis; (3) accommodating women in sports programmes on a sex-integrated basis; and (4) permitting women to choose whether they prefer a sex-integrated or sex-segregated context for their sports activities (i.e. on the basis of voluntary, rather than coercive, sex segregation). The problem is that it is not a straightforward process, but one based on struggles that can mean setbacks as well as forward momentum (Hofmann 2011; Hofmann and Preuss 2005). A report for the Women's Sports Foundation (WSF) (2009), *Women in the 2000, 2004 and 2008 Olympic and Paralympic Games*, concluded that:

> While progress has been made, the Olympic Games are an enormous undertaking where progress and inequalities co-exist. In 2008, the IOC projected 45% for women, but it appears that this increase in percentage was the result of a modest participation increase for women and a decrease in the participation of male athletes. The participation gap between female and male athletes has closed over the last two Olympiads primarily by cutting the men's field. This is also true of the gap between female and male Paralympians. Several adjustments were made in the 2008 Paralympic program, which offers fewer classifications for male athletes, while increasing the number of classifications for female athletes.
>
> (WSF 2009: 3)[1]

The WSF report noted that certain countries have not incorporated more females into their Olympic teams. Whilst the Olympic Solidarity Program is available to assist with funding for nations facing financial difficulties, some countries claim cultural and religious sanctions preclude the inclusion of women on their Olympic teams. Nonetheless, some countries with religious constraints have been able to send women to the Games. For example, Egypt sent 16 women (over 16% of the total team) to the 2004 Summer Olympics. Egypt has been cited as being different from other Islamic countries because of its secular interpretation of Islam (Walseth and Fasting 2003), but other Muslim nations have also increased the number of female athletes (accounting for 60% of Senegal's delegation in 2004). Despite these increases, a relatively low number of Muslim women competed in the 2004 Olympic Games (WSF 2009: 2).

Testing of sex type remains one of the most significant markers of sport, and elite Olympic sport especially, as a gendered activity. Mokgadi Caster Semenya, the South African middle-distance runner and world champion, won the gold medal in the women's 800 metres at the 2009 World Championships. Afterwards, questions were raised about whether Semenya has an intersex condition that might give her an unfair advantage over the other racers. She was withdrawn from international competition until 6 July 2010, when the IAAF cleared her to return to competition. Analysis of international newspaper coverage before and during the 2004 Summer Olympics in Athens demonstrated that the media still tend to focus on women's appearance and bodies rather than their athletic performance (Markula 2009). Women competitors in more 'feminine' sports – such as archery, badminton, swimming, diving, gymnastics and volleyball – tended to attract more attention than women in 'masculine' ones that exhibit size, power, strength, speed and contact.

The WSF (2009: 2) report concludes that the IOC has recently 'made noteworthy attempts to support the inclusion of greater numbers of women in the international sporting scene'. Initiatives include the Women and Sport Commission and the Fourth IOC World Conference on Women and Sport, held in 2008. However, changes have been less far reaching in the National Olympic Committees, the International Federations and the International Paralympic Committee. The WSF report considers that most of them still 'struggle to meet the IOC's request that women be represented at a minimal 20% standard in leadership positions' (WSF 2009: 2).

The need to encourage women to be involved in leadership positions and organisations – from the grassroots levels to the upper echelons of competitive Olympic and Paralympic sport – remains ongoing. One of the barriers to this is that the marketing of exercise – evidenced in health and fitness magazines as well as mainstream women's magazines – is often not for physiological fitness or psychological health, but in pursuit of physical perfection or sexual attractiveness. Women are more likely to engage in exercise – non-competitive physical activity – rather than sport. The image-making and commercialisation of the sexual body in sport have developed for both men and women athletes (Whannel 2000) but do they have an equal impact? Research by Sassatelli (1999) and Fishwick (2001) suggests that some women are able to find in exercise and health clubs an important space for self-development lacking in other parts of their lives. Yet fewer opportunities exist for women to work in professional sport. Sport offers women new ways of spending leisure time and exercising economic power. But it arguably also helps to confirm and reinforce their role and position in society. It offers both liberation and constraint, challenging some social norms or conventions whilst incorporating some people into others. The recent attempt to encourage women as consumers of sportswear, as well as spectators at big events, may suggest a decline in the peripheral nature of sport to women compared with men. But there are many ways that women remain on the outside of sport – and Olympic sport especially.

174

DISABILITY SPORT: PARALYMPISM AS A VEHICLE FOR BLURRING DIFFERENCES

The London 2012 Games has (thankfully perhaps) only two official mascots: Wenlock and Mandeville. Readers of Chapter 4 will recognise where the first name comes from – Much Wenlock in Shropshire, which hosted games in the nineteenth century, and was visited by Coubertin as he was searching for models for his modern Olympics. Mandeville on the other hand derives from the name of the hospital that hosted the first ever 'Paralympic' Games – Stoke Mandeville Hospital in Aylesbury, Buckinghamshire, a few miles to the north of London.

Sainsbury's, the large British supermarket chain, is acting as sponsor of the 2012 Paralympics, and Channel 4 is to cover the Paralympics exclusively. It is now a requirement of potential Olympic hosts that the Paralympics and 'regular' event must be included in any candidacy file. In the past decade the IOC has embraced the International Paralympic Committee (Cashman and Darcy 2009). Do these developments mark a significant move from the two events existing in separate spheres to consecutive staging of the Games? In the future will we see a genuinely combined Games? This section marks a note of caution about these developments and suggests that struggles over the meaning and place of disability sport will continue (Howe 2008).

According to Colin Barnes (1992), disabled people have identified ten commonly recurring disabling stereotypes in the mass media. These are the disabled person as:

1 pitiable and pathetic;
2 an object of curiosity or violence;
3 sinister or evil;
4 super cripple;
5 adding atmosphere;
6 laughable;
7 his/her own worst enemy;
8 a burden;
9 non-sexual;
10 unable to participate in daily life.

Studies of impairment and disability representation took off in the 1980s. Disabled people were found, to a large extent, to be absent from much of the mainstream media. There were few, if any, disabled characters in soap operas or other long-running TV dramas. When they did appear little attention was paid to the ordinary features of their lives – love, romance or sex – and the focus was primarily on the interaction of disabled people with health and social care professionals. Drama was focused on how they managed their impairment. Television portrayals seemed to be underpinned by themes such as pity, fear, menace, loathing, innocence and courage (Cumberbatch and Negrine 1992). They dealt with personal tragedies and special achievements.

Similar critiques have been made of newspaper coverage of disability. The press tended to focus on health, fundraising and charity as well as on the personal tragedy dimensions of stories about people with disabilities. Researchers identified a fairly consistent negative cultural stereotyping of people with impairments. Media representations have tended to be underpinned by cultural rules about 'able-bodiedness' (Barnes 1992). Attempts to offer alternative counter-representations could run the risk of alienating the audience and producing fear. Historical research into media representations of people with disabilities reveals a fascination with what have been described as 'spectacles of difference'. These serve to reinforce the image of a disabled person either as a tragic but brave victim of a crippling condition or as a pitiable and pathetic individual. Reviewing research into media representations of disabled people, Barnes and Mercer (2003) identify the issue of *cultural domination* – 'in which groups experience symbolic devaluation' (Barnes and Mercer 2003: 88) – as a central concern. But they also suggest that there has been a change in the way that disabled people are represented, with more disabled people appearing in soap operas and drama series as 'ordinary' (Barnes and Mercer 2003). The coverage of disabled sport may be another area where changes are under way.

Despite the acknowledgement that the mass media and other cultural representations play a constitutive role in the social definition and reproduction of meanings of disability, compared to research into the representation of women and black and ethnic minority people in sport, there has been very little that focuses on the media representation of disabled athletes or people with disabilities participating in sport (Goggin and Newell 2000). As Anderson (2000: 107) notes, 'Throughout history, disabled sport has been somewhat marginalised by the media. Although as exciting and emotive as any sport, disabled sport has not received much media coverage'. In fact, film archives do demonstrate that disabled sports people were often represented as examples of 'the super cripple'.

Systematic analysis of the media coverage of the Paralympic Games and disability sport in general has only recently begun to develop (see for example Schantz and Gilbert 2001; Schell and Duncan 1999). Thomas and Smith (2003) have published an analysis of the British media coverage of the 2000 Paralympic Games held in Sydney. Their study focused on the print media and examined the language and images used to portray athletes' performances. They reached four main conclusions:

1   There was a tendency for the print media to provide medicalised descriptions of disability (with an emphasis placed on the athletes overcoming their medical problems).
2   The photographic images often hid the athletes' impairments.
3   Female Paralympic Games athletes were less likely to be portrayed in active poses than male athletes.
4   The images tended to reinforce stereotypical perceptions of disability and reaffirm notions of able-bodiedness (through an emphasis, for example, on how Paralympic Games athletes sought to emulate able-bodied athletes).

Hence the eight British newspapers that Thomas and Smith gathered data from produced a view of disability as individualised rather than socially constructed and tended, they argued, to trivialise disabled people's athletic performances. The portrayal of disabled people often produces an individualised account of disability. Disabled people are often viewed as dependent, reported in a way which is patronising and objectifying, and with images that tend to direct attention away from the social factors that create disability. These tendencies are a feature of much news and documentary reporting, of which sports reporting can be considered a part. It also may be because disabled people are rarely involved in the decision-making processes in the media about what should and should not be shown or reported.

176

When asked how she felt her sport was covered in the media, Tanni Grey-Thompson, the winner of nine Paralympic gold medals for Britain, said:

> We do pretty well, for a minority sport. The coverage is still probably a bit too nice. The print media are getting bolder but there is a feeling that broadcasters don't want the criticism to seem too harsh.
>
> (*Daily Telegraph* 16 September 2003)

Yet, as research has revealed, disabled female athletes have less coverage (Schantz and Gilbert 2001; Schell and Duncan 1999) than disabled male athletes, those with cerebral palsy and learning difficulties have less coverage than other disabled athletes, and wheelchair athletes receive greater media attention than others – possibly because they are perceived to deviate less from cultural notions of able-bodiedness than the others.

Whilst Thomas and Smith (2003) offer a welcome contribution to the literature, there are a number of omissions. As noted above, they focused on representations of the 2000 Paralympic Games from a selection of only eight national English newspapers (and adopted an unusual classification system that linked the *Guardian* and the *Sun/News of the World* together as 'liberal' and the *Daily Mail* and *The Times* together as 'conservative'). Because of this, they ignored regional daily newspapers, the local press and magazines (including niche sports magazines). In addition, they did not consider reporting of the 2000 Paralympic Games by television, radio or the internet (Goggin and Newell 2000). The focus on representations, whilst consistent with much of the international research previously cited, ignores the production of sport as news and entertainment (Whannel 1992; Horne *et al.* 1999: ch. 6) in the broadcast media. In addition, by failing to take into account audience reception and readings of the media messages, they ignore important developments in media analysis that have occurred in the past decade.

In a consideration of sports journalism, difference and identity, Tudor (1998) notes that there have been three typical defences against the suggestion that sports reporting sustains patterns of inferential racism: 'lazy journalism'; 'reflecting society'; and 'things are improving'. We would suggest that the twin of 'inferential racism' might be called 'inferential handicapism' and that these three defences have been deployed when accusations have been made about the marginalisation of disabled people in the mainstream media and the coverage, or lack of it, of disabled sport. Yet as Tudor shows, each of these responses can be shown to be deficient. The first tends to individualise the issue when it is a more collective phenomenon. The second ignores the selecting, amplifying and spreading role of the media – the tabloid press, for example, often tends to assume a homogeneous public in appealing to crude populist assumptions. The third, whilst acknowledging problems in the past, fails to consider the extent to which the media have failed to challenge racism (or handicapism) in the present. There are some examples of media coverage of people with disabilities being discriminated against in sport or in sport situations – for example, Casey Martin, the American golf player who sued the Professional Golf Association for the right to use a golf cart in tournaments (reported in the *Guardian* 16 January 1998), and Shelley Anne Emery, the woman in a wheelchair whose image was digitally removed from a photograph of the England cricket team celebrating a Test Match win over South Africa published in the *Sun* (reported in the *Guardian* 19 August 1998). There are also examples of disabled people being praised for their accomplishments in sport. Some might argue that this is merely perpetuating a culture of pity towards the disabled. An understanding of the history of the representations of disabled athletes in the media in all its forms is an essential prerequisite for assessing the impact of these changes. To date there has been very little research undertaken into the history of the mass media involvement in disability sport in Britain, or, despite its prominence in the disability sports calendar, the social significance of the Paralympic Games.

With the growth of the Paralympic Games, and in the USA programmes such as 'Sporting Chance', which provide disabled people with opportunities to participate in sport, 'marketers are now addressing this market', according to Shank (2002: 412). In the USA, Nixon notes (2000: 425) that 'We have even seen athletes with disabilities on "Wheaties" cereal boxes, a site where some of the most prominent American sports heroes have been displayed'. It can be argued that the development of the Paralympic Games has involved a transformation of their purpose from making disabled people into good worker-citizens, via participation in wholesome sport, into making them good consumer-citizens through their consumption of the expanded sports spectacle. Sport may become a major conduit for the production of what can be termed 'commodity disabilism' or the treatment of disability as a commodity. This will be accompanied by changes in the representation of disabled athletes in the media in all its forms. Some researchers have identified how this is already under way (Duncan and Aycock 2005).

CONCLUSION

We began this chapter by referring to Maurice Roche. He argues that, in addition to being a movement, the Olympics offered several other forms of global citizenship. With regard to universal citizenship, he suggests, 'arguably the negatives outweigh the positives in the Olympic record' (Roche 2000: 203). That within 27 years of the cessation of hostilities in 1945 all three Axis powers (Italy, Japan and (West) Germany) had hosted at least one Olympic Games might suggest otherwise, but Roche argues the IOC has not tended to take 'a consistent and strong line on the human rights record' of the host nations. Equally, the likelihood that the Olympics as a media event will become fully available to all people in the world, via the internet, is another of those arguments about new media technologies that is based as much on hope as on experience. It is difficult to imagine that the IOC will allow internet coverage of the Games to compromise the major element in its funding – exclusive broadcasting rights revenue. Hence the media coverage of the mega-event has tended to be both commercialised and nationalised – insofar as the sports covered (the 'feed') tends to be determined by national TV companies' choices in line with the involvement of its athletes and the anticipated tastes of its viewers. It is in this way that international mega-events can be transformed into forums for national(ist) introspection.

As a collective actor in global civil society, the IOC has had to deal with another two issues concerning its integrity: the process of bidding to act as host and the development of the idea of an 'Olympic truce'. Regarding the first, as we have seen, Olympic city bidding corruption and the role of agents in helping to win bids was a focus of investigative journalism for much of the 1990s, and especially after 1998 and the revelations surrounding the bribes that enabled the success of Salt Lake City in obtaining the 2002 Winter Olympic Games. The Olympic truce idea, in conjunction with the United Nations, is a contribution to international civil society insofar as it seeks the preservation of human life and peaceful coexistence. Yet through this the UN risks 'being associated with an association which is committed to commercialism, global capitalism and consumer culture' (Roche 2000: 214–215).

Roche also draws attention to the phenomenological impacts of sports mega-events. In particular he looks at their role in providing time-structuring resources – both interpersonal and public – and suggests that the 'once in a lifetime' opportunity is one of the main reasons for their popularity, at least amongst those who live in the cities and places that host them. Roche (2003) argues that mega-events are socially memorable and culturally popular precisely because they mark time between generations and thus provide a link between the everyday life-world (micro social sphere) and the meso and macro social spheres. They are 'a special kind of time-structuring institution in modernity' (Roche 2003: 102). Hughes (1999) too notes that underpinning the economic strategies captured by such notions as 'selling places', 'place marketing' and the 'creative city', the idea that ludic space might be an economically valuable use of land has come to the fore. The ludic city, though, might also be seen as valuable for the growth of sociality and the consideration of alternative ways of relating to each other as human beings (see Latham 2003).

Consumer identities and consumer spaces are produced by trademarked mega-events, including the Olympic Games (Magdalinski *et al.* 2005). At the same time sport, culture and (pop) music events enable flows and mobilities of people and non-human entities. In the midst of these, new social identities and understandings – interlinked through social class, gender, ethnic and national differences – may be produced, resisted or sustained. Cashman (2006: 21–22) suggests that memory regarding sports mega-events such as the Olympic Games can take three forms – individual or private memory, spontaneous collective memory, and cultivated public memory. This begs the question, however, about who does the sustaining of memory – at the grassroots, citizens, the media or politicians – and for what ends. There can be a tendency when recalling events towards what Cashman refers to as 'Olympic reductionism' (2006: 25). Here memories are reduced to the highlights – 'a few events which are repeatedly mentioned in public discourse' – and usually only the official achievements. In the popular memory of sports mega-events how it is possible to go beyond these official accounts is an important question that needs to be addressed, and this leads us to consideration of the politics of legacy which is the focus of the final chapter.

FURTHER READING

Carrington, B. (2010) *Race, Sport and Politics*, London: Sage.
Coalter, F. (2004) 'Stuck in the blocks? A sustainable sporting legacy' in A. Vigor, M. Mean and C. Tims (eds) *After the Gold Rush: A Sustainable Olympics for London*, London: Institute for Public Policy Research/ Demos, pp. 91–108.
Howe, P. D. (2008) *The Cultural Politics of the Paralympic Movement*, London: Routledge.
Markula, P. (ed.) (2009) *Olympic Women and the Media: International Perspectives*, London: Palgrave.

CHAPTER 10

THE OLYMPICS AND URBAN DEVELOPMENT: IMAGINING AND ENGINEERING CITIES AND SPORT SPECTACLES

Cities are spatial manifestations of broader social forces and struggles. The built environment and architecture play their part as both metric and motor of change. In the West for the past 250 years the urban environment has been created by industrial capitalist modernity. Space has been restructured in line with changes in capitalism. 'Selling places is now a well-known feature of contemporary urban societies' (Philo and Kearns 1993: 18). In the past 30 years most of the developed and developing world, including the so-called BRIC emerging economies (Brazil, Russia, India and China), have joined in the competitive marketing of places as social and economic opportunities seeking capital investment. Places have become commodities and 'converted into products to be sold in competitive markets' (Philo and Kearns 1993: 19). Related to this is the globalisation of what sociologist John Urry (2002: 115) calls the 'tourist gaze': 'all sorts of places (indeed almost everywhere) have come to construct themselves as objects of the tourist gaze . . . not as centres of production or symbols of power but as sites of pleasure'. Hence, in central Beijing in 2006, although a Starbucks coffee franchise was forced to close in its Forbidden City (a World Heritage site) location after some tens of thousands of people campaigned against its presence, just around the corner was a more legitimate retail outlet: a Beijing 2008 Olympic Games official store.

The city of Beijing has been transformed enormously since 1989 (Broudehoux 2004; Sudjic 2005: 106ff.). During the past decade the focus of urban redevelopment gradually shifted from the centre around Tiananmen Square to the north of the city and the site of the 2008 Olympics. Broudehoux shows how the city's development in the past 30 years has been driven by a larger national agenda to consolidate a new political regime and compete in global marketplaces for capital investment and economic influence. During this time Beijing has come under the influence of local governmental boosters and private (mainly foreign) development interests which operate according to the same patterns that 'growth coalitions' have exhibited in cities around the world (see Schimmel 2001). This has led to the trivialising and commercialising of local history, the fragmentation and privatisation of the public realm, and the catering to business elites and tourists at the expense of local communities and less empowered members of society.

Hence key members of what architectural critic Sudjic (2005: 117) called the 'flying circus of the perpetually jet-lagged' were invited on to the 13-strong jury that judged the architectural competition to design the Olympic (Beijing National) Stadium. The winners, Jacques Herzog and Pierre de Meuron, also designed the Allianz Arena football stadium in Munich before the 2006 football World Cup, the Tate Modern in London and the Forum Building in Barcelona.

the spectacle of modernity

Sudjic (2005: 117) considered their proposed Bird's Nest stadium would be the most distinctive Olympic stadium since 'Munich's Teflon-coated tents' in 1972. In addition to the Olympic stadium, nearby was the National Aquatics Centre (the 'Water Cube'), designed by Australian architectural firm PTW, and Digital Beijing, the information control and data centre for the Games. The building of Terminal 3 of Beijing Airport (designed by Lord (Norman) Foster, who also helped design the new Wembley Stadium in London), the National Theatre, and the headquarters of China Central Television (CCTV) designed by Rem Koolhaas, completes a list of some of the most iconic architectural structures that have been built in Beijing since the awarding of the Olympic Games in 2001.

It is clear that sports and other mega-events have long provided opportunities for nations to signal emergence or re-emergence on the international stage. Whilst there are and can only be a few 'global cities' (Sassen 1991), attempts to promote locations are a commonplace of the past 30 years. Whether as new hubs for business and finance or as tourist destinations, cities increasingly build and utilise iconic architecture and urban spaces to flag their presence in the world. Sports mega-events play their part in this competition for global promotion and branding. But this is only one of their contributions. As Eisinger (2000) notes, the 'politics of bread and circuses' is about building cities for the wealthy 'visitor class'; iconic stadium construction is about flagging transnational places and creating symbolic capital to attract middle- and upper-middle-class visitors.

Figure 10.1 Birds Nest interior. The main stadium, or Bird's Nest, in use during the 2008 Summer Olympics.

Figure 10.2 Water Cube interior. Inside the Water Cube swimming pool, one of the other specially built facilities for the 2008 Beijing Olympic Games.

Some sociologists of sport have identified these developments and begun to explore them critically (see for example Friedman *et al.* 2004; Silk and Amis 2005; Zhang and Silk 2006). Reviews of the impact of sports mega-events on the urban environment have noted at least three vested interests involved in their production: sport, corporate and urban. With a focus on 'impacts', 'legacy' or, as Hiller (2003) prefers, 'outcomes', studies have considered the different phases (Essex and Chalkley 2003) and patterns (Liao and Pitts 2006) of urban development that have resulted from the Olympic Games. We agree with Hiller (2003) that it is important to consider the controversial nature of urban developments related to sports mega-events. 'Legacies' cannot be considered to be simply positive ones. As Jonathan Glancey remarked in his review of architecture for 2008 in the *Guardian*, the Beijing National Stadium was 'the architectural star of the Olympics' (Glancey 2008b: 23). Looking back a year later he included the Bird's Nest in his top ten list of buildings of the decade, yet also noted that since the Olympics, 'this charismatic structure has been largely redundant' (Glancey, 2009: 19).

Rather than rehearse various 'knowns' about sports mega-events (Horne 2007), such as the likely production of 'white elephants' and the overestimation of benefits and underestimation of costs, this chapter discusses the Olympic sports mega-events as an active expression of a globalising neoliberal political economy.[1]

One of the Olympic Games' well-known features is that, for a limited period of time, they create restrictions on certain forms of movement, public (and commercial) expression, and other cultural, artistic and sporting projects. Indeed, critical studies of Olympic developments have typically focused on the displacement of settled populations and the disruption of accepted legal and social norms in order to ensure a beautified, redeveloped and efficient event space. Localised land ownership and use conflicts are an ingrained (and seemingly endemic) feature of the contemporary Olympics story, whose features are: the mass eviction of (often poor or migrant) resident populations and the reform or de facto suspension of established planning procedures in the pre-event phase; the introduction of highly restrictive regulatory and legal instruments to ensure public compliance with the stipulations of local and global organisers during the event itself; and the continued displacement of the previously settled populations through infrastructural transformation and social gentrification in the post-event phase. COHRE, a Geneva-based NGO, has worked since Seoul (1988) on evictions, producing a series of critical reports (COHRE 2007, 2008), academic studies (Olds 1998; Greene 2003) and interventions with global institutional actors (Rolnik 2009). The non-respect of planning procedures has been highlighted in a series of studies (e.g. Hall 2001 on Sydney; Karamichas 2005 on Athens; Whitson 2011 on Vancouver). The securitisation and corporatisation of event space at successive Games, and the concomitant suspension of civil liberties, have similarly been highlighted (e.g. Tajima 2004 on Nagano; Cunneen 2000 on Sydney; Schimmel 2006 on Salt Lake; Klein 2008 on Beijing).

Between Beijing in 2008 and London in 2012 we have moved from CCTV to cctv (closed-circuit television) and the use of unmanned aerial vehicles (UAVs) to monitor people's movement, as the tangible security risk that sports mega-events pose leads to an accompanying array of novel security and surveillance measures (Boyle and Haggerty 2009). Restrictions on the use of certain phrases and words are required to avoid ambush marketing when the IOC and the OCOG rely so heavily on the sponsorship of global corporations. Whilst the Olympics are meant to be about much more than simply sport, the cultural activities associated with the Games tend to take second place, whilst other sporting events have to accommodate the event by changing their schedules.

In several ways then, as we argued in Chapter 7, the staging or hosting of sports mega-events promotes neoliberal forms of governance and the neoliberalisation of space (Peck and Tickell 2002), and thus has clear similarities with the 'shock doctrine' informing public policy in the wake of social, 'natural' and economic disasters (Klein 2007). Although the idea that capitalism advances on the back of disasters, or violent circumstances, is not a new one – Marx (1976 [1867]) wrote at length in *Capital* about the extra-economic coercion required to bring about primitive accumulation in the eighteenth century in Western Europe for example – Klein's book is a valuable insight into recent history, arguing that the use of shock is a technique for imposing an ideology (what she calls the free market fundamentalist ideas underpinning neoliberal economic thought and policy). The shock doctrine is also a philosophy of how political change can happen and be brought about. Charting the rise of free market fundamentalism over the past 40 years reveals that when ideas are unpopular, advocates of free market neoliberalism have exploited shocks to help push through their policies without popular democratic consent. The product is what Klein calls 'disaster capitalism' – a form of capitalism that uses large-scale disasters in order to push through radical neoliberal capitalist policies – and its related privatisation agenda for (formerly) public services.

We want to suggest that sports mega-events can be viewed as the apparently benign twin of disaster capitalism's shock therapy, involving their own shocks and generating their own forms

Figure 10.3 London Olympic site, looking west. In Stratford, East London, the stadium and the swimming pool for the 2012 Summer Olympics are constructed against a cityscape of other iconic buildings, such as The Gherkin (Swiss Re) office building in the City of London.

of awe. Substantial parts of cities and other areas designated for the events are disturbed for years by the construction projects, debt accumulation, restructuring and other disruptions of space and time. Indeed, despite the IOC's apparent wish under Jacques Rogge to move away from favouring gigantism in Games staging (see, for example, the recommendations of the 'good governance' Study Commission to the 2003 Prague IOC meeting, Pound 2003: 23, 35), recent decisions for Summer Games hosting have consistently chosen the most expensive and extensive project on offer (Beijing, London, Rio de Janeiro), whilst overlooking relatively compact bids (Paris and, especially, Madrid). We want to suggest that these decisions reveal a fundamental tension between the requirements of event staging and of legacy creation, between short-term demands and the impact necessary for transformative cultural change and infrastructural development. Affected urban areas accordingly face the imposition of temporary extra-legal forms of governance, which then dissolve after the event, leaving 'legacies' that have to be dealt with. In London, the ODA, charged with building the site and facilities, with the powers of an urban development corporation, can act as its own planning authority within the Olympic precinct area, whilst LOCOG is a private company established to run the events until they finish in September 2012. Sports mega-events promote the use of vast amounts of public money for private gain into a civic obligation (and therefore make it difficult to criticise without being portrayed as unpatriotic or a 'naysayer'). With sports mega-events, however, the shock is largely perceived not as trauma but as a festival and global media spectacular (Gaffney 2010). Winning a bid to host a mega-event, putting the fantasy financial figures of a bid document into operation, dealing with the proposed location both before

184

and after the event are just some of the moments where shock and awe are generated by sports mega-events.

The remainder of this chapter considers three issues. First, just who are the agents and institutions that assemble, build and especially design the material infrastructure, including the stadiums and facilities, for sports mega-events such as the Olympic Games? Adopting a 'production of consumption' approach to the study of sport in consumer culture, related to, but not completely informed by, the critical political economy of sport (to be found, for example, in the work of Belanger 2009, Whannel 2008, and Whitson and Macintosh 1993), we discuss the creators of the emblematic buildings and the leisure and sport spaces constructed to assist in the pursuit or maintenance of 'world-class' status. Second, why do cities like London and Paris, which do not need the Games to attract tourist visitors, still bid to host them? Ever since Barcelona in 1992, bids to host the Olympic Games have emphasised the marketing of a city as a tourist destination and urban development and legacy have also become familiar terms in the bidding context. It seems that winning the Games functions to enable a whole range of giant infrastructural projects that would otherwise struggle to win support. The Games stimulate the dreams of architects and mayors, builders and planners, leaders and entrepreneurs, as well as politicians (such as President Lula of Brazil). 'Legacy' has become justification in the rhetoric of 'major event speak'. We consider this development, after the apparent success of Barcelona, in terms of the shift from (inter-)national politics to (inter-)city politics as the rationale for Olympic bid funding. Third, we conclude with a summative discussion about the place, role, function and relevance of the Olympic Games in the twenty-first century, and ask in particular if sustainability and the 'greening of the Games' are doing more than simply sustaining the unsustainable.

ARCHITECTS AND THE PRODUCTION OF THE MATERIAL INFRASTRUCTURE OF CITIES

Previous research has identified the stadium as a site for multidisciplinary investigations into the meanings of urban leisure, and the economy and politics of sports spaces (Bale and Moen 1995; Marschik *et al.* 2005; Trumpbour 2007; Gaffney 2008). The focus here is on the builders – especially the project and design architects – responsible for the production and design of the material infrastructure that is increasingly required to be in some way as iconic as the people who are expected to perform in it.[2] In this section we consider the production of the material infrastructure and, particularly, debates about the political economy of architecture and architects. Included here is an outline of the growth of what Leslie Sklair (2001) calls the 'transnational capitalist class' and the place of architects in this class. The leading firms and architects that build sport stadiums, and especially stadiums for sports mega-events, are briefly discussed and their key characteristics identified. The changing profile of architecture and architects in relation to the urban sport spectacle in both the UK and North America is also discussed. The conclusion summarises the discussion and identifies future research questions for a critical sociology of sports architecture.

Until recently, architecture – and the social role of architects in particular – have not been a significant topic for sociological analysis. Partly this has been supported by the view that architecture is an artistic practice, the creation of individual genius, and therefore cannot be adequately comprehended by sociological theories. Three books published in the last 12 years, however, demonstrate that it is possible to produce a sound understanding of the social world of architecture, architects and architectural education, utilising contemporary social theories. Garry Stevens (1998) found great value in Pierre Bourdieu's work for understanding the way the architectural 'field' produces cultivated individuals with distinctive styles and tastes, and thus the way in which individual architectural creativity is derived from a social process. Like other artistic practices, contemporary architecture can be examined in Marxist and sociological terms by looking at the social relations of production within which it emerges and operates. These approaches pay attention to the institutions through which architects are educated, how building designs are produced and hence how architecture is socially constructed. Architects may operate today within conditions that are determined by the market for design and iconicity but also, as Donald McNeill (2009) suggests in his important book, architecture is a *heteronomous* practice – it is reliant on other agents and practices in order to take place. As the managing principal at the world's largest architectural practice in 2008, Chris Johnson of Gensler, told *Building Design* magazine, 'we don't really do projects, we do relationships' (*Building Design* 2008: 6). Taking this notion of architectural dependency further is the study *Architecture Depends* by Jeremy Till (2009), which demonstrates the *contingency* of architecture and architects via a discussion of the sociological ideas of Zygmunt Bauman, Henri Lefebvre and Bruno Latour, amongst others.[3]

As McNeill (2009) suggests, architecture needs to be understood from the perspectives of the firm, fame and form. Which are the firms involved in the building of sport facilities and stadiums? Whilst Ewen (1988) alludes to the changing celebrity status of architects and architecture during the twentieth century, Till (2009: 42) comments that 'the values and currency of the famous' dominate architectural culture, and the production and marketing of architectural icon buildings and signature architects (Larson 1994: 470), or 'starchitects', has certainly grown since the 1980s. Whilst architecture may have a cultural and aesthetic existence independent of those paying for it, it is unquestionably the case that 'architecture is about power' (Sudjic 2005: 6). As Stevens notes:

> The field of architecture is responsible for producing those parts of the built environment that the dominant classes use to justify their domination of the social order. Buildings of power, buildings of state, buildings of worship, buildings to awe and impress.
>
> (Stevens 1998: 86)

Politically, architecture tells a story about those who determine that something is built. Whether democratic or totalitarian, a regime utilises architecture as a tool of 'statecraft' (Sudjic 2005: 8; see also Marvin 2008 for the role of architecture in Chinese statecraft). One very important economic feature is the growth of the marketplace for building design. The market provides the basic economic structure that encloses and also creates the experiences of architects. The structure makes some aspirations possible, and others inconceivable. A brief consideration of the political economy of architecture would reveal that whilst architects design buildings, they do not do so under circumstances of their own choosing. As Till (2009: 123) states, 'qualities of hard space that dominate architectural production allow that space to be easily appropriated by the market'. This is exacerbated by the architects' code of conduct, whereby they provide a service for clients (not users) whose own demands are most often driven by market and 'short-term opportunism'. If 'architects can never fully control the actions of users' (Till 2009: 41) they most certainly cannot easily dictate to those for whom they provide a service. This is one of the ways in which the position and role of architects are contingent.

Architects are involved in the construction of 30–50% of the contract value of buildings in the developed world (Stevens 1998: 228 n. 64). Traditionally it has been considered that there are three types of architectural firm: 'strong delivery', 'strong service' and 'strong ideas' firms (Gutman 1988). The first type are highly commercial and rarely win awards – but build a lot. The second includes architectural practices such as Skidmore, Owings and Merrill which designed Canary Wharf in London and are currently designing the Freedom Tower at 'Ground Zero' in Manhattan. The third type of firm contains well-known starchitects such as Frank Gehry, Norman Foster and Robert Venturi, all famous for producing iconic buildings. Gehry's design for the Guggenheim Museum in Bilbao, for example, became the world's most famous new building in the 1990s and led to calls to replicate the 'Bilbao effect'. The building – a titanium-covered museum juxtaposed against central Bilbao's river valley and built on the site of a former steelworks – 'brought together deeply politicized place marketing, the architectural branding of an aspirational art institution, and the worldwide projection of Frank Gehry as a celebrity architect' (McNeill 2009: 81–82). Gehry even featured in an episode of 'The Simpsons'.

Despite the symbolic value of such iconic architecture designed by celebrity architects, Sklair (2005: 487) noted that entry level to the *Fortune* Global 500 – the annual list of the world's largest transnational corporations identified by *Fortune* magazine – was $10 billion in 2003, and no leading architectural firm reached anywhere near this figure. Even strong delivery firms, which produce a lot of buildings but few icons, operate in consortia chasing mega-projects (here defined as construction projects estimated to involve expenditures over $1 billion). The two main locations for most mega-projects in the past decade have been the USA and China. In 2006 the USA had an estimated 150 projects that provided the bulk of opportunities for engineering, architectural and construction firms there (RKMA 2006: 46). The restructuring of the financial sector globally has had an impact on these projects, yet economic growth in Pacific-Asia (especially stimulated by China's building boom since the 1990s, see Olds 2001 and 1997) and the Middle East (until recently) has encouraged more celebrity architects to operate globally. These 'starchitects' have taken on an increased role in planning and building in cities in the Asia-Pacific. The so-called 'Global Intelligence Corps', including architectural celebrities, have been used to brand local developments by indigenous developers, politicians and bureaucrats, who thus in turn gain symbolic capital by association (Olds 1997; Larson 1994; Rimmer 1991). As Broudehoux (2004: 21) notes, since the death of Mao Zedong Beijing has been 'turning itself into a scenographic venue for the hosting of world class media events and the staging of grand urban spectacles'. This works in sport as much as any other form of spectacle, as we will see below.[4]

Production relations in architecture can be understood as 'a field of cultural contestation' (Jones 2006: 550) or, as Ulrich Beck (1998: 115) once put it, 'politics with bricks and mortar', in the midst of global-local processes. In the contemporary globalising world, starchitects producing iconic buildings have increasingly become useful to what Leslie Sklair (2006, 2005, 2002, 2001) refers to as the transnational capitalist class (TCC).

Sklair (2005) argues that the emergence of contemporary 'iconic architecture' is a result of transformations in the production, marketing and reception of architecture, which is itself a consequence of capitalist globalisation. 'Iconic architecture' refers to two things – buildings and spaces that are famous because of the architects who design them, and buildings and spaces with special symbolic/aesthetic significance attached to them. Architects can be iconic in this sense – hence the media label 'starchitect'. Before the 1950s – which in Sklair's formulation is the pre-globalisation era – the interests of the state and/or religion drove iconic architecture. In the globalisation era he argues that the dominant force driving iconic architecture is 'the transnational capitalist class' (Sklair 2005: 485).

Architecture has been internationalised as its source of patronage and sponsorship has altered (King 2004). Modes of production and associated ideologies increasingly shape architectural design rather than the nation-state (although see Brownell (1995) on stadium building in Beijing). Globalised production, aided by new technologies of communication and design in addition to an already internationalised profession (formalised by the formation of the International Union of Architects in 1948), led to the growth of architecture as a global cultural form. The 1950s and 1960s saw the building of American-style hotels throughout the world, prompting debates about homogenisation and plurality that became familiar in subsequent decades with respect to the notion of sociocultural globalisation.

According to Sklair, the TCC comprises people with globalising as well as localising agendas, who have a home in more than one place, and who have a cosmopolitan outlook. The TCC seeks to secure the conditions under which its largely capitalist interests are furthered in global and local contexts. The TCC has four fractions: corporate, state, technical and consumerist. The corporate fraction owns and controls major transnational corporations and their local affiliates. In architecture these are the major architectural, architecture-engineering and architecture-developer-real estate firms listed in such magazines as the (now defunct) *World Architecture* and *Building Design's World Architecture 100*. As we have suggested, the revenues of these companies are relatively small compared to firms in the *Fortune* 500, and the number of starchitects with the biggest firms is also small, but they have great significance for the built environment and their cultural importance for cities outweighs their financial muscle. This is one reason why Preuss (2004: 235–236) is mistaken to ignore the symbolic role and value of architectural design in sports mega-events such as the Olympic Games. Nor is it enough, without further investigation, to say that the impacts of sports mega-events on the urban, spatial, architectural and built form of cities (including negative ones such as mass evictions, see COHRE 2007) are 'obvious' (King 2004: 35).

The state fraction of the TCC includes politicians and bureaucrats who decide what gets built where, and how changes to the built environment are regulated (at central, regional and municipal levels of government). The technical TCC comprises the professionals involved in the design of structural features and services of new buildings, as well as the education of students and the public in architectural discourse. The consumerist TCC includes the merchants and media responsible for the marketing and the consumption of architecture (Sklair 2005: 485–486). The involvement of the various fractions of the TCC in the shaping of the built environment relates to sports facilities and stadiums as much as to any other public building. Which firms build these monuments? How do they make their buildings mean something? The following paragraphs provide initial answers to these questions.

Building Design magazine's *World Architecture 100* ranks architectural practices by size (number of architects and other 'creative' staff employed), regional prominence by fee income and market sector share. Of the leading companies in the sector, four had their headquarters in the USA, two in Europe, two in Japan and one each in Australia and the People's Republic of China. The leading company in the design of sports facilities was HOK International (Hellmuth, Obata and Kassabaum). In the *World Architecture 100* for 2008, overall HOK was the second largest architectural practice, with total fee income in excess of $250 million and 2,500 employees. Founded in 1955 by George Hellmuth, Gyo Obata and George Kassabaum, HOK had 26 regional offices on four continents (North America, Europe, Asia and Australia).[5] A specialist company division – HOK Sport + Venue + Event (HOKSVE) – dealt with sport venues and event management, following a merger with the Lobb Partnership in 1999 and Anderson Consulting in 2002. As the division's website noted:

> Our global client list is diverse and comprehensive, and it includes 24 Major League Baseball franchises, 30 NFL franchises, 80 professional and civic arena clients, 40 soccer and rugby teams and 120 colleges and universities. Our reach is worldwide. Our passion is undeniable and we approach the architecture of sport unlike anyone else.[6]

HOKSVE employed over 70 principal and senior principal architects (although only three of them were women). It has engaged in projects covering most sports – aquatic, athletics (track and field), Australian Football League, baseball (major league and minor league), basketball (including collegiate), cricket, equine, field and ice hockey, American football, football (soccer), motor racing, speed skating, and tennis – over a 25-year period. In 2008, HOK's apparent ascendancy as the 'Number 1' sports stadium architectural firm was reflected in terms of its regional status. HOK appeared in the top ten practices in Australasia, the Middle East, Central Asia, and North and South Central America in the 2008 *World Architecture 100*.

In the second half of 2008, HOKSVE was subject to a management buyout (led by senior principal architect Rod Sheard). It was relaunched with the new corporate name and brand as 'Populous™' in March 2009. The webpage of the new practice states that: 'Populous™ is a global design practice specialising in creating environments that draw people and communities together for unforgettable experiences'. It continues to achieve considerable success in attracting commissions – including both the main stadium for the Winter Olympic and Paralympic Games to be held in Sochi (Russia) in 2014 and London's 2012 Olympic Stadium.[7]

None of the other companies in the sports stadium sector has such a global presence as HOK/Populous™, although NBBJ – tenth in the sports stadium sector but seventeenth largest architectural firm in the world in 2008 – featured in both North America and Central and Eastern Europe regional 'top tens'. Dallas-based HKS, in addition to their commission to build the new Liverpool FC stadium, were selected to design a multi-sport stadium scheduled to be built on the site of the former Maze/Long Kesh prison in Belfast, Northern Ireland. The project was cancelled in 2008 owing to the political situation. Most of the other sports stadium sector leaders have a more regional, rather than global, presence. Cox was ranked second overall in the Australasia region, ACXT-IDOM and JSK were ninth and tenth in Western Europe, Leo Daly and HKS are third and fourth biggest in North America, whilst Nikkon Seikei, Kume Seikei, and Leigh & Orange were first, fourth and ninth respectively in the Pacific Rim region (*Building*

Figure 10.4 Sydney Telstra Stadium in 2007. Following the Sydney Summer Olympics in 2000 the main stadium was reconfigured to shorten the north and south wings and hold fewer spectators. It has been renamed twice – Telstra (at the time of this photograph) and now ANZ Stadium after sponsors with naming rights.

Design 2008: 35, 37). Nikkon Seikei, the largest firm in Japan, whose major projects range from golf course and country club design to bridge and road building, has nearly all its projects in Asia.

The website of Leo Daly, a large Omaha-based practice, responsible for several sports arenas and public venues, outlines the complexity of the sector's needs:

> Whether they serve as anchor for a civic complex that revitalizes a downtown area or become a symbol of school pride, public assembly and sports venues must be exceptional and generate excitement . . . Their multipurpose nature requires flexibility to accommodate and rotate activities . . . Our designers work closely with owners, municipalities, operators, food service providers, sports teams and performers because they understand these facilities must meet the goals of multiple stakeholders.[8]

Five features are immediately noticeable about sport sector architectural firms, practices and projects. First, as with most other architectural work, as McNeill (2009) and Till (2009) both

190

the spectacle of modernity

demonstrate well, is the necessity of working in partnership with other architectural practices and construction and design services – such as service and structural engineers, project managers and building contractors. Both JSK and Cox have worked in collaboration with HOK on projects in Germany (World Arena, Berlin) and Australia (MCG, Melbourne) respectively. Dependence also applies with respect to the necessity of conformity to local building regulations and safety guidelines (e.g. DCMS 2008) which are as much a feature of the sports facilities and stadiums sector as of other areas of architectural practice. Second, as the quotation from Leo Daly above affirms, the stakeholders'/clients' needs come before those of potential users or citizens of the locations where stadiums or arenas are built. Third, the leading firms tend to be those with a more global presence. Those that seek a global presence will use any successes in design competitions to enhance their reputation and thus sustain their presence in the market sector. Fourth, despite apparent globalisation, there has been a tendency for most sports-related work in North America, Europe and the Pacific Rim region (including East Asian countries) to be designed by 'local' companies, although the Beijing Olympic Stadium and the associated Water Cube aquatic centre were exceptions to this. Fifth, and finally, high-profile starchitects and well-respected companies, such as Foster & Partners and Herzog & de Meuron, are not part of the sport stadium 'top ten' even though they have been and will be involved in some highly significant developments in the sector.

Ren (2008: 176) suggests 'social scientists have just begun to explore the linkage between architectural mega-projects and nation-building practices in global or globalising cities'. Next we sketch some examples of how stadium architects contribute to the construction of not only sport stadiums and spectacles, but also urban built environments, and thus help to produce symbolic capital for localities seeking a global profile.

SPORTS MEGA-EVENTS AND URBAN DEVELOPMENT

The allure of hosting sports mega-events has increased greatly in the past 25 years. When Los Angeles hosted the Summer Olympics in 1984 there were no competitor nations. Nagoya was the only rival to Seoul to host the Summer Games in 1988. Clearly the significant alteration in the global geopolitical landscape – the collapse of the Soviet Union, the highly symbolic but material demolition of the Berlin Wall, and the associated break-up of the East European bloc of nations at the end of the 1980s – has helped the Olympic 'mega' develop into the position it now holds in the global imagination and the global economy of appearances. As noted earlier, journalist and architectural critic Deyan Sudjic (2005: 326) suggests that architecture 'is constantly about . . . power, glory, spectacle, memory, identity' whilst it always changes in form. That this is as true for the buildings and facilities underpinning sport and sports mega-events as it is for other construction projects can be seen through a brief examination of selected buildings designed for Summer Olympic Games.

As we have suggested, the role of architects in the creation of memorable Olympic infra-structures has not been analysed much until relatively recently. This may partly be to do with the fact that whilst a list of stadiums built prior to 1984 includes the well-received Tokyo and Munich projects, it also includes Montreal, which stands out as one of the most negative examples of contemporary architectural ambition. This complex design and ambitious *grand projet* left the city with an enormous debt, only paid off completely 30 years later in 2006.[9] Use of the Montreal site has largely been restricted to non-sports events and a zoological garden.

191

It is clear that the Olympic Games and other sports mega-events have long provided opportunities for nations to signal emergence or re-emergence on the international stage. Whilst there are – and can only be – a few 'global cities', attempts to promote locations has become a commonplace of the past 20 years. Whether as new hubs for business and finance or as tourist destinations, cities increasingly build and utilise iconic architecture and urban spaces to flag their presence in the world. Sports mega-events play their part in this competition for global promotion and branding.

Researchers have noted that the attraction of hosting sports mega-events has grown since the 1980s because it enables multiple sets of agendas to be addressed. The main ones are place promotion, internal (social, cultural and economic) development, and global status. The hosting of a major event enables symbolic as well as material nation-building to take place. Short (2004: 68ff.) identifies four modalities of global cities: transport hubs and networks; global cultures and cosmopolitanism; global imaginings and place marketing; and global spectacles, signature architects and cosmopolitan urban semiotics. The Summer Olympic Games are 'the mega-event with the ability to create, reinforce and consolidate global city status' (Short 2004: 108) as it condenses these modalities. The summer Olympics are 'global spectacles, national campaigns and city enterprises' at one and the same time (Short 2004: 86).

Globally, the International Olympic Committee, prompted by concerns about its environmental impact, wavering public opinion in the light of corruption revelations, and interest in the amorphous concepts of 'legacy' and 'sustainability' which developed in the 1990s, has helped shape the environment in which the change in the role of architecture and stadium architects in sport has taken place. Concerns about legacy have been the focus of an IOC conference and transfer of knowledge has become a vital part of the organisation of Olympic events. The related concern with 'sustainability' has existed since 1994 when the IOC adopted the environment as the third pillar of the Olympic movement. Former IOC President Samaranch and current President Rogge have written highly positive forewords to books on stadium design (see John and Sheard 2000; John et al. 2006).

With regard to a healthy legacy, campaigners have warned that attempts to use the London 2012 Olympics to improve public health may be undermined by the fact that one in five meals served to fans at the Games will come from sponsor McDonald's. Games organisers said that 3 million of the 14 million meals served during the event will be prepared by the fast food chain. All branded soft drinks will be provided by Coca-Cola, and the only other branded food on sale will be Cadbury's chocolate. McDonald's and Coca-Cola both sponsor the IOC, which passes several million pounds of those revenues to London's organisers, while Cadbury pays £20 million as a direct sponsor of the 2012 games. The British Heart Foundation (BHF) and the National Obesity Forum said the policy undermined claims from Lord Coe, the chairman of the London organising committee, and Tessa Jowell, the former Olympics minister, that one of the main legacies of hosting the Olympics will be improved health across the nation. McDonald's outlets will be erected across the athletes' village, the main Olympic Park and in the media centre. 'Health does not seem to be high on their agenda', said Ruairi O'Connor, head of policy at the BHF. 'The focus on fast food, where the primary products are high in fat, sugar and salt, means we question whether the health legacy which has been promised will be fulfilled.'[10]

Sklair argues that starchitects assist the TCC through the construction of transnationally attractive consumption spaces and the production of iconic architectural forms. Since the

1980s, starchitects have been invited to build iconic buildings and consumption spaces and the ideological role of these reflects other processes going on in cities. This includes: the re-imagining/imagineering of cities as consumption centres, rather than centres of production; the building of urban entertainment destinations and other themed environments; and the construction of spaces for the consumption of experiential commodities, such as sports and recreational events, concerts and other commercial gatherings, which include stadiums – or 'tradiums', often increasingly named after a sponsor rather than their location in the city (Rutheiser 1996; Hannigan 1998). Saunders (2005: viii) suggests that '*Spectacle* is the primary manifestation of the commodification or commercialisation of design'. This has involved a simulated de-McDonaldisation in some places and the creation of ballparks as theme parks in the United States especially (Ritzer and Stillman 2001). The end result is 'a heavily themed environment rationally organised to maximise consumption' (Giulianotti 2005: 134). In addition, this process has seen architects become brands in their own right (Frampton 2005), creating 'architainment' for some.

As noted, some sociologists have already responded to these developments critically. In North America journalist Dave Zirin has also identified the building of iconic sports and leisure spaces as a poor 'substitute for anything resembling an urban policy in this country' (Zirin 2009: 262). He describes the way that the Louisiana Superdome became a shelter for 30,000 of New Orleans's poorest residents left homeless by the effects of Hurricane Katrina in August 2005. Although it was built from public funds 30 years earlier, it would normally have been beyond their means to enter the arena. The homeless people were then moved on from there to the Houston Astrodome in Texas, not to government housing, public shelters or somewhere nearer to their devastated homes. Zirin (2009: 262) argues, 'stadiums are sporting shrines to the dogma of trickle-down economics'. US public money amounting to $16 billion has been spent on stadium construction and upkeep in the last decade. Despite no evidence that they function as financial cash cows, 'the domes keep coming' (Zirin 2009: 262). The opening of two new baseball arenas in 2009 in New York, Citi Field (New York Mets) and the new Yankee Stadium (New York Yankees) – the latter the most expensive sport stadium in the world (ahead of the new Wembley Stadium) – testifies to the continuing lure of sports facilities (Cornwell 2009).

In the UK, Inglis (2005, 2000) identifies two moments when sport stadium architecture underwent fundamental changes – at the end of the nineteenth century and at the end of the twentieth century. The 'local' stimulus to the most recent shift in Britain has been the sustained investment in the infrastructure of football stadiums in England, Wales and (to a lesser extent) Scotland since the publication of the Taylor Report (1990) into the Hillsborough Stadium disaster in 1989, which recommended, amongst other things, the move towards all-seat football stadiums.[11] One of the first fruits of this tragic stimulus was the Alfred McAlpine (now Galpharm) Stadium built in Huddersfield, designed by Rod Sheard, which became the first sports venue to win a Royal Institute of British Architects 'building of the year' award in 1995. As we have seen, following the merger of Sheard's Lobb Partnership and HOK in 1999, Sheard and HOK Sport (and now known as Populous™) have become even more prominent in promoting sports architecture.

Belanger (2009) identifies several contradictory and contested features of the urban sport spectacle that architects can become enmeshed in as they produce (trans)national sport spaces. First, the paradox of distinctiveness is that if everywhere has iconic architecture then there is a global sameness to the pursuit of distinction. This can lead to the creation of unspectacular spectacles, or the predictable monotony of the spectacular in commodified space, as geographer David Harvey once argued was the case with respect to postmodernist architecture (see Merrifield 2002: especially 144–155).

Second, there are various urban narratives, imaginaries and themes that can create a division, in architectural as well as other terms, between the spectacular global and the vernacular local. This in turn can lead to spectacular local resistance to and/or negotiation with the global spectacle through novel uses and vernacular appropriation of the built environment (Stevens 2007). With Brazil hosting the two biggest sports events in the world – the 2014 FIFA football World Cup and the 2016 Summer Olympic and Paralympic Games in Rio de Janeiro – it is likely that various struggles will develop over urban projects planned to transform stadiums, roads and neighbourhoods close to key sports facilities and sites.

Third, the production of consumption spaces, such as the 'new made to look old' nostalgic baseball parks in the US (such as Camden Yards in Baltimore or PNC Park in Pittsburgh), uses

Figure 10.5
Diga Não: 'Say no to removals' reads this sign used by residents of Vila Autódromo in Rio de Janeiro in their campaign to prevent eviction from their homes adjacent to one of the sites to be developed for the 2016 Summer Olympic Games.

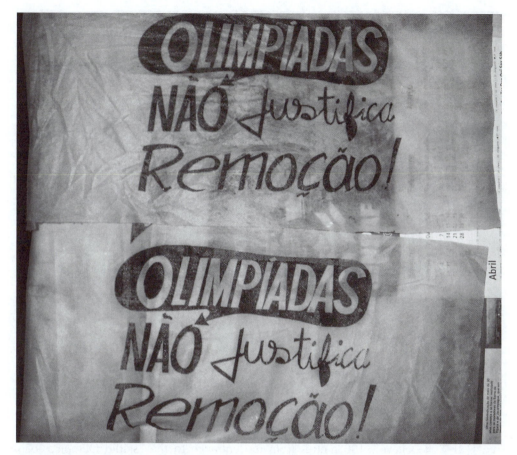

Figure 10.6 Não justifica. 'The Olympics do not justify evictions': another sign used by residents of Vila Autódromo in Rio de Janeiro in their campaign to prevent eviction from their homes.

collective memory to reformulate a new consumerised public sphere. Yet, as spaces, sports stadiums are both public and private – both popular and disciplining, intimate as well as commercial. They are shaped by public meanings and form the basis of popular memories, at times of disaster, becoming the forum for cultures of commemoration (Russell 2006). Hence Belanger alerts us to the ever present gap between capital's intentions and the use-values of spectacular urban sport spaces.[12] The local population are asked to believe in the promises of urban development associated with hosting sports mega-events such as the Olympic Games.

THE SPATIAL AND POLITICAL IMPACT OF SPORTS ARCHITECTURE AND ARCHITECTS

Individuals, companies, practices and consortia are required to produce sports mega-events and their material infrastructure. Yet in building and designing for sport, firms such as

Figure 10.7 'I believe': 100 metres from the entrance to the Estádio Olímpico João Havelange, also known by its nickname Engenhão (or big sugar mill), the multi-sport use (hence Olympic) stadium located in the Engenho de Dentro neighbourhood in Rio de Janeiro, graffiti artists offer reflections on hosting the Pan-American Games in 2007 and their aspirations looking forward to the 2016 Olympic Games.

Populous™ have come to dominate international stadium design by 'turning out an inter-changeable series of huge spectator machines that can process crowds quickly and efficiently yet entirely lack personality or charisma', according to Sudjic (2005: 117). As some starchitects have taken on an increased role in planning and building in cities in the Asia-Pacific, as well as the rest of the developed world, their global influence can be seen in stadium architecture as much as in any other form of iconic architecture. That the design of the built environment has been increasingly 'engulfed in and made subservient to the goals of the capitalist economy' in the past 30 years is almost a truism (Saunders 2005: vii).

Nonetheless, whilst architects are caught in the dilemmas of involvement in the market, some seek to imbue their designs with greater public access (Bauman Lyons Architects 2008; McNeill 2009). According to architect Irena Bauman, 'Architects need to become sociologists as well as researchers' (Wainwright 2008: 2). Jones (2006: 550) suggests that architecture may have

196

become an increasingly significant expression of diverse collective identities in recent years. Whilst landmark buildings were once a central way of 'expressing and developing the national code', Jones notes that they are now increasingly sites of symbolic conflict and competition over identities. In what he considers could be a post-national context, architecture can provide a cultural space for new identities to be expressed and contested. The role of architects as cultural intermediaries in all this is to make their buildings meaningful to non-architects. The 'architect's role in translating and disseminating meanings is key' (Jones 2006: 556). They do this by reflexively situating their buildings in terms of identity projects.

We might ask: How can architects align their buildings with various identity discourses? There are three ways in which architects can engage with their designs' meanings – interpreting the buildings they design, conveying the meaning of the buildings, and linking the buildings to identities – collective and personal. First, architects have become more active in disseminating their interpretations of their buildings (Jones 2006: 551–553). They appear more on television, give more lectures, write more books and letters to newspapers, and generally have a higher media profile. Rod Sheard's recent output is one good example of this. In his books, contributions to collections, and articles discussing his work he has even developed a theory of the development of stadiums – 'the five generations of stadiums' theory (Sheard 2005: 100ff., 2001a, 2001b; Culf 2005; Inglis 2000). This firmly places the contemporary stadium at the centre of urban regeneration projects – with the potential for inspiring urban change through the building of iconic sports architecture.

A second way architects communicate the meaning of their work is to create symbolic narrative associations between their work and positive or warm political concepts – such as 'democracy', 'transparency' and 'openness' (for example, this was especially evident in the relationship between architects EMBT headed by Enric Miralles and the design of the new Scottish Parliament building). With respect to stadium architecture, the guided tour of the new Wembley Stadium building given by Lord (Norman) Foster which was broadcast during the FA Cup Final Preview on 19 May 2007 on BBC TV was another example of this. Throughout, Foster referred to the stadium as 'intimate', praised the 'closeness' of the 'fantastic views' (even from the 'cheap seats') and emphasised how much more the new stadium resembled 'a spa', 'a luxury hotel' or 'a cultural building like an opera house or a hotel' than a football stadium. The arch, on the other hand, was 'one of those inspirational things'.

The third way architects make their buildings mean something is to avoid privileging one collective identity over another – focusing instead upon concepts such as 'multiculturalism', 'diversity' and 'accessibility'. In this way the architects create links between buildings and collective identities, even though some are very exclusive and privileged identities. Meanings can change, and values linked to buildings can be detached. Architecture reflects tensions in global and local identity. So how buildings are coupled to collective identities is best understood as a process over time, involving a 'complex web of highly charged discourses about identities' (Jones 2006: 562). Since meanings are not self-evident they have to be identified, translated, interpreted and communicated.

Some architects can also be producers of alternative, protest, hybrid and more locally relevant meanings and identities. Ai Wei Wei, consultant designer on the Beijing Bird's Nest project with Herzog & de Meuron, referred to it as a 'public relations sham' and the 2008 Olympics as 'a pretend smile' (Glancey 2008a). Shortly before the event in August 2008 he clarified his

197

position towards the stadium. 'I don't criticize the stadium. I criticize the government's use of the Olympics for propaganda. I am disappointed that the system is not able to turn this historical event into political reform' (Watts 2008).

In sum, the role of architects in contemporary culture is to act as conveyors of meaningful discourses about the buildings and the cultural spaces they produce. The same can be said for the designers and architects of sports facilities and stadiums. Through sustaining and perpetuating the global sports mega-event cycle they contribute to and form part of the culture of consumption. Yet, whilst for some consumption has been seen as a means of overcoming many urban problems, investment in the cultural economy 'cannot single-handedly save the city' (Miles and Miles 2004: 2). As Miles and Miles suggest, 'consumption divides as much as it provides'. Likewise, among writers on the commodification of architecture, it remains a central debate whether it is indeed possible 'for designers to resist, escape or offer substantial alternatives to the dominant commercial culture' (Saunders 2005: viii).

Both critics and boosters of spectacular sports mega-events now conduct research into the organisation and networks surrounding them and their impacts, legacies and outcomes (see, for example, Cashman (2006) for a critical yet generally enthusiastic discussion of the IOC-funded Olympic Games Global Impact project). Research by academics and investigative journalists has also looked at the workings of international sports organisations and international sports federations in examining the background to sports mega-events (e.g. Chappelet and Kubler-Mabbott 2008; Sugden and Tomlinson 1998; Jennings 2006, 1996). In addition to the IOC and FIFA, media corporations, transnational sponsors, politicians, members of bid teams and national sport organisations have been considered as constituent parts of the networks of power and influence that produce, mediate and transact sports mega-events. Yet as well as their political, economic, cultural and symbolic impacts – through showing off places as global – sports mega-events as spectacles have a spatial impact, in particular upon the built environment, which is generally urban, modernist and consumerist.

There is nothing new about commercial relations and sports and sport mega-events, or about explicit relationships between sport and politics. What has happened is that the way in which sport and sports events are related to both economic and political processes has changed. Sport and sports mega-events, especially the Olympics since the 1980s, have become more commercial and implicated in market relationships. Sport and sports mega-events are experiential commodities and have many attractions for both corporate and governmental agencies seeking a presence in the globalised world. Sports mega-events are also part of the promotional culture of contemporary capitalism. Hence an increased supply of spectacle creates opportunities to attract inward investment and generate consumption spending.

Architecture – especially via airport terminal buildings, tall towers and domes – has become one of the major means of acquiring an identity for cities and urban spaces in an age of uncertainty and the 'institutionalised precariousness' that currently pervades all countries (Horne 2006: 13). Architecture 'has long been a means used by small countries to project their presence on a world stage' (Sudjic 2005: 154). It is not only small countries that use architecture to signal their existence. As a result of this and the associated growth and spread of the culture-ideology of consumerism (Sklair 2005: 498), architecture and architects increasingly have a higher public profile. Globalisation works through agency and it is the agency of the consumerist fraction of the TCC in architecture that has promoted the role of architects.

198

The basic message of this chapter has been that the relationship between sports mega-events and the urban infrastructure may be 'obvious' but it needs examining. Buildings are part of the legacy of sport and sports mega-events – both negative and positive. Architects act as interpreters of the transnational sport spaces they help to design and in so doing they may sustain the work of the TCC and the maintenance of the culture-ideology of consumerism or, on some occasions, challenge it. As Hannigan (1998) suggests, seeing the city as a centre of consumption is not new, but the way we are currently encouraged to consume is. The dreams created through forms of urban development associated with sports mega-events tend not to be those of local, average or low-waged residents, but those of the wealthy, the mobile and transnational corporations (Rutheiser 1996). Just as late modern baseball stadiums (ballparks) in the USA have become colonised by consumer culture (Ritzer and Stillman 2001) so too are the other stadiums and spaces being built for sports mega-events increasingly often seen as places with a 'sports theme'. It is in these contested spaces that architects play their part and also might face challenges. Whether architects simply impose the will of the marketised world of sport on consumer culture through their designs – and hence for example perpetuate the divisions within sport between the 'haves' and the 'have nots' – or whether they provide opportunities to challenge such divisions in socially meaningful ways will be the subject of future investigations.

The Summer Olympic Games are a mega-event with the 'ability to create, reinforce and consolidate global city status' (Short 2004: 108). Yet, as Broudehoux suggests about urban entrepreneurialism:

> The ready-made identities assigned by city boosters and disseminated through the mass media often reduce several different visions of local culture into a single vision that reflects the aspirations of a powerful elite and the values, lifestyles, and expectations of potential investors and tourists. These practices are thus highly elitist and exclusionary, and often signify to more disadvantaged segments of the population that they have no place in this revitalised and gentrified urban spectacle.
>
> (Broudehoux 2004: 26)

The conflicts, resistances and negotiations involved in, in this case, the East Asian experience of hosting sports mega-events can be found amongst the debates about architecture elsewhere. This suggests that two issues worthy of future research in the sociology of sport architecture are, first, 'whether and to what extent it is possible for designers to resist, escape, or offer substantial alternatives to the dominant commercial culture' (Saunders 2005: viii) and second, the power relations involved in local and global forces that collide in the production of sport stadiums. As Short (2004) remarks, winners and losers can be identified. Winners include: political regimes seeking to redevelop a city's image; subtle place-specific discourses; and real estate and building companies. The losers are the marginal and weaker social groups – those living in poorer inner-city sites who often face relocation without adequate (or any) compensation. Crilley (1993: 249) has argued that the architecture of redevelopment can perform 'an effective screening role conducive to geographical and social myopia'.

CONCLUSION

OLYMPIC FUTURES?

This conclusion consolidates and reviews some key arguments, identifies current trends, and poses some questions. We have already alluded, in Chapter 4, to that fateful period in the last quarter of the nineteenth century when chain stores, branded goods, the modern mass media, elite sport and the first globalising organisations came to occupy centre stage in the development of popular culture. The world has, of course, changed dramatically since that period, and yet has been profoundly marked by it. The Olympic Games represent a peculiarly contradictory social institution, in which a club for European aristocracy is the owner, steward and in effect sole beneficiary of a billion-dollar enterprise. For such an institution to have survived, a constant process of careful and cautious adaptation to change has been required. Unlike many other social institutions, it has not thus far been damaged by schisms nor challenged by rivals. However, few social institutions can maintain this process indefinitely, and despite its great economic power, the Olympic movement faces some challenging times, managing risk, climate change, changing balances between world powers, and changing cultural attitudes to success, celebrity and performance.

We want to conclude by reviewing some of the themes of the book in terms of four 'Cs' – capitalism, connections, citizenship and contradictions – and consider their significance for understanding sports mega-events such as the Olympic Games. The developments relating to the staging of sports mega-events in the past 30 or so years, alongside the pursuit of enhanced or even 'world class' status by politicians and businesses, outlined in this book, raise questions about the social distribution of the supposed benefits of urban development initiatives. Which social groups actually benefit, which are excluded, and what scope there is for contestation of these developments are three important questions that are often ignored (Lowes 2002). In the build-up to bidding for mega-events, Gruneau (2002: ix–x) argues that local politicians and media often focus on the interests and enthusiasms of the developers, property owners and middle-class consumers as 'synonymous with the well-being of the city'. As a result, sectional interests are treated as *the* general interest, and ongoing 'class and community divisions regarding the support and enjoyment of spectacular urban entertainments' are downplayed, if not ignored altogether (Gruneau 2002: ix–x).

This downplaying is what we can call, after Slavoj Žižek's retort to the former US Defense Secretary Donald Rumsfeld, one of the 'known unknowns' of sports mega-events (Horne 2007). Rumsfeld, engaging in speculation about the situation in Iraq in March 2003, had stated:

> There are known knowns; there are things we know we know. We also know there are known unknowns; that is to say we know there are some things we do not know. But there are also unknown unknowns – the ones we don't know we don't know.

Žižek (2005) felt that Rumsfeld had forgotten to add a crucial fourth term, '"unknown knowns", things we don't know that we know'. We agree with Zizek and consider that it is an academic's duty to look critically and self-critically at the assumptions, beliefs and sometimes obscene practices undertaken by those involved with sports mega-events that are often suppressed or, perhaps more accurately, repressed – the 'unknown knowns'.

When it comes to sports mega-events, politicians, senior administrators of sport, corporate leaders and even some academic researchers encourage the pretence that we do not know about many of the most significant things that actually form the background to them. This is the case because, just as with other aspects of urban planning, sports mega-events are highly political affairs, surrounded by sports, urban and corporate interests. Even the language used is highly nuanced – as Hiller (2003) amongst others has pointed out, the aftermath or repercussions of sports mega-events are often discussed now in terms of their 'legacies', rather than their 'impacts'. Yet legacy is a warm word, sounding positive, whereas if we consider the word 'outcomes' it is a more neutral word, permitting the discovery of both negative and positive outcomes. Whilst outcomes can be tangible and material or intangible and symbolic – and economists and urban planners have tended to focus their research attention on the former (Gratton et al. 2006), whereas sociologists, political scientists and social geographers have often been more interested in the intangible, symbolic and representational outcomes (Manzenreiter 2006; McNeill 2004) – the relationship of sports mega-events to developments in contemporary capitalism is evident.

Contemporary capitalist development has been underpinned by 'the shock doctrine', according to journalist Naomi Klein (2007). She argues that the use of shock – or violence – is a technique or tool in order to impose an ideology – what she calls the free market fundamentalist ideas underpinning neoliberal economic thought and policy. The shock doctrine is also a philosophy of how political change can happen and be brought about. Charting the rise of free market fundamentalism over the past 35 years reveals that when ideas are unpopular advocates of free market neoliberalism have exploited shocks to help push through their policies without popular democratic consent. The product is what Klein calls 'disaster capitalism' – a form of capitalism that uses large-scale disasters in order to push through radical neoliberal capitalist policies and the related privatisation agenda for (formerly) public services. In addition, disaster capitalism also creates disasters, and responses to them, in what Klein refers to as its 'postmodern' form (Klein 2007).

Klein in her investigation explores the roots of disaster capitalism back to General Pinochet's military coup on 11 September 1973 and monetarist economist Milton Friedman's prescriptions for Chile afterwards. In addition to the use of torture, and the imprisonment and murder of dissenters in Latin America, Klein views Thatcher's Falklands/Malvinas War in the 1980s as an equivalent shock that enabled privatisation to be implemented in the UK. More recently, environmental disasters, terrorist attacks (such as the other 11 September, in 2001 when the World Trade Center in Manhattan was destroyed) and economic crises have been used to bring about free market reforms. Hence another of Klein's arguments is that the

202

equation of the free market with democracy and freedom is misplaced – privatisation and the spread of capitalist market relations more generally have often been accompanied by violence, terror and crises. The idea that capitalism advances on the back of disasters or violent circumstances is not a new one. Marx (1976 [1867]) wrote at length in *Capital* about the extra-economic coercion required to bring about primitive accumulation in the eighteenth century in Western Europe, for example. But Klein's book is a valuable insight into recent history.

What relationship does sport – and specifically sports mega-events – have with disaster capitalism? Within the 35-year period that Klein refers to, sports mega-events have become more prominent, as we have seen. Since the 1980s Anderson (2007) writes that America's 'two great protagonists of the Cold War period, China and Russia' have been 'integrated into the festivities of the global spectacle'. One can cite the St Petersburg summit, the Beijing Olympics of 2008, the Sochi Winter Olympics of 2014, and we can now add Russia, selected as host of the 2018 World Cup, to this list. So we suggest that these sporting spectaculars can be viewed as the twin of disaster capitalism's shock therapy, involving their own shocks and generating their own forms of awe. Winning a bid to host a mega-event, putting the fantasy financial figures of the bid document into operation, dealing with the proposed location before and dealing with it after the event has taken place, are just some of the moments when shock and awe are generated by sports mega-events. The city of Rio de Janeiro offers an interesting study on the extent to which an Olympic Games and a World Cup will impact, positively and negatively, on the ecology of a city with massive poverty, crime and drug use.

Appadurai (1996) recognised that there are economic, technological, financial, ethnic and image mobilities that help construct the contemporary globalising social 'scape'. Sport can be seen as both a metric and a motor of this globalisation process (Giulianotti and Robertson 2007). Sport – in its professional, commercial and consumer-oriented forms – is inevitably part of the expansion of capitalist social relations on a global basis. Sport has become increasingly commodified. Sport reflects this in many ways, including in terms of the unequal distribution of involvement and participation and the growth of the global sports market. Sports mega-events have perhaps their greatest contemporary allure as an element in these globalising processes. For athletes, sports fans and many citizens, the appeal of hosting a 'once in a lifetime' experience on home soil is palpable. The ability to make connections with global flows, possibly as a new hub in the networks of financial, media or tourist flows, is a primary motivation for city, regional and national governments' involvement in the competitions to host sports mega-events. Sports mega-events both have promotional leverage and enable (transnational and national) corporations to leverage business opportunities out of them. But in so doing the risky nature of sports mega-events also comes into focus.

Along with Rick Gruneau, previously mentioned, many other writers including Whitson and Horne (2006) have raised concerns about the distribution of the benefits and the costs of sports mega-events. As Michael Hall (2005) points out, the selling of a city in order to host a sports mega-event or develop it in ways to attract inward investment can lead to some local citizens being sold short. Modern Western cities are based in large part on activities of 'repair and maintenance', according to Nigel Thrift (2005). Citizens there are 'surrounded by the hum of continuous repair and maintenance'. Cities in the Global South may be in a continuous state of emergency; they operate repair and maintenance on the basis of social networks, based on kin and friendships (Thrift 2005: 135–138). A key feature of repair and maintenance is the idea of 'regeneration', and this takes material and representational forms, just like legacies or outcomes promised from mega-events. The promotional values of sports mega-events for cities in the Global North, and some in the South, relates to the search for international esteem and 'world class' ranking, via image generation and both external and internal promotion. For example, the use of the phrase 'Expect EMotions' as the slogan for UEFA EURO 2008™ reminds us that, 'the systematic engineering of affect has become central to the political life of Euro-American cities' (Thrift 2004). Cleverly, the word 'EMotions' also enabled the co-organisers of Euro 2008 to allude to the abbreviation of the competition (EM, short for Europameisterschaft 2008), fully understood by their German-speaking populations. As Bennett (1991) with respect to Australian cities and more recently Whitson (2004) with respect to Canada have suggested, staging sports mega-events is as much about engineering the emotions of the local populations as welcoming foreign visitors. We speculated at the conclusion of Chapter 1 (and will soon know, of course) to what extent the 2012 Games might contribute to the engineering of a post-recession feel-good factor in the UK.

Mega-events are short-life events with longer-life pre- and post-event social dimensions, not least because of their scale, their occupation and maintenance of a time cycle and their impacts (whether conceived of as positive or negative). As sports mega-events have become global media events they have assumed a greater public profile than world's fairs and expos (even though world's fairs do attract large numbers of visitors, they have far less media presence). Following improvements in global mediation, corporations use sports mega-events to leverage business opportunities more than ever before, and this neatly sums up one of the major concerns about them. To add to these we might mention the following four significant contradictions: the potential for patriotic promotional discourse to sow the seeds for heightened xenophobia, the imbalance between local democratic control and autocratic (international) sports and other organisational demands, the growing imbalance between dependency on global media rights on the part of organisers and internet streaming of content, and the way that the biggest multi-sport mega-event (the Olympic Games) relies upon the veneer of its anti-commercial ideology (no arena advertising) as one of its major commercial assets. In addition to the overestimation of their benefits and underestimation of their costs, the related uneven internal development, as the host location benefits from the 'lightning rod' effect of the mega-event on public infrastructural spending decisions, makes the hosting of sports mega-events one of the most fundamentally political acts of the current age.

We hope that this book has enabled interested readers, researchers and students to develop an understanding of the Olympic Games that goes beyond keeping the score and noting the records, and to appreciate how sport is thus now fully interconnected economically, ideologically and politically into society through one of its mega-events.

NOTES

1 LONDON, THE OLYMPICS AND THE ROAD TO 2012

1 *London Marathon History*, www.virginlondonmarathon.com (accessed 29 September 2009).
2 Tony Travers: GLC Leaders, 1965 to 1986, http://www.lse.ac.uk/collections/london DevelopmentWorkshops/lselondondevelopmentworkshops2/glctothegla/glc_leaders_1965-1986.pdf (accessed 29 September 2009).
3 *London Marathon History*, www.virginlondonmarathon.com (accessed 29 September 2009).
4 These presentations were observed by Whannel, who was in the hall during the IOC Session, working for a television company on a documentary about the Games.
5 Renaissance that never was: Birmingham's new leader snubs prestige building projects, Nick Cohen, *The Independent*, 10 October 1993, http://www.independent.co.uk/news/uk/renaissance-that-never-was-birminghams-new-leader-snubs-prestige-building-projects-1509856.html (accessed 30 June 2010).
6 Whannel recalls him, during an International Olympic Academy event in Olympia, in 1992, briefly commandeering a small electric vehicle, which was retailing fruit and vegetables, to broadcast through its tannoy speaker the strident clarion call 'Vote for Manchester !'
7 Gavin Poynter, 'The economics of the Olympics bid', *Rising East Online,* No. 1, January 2005.
8 It must be acknowledged, however, that the Channel Tunnel line was only completed 15 years after the tunnel was opened, whereas the French high-speed link, ready when the tunnel opened, was only one part of a whole network of modern high-speed rail routes built for the ultra-fast TGV (Train Grande-Vitesse). Stratford International station was conceived, planned and built as an international station, with passport control and customs, at which some Eurostar trains would stop. However, in 2010 it became clear that Eurostar would not be even contemplating opening this station until all building work was complete. There may well be questions about the economic case for a separate international station only a few minutes from the St Pancras terminal.
9 As a result of the Local Government Act of 1985.
10 Government of London, House of Commons Debate 5 June 1991 vol. 192 cc285-338 http://hansard.millbanksystems.com/commons/1991/jun/05/government-of-london (accessed 29 September 2009).

11 As a result of the Greater London Authority Act 1999.

12 http://www.olympics.org.uk

13 http://www.olympics.org.uk

14 Westminster Media Forum Projects (2006) *Westminster Media Forum Keynote Seminar Media Countdown to the Games*, Bagshot: Westminster Media Forum Projects.

15 Press release from London Mayor's office, http://www.london.gov.uk/view_press_release.jsp?releaseid=10029.

16 Olympics win proves golden for Carillion, *Construction Plus*, 26 August 2008, htttp://www.cnplus.co.uk/insideknowledge/2008/08/olympics_win_proves_golden_for_carillion.html

17 *Building*, 5 September 2008, Sarah Richardson, http://www.building.co.uk/story.asp?sectioncode=659&storycode=3121522&c=1

2 THE IOC AND THE BIDDING PROCESS

1 http://www.olympic.org/en/content/The-IOC/The-IOC-Institution1/IOC-Members-list/ (accessed 22 September 2010).

2 http://www.olympic.org/Documents/Olympic%20Charter/Charter_en_2010.pdf (accessed 9 December 2010).

3 http://ioa.org.gr/en/ioa-information/history (accessed 18 October 2010).

4 http://multimedia.olympic.org/pdf/en_report_696.pdf (accessed 18 October 2010).

5 See: LA84 Foundation for all reports: www.la84foundation.org/5va/reports_frmst.htm.

3 TELEVISION AND THE COMMERCIALISATION OF THE OLYMPICS

1 This estimate is derived from television schedule analysis conducted in 1979–80, 1989–90 and 1999–2000. A similar analysis is currently being conducted for 2009–10. On preliminary calculations, based on our current research on terrestrial television sport, between January and May 2010, football, motor sport, snooker and horse racing accounted for 48% of all sport programmes on British television, whilst athletics, swimming, cycling and gymnastics accounted for 5% of all sport programmes.

2 ONS 2002 Sport and Leisure: Results from the sport and leisure module of the 2002 General Household Survey.

3 *Official Olympic Games Report* 1932 Los Angeles, pp. 186–222. Also see Shen Yalin (2007) 'The Development of the Olympic Press Centre', unpublished MA dissertation, University of Luton (now Bedfordshire). Shen Yalin's work on the historical development of the press centre was a valuable resource for this account of Olympic press and radio.

4 *Official Olympic Games Report* 1936 Berlin, Vol. I, pp. 301–350.

5 *Official Olympic Games Report* 1948 London, pp. 114–120.

6 Source: http://www.terramedia.co.uk/media/change/olympic_Games_1956.htm Terramedia (*The Olympic Media dossier*).

7 http://www.terramedia.co.uk/media/change/olympic_Games_1956.htm Terramedia (*The Olympic Media dossier*). The audiences were small, but the enormous effort put into covering the Games gave great impetus to the technological development of television.

8 http://www.museum.tv/eotvsection.php?entrycode=olympicsand (accessed 30 November 2009).
9 *Official Olympic Games Report* 1988 Seoul, Vol. I, pp. 689–706.
10 *Official Olympic Games Report* 1964 Tokyo, Vol. I, pp. 372–374, quoted in Yalin 2007.
11 *Official Olympic Games Report* 1976 Montreal, p. 175, quoted in Yalin 2007.
12 IOC website (http://www.olympic.org/)
13 http://www.museum.tv/eotvsection.php?entrycode=olympicsand (accessed 30 November 2009).
14 Olympic Broadcasting Services www.obs.es (accessed 14 September 2009).
15 IOC marketing fact file.
16 *Official Olympic Games Report* 1996 Atlanta, Vol. I, p. 106, and see Yalin 2007.
17 For studies of the power of US TV, see Spence 1988, Wilson 1988, McPhail and Jackson 1989, O'Neil 1989, Real 1989; and for studies of sport and the media, see Moragas *et al.* 1996a and Rowe 1996, 1999.
18 See Tomlinson 1996, 1999, Hall and Hodges 1997, Wilson and Sinclair 2000 and Roche 2000.
19 23/8/08 http://sportsbiznews.blogspot.com/2008/08/2008-beijing-summer-olympics-credit.html (accessed 30 November 2009).
20 Interview with Roger Mosey, BBC Olympics Director, in *Convergence: the International Journal for Research on New Media Technologies*, Autumn 2010.
21 Interview with Roger Mosey, BBC Olympics Director, in *Convergence: the International Journal for Research on New Media Technologies*, Autumn 2010.
22 Conversation with ISL executive, 1986.
23 Ewing 2006: 13, quoting the London Host City Contract 2012.
24 Malcolm Davies, Partner, Berry Davies LLP, 'Intellectual Property and the London 2012 Olympic Games: What businesses need to know', http://www.ipo.gov.uk/news/news letters/ipinsight/ipinsight-200911/ipinsight-200911-4.htm (accessed 10 July 2010).
25 London Olympic Games and Paralympic Games (Protection) Act 2006. Can be found at http://www.opsi.gov.uk/acts/acts2006/ukpga_20060012_en_1
26 Malcolm Davies, Partner, Berry Davies LLP, 'Intellectual property and the London 2012 Olympic Games: what businesses need to know', http://www.ipo.gov.uk/news/news letters/ipinsight/ipinsight-200911/ipinsight-200911-4.htm (accessed 10 July 2010).

4 REVIVING THE OLYMPICS

1 Bill Mallon, *Track and Field News*, http://mb.trackandfieldnews.com/discussion/view topic.php?p=412657 (accessed 9 July 2010).
2 http://industrielles-gartenreich.com/english/03_projekte/311_drehberg.htm (accessed 10 July 2010).
3 The Olympics of 1777, http://www.garyschwartzarthistorian.nl/schwartzlist/?id=65 (accessed 10 July 2010). See also http://www.gartenreich.com
4 See http://www.shd.org.rs/ESSEE4/AboutPalic.html
5 Cirque Olympique http://www.hberlioz.com/Paris/BPOlympique.html (accessed 30 June 2010); http://www.circopedia.org/index.php/Cirque_d'Hiver (accessed 30 June 2010).
6 Franconi's Hippodrome: New York's Roman Coliseum (http://thevirtualdimemuseum.

blogspot.com/2010/01/franconis-hippodrome-new-yorks-roman.html accessed 30 June 2010).

7 http://www.mccord-museum.qc.ca/scripts/explore.php?Lang=1andtableid=11andtable name=themeandelementid=26__trueandcontentlong (accessed 9 July 2010). By Karine Rousseau, http://www.thecanadianencyclopedia.com/index.cfm?PgNm=TCEandParams =A1ARTA0008078 (accessed 9 July 2010).

8 http://www.liverpooldailypost.co.uk/liverpool-life-features/liverpool-special-features/ 2008/08/08/how-we-lit-the-olympic-flame-64375-21490142/(accessed 30 June 2010).

9 According to Ray Physick (2007) *Played in Liverpool: Charting the Heritage of a City at Play*, London: English Heritage.

10 http://www.liverpooldailypost.co.uk/liverpool-life-features/liverpool-special-features/ 2008/08/08/how-we-lit-the-olympic-flame-64375-21490142/ (accessed 30 June 2010).

11 Peter McCusker, 'Bring back the Morpeth Olympics', 11 April 2008, *The Journal* http://www. nebusiness.co.uk/business-news/latest-business-news/journal-business-news/2008/ 04/11/bring-back-the-morpeth-olympics-51140-20749347/ (accessed 10 July 2010).

12 *Morpeth Herald,* 10 July 2010, http://www.morpethherald.co.uk/CustomPages/Custom Page.aspx?PageID=40295 (accessed 10 July 2010). See J. Thielgen, 'Genesis and history of the Morpeth Olympic Games' (Germany) and J. Ruhl, 'History and development of the Morpeth Olympic Games', 1999 conference proceedings, for more information.

13 John MacAloon, in a preface to a new edition of *This Great Symbol* (2006), acknowledges that Dietrich Quanz demonstrates close ties between the Olympic movement and the international peace movement. He agrees with Quanz's speculation that the organisational design of the new IOC owed something to the International Peace Bureau. MacAloon (2006: 334) comments that

> At a time of worry that the new IOC regime in Lausanne is turning away from formal relations with peace organizations and with universities under the pressure of or in preference to its sports business responsibilities, it is important to be reminded of how inseparable educational sport, international understanding and peace activism were at the outset for the modern Olympic Games.

14 Confusingly, in England the term 'public school' literally means a fee-paying school. In practice the term is reserved for the elite schools that flourished during the nineteenth century as the means of educating the sons of the social elite. They were 'public' in contrast to the earlier aristocratic tradition of educating children at home. The public schools were originally largely aristocratic, but, following the reforms of the 1840s, became increasingly popular with the new Victorian bourgeoisie. Other fee-paying schools of lesser status are generally referred to as private schools. The schools that in other societies would be known as 'public' schools are called in the UK 'state schools'. Free state education began to develop in the 1870s following the 1870 Education Act. Throughout the twentieth century the dominant proportion of the political class in the UK were educated at public schools. After a more egalitarian shift with the Prime Ministers Heath, Callaghan, Thatcher and Major all products of state schools, the UK appears to have reverted to tradition with Tony Blair and the current Prime Minister David Cameron both former public schoolboys.

15 See Coubertin (1890) for an account of his trip to the USA and American education. In the light of his passionate advocacy of the British system, this perspective cannot be taken

208

as neutral, balanced or dispassionate. See also Coubertin (1917) which contains material on English education, Arnold and sport.

16 http://www.wenlock-olympian-society.org.uk/william-penny-brookes/wpb-book.shtml (accessed 12 August 2010).

17 For more on this, see Katharine Moore (1989) 'The warmth of comradeship: The first British Empire Games and imperial solidarity', in *International Journal of the History of Sport*, Vol. 6 No. 2: 242–251; Katharine Moore (1991) 'A neglected imperialist: the promotion of the British Empire in the writing of John Astley Cooper', in *International Journal of the History of Sport*, Vol. 8 No. 2: 256–269; Katharine Moore (1986) 'Sport, politics andimperialism: British Empire Games, 1881–1930', in *Proceedings of the Fourth Annual Conference*, London: British Society of Sports Historians; Katharine Moore (1987) 'The Pan-Britannic festival: a tangible but forlorn expression of imperialism', in J. A. Mangan (ed.) *Pleasure Profit Proselytism*, London: Frank Cass (pp. 144–162).

5 FROM WORLD'S FAIRS TO MEGA-EVENTS

1 http://www.olympics.org.uk/contentpage.aspx?page=410 (accessed 17 November 2010).

2 Abandoned Lines and Railways, n/d http://www.urban75.org/railway/wood-lane-station.html (accessed 18 August 2010).

3 Exploring Twentieth Century London, Museum of London, http://www.twentiethcentury london.org.uk/server.php?show=conObject.5720 (accessed 18 August 2010).

4 Japanese Embassy, 2010, http://www.uk.emb-japan.go.jp/en/event/webmagazine/1910_ exhibition.html (accessed 18 August 2010).

5 Exploring Twentieth Century London, Museum of London, http://www.twentiethcentury london.org.uk/server.php?show=conObject.5718) (accessed 18 August 2010).

6 L. H. Officer (2010) 'Five ways to compute the relative value of a UK pound amount, 1830 to present', *Measuring Worth*, http://www.measuringworth.com/ukcompare/ (accessed 18 August 2010).

7 Exploring Twentieth Century London, Museum of London, http://www.twentiethcentury london.org.uk/server.php?show=conInformationRecord.262 (accessed 18 August 2010).

8 Leicestershire County Council, 2008, http://prints.leics.gov.uk/pictures_672460/Rushton-excavator-at-work-near-Wembley-Park-steel-tower.html (accessed 18 August 2010).

9 http://www.engineering-timelines.com (accessed 18 June 2008).

10 Hurst Peirce + Malcolm, n/d, http://hurstpm.net/page_33 (accessed 18 August 2010).

6 THE INTERNATIONALIST SPIRIT AND NATIONAL CONTESTATION

1 Avery Brundage was President of the United States Olympic Committee, Vice-President of the IAAF, and a future President of the IOC.

2 Sigfrid Edstrom was President of the IAAF, and Vice-President and a future President of the IOC.

3 Baillet-Latour was IOC President from 1925 to 1942.

4 See Guttmann 1984: 72–73. Brundage, like other right-wing Americans of the period, came to blame many of the problems of the world on Jews and communists who were,

in some ill-defined way, in league. He was an active isolationist during the early 1940s, associating with aviator Charles Lindbergh, who was suspected of pro-Nazi views. After the war he corresponded with Swedish IOC member Count von Rosen, one of whose letters to Brundage proclaimed that Jews were responsible for all the world's troubles, and that communism was the political form of Judaism (see Guttmann 1984: 92).

5 BBC Sound Archives, Berlin Olympics Live broadcast of the Opening Ceremony.
6 See Riordan in Tomlinson and Whannel 1984.
7 See, for example, the *LA Times* 30 September 1986).
8 http://www.meor1996.org/ (accessed 10 July 2010).

7 POLITICS AND THE OLYMPICS

1 At the same time American athlete Leahseneth ('Lacey') O'Neal coined the less widely used term 'girlcott'. Speaking for black women athletes, she advised that the group would not 'girlcott' the Olympic Games as they were still focused on being recognised, http://www.sports-reference.com/olympics/athletes/on/lacey-oneal-1.html (accessed 19 August 2010).
2 They continue to be counted officially by the IOC as the sixth Olympic Games.
3 See for example this newspaper report from the time: http://www.guardian.co.uk/politics/1948/jul/29/past.comment (accessed 25 October 2010).
4 As with much of this book, the focus of this chapter is on the Summer Olympic Games. The Winter Olympics have not had so many instances of boycotts, although at the 1980 Winter Olympics Taiwan (referring to itself as the Republic of China, ROC) refused to compete under the name of 'Chinese Taipei'. It is the only case of boycotting the Winter Olympic Games. In August 2008, however, the government of Georgia called for a boycott of the 2014 Winter Olympics, set to be held in Sochi, Russia, in response to Russia's participation in the 2008 South Ossetia war. Sochi is within 20 miles of Abkhazia, a disputed territory claimed by Georgia. The IOC responded to concerns about the status of the 2014 Games by stating that it is 'premature to make judgments about how events happening today might sit with an event taking place six years from now'.
5 This did not, however, apply to the Paralympic Games. South Africa made its Paralympic Games début in 1964, and continued to compete until 1976.
6 The following section derives from Coffey 2010, Jacob 2010 and Williamson 2010.
7 In the case of Chicago, protests held in the city just days before the decision resulted in six arrests. Citizens organised No Games, a website to share information and ideas around protesting the Games, where they now celebrate: 'No Games Chicago helped turn back a bad plan for our future.' See http://nogames.wordpress.com/ (accessed 22 November 2010).
8 Coffey 2010. For a slideshow about Vila Autódromo, see http://www.globalpost.com/dispatch/study-abroad/100519/brazil-olympics-rio-favelas (accessed 20 November 2010).
9 On the IOC website 'Olympics in Action' promises 'to build a better world through sport' via six component slogans: http://www.olympic.org/en/content/Olympism-in-Action/Development-through-sport/Development-through-Sport-First-UN-IOC-Forum-shows-way-forward/ (accessed 19 November 2010).
10 Theresa Williamson, Executive Director of Catalytic Communities, a Rio-based not-for-profit organisation working to recognise, share, strengthen and project community

solutions within favelas and elsewhere, suggests that this is an opportunity for Rio to create a best practice in Olympic planning. 'If you just had some creative planning, there's no reason that Vila Autódromo can't be integrated into the fabric of the Olympics', Williamson said. She suggested solutions might include urbanising the community, employing residents in the Olympic venues, and ensuring that infrastructure projects be given a social use to directly benefit the community after the Games (cited in Coffey 2010). Information about other recent related forced evictions in Rio can be found at: http://rioonwatch.org/?tag=forced-evictions (accessed 20 Novembe 2010). Meanwhile the IOC and the United Nations reached an apparent accord about the positive role of sport for social development: http://www.un.org/News/Press/docs/2010/ga11012.doc. htm (accessed 20 November 2010).

11 'Building better global economic BRICs' (Goldman Sachs, Global Economics Paper No. 66, 30 November 2001).

12 For example, much of the funding – and, indeed, the labour – to build cricket stadiums in the Caribbean for the 2007 Cricket World Cup came from abroad. Taiwan put money into Warner Park on St Kitts, the Indian government contributed to building Guyana's Providence Stadium, and money and labour from the People's Republic of China helped build stands and pavilions in Grenada and Jamaica, as well as Antigua's stadium (see Horne 2007b for details).

8 FESTIVAL, SPECTACLE, CARNIVAL AND CONSUMPTION

1 Source: http://www.culturalolympics.org.uk/ (accessed 2 September 2010).
2 A Report on the Surveillance Society (for the Information Commissioner by the Surveillance Studies Network) September 2006, London.
3 *The Times*, assorted stories between October and December 2004; and Multiplex, http://www.multiplex.com.au/page.asp?partid=294andID=170
4 http://www.multiplex.com.au/page.asp?partid=294andID=170
5 http://www.reubenbrothers.com/news_acquistions.html
6 http://news.independent.co.uk/business/news/article423001.ece
7 ODA Media Release 2 March 2007.
8 ODA: Minutes of 23rd Board Meeting, 28 February 2008.
9 ODA: Minutes of 24th Board Meeting, 27 March 2008.
10 ODA: Minutes of 25th Board Meeting, 24 April 2008.
11 ODA Media Release 2 March 2007.
12 TfL Board Meeting 6 February 2008.
13 Keeping the environment at the top of the agenda, in James Morris and Natalie Evans (eds) (2008) *The Million Vote Mandate*, London: Policy Exchange and Localis.

9 LEVEL PLAYING FIELDS

1 http://www.womenssportsfoundation.org/Content/Research-Reports/2008-Olympic-Report.aspx (accessed 27 October 2010).

10 THE OLYMPICS AND URBAN DEVELOPMENT: IMAGINING AND ENGINEERING CITIES AND SPORT SPECTACLES

1 The following six paragraphs draw on Hayes and Horne 2011.
2 Whilst Stevens (1998: 137) estimated that less than 1% of the buildings designed by architects listed in the *Macmillan Encyclopedia of Architects* were for sports, these figures relate to the late 1970s. Preuss (2004: 235–236) in his study of the economics of the Olympics suggests that architectural design 'applies less to sports venues and Olympic villages than to the smaller ticket-selling information stands'. We propose that both authors underestimate the symbolic power and economy of the sports mega-events infrastructure.
3 The architectural connection of Bauman's work is also commented upon by those who know that his daughter Irena is an architect; see Bauman Lyons Architects 2008.
4 Trumpbour 2007 provides an interesting focus on the stadium construction boom that has beset the USA since the late 1990s. As cities in the USA have competed to retain or gain 'major league' or 'world class' status, association with a professional sports franchise is seen as a valuable source of symbolic capital.
5 http://www.hok.com (accessed 9 December 2010).
6 http://www.hoksport.com/ (accessed 29 May 2007).
7 http://www.worldarchitecturenews.com/index.php?fuseaction=wanappln.projectview andupload_id=12441# (accessed 16 December 2009).
8 www.leoadaly.com/markets (accessed 10 December 2008).
9 http://www.cbc.ca/canada/montreal/story/2006/12/19/qc-olympicstadium.html; also see Morin 1998, Whitson and Horne 2006.
10 Robert Booth, guardian.co.uk, 7/12/09 (accessed 8 December 2009).
11 Trumpbour (2007: 57) notes that if the pace of stadium building in the USA continues at the same rate as it commenced the twenty-first century then it will have surpassed the value for the entire twentieth century by 2015. The situation in England is not much different, although the rebuilding began in the 1990s.
12 On the rise of privatised 'cities within cities' in twenty-first-century UK, however, see Minton 2009a, 2009b.

BIBLIOGRAPHY

Allison, L. (ed.) (1986) *The Politics of Sport*, Manchester: Manchester University Press.

Allison, L. (ed.) (1993) *The Changing Politics of Sport*, Manchester: Manchester University Press.

Anderson, B. (1983) *Imagined Communities*, London: Verso.

Anderson, B. (1991) *Imagined Communities: Reflections on the Origin and Spread of Nationalism*, London: Verso.

Anderson, J. (2000) 'Disability sports' in R. Cox, G. Jarvie and W. Vamplew (eds) *Encyclopedia of British Sport*, Oxford: ABC-CLIO (pp. 105–107).

Anderson, P. (2007) 'Jottings on the conjuncture', *New Left Review* 48 (second series) November/December: 5–37.

Andrews, D., Schulz, J. and Silk, M. (2010) 'The Olympics and terrorism' in A. Bairner and G. Molnar (eds) *The Politics of the Olympics*, London: Routledge (pp. 81–92).

Anthony, D. (1986) *Britain and The Olympic Games: Rediscovery of a Heritage*, Birmingham: City of Birmingham.

Anthony, D. (1997) 'Coubertin, Britain and the British: a chronology', *Journal of Olympic History* 5 (3): 18.

Appadurai, A. (1996) *Modernity at Large*, Minneapolis: University of Minnesota Press.

Archer, R. and Bouillon, A. (1982) *The South African Game: Sport and Racism*, London: Zed Press.

Aris, S. (1990) *Sportsbiz: Inside the Sports Business*, London: Hutchinson.

Arnstein, W. L. (1975) 'The survival of the Victorian aristocracy' in F. C. Jaher (ed.) *The Rich, the Well Born, and the Powerful: Elites and Upper Classes in History*, Secaucus, NJ: Citadel Press (pp. 202–257).

Bairner, A. and Molnar, G. (2010) 'The politics of the Olympics: an introduction' in A. Bairner and G. Molnar (eds) *The Politics of the Olympics*, London: Routledge (pp. 3–14).

Bakhtin, M. (1965) *Rabelais and his World*, Cambridge, MA: MIT Press.

Bale, J. (2008) 'From the Anthropological Days to the Anthropological Olympics' in S. Brownell (ed.) *The 1904 Anthropology Days and Olympic Games: Sport, Race, and American Imperialism*, Lincoln, NE, and London: University of Nebraska Press (pp. 324–342).

Bale, J. and Moen, O. (eds) (1995) *The Stadium and the City*, Keele: Keele University Press.

Bandy, S. (2010) 'Politics of gender through the Olympics: the changing nature of women's involvement in the Olympics' in A. Bairner and G. Molnar (eds) *The Politics of the Olympics*, London: Routledge (pp. 41–57).

Barnes, C. (1992) *Disabling Imagery and the Media*, Halifax: Ryburn Publishing.

Barnes, C. and Mercer, G. (2003) *Disability*, Cambridge: Polity Press.

Barney, R. K., Wenn, S. R. and Martyn, S. G. (2002) *Selling the Games: The IOC and the Rise of Olympic Commercialism*, Salt Lake City: University of Utah Press.

Bateman, D. and Douglas, D. (1986) *Unfriendly Games: Boycotted and Broke*, Glasgow: Mainstream.

Bauman Lyons Architects (2008) *How to Be a Happy Architect*, London: Black Dog.

Beamish, B. (2010) 'The politics of performance enhancement in the Olympic Games' in A. Bairner and G. Molnar (eds) *The Politics of the Olympics*, London: Routledge (pp. 58–68).

Beck, U. (1998) *Democracy without Enemies*, Cambridge: Polity.

Belanger, A. (2009) 'The urban sport spectacle: towards a critical political economy of sports' in B. Carrington and I. McDonald (eds) *Marxism, Cultural Studies and Sport*, London: Routledge (pp. 51–67).

Bennett, T. (1991) 'The shaping of things to come: Expo '88', *Cultural Studies* 5: 30–51.

Billings, A. (2008) *Olympic Media: Inside the Biggest Show on Television*, London: Routledge.

Billings, A. C., Eastman, S. T. and Newton, G. D. (1998) 'Atlanta revisited: prime–time promotion in the 1996 Summer Olympics', *Journal of Sport and Social Issues* 22 (1): 65–78.

Birley, D. (1993) *Sport and the Making of Britain*, Manchester: Manchester University Press.

Bocock, R. (1994) *Consumption,* London: Routledge.

Boix, J., Espada, A. and Pointu, R. (1994) *L'héritage trahi*, Paris: Editions Romillat.

Boje, D. M. (2001) 'Carnivalesque resistance to global spectacle: a critical postmodern theory of public administration', *Administrative Theory and Praxis* 23 (3): 431–458.

Boorstin, D. (1961) *The Image: A Guide to Pseudo-Events in America*, New York: Harper & Row.

Bourdieu, P. (1978) Sport and social class, *Social Science Information* 17 (6): 819–840.

Bowlby, R. (1985) *Just Looking: Consumer Culture in Dreiser, Gissing and Zola*, London: Methuen.

Boyle, P. and Haggerty, K. (2009) 'Olympic-size questions about surveillance and privacy', http://www.straight.com/article–273017/vancouver/philip–boyle–and–kevin–d–haggerty olympicsize–questions–about–surveillance–and–privacy (accessed 15 July 2010).

Brent Heritage (2002) 'Wembley', http://www.brent–heritage.co.uk/wembley.htm (accessed 18 August 2010).

Briggs, A. (1991) 'Mass entertainment: the origins of a modern industry' in A. Briggs, *Serious Pursuits: Communications and Education. Collected Essays Vol. 3*, Hemel Hempstead: Harvester Wheatsheaf (pp. 38–61).

Brohm, J.-M. (1978) *Sport: A Prison of Measured Time*, London: Ink Links.

Brookes, R. (2002) *Representing Sport*, London: Hodder.

Brooks-Buck, J. and Anderson, E. (2001) 'African American access to higher education through sports: following a dream or perpetuating a stereotype?' *Widening Participation and Lifelong Learning* 3: 26–31.

Broudehoux, A.-M. (2004) *The Making and Selling of Post-Mao Beijing*, London: Routledge.

Broudehoux, A.-M. (2007) 'Spectacular Beijing: the conspicuous construction of an Olympic metropolis', *Journal of Urban Affairs* 29 (4): 383–399.

Brownell, S. (1995) 'The stadium, the city and the state: Beijing' in J. Bale and O. Moen (eds) *The Stadium and the City*, Keele: Keele University Press (pp. 95–110).

Brownell, S. (ed.) (2008) *The 1904 Anthropology Days and Olympic Games: Sport, Race, and American Imperialism*, Lincoln, NE, and London: University of Nebraska Press.

Building Design (2008) 'World Architecture 100', http://emag.digitalpc.co.uk/cmpi/world arch08.asp (accessed 17 December 2009).

Burstyn, V. (1999) *The Rites of Men: Manhood, Politics and the Culture of Sport*, Toronto: Toronto University Press.

Carrington, B. (2004) 'Cosmopolitan Olympism, humanism and the spectacle of "race"' in J. Bale and M. K. Christensen (eds) *Post-Olympism? Questioning Sport in the 21st Century*, Oxford: Berg (pp. 81–98).

Carrington, B. (2010) *Race, Sport and Politics*, London: Sage.

Carrington, B. and McDonald, I. (eds) (2001) *'Race', Sport and British Society*, London: Routledge.

Cashman, R. (2006) *The Bitter-Sweet Awakening*, Sydney: Walla Walla Press.

Cashman, R. and Darcy, S. (2008) *Benchmark Games*, Sydney: Walla Walla Press.

Cashman, R. and Darcy, S. (2009) *Benchmark Games: The Sydney 2000 Paralympic Games*, Sydney: Walla Walla Press.

Chappelet, J.-L. and Kubler-Mabbott, B. (2008) *The International Olympic Committee and the Olympic System: The Governance of World Sport*, London: Routledge.

Charpentier, H. and Boissonnade, E. (1999) *La Grande Histoire des Jeux Olympiques*, Paris: Editions France-Empire.

Clendinning, A. (2006) 'Exhibiting a nation: Canada at the British Empire Exhibition, 1924–1925', *Histoire sociale / Social History* XXXIX (77) May: 79–107.

Coakley, J. (2003) *Sports in Society*, New York: McGraw-Hill (8th edition).

Coalter, F. (2004) 'Stuck in the blocks? A sustainable sporting legacy' in A. Vigor, M. Mean and C. Tims (eds) *After the Gold Rush: A Sustainable Olympics for London*, London: Institute for Public Policy Research/Demos (pp. 91–108).

Coffey, A. (2010) 'Brazil Olympics may send poor families packing', http://www.globalpost. com/dispatch/study–abroad/100519/brazil–olympics–rio–favelas (accessed 20 November 2010).

Cohen, P. (2005) 'The Olympics story', *Rising East Online* 1, January 2005.

COHRE (2007) *Fair Play for Housing Rights: Mega-events, Olympic Games and Housing Rights*, Geneva: Centre on Housing Rights and Evictions.

COHRE (2008) *One World, Whose Dream? Housing Rights Violations and the Beijing Olympic Games*, Geneva: Centre on Housing Rights and Evictions.

Cook, T. A. (1908) *The Cruise of the Branwen (Being a Short History of the Modern Revival of the Olympic Games)*, London: privately published 7 May 1908, copy in British Library.

Cornwell, R. (2009) 'Yield of dreams', *The Independent* 17 April, p. 48.

Coubertin, P. de (1890) *Universités trans-Atlantiques*, Paris: Libairie Hachette.

Coubertin, P. de (1917) *Un artisan d'energie française*, Paris: Henri Didier, Libraire Éditeur.

Coubertin, P. de (2000) *Pierre de Coubertin 1863–1937, Olympism: Selected Writings*, Lausanne: IOC.

Crilley, D. (1993) 'Architecture as advertising: constructing the image of redevelopment' in G. Kearns and C. Philo (eds) *Selling Places: The City as Cultural Capital, Past and Present*, Oxford: Pergamon Press (pp. 231– 252).

Culf, A. (2005) 'The man who is making a £2bn mark on London', *Guardian*, 27 October, Sport section, p. 8.

Cumberbatch, G. and Negrine, R. (1992) *Images of Disability on Television*, London: Routledge.

Cunneen, C. (2000) 'Public order and the Sydney Olympics: forget about the right to protest', *Indigenous Law Bulletin* 5 (1): 26–27.

Curran, J., Gaber, I. and Petley, J. (2005) *Culture Wars: The Media and the British Left*, Edinburgh: Edinburgh University Press.

Darnell, S. (2010) 'Mega sport for all? Assessing the development promises of Rio 2016' in R. Barney, J. Forsyth and M. Heine (eds) *Rethinking Matters Olympic*, 10th International Symposium for Olympic Research, London, Ontario (pp. 498–507).

Davis, A. (2000) 'Public relations, political communication and national news production in Britain 1979–1999', PhD thesis, Goldsmiths College, University of London.

Davison, P. (ed.) (1998) *I Belong to the Left, 1945: The Complete Works of George Orwell, Vol. 17*, London: Secker & Warburg.

Day, I. (1990) *'Sorting the Men out from the Boys': Masculinity, a Missing Link in the Sociology of Sport*, Sheffield: Sheffield City Polytechnic.

Dayan, D. and Katz, E. (1992) *Media Events: The Live Broadcasting of History*, Cambridge, MA: Harvard University Press.

DCMS (2008) *Guide to Safety at Sports Grounds*, London: Department of Media, Culture and Sport.

de S. Honey, J. R. (1975) 'Tom Brown's universe: the nature and limits of the Victorian public schools community' in B. Simon and I. Bradley (eds) *The Victorian Public School*, Dublin: Gill & Macmillan (pp. 19–33).

Debord, G. (1967/1970) *Society of the Spectacle*, Detroit, MI: Black & Red.

Dimeo, P. and Kay, J. (2004) 'Major sports events: image projection and the problems of the "semi periphery": a case study of the 1996 South Asia Cricket World Cup', *Third World Quarterly* 25 (7): 1263–1276.

Donnelly, P. (1996) 'Prolympism: sport monoculture as crisis and opportunity', *Quest* 48 (1): 25–42.

Donnelly, P. (2009) 'Own the podium or rent it? Canada's involvement in the global sporting arms race', *Options Politiques/Policy Options* December: 41–44.

Duncan, M. C. (2001) 'The sociology of ability and disability in physical activity', *Sociology of Sport Journal* 18 (1): 1–4.

Duncan, M. C. and Aycock, A. (2005) 'Fitting images: advertising, sport and disability' in S. Jackson and D. Andrews (eds) *Sport, Culture and Advertising*, London: Routledge (pp. 136–153).

Dunning, E. (1975) 'The origins of modern football and the public school ethos' in B. Simon and I. Bradley (eds) *The Victorian Public School*, Dublin: Gill & Macmillan (pp. 168–176).

Durry, J. (undated) *Pierre de Coubertin: The Visionary*, Lausanne: IOC.

Dyer, R. (1978) 'Entertainment and utopia', *Movie* 24: 2–13.

The Economist (1996) 'The zillion dollar games', 22 July: 13.

Eichberg, H. (1998) *Body Cultures: Essays on Sport, Space and Identity*, London: Routledge.

Eisinger, P. (2000) 'The politics of bread and circuses: building a city for the visitor class', *Urban Affairs Review*, January: 316–333.

English Sports Council (1998) *The Development of Sporting Talent 1997: An Examination of the Current Practices for Talent Development in English Sport*, London: English Sports Council.

Entine, J. (2000) *Taboo*, New York: Public Affairs.

Espy, R. (1979) *The Politics of the Olympic Games*, Berkeley, CA: University of California Press.

Essex, S. and B. Chalkley (1998) 'Olympic Games: catalyst of urban change', *Leisure Studies* 17 (3): 187–206.

Essex, S. and Chalkley, B. (2003) 'Urban transformation from hosting the Olympic Games', Barcelona: Centre d'Estudis Olimpics (UAB) available at http://olympicstudies.uab.es/lectures/web/pdf/essex.pdf

European Tour Operators Association (2006) *Olympic Report*, London: ETOA.

Ewen, S. (1988) *All Consuming Images*, New York: Basic Books.

Ewing, K. D. (2006) *Global Rights in Global Companies: Going for Gold at the UK Olympics* (Background Report 1), London: Institute of Employment Rights.

Featherstone, M. (2007) *Consumer Culture and Postmodernism*, 2nd edition, London: Sage.

Finley, M. and Pleket, H. (1976) *The Olympic Games: The First Thousand Years*, London: Chatto & Windus.

Fischer, E. and Gainer, B. (1994) 'Masculinity and the consumption of organised sports' in J. A. Costa (ed.) *Gender Issues and Consumer Behaviour*, London: Sage (pp. 84–103).

Fishwick, L. (2001) 'Be what you wanna be: a sense of identity down at the local gym' in N. Watson and S. Cunningham-Burley (eds) *Reframing the Body*, Basingstoke: Palgrave (pp. 152–165).

Fleming, S. (1995) *'Home and Away': Sport and South Asian Male Youth*, Aldershot: Avebury (pp. 152–165).

Frampton, K. (2005) 'Introduction: the work of architecture in the Age of Commodification' in W. Saunders (ed.) *Commodification and Spectacle in Architecture*, Minneapolis: University of Minnesota Press (pp. ix–xviii).

Friedman, M., Andrews, D. and Silk, M. (2004) 'Sport and the façade of redevelopment in the postindustrial city', *Sociology of Sport Journal* 21 (1): 119–139.

Frow, J. (1997) *Time and Commodity Culture: Essays in Cultural Theory and Postmodernity*, Oxford: Clarendon Press.

Gaffney, C. (2008) *Temples of the Earthbound Gods: Stadiums in the Cultural Landscapes of Rio de Janeiro and Buenos Aires*, Austin: University of Texas Press.

Gaffney, C. (2010) 'Mega-events and socio-spatial dynamics in Rio de Janeiro, 1919–2016', *Journal of Latin American Geography* 9 (1): 7–29.

Garcia, B. (2001) 'Enhancing sport marketing through cultural and arts programmes: lessons from the Sydney Olympic Arts Festivals', *Sport Management Review* (the official journal of the Sport Management Association of Australia and New Zealand), 4 (2): 193–219.

Garcia, B. and Miah, A. (2006) 'Ever-decreasing circles: the profile of culture at the Olympics', *Locum Destination Review*, July: 60–62.

Gathorne-Hardy, J. (1977) *The Public School Phenomenon*, Harmondsworth: Penguin.

Gems, G. (2008) 'Anthropology Days, the construction of whiteness, and American imperialism in the Philippines' in S. Brownell (ed.) *The 1904 Anthropology Days and Olympic Games: Sport, Race, and American Imperialism*, Lincoln, NE, and London: University of Nebraska Press (pp. 189–216).

Girginov, V. (ed.) (2010) *The Olympics: A Critical Reader*, London: Routledge.

Girginov, V. and Hills, L. (2008) 'A sustainable sports legacy: creating a link between the London Olympics and sports participation', *International Journal of the History of Sport* 25 (14): 2091–2116.

Girginov, V. and Parry, J. (2005) *The Olympic Games Explained*, London: Routledge.

217

Giulianotti, R. (2005) *Sport: A Critical Sociology*, Cambridge: Polity.

Giulianotti, R. and Robertson, R. (eds) (2007) *Globalization and Sport*, Oxford: Blackwell.

Glancey, J. (2008a) 'Secrets of the Bird's Nest', *Guardian*, G2, 11 February, pp. 23–27.

Glancey, J. (2008b) 'Architecture', *Guardian*, G2, 11 December, pp. 22–23.

Glancey, J. (2009) 'The wow years', *Guardian*, G2, 8 December, pp. 17–20.

Goffman, E. (1974) *Frame Analysis: An Essay on the Organization of Experience*, New York: Harper & Row.

Goggin, G. and Newell, C. (2000) 'Crippling Paralympics? Media, disability and Olympism', *Media International Australia* 97: 71–84.

Gold, J. and Gold, M. (eds) (2007) *Olympic Cities* London: Routledge.

Graham, C. G. (1986) *Leni Riefenstahl and Olympia*, Metuchen, NJ, and London: Scarecrow Press.

Gratton, C., Shibli, S. and Coleman, R. (2006) 'The economic impact of major sports events: a review of 10 major UK sports events' in J. Horne and W. Manzenreiter (eds) *Sports Mega-Events: Social Scientific Analyses of a Global Phenomenon*, Oxford: Blackwell (pp. 41–58).

Gravelaine, F. de (1997) *Le Stade de France: Au coeur de la ville pour le sport et le spectacle*, Paris: Le Monteur.

Greenberg, S. (1987) *Guinness Olympic Games. The Records*, London: Guinness Superlatives.

Greene, S. J. (2003) 'Staged cities: mega-events, slum clearance, and global capital', *Yale Human Rights and Development Law Journal* 6: 161–187.

Gruneau, R. (1981) 'Elites, class and corporate power in Canadian sport: some preliminary findings' in J. Loy, G. Kenyon and B. McPherson (eds) *Sport, Culture and Society: A Reader on the Sociology of Sport*, Philadelphia, PA: Lea & Febiger (pp. 348–371).

Gruneau, R. (1984) 'Commercialism and the modern Olympics' in A. Tomlinson and G. Whannel (eds) *Five Ring Circus: Money, Power and Politics at the Olympic Games*, London: Pluto Press (pp. 1–15).

Gruneau, R. (2002) 'Foreword' in M. Lowes, *Indy Dreams and Urban Nightmares,* Toronto: Toronto University Press (pp. ix–xii).

Gruneau, R. and Neubauer, R. (2011) 'A gold medal for the market: the 1984 Los Angeles Olympics, the Reagan era, and the politics of neoliberalism' in S. Wagg and H. Lenskyj (eds) *Handbook of Olympic Studies*, Basingstoke: Palgrave Macmillan.

Gutman, R. (1988) *Architectural Practice: A Critical View*, Princeton, NJ: Princeton Architectural Press.

Guttmann, A. (1978) *From Ritual to Record*, London: Columbia University Press.

Guttmann, A. (1984) *The Games Must Go On: Avery Brundage and the Olympic Movement*, New York: Columbia University Press.

Guttmann, A. (1992) *The Olympics: A History of the Modern Games*, Chicago: University of Illinois Press.

Guttmann, A. (2006) 'Berlin 1936: the most controversial Olympics' in A. Tomlinson and C. Young (eds) *National Identity and Global Sport Events: Culture Politics and Spectacle in the Olympics and World Cup*, New York: SUNY (pp. 65–82).

Hain, Peter (1970) *Don't Play With Apartheid*, London: Allen & Unwin.

Hall, C. M. (2001) 'Imaging, tourism and sports event fever: the Sydney Olympics and the need for a social charter for mega-events' in C. Gratton and I. Henry (eds) *Sport in the City*, London: Routledge (pp. 166–183).

Hall, C. M. (2005) 'Selling places: hallmark events and the reimaging of Sydney and Toronto' in J. Nauright and K. Schimmel (eds) *The Political Economy of Sport*, Basingstoke: Palgrave (pp. 129–151).

Hall, C. M. and Hodges, J. (1997) 'The politics of place and identity in the Sydney 2000 Olympics: sharing the spirit of corporatism' in M. Roche (ed.) *Sport, Popular Culture and Identity*, Oxford: Meyer & Meyer (pp. 95–111).

Hall, S., Critcher, C., Jefferson, T., Clarke, J. and Roberts, B. (1978) *Policing the Crisis: Mugging, the State and Law and Order*, London: Macmillan.

Hampton, J. (2008) *The Austerity Olympics: When the Games Came to London in 1948*, London: Aurum Press.

Hannigan, J. (1998) *Fantasy City: Pleasure and Profit in the Postmodern Metropolis*, London: Routledge.

Hardin, B. and Hardin, M. (2003) 'Conformity and conflict: wheelchair athletes discuss sport media', *Adapted Physical Activity Quarterly* 20 (3): 246–259.

Hargreaves, J. A. (1984) 'Women and the Olympic phenomenon' in A. Tomlinson and G. Whannel (eds) *Five-Ring Circus: Money, Power and Politics at the Olympic Games*, London: Pluto Press (pp. 53–70).

Hargreaves, J. A. (1994) *Sporting Females: Critical Issues in the History and Sociology of Women's Sport*, London: Routledge.

Hargreaves, J. A. (2000) *Heroines of Sport: The Politics of Difference and Identity*, London: Routledge.

Hart-Davis, D. (1986) *Hitler's Games*, London: Century.

Harvey, D. (1989) *The Condition of Postmodernity*, Oxford: Blackwell.

Hayes, G. and Horne, J. (2011) 'Sustainable development, shock and awe? London 2012 and civil society', *Sociology* 45.

Hill, C. (1992) *Olympic Politics*, London: Manchester University Press.

Hill, C. (1994) 'The politics of Manchester's Olympic bid', *Parliamentary Affairs* 47: 338–355.

Hill, C. (1996) *Olympic Politics: Athens to Atlanta 1896–1996*, 2nd edition, Manchester and New York: Manchester University Press.

Hiller, H. (2003) 'Toward a science of Olympic outcomes: the urban legacy', in M. de Moragas, C. Kennett, and N. Puig (eds) *The Legacy of the Olympic Games 1984–2000*, Lausanne: IOC (pp. 102–109).

Hilvoorde, van I., Elling, A. and Stokvis, R. (2010) 'How to influence national pride? The Olympic medal index as a unifying narrative', *International Review for the Sociology of Sport* 45 (1): 87–102.

Hoberman, J. (1995) 'Toward a theory of Olympic internationalism', *Journal of Sport History* 22: 1–37.

Hoberman, J. (1997) *Darwin's Athletes: How Sport Has Damaged Black America and Preserved the Myth of Race*, Boston: Houghton Mifflin.

Hofmann, A. (2011) 'A never ending story: women's struggle for acceptance in ski jumping', *Journal of the New England Ski Museum* 80, Winter: 1–11 (available at http://www.ski museum.org/doc198.html).

Hofmann, A. and Preuss, A. (2005) 'Female eagles of the air: developments in women's ski-jumping' in M. Lämmer, E. Mertin and T. Terret (eds) *New Aspects of Sport History: Proceedings of the 9th ISHPES Congress, Cologne, Germany*, Cologne: Academia Verlag (pp. 202–209).

Holt, Oliver (2005) 'Bored of the rings', *GQ Sport* 1 (1): 16–20.

Holt, R. (1989) *Sport and the British: A Modern History*, Oxford: Oxford University Press.

Holt, R. and Mason, A. (2000) *Sport in Britain, 1945–2000*, Oxford: Blackwell.

Horne, J. (2006) *Sport in Consumer Culture*, Basingstoke: Palgrave.

Horne, J. (2007) 'The "four knowns" of sports mega–events', *Leisure Studies* 26 (1): 81–96.

Horne, J. (2007a) 'World Cup Cricket and Caribbean aspirations: from Nello to Mello', *North American Congress on Latin America (NACLA) Report on the Americas* 40 (4): 10–14.

Horne, J. (2010) 'The politics of hosting the Olympic Games' in A. Bairner and G. Molnar (eds) *The Politics of the Olympics*, London: Routledge (pp. 27–40).

Horne, J. (2011a) 'The four "Cs" of sports mega-events: capitalism, connections, citizenship and contradictions' in G. Hayes and J. Karamichas (eds) *Olympic Games, Mega-Events, and Civil Societies: Globalisation, Environment, and Resistance*, Basingstoke: Palgrave.

Horne, J. (2011b) 'Architects, stadia and sport spectacles: notes on the role of architects in the building of sport stadia and making of world-class cities', *International Review for the Sociology of Sport* 46 (2): 205–227.

Horne, J. (2011c) 'Sports mega-events and the shaping of urban modernity in East Asia' in M. Baskett and W. M. Tsutsui (eds) *Olympian Desires: Building Bodies and Nations in East Asia*, Folkestone: Global Oriental.

Horne, J. and Manzenreiter, W. (2006) 'An introduction to the sociology of sports mega-events' in J. Horne and W. Manzenreiter (eds) *Sports Mega-Events: Social Scientific Analyses of a Global Phenomenon*, Oxford: Blackwell (pp. 1–24).

Horne, J. and Manzenreiter, W. (2011) 'Tales from the East' in H. Lenskyj and S. Wagg (eds) *Handbook of the Olympic Games*, Basingstoke: Palgrave.

Horne, J. and Whannel, G. (2010) 'The "caged torch procession": celebrities, protesters and the 2008 Olympic torch relay in London, Paris and San Francisco', *Sport in Society* 13 (5): 760–770.

Horne, J., Tomlinson, A. and Whannel, G. (1999) *Understanding Sport: An Introduction to the Sociological and Cultural Analysis of Sport*, London: E & FN Spon.

Howe, P. D. (2008) *The Cultural Politics of the Paralympic Movement*, London: Routledge.

Howe, P. D. (2010) 'Disability, Olympism and Paralympism' in A. Bairner and G. Molnar (eds) *The Politics of the Olympics*, London: Routledge (pp. 69–80).

Howell, D. (1990) *Made in Birmingham: The Memoirs of Denis Howell*, London: Queen Anne Press.

Hughes, G. (1999) 'Urban revitalization: the use of festive time strategies', *Leisure Studies* 18 (2): 119–135.

Hutchins, B. and Mikosza, J. (2010) 'The Web 2.0 Olympics: athlete blogging, social networking and policy contradictions at the 2008 Beijing Games', *Convergence: The International Journal of Research into new Media Technologies*, Special issue on Sport in new media cultures, 16 (3): 163–183.

Hylton, K. (2009) *'Race' and Sport: Critical Race Theory*, London: Routledge.

Inglis, S. (2000) *Sightlines: A Stadium Odyssey*, London: Yellow Jersey.

Inglis, S. (2005) *Engineering Archie: Archibald Leitch – Football Ground Designer*, London: English Heritage/HOK.

IOC (2004) *Olympic Charter*, Lausanne: IOC.

IOC (2007a) *Olympic Charter*, revised 7 July, Lausanne: IOC.

IOC (2007b) *Sexual Harassment and Abuse and Abuse in Sport: Consensus Statement* (February), IOC Medical Commission Expert Panel, Lausanne: IOC.

IOC (2009) *Olympic Marketing Fact File*, Lausanne: IOC.

IOC (2010) http://www.olympic.org/en/content/Olympic–Games/All–Past–Olympic–Games/Summer/Beijing–2008/ (accessed 19 August 2010).

IOC (2010a) *The Olympic Summer Games: Factsheet* (January), Lausanne: IOC.

IOC (n/d) *Sponsor Handbook: A Celebration of the Olympic Centennial*, Lausanne: The Olympic Programme.

Jacob, S. (2010) 'In a meeting with the Mayor of Rio, Vila Autódromo reaffirms desire to stay', http://www.catcomm.org/en/?p=2642 (accessed 20 November 2010).

James, C. L. R. (1963) *Beyond a Boundary*, London: Stanley Paul.

Jarvie, G. (1991) *Highland Games: The Making of the Myth*, Edinburgh: Edinburgh University Press.

Jarvie, G. (1992) 'Highland gatherings, Balmorality, and the glamour of backwardness', *Sociology of Sport Journal* 9 (2): 167–178.

Jarvie, G. (2006) *Sport, Culture and Society*, London: Routledge.

Jarvie, G. (ed.) (1991) *Sport, Racism and Ethnicity*, London: Falmer.

Jennings, A. (1996) *The New Lords of the Rings*, London: Pocket Books.

Jennings, A. (2000) 'The great Olympic illusion', programme broadcast on BBC2, 29 August (transcript: http://news.bbc.co.uk/1/hi/programmes/correspondent/901405.stm).

Jennings, A. (2006) *Foul! The Secret World of FIFA: Bribes, Vote Rigging and Ticket Scandals*, London: HarperSport.

Jennings, A. and Sambrook, C. (2000) *The Great Olympic Swindle*, London: Simon & Schuster.

John, G. and Sheard, R. (2000) *Stadia: A Design and Development Guide*, 3rd edition, Oxford: Architectural Press.

John, G., Sheard, R. and Vickery, B. (2006) *Stadia: A Design and Development Guide*, 4th edition, Oxford: Architectural Press.

Jones, P. (2006) 'The sociology of architecture and the politics of building', *Sociology* 40 (3): 549–565.

Karamichas, J. (2005) 'Risk versus national pride: conflicting discourses over the construction of a high voltage power station in the Athens metropolitan area for demands of the 2004 Olympics', *Human Ecology Review* 12 (2): 133–142.

Kellner, D. (2003) *Media Spectacle*, London: Routledge.

Keys, B. (2006) *Globalizing Sport: National Rivalry and International Community in the 1930s*, Cambridge, MA and London: Harvard University Press.

Kidd, B. (1984) 'The myth of the ancient games', in A. Tomlinson and G. Whannel (eds) *Five Ring Circus*, London: Pluto (pp. 71–83).

Kidd, B. (1992) 'The Toronto Olympic commitment: towards a social contract for the Olympic Games', *Olympika: International Journal of Olympic Studies* 1: 154–167.

Kidd, B. (2010) 'Epilogue: the struggles must continue', *Sport in Society* 13 (1): 157–165.

Kidd, B. and Donnelly, P. (2000) 'Human rights in sports', *International Review for the Sociology of Sport* 35 (2): 131–148.

King, A. (2004) *Spaces of Global Cultures: Architecture Urbanism Identity*, London: Routledge.

Klein, N. (2007) *The Shock Doctrine*, London: Penguin/Allen Lane.

Klein, N. (2008) 'The Olympics: unveiling police state 2.0', *The Huffington Post*, http://www.

huffingtonpost.com/naomi–klein/the–olympics–unveiling–po_b_117403.html, posted 7/8/08 (accessed 10 December 2010).

Knight, D. R. (1978) *The Exhibitions: Great White City 70th Anniversary*, London: Barnard & Westwood.

Knott, S. M. (2008) 'Germans and others at the "American Games". Problems of national and international representation at the 1904 Olympics' in S. Brownell (ed.) *The 1904 Anthropology Days and Olympic Games: Sport, Race, and American Imperialism*, Lincoln, NE, and London: University of Nebraska Press (pp. 278–300).

Krüger, A. (1993) Book review of J. Boix and A. Espada *El deporte del poder: vida y milagro de Juan Antonio Samaranch* (Madrid: Ediciones temas de hoy, 1991), *International Journal of Sports History* 10: 291–293.

Krüger, A. (2003) 'Germany: the propaganda machine', in M. William and A. Krüger (eds), *The Nazi Olympics*, Urbana and Chicago: University of Illinois Press (pp. 17–43).

Krüger, A. and Riordan, J. (1996) *The Story of Worker Sport*, Leeds: Human Kinetics.

Krüger, A. and Murray, W. (eds) (2003) *The Nazi Olympics: Sport, Politics and Appeasement in the 1930s*, Champaign and Urbana: University of Illinois Press.

Larson, J. and Heung-Soo Park (1993) *Global Television and the Politics of the Seoul Olympics*, Boulder, CO: Westview.

Larson, M. (1994) 'Architectural competitions as discursive events', *Theory and Society* 23 (4): 469–504.

Latham, A. (2003) 'Urbanity, lifestyle and making sense of the new urban cultural economy', *Urban Studies* 40 (9): S. 1699–1724.

Lee, M. (1993) *Consumer Culture Reborn*, London: Routledge.

Lee, M. (2006) *The Race for the 2012 Olympics: The Inside Story of How London Won the Bid*, London: Virgin.

Lee, P.-C., Bairner, A. and Tan, T.-C. (2010) 'Taiwanese identities and the 2008 Beijing Olympic Games' in A. Bairner and G. Molnar (eds) *The Politics of the Olympics*, London: Routledge (pp. 129–144).

Lennartz, K. (1983) *Deutschlands an den Olympischen Spielen 1900 in Paris und 1904 in St Louis (German Participation at the Olympic Games: 1900 in Paris and 1904 in St Louis)*, Bonn: Carl Diem Institut.

Lenskyj, H. (2000) *Inside the Olympic Industry*, Albany, NY: SUNY Press.

Lenskyj, H. (2002) *The Best Olympics Ever? Social Impacts of Sydney 2000*, Albany, NY: SUNY Press.

Lenskyj, H. (2008) *Olympic Industry Resistance*, Albany, NY: SUNY Press.

Levy, A. (2004) *Small Island*, London: Headline.

Liao, H. and Pitts, A. (2006) 'A brief historical review of Olympic urbanization', *International Journal of the History of Sport* 23 (7): 1232–1252.

Lippe Gerd, von der (2008) 'Female ski-jumpers in Norway: against nature' in M. Lämmer, E. Mertin and T. Terret (eds) *New Aspects of Sport History: Proceedings of the 9th ISHPES Congress, Cologne, Germany*, Cologne: Academia Verlag (pp. 331–335).

London 2012 (2004) *Candidate File*, London: London 2012.

Long, J., Hylton, K., Spracklen, K., Ratna, A. and Bailey, S. (2009) *Systematic Review of the Literature on Black and Minority Ethnic Communities in Sport and Physical Recreation*, Leeds: Sporting Equals and the Sports Councils / Carnegie Research Institute, Leeds Metropolitan University.

Lovesey, P. (1979) *The Official Centenary History of the AAA*, London: Guinness Superlatives.

Lowerson, J. (1993) *Sport and the Middle Classes, 1870–1914*, Manchester: Manchester University Press.

Lowes, M. (2002) *Indy Dreams and Urban Nightmares*, Toronto: Toronto University Press.

Maas, K. and Hasbrook, C. (2001) 'Media promotion of the paradigm citizen/golfer: an analysis of golf magazines' representations of disability, gender and age', *Sociology of Sport Journal* 18 (1): 21–36.

MacAloon, J. J. (1981) *This Great Symbol: Pierre de Coubertin and the Origins of the Modern Olympic Games*, Chicago: University of Chicago Press.

MacAloon, J. J. (1984) 'Olympic Games and the theory of spectacle in modern societies' in J. J. MacAloon (ed.) *Rite, Drama, Festival, Spectacle: Rehearsals Toward a Theory of Cultural Performance*, Philadelphia, PA: Institute for the Study of Human Issues (pp. 241–280).

MacAloon, J. J. (1996) 'Humanism as political necessity? Reflections on the pathos of anthropological science in Olympic contexts', *Quest* 48 (1): 67–81.

MacAloon, J. J. (1999) 'Anthropology at the Olympic Games' in A. M. Klausen (ed.) *Olympic Games as Performance and Public Event*, New York and Oxford: Berghahn Books (pp. 9–26).

MacAloon, J. J. (2006) *This Great Symbol: Pierre de Coubertin and the Origins of the Modern Olympic Games*, 2nd edition. London: Routledge.

MacAloon, J. J. (ed.) (1984) *Rite Drama Festival Spectacle*, Philadelphia: Institute for the Study of Human Issues.

McDonagh, E. and Pappano, L. (2008) *Playing With the Boys: Why Separate is Not Equal*, New York: Oxford University Press.

McFee, G. (1990) 'The Olympic Games as tourist event' in A. Tomlinson (ed.) *Sport in Society: Policy, Politics and Culture*, Brighton: Leisure Studies Association.

McIntosh, P. (1952) *Physical Education in England since 1800*, London: Bell.

McLeod-Roberts, L. (2007) 'Paramilitary games', *NACLA Report on the Americas* 40 (4): 20–25.

McNeill, D. (2004) *New Europe: Imagined Spaces*, London: Hodder Arnold.

McNeill, D. (2009) *The Global Architect*, London: Routledge.

McPhail, T. and Jackson, R. (eds) (1989) *The Olympic Movement and the Mass Media*, Calgary, Canada: Hurford Enterprises.

Magdalinski, T., Schimmel, K. and Chandler, T. (2005) 'Recapturing Olympic mystique: the corporate invasion of the classroom' in J. Nauright and K. Schimmel (eds) *The Political Economy of Sport*, London: Palgrave Macmillan (pp. 38–54).

Mallon, B. and Buchanan, I. (2000) *The 1908 Olympic Games: Results for All Competitors in All Events with Commentary*, Jefferson, NC, and London: McFarland.

Mandell, R. (1976) *The First Modern Olympics*, Berkeley: University of California Press.

Mandell, R. (1987) *The Nazi Olympics*, Urbana: University of Illinois Press.

Mangan, J. A. (1975) 'Athleticism: a case study of the evolution of an educational ideology' in B. Simon and I. Bradley (eds) *The Victorian Public School: Studies in the Development of an Educational Institution*, Dublin: Gill & Macmillan (pp. 147–167).

Mangan, J. A. (1981) *Athleticism in the Victorian and Edwardian Public School*, Cambridge: Cambridge University Press.

Mangan, J. A. (1987) 'Social Darwinism and upper class education in late Victorian and Edwardian England' in J. A. Mangan and J. Walvin (eds) *Manliness and Morality: Middle Class Masculinity in Britain and America*, Manchester: Manchester University Press (pp. 135–159).

Mangan, J. A. (2000) *Athleticism in the Victorian and Edwardian Public School*, revised edition, London: Frank Cass.

Manzenreiter, W. (2006) 'Sport spectacles, uniformities and the search for identity in late modern Japan' in J. Horne and W. Manzenreiter (eds) *Sports Mega-Events: Social Scientific Analyses of a Global Phenomenon*, Oxford: Blackwell (pp. 144–159).

Markula, P. (ed.) (2009) *Olympic Women and the Media: International Perspectives*, London: Palgrave.

Marschik, M., Mullner, R., Spitaler, G. and Zinganel, M. (eds) (2005) *Das Stadion: Geschicte, Architektur, Politik, Okonomie*, Vienna: Turia & Kant.

Marshall, P. D., Walker, B. and Russo, N. (2010) 'Mediating the Olympics', *Convergence: The International Journal of Research into new Media Technologies*, Special Issue on Sport in New Media Cultures 16 (3): 263–278.

Marvin, C. (2008) '"All Under Heaven" – Megaspace in Beijing' in M. Price and D. Dayan (eds) *Owning the Olympics: Narratives of the New China*, Ann Arbor: University of Michigan Press (pp. 229–259).

Marx, K. (1976 [1867]) *Capital, Vol. I*, Harmondsworth: Penguin.

Matthews, G. R. (2005) *America's First Olympics: The St Louis Games of 1904*, Columbia and London: University of Missouri Press.

Merrifield, A. (2002) *Metromarxism: A Marxist Tale of the City*, New York: Routledge.

Miah, A., Garcia, B. and Zhihui, T. (2008) '"We are the media": non-accredited media and citizen journalists at the Olympic Games' in M. E. Price and D. Dayan (eds) *Owning the Olympics: Narratives of the New China*, Ann Arbor: University of Michigan Press (pp. 320–345).

Miles, S. (2010) *Spaces for Consumption: Pleasure and Placelessness in the Post-Industrial City*, London: Sage.

Miles, S. and Miles, M. (2004) *Consuming Cities*, Basingstoke: Palgrave.

Miller, D. and Dinan, W. (2007) *A Century of Spin: How Public Relations Became the Cutting Edge of Corporate Power*, London: Pluto.

Minton, A. (2009a) *Ground Control: Fear and Happiness in the Twenty-First-Century City*, London: Penguin.

Minton, A. (2009b) 'These cities within cities are eating up Britain's streets', *Guardian* 16 December, p. 30.

Montalban, M. V. (2004 [1991]) *An Olympic Death*, London: Serpent's Tail.

Moore, K. (1987) 'The Pan-Britannic Festival: a tangible but forlorn expression of Imperialism' in J. A. Mangan (ed.) *Pleasure Profit Proselytism*, London: Frank Cass (pp. 144–162).

Moragas, M. de, MacAloon, J. and Llinés, M. (1996) *Olympic Ceremonies: Historical Continuity and Cultural Exchange*, Barcelona and Lausanne: Olympic Museum, IOC.

Moragas, M. de, Rivenburgh, N. K. and Larson, J. F. (eds) (1996a) *Television in the Olympics*, London: John Libbey.

Morin, G. (1998) *La Cathédrale inachevée*, Montreal: XYZ editeur.

Müller, F., van Zoonene, L. and de Roode, L. (2008) 'The integrative power of sport: imagined and real effects of sports events on multicultural integration', *Sociology of Sport Journal* 25 (4): 387–401.

Munoz, F. (2006) 'Olympic urbanism and Olympic villages: planning strategies in Olympic host cities, London 1908 to London 2012' in J. Horne and W. Manzenreiter (eds) *Sports Mega-Events: Social Scientific Analyses of a Global Phenomenon*, Oxford: Blackwell (pp. 175–187).

Murray, W. J. (1987) 'The French workers sports movement and the Popular Front victory (1939)', *International Journal of the History of Sport* 4 (2): 203–230.

National Audit Office (2008) *Preparing for Sporting Success at the London 2012 Olympic and Paralympic Games and Beyond*, London: Stationery Office.

Nixon H. L. (2000) 'Sport and disability' in J. Coakley and E. Dunning (eds) *Handbook of Sports Studies*, London: Sage (pp. 422–438).

Office for National Statistics (1998) *Living in Britain: Results from the 1996 General Household Survey*, London: Stationery Office.

Official Report (1948) *The Official Report of the Organising Committee for the XIV Olympiad*, London: Organising Committee for the XIV Olympiad.

O'Neill, B. (2005) 'Fortress Olympics', *Rising East Online* 1, January.

Olds, K. (1997) 'Globalizing Shanghai; the "Global Intelligence Corps" and the building of Pudong', *Cities* 14 (2): 109–123.

Olds, K. (1998) 'Urban mega-events, evictions and housing rights: the Canadian case', *Current Issues in Tourism* 1 (1): 2–46.

Olds, K. (2001) *Globalization and Urban Change: Capital, Culture and Pacific Rim Mega-Projects*, Oxford: Oxford University Press.

O'Neil, T. (1989) *The Game Behind the Game: High Stakes, High Pressure in TV Sports*, New York: Harper & Row.

Osmond, G. (2010) 'Photographs, materiality and sport history: Peter Norman and the 1968 Mexico City Black Power salute', *Journal of Sport History* 37 (1): 119–137.

Payne, M. (2005) *Olympic Turnaround*, London: London Business Press.

Peck, J. and Tickell, A. (2002) 'Neoliberalizing space', *Antipode*, 34 (3): 380–404.

Phillips, B. (2000) *Honour of Empire, Glory of Sport: The History of Athletics at the Commonwealth Games*, Manchester: Parrs Wood Press.

Philo, C. and Kearns, G. (1993) 'Culture, history, capital: a critical introduction to the selling of places' in G. Kearns and C. Philo (eds) *Selling Places: The City as Cultural Capital, Past and Present*, Oxford: Pergamon Press (pp. 1–32).

Pierson, D. (2010) 'China gushes over high-tech toilets', *The Daily Yomiuri*, 11 October, p. 11.

Pound, D. (2004) *Inside the Olympics*, Canada: John Wiley.

Pound, R. W. (2003) *Olympic Games Study Commission* (Report to the 115th IOC Session, Prague, July), Lausanne: International Olympic Committee.

Poynter, G. (2005) 'The economics of the Olympic bid', *Rising East Online* 1, January.

Poynter, G. and MacRury, I. (eds) (2009) *Olympic Cities: 2012 and the Remaking of London*, London: Ashgate.

Preuss, H. (2004) *The Economics of Staging the Olympic Games: A Comparison of the Games 1972–2008*, Cheltenham: Edward Elgar.

Price, M. E. (2008) 'On seizing the Olympic platform' in M. E. Price and D. Dayan (eds) *Owning the Olympics: Narratives of the New China*, Ann Arbor: University of Michigan Press (pp. 86–114).

Puijk, R. (1997) *Global Spotlights on Lillehammer*, Luton: University of Luton Press.

Quanz, D.. (1993) 'Civic pacifism and sports-based internationalism: framework of the founding of the International Olympic Committee', *Olympika* 2: 1–24.

Ramsamy, S. (1982) *Apartheid, the Real Hurdle*, London: International Defence and Aid Fund for South Africa.

Ramsamy, S. (1984) 'Apartheid, boycotts and the Games' in A. Tomlinson and G. Whannel

225

(eds) *Five Ring Circus: Money, Power and Politics at the Olympic Games*, London: Pluto Press (pp. 44–52).

Real, M. (1986) *Global Ritual: Olympic Media Coverage and International Understanding*, Paris: UNESCO.

Real, M. (1989) *Super Media*, London: Sage.

Ren, X. (2008) 'Architecture and nation building in the age of globalization: construction of the national stadium of Beijing for the 2008 Olympics', *Journal of Urban Affairs* 30 (2): 175–190.

Rimmer, P. (1991) 'The global intelligence corps and world cities: engineering consultancies on the move' in P. Daniels (ed.) *Services and Metropolitan Development: International Perspectives*, London: Routledge (pp. 146–172).

Riordan, J. (1984) 'The Workers' Olympics' in A. Tomlinson and G. Whannel (eds) *Five Ring Circus: Money, Power and Politics at the Olympic Games*, London: Pluto Press (pp. 98–112).

Ritzer, G. and Stillman, T. (2001) 'The postmodern ballpark as a leisure setting: enchantment and simulated de-McDonaldization', *Leisure Sciences* 23 (2): 99–113.

RKMA (Richard K. Miller & Associates) (2006) *The 2007 Architectural/Engineering/Construction Market Research Handbook*, Loganville, GA: Richard K. Miller & Associates.

Roche, M. (2000) *Mega-Events and Modernity: Olympics and Expos in the Growth of Global Culture*, London: Routledge.

Roche, M. (2003) 'Mega-events, time and modernity: on time structures in global society', *Time and Society* 12 (1): 99–126.

Rolnik, R. (2009) *Report of the UN's Special Rapporteur on Adequate Housing as a Component of the Right to an Adequate Standard of Living, and on the Right to Non-discrimination in this Context*, New York: United Nations General Assembly, A/HRC/13/20.

Rowe, D. (1995) 'Big defence: sport and hegemonic masculinity' in A. Tomlinson (ed.) *Gender, Sport and Leisure: Continuities and Challenges*, Chelsea School Research Centre Topic Report 4 Eastbourne: University of Brighton (pp. 123–133).

Rowe, D. (1996) 'The global love-match: sport and television', *Media Culture and Society* 18 (4): 565–582.

Rowe, D. (1999) *Sport, Culture and the Media*, Milton Keynes: Open University Press.

Rowe, N. and Moore, S. (2004) *Participation in Sport – Results from the General Household Survey 2002*, Sport England Research Briefing Note, London: Sport England.

Russell, D. (2006) '"We all agree, name the stand after Shankly": cultures of commemoration in late twentieth–century English football culture', *Sport in History* 26 (1): 1–25.

Rutheiser, C. (1996) *Imagineering Atlanta: The Politics of Place in the City of Dreams*, New York and London: Verso.

Sassatelli, R. (1999) 'Interaction order and beyond: a field analysis of body culture within fitness gyms', *Body and Society* 5 (2/3): 227–248.

Sassen, S. (1991) *The Global City*, Princeton, NJ: Princeton University Press.

Saunders, W. (2005) 'Preface' in W. Saunders (ed.) *Commodification and Spectacle in Architecture*, Minneapolis: University of Minnesota Press (pp. vii–viii).

Schantz, O. and Gilbert, K. (2001) 'An ideal misconstrued newspaper coverage of the Atlanta Paralympic Games in France and Germany', *Sociology of Sport Journal* 18 (1): 69–94.

Schell, L. A. and Duncan, M. C. (1999) 'A content analysis of CBS's coverage of the 1996 Paralympic Games', *Adapted Physical Activity Quarterly* 16 (1): 27–47.

226

Schell, L. A. and Rodriguez, S. (2001) 'Subverting bodies/ambivalent representations: media analysis of Paralympian, Hope Lewellen', *Sociology of Sport Journal* 18 (1): 127–135.

Schimmel, K. (2001) 'Sport matters: urban regime theory and urban regeneration in the late-capitalist era' in C. Gratton and I. Henry (eds) *Sport in the City*, London: Routledge (pp. 259–277).

Schimmel, K. (2006) 'Deep play: sports mega-events and urban social conditions in the USA' in J. Horne and W. Manzenreiter (eds) *Sports Mega-Events*, Oxford: Blackwell (pp. 160–174).

Schmidt, C. (2007) *Five Ring Circus: The Untold Story of the Vancouver 2010 Games* (documentary film) available from www.TheFiveRingCircus.com.

Schweid, R. (1994) *Barcelona: Jews, Transvestites and an Olympic Season*, Berkeley, CA: Ten Speed Press.

Shank, M. D. (2002) *Sports Marketing: A Strategic Perspective*, Upper Saddle River, NJ: Prentice Hall.

Shaw, C. (2008) *Five Ring Circus: Myths and Realities of the Olympic Games*, Gabriola Island, BC: New Society Publishers.

Sheard, R. (2001a) *Sports Architecture*, London: Spon.

Sheard, R. (2001b) 'Olympic stadia and the future' in International Union of Architects/IOC *The Olympic Games and Architecture: The Future for Host Cities*, Lausanne: IOC (pp. 43–47).

Sheard, R. (2005) *The Stadium: Architecture for the New Global Culture*, Singapore: Periplus.

Shilling, C. (2004) 'Physical capital and situated action: a new direction for corporeal sociology', *British Journal of Sociology of Education* 25 (4): 473–487.

Shilling, C. (2007) 'Sociology and the body: classical traditions and new agendas' in C. Shilling (ed.) *Embodying Sociology: Retrospect, Progress, Prospects* (*Sociological Review* Monograph Series), Oxford: Blackwell (pp. 2–17).

Short, J. R. (2004) *Global Metropolitan: Globalizing Cities in a Capitalist World*, London: Routledge.

Silk, M. and Amis, J. (2005) 'Sport tourism, cityscapes and cultural politics', *Sport in Society* 8 (2): 280–301.

Simon, B. (1975) 'Introduction' in B. Simon and I. Bradley (eds) *The Victorian Public School: Studies in the Development of an Educational Institution*, Dublin: Gill & Macmillan (pp. 1–18).

Simon, B. and Bradley, I. (eds) (1975) *The Victorian Public School. Studies in the Development of an Educational Institution*, Dublin: Gill & Macmillan.

Simson, V. and Jennings, A. (1992) *The Lords of the Rings: Power, Money and Drugs in the Modern Olympics*, London: Simon & Schuster.

Sinclair, I. (2008) 'The Olympics scam', *London Review of Books* 30 (12): 17–23.

Sklair, L. (2001) *The Transnational Capitalist Class*, Oxford: Blackwell.

Sklair, L. (2002) *Globalization: Capitalism and its Alternatives*, Oxford: Oxford University Press.

Sklair, L. (2005) 'The transnational capitalist class and contemporary architecture in globalizing cities', *International Journal of Urban and Regional Research* 29 (3): 485–500.

Sklair, L. (2006) 'Iconic architecture and capitalist globalization', *City* 10 (1): 21–47.

Smit, B. (2006) *Pitch Invasion: Adidas, Puma and the Making of Modern Sport*, London: Allen Lane.

Spence, J. (1988) *Up Close and Personal*, New York: Atheneum.

Spiegel, F. (2007) 'Watkin's Folly to Wembley Stadium', http://britishhistory.suite101.com/article.cfm/watkins_folly_to_wembley_stadium (accessed 18 August 2010).

Sport England (1999a) *Participation in Sport in Great Britain 1996*, London: Sport England.

Sport England (1999b) *Survey of Sports Halls and Swimming Pools in England 1997*, London: Sport England.

Sport England (2000) *Sports Participation and Ethnicity in England National Survey 1999/2000*, London: Sport England.

sportscotland (2002) *Sports Participation in Scotland 2001,* Edinburgh: sportscotland.

Stallard, P. (1996) 'A fractured vision: the world fair comes to Wembley', unpublished paper, Sheffield: University of Sheffield Geography Department.

Steinberg, D. A. (1978) 'The Workers Sport Internationals 1920–28', *Journal of Contemporary History* 13: 233–251.

Stevens, G. (1998) *The Favored Circle: The Social Foundations of Architectural Distinction*, Cambridge, MA: MIT Press.

Stevens, Q. (2007) *The Ludic City: Exploring the Potential of Public Spaces*, London: Routledge.

Stevenson, D. (1977) 'Olympic arts: Sydney 2000 and the Cultural Olympiad', *International Review for the Sociology of Sport* 32 (3): 227–238.

Sudjic, D. (2005) *The Edifice Complex: How the Rich and Powerful Shape the World*, London: Penguin.

Sugden, J. and Tomlinson, A. (1998) *FIFA and the Contest for World Football*, Cambridge: Polity.

Taine, Hippolyte (1872) *Notes sur l'Angleterre*, Paris.

Tajima, A. (2004) '"Amoral universalism": mediating and staging global and local in the 1998 Nagano Winter Olympic Games', *Critical Studies in Media Communication* 21 (3): 241–260.

Thomas, N. and Smith, A. (2003) 'Preoccupied with able–bodiedness? An analysis of the British media coverage of the 2000 Paralympic Games', *Adapted Physical Activity Quarterly* 20 (2): 166–181.

Thrift, N. (2004) 'Intensities of feeling: towards a spatial politics of affect', *Geografiska Annaler* Series B, 86, 1: 57–78.

Thrift, N. (2005) 'But malice aforethought: cities and the natural history of hatred', *Transactions of the Institute of British Geographers* 30: 133–150.

Till, J. (2009) *Architecture Depends*, Cambridge, MA: MIT Press.

Tomlinson, A. (1996) 'Olympic spectacle: opening ceremonies and some paradoxes of globalisation', *Media Culture and Society* 18 (4): 583–602.

Tomlinson, A. (1999) 'Staging the spectacle: reflections on Olympic and World Cup ceremonies, *Soundings* 13: 161–171.

Tomlinson, A. (2005a) 'Olympic survivals' in L. Allison (ed.) *The Global Politics of Sport*, London: Routledge (pp. 46–62).

Tomlinson, A. (2005b) 'The making of the global sports economy: ISL, adidas, and the rise of the corporate player in world sport' in M. L. Silk, D. L. Andrews and C. L. Cole (eds) *Sport and Corporate Nationalisms*, Oxford: Berg (pp. 35–65).

Tomlinson, A. and Whannel, G. (eds) (1984) *Five Ring Circus: Money, Power and Politics at the Olympic Games,* London: Pluto.

Tomlinson, A. and Young, C. (eds) (2006) *National Identity and Global Sports Events*, Albany, NY: State University of New York Press.

Toohey, K. and Veal, A. (2007) *The Olympic Games: A Social Science Perspective*, 2nd edition, Oxford: CABI.

Trory, E. (1980) *Munich, Montreal and Moscow: A Political Tale of Three Olympic Cities*, Hove, Sussex: Crabtree Press.

Trumpbour, R. (2007) *The New Cathedrals: Politics and Media in the History of Stadium Construction*, Syracuse, NY: Syracuse University Press.

Tudor, A. (1998) 'Sports reporting: race, difference and identity' in K. Brants, J. Hermes and L. van Zoonen (eds) *The Media in Question: Popular Cultures and Public Interests*, London: Sage (pp. 147–156).

Ueberoth, P. (1985) *Made in America: His Own Story*, New York: Morrow.

Urry, J. (2002) *The Tourist Gaze*, 2nd edition, London: Sage.

Vertinsky, P., Jette, S. and Hofmann, A. (2009) '"Skierinas" in the Olympics: gender justice and gender politics at the local, national and international level over the challenge of women's ski jumping', *Olympika*, XVIII: 43–74.

Wainwright, M. (2008) 'The happy architect' *Guardian*, Society, 19 November, pp. 1–2.

Walseth, K. and Fasting, K. (2003) 'Islam's view on physical activity and sport: Egyptian women interpreting Islam', *International Review for the Sociology of Sport* 38 (1): 45–60.

Walters, G. (2006) *Berlin Games: How Hitler Stole the Olympic Dream*, London: John Murray.

Watts, J. (2008) 'China using Games as "warfare", says stadium designer', *Guardian*, 2 August, p. 26.

Weber, M. (1970) *From Max Weber: Essays in Sociology*, edited by H.H. Gerth and C. Wright Mills, London: Routledge & Kegan Paul.

Wellard, I. (2002) 'Men, sport, body performance and the maintenance of 'exclusive masculinity', *Leisure Studies* 21 (3/4): 235–247.

Whannel, G. (1984) 'The television spectacular' in A. Tomlinson and G. Whannel (eds) *Five Ring Circus: Money, Power and Politics at the Olympic Games*, London: Pluto (pp. 30–43).

Whannel, G. (1992) *Fields in Vision: Television Sport and Cultural Transformation*, London: Routledge.

Whannel, G. (1999) 'From "motionless bodies" to acting moral subjects: Tom Brown, a transformative romance for the production of manliness', *Diegesis: Journal for the Association for Research in Popular Fictions* 4: 14–21.

Whannel, G. (2000) 'Sport and the media' in J. Coakley and E. Dunning (eds) *Handbook of Sport Studies*, London: Sage (pp. 291–308).

Whannel, G. (2002) *Media Sport Stars: Masculinities and Moralities*, London: Routledge.

Whannel, G. (2008) *Culture, Politics and Sport: Blowing the Whistle Revisited*, London: Routledge.

Whannel, G. (2010) 'News, celebrity and vortextuality: a study of the media coverage of the Jackson verdict', *Cultural Politics* 6 (1): 65–84.

Wheeler, R. F. (1978) 'Organised sport and organised labour: the workers' sport movement', *Journal of Contemporary History* 13: 191–210.

Whitson, D. (1994) 'The embodiment of gender: discipline, domination and empowerment' in S. Birrell and C. Cole (eds) *Women, Sport and Culture*, Champaign, IL: Human Kinetics (pp. 353–371).

Whitson, D. (2004) 'Bringing the world to Canada: "the periphery of the centre"', *Third World Quarterly* 25 (7): 1215–1232.

Whitson, D. (2011) 'Vancouver 2010: the saga of Eagleridge Bluffs' in G. Hayes and

J. Karamichas (eds) *Olympic Games, Mega-Events, and Civil Societies: Globalisation, Environment, and Resistance*, Basingstoke: Palgrave.

Whitson, D. and Horne, J. (2006) 'Underestimated costs and overestimated benefits? Comparing the impact of sports mega-events in Canada and Japan' in J. Horne and W. Manzenreiter (eds) *Sports Mega-Events: Social Scientific Analyses of a Global Phenomenon*, Oxford: Blackwell (pp. 73–89).

Whitson, D. and Macintosh, D. (1993) 'Becoming a world-class city: hallmark events and sport franchises in the growth strategies of Western Canadian cities', *Sociology of Sport Journal* 10 (3): 221–240.

Wilkinson, R. (1964) *The Prefects: British Leadership and the Public School Tradition: A Comparative Study in the making of Rulers*, London: Oxford University Press.

Williams, J. (2009) 'The curious mystery of the Cotswold 'Olimpick' games: did Shakespeare know Dover . . . and does it matter?', *Sport in History* 29 (2): 150–170.

Williamson, T. (2010) 'The 2016 Olympics: a win for Rio?' A five-part series of articles available at http://rioonwatch.org/?p=83 (accessed: 20 November 2010).

Wilson, H. and Sinclair, J. (eds) (2000) 'The Olympics: media, myth, madness', special issue of *Media International Australia* 97, Nathan, Queensland: Australian Key Centre for Cultural and Media Policy, Griffiths University.

Wilson, N. (1988) *The Sports Business*, London: Piatkus.

Women's Sports Foundation (WSF) (2009) *Women in the 2000, 2004 and 2008 Olympic and Paralympic Games*, New York: WSF.

Wong, D. S. Y. (forthcoming) 'The youth Olympic Games', *International Journal of the History of Sport*.

Yalin, S. (2007) 'The development of the Olympic Press Centre', unpublished MA dissertation, Luton: University of Luton (now the University of Bedfordshire).

Young, C. (2010) 'Berlin 1936' in A. Bairner and G. Molnar (eds) *The Politics of the Olympics*, London: Routledge (pp. 93–105).

Young, D. C. (1984) *The Olympic Myth of Greek Amateur Athletics*, London: ARS Publishing.

Young, David C. (1996) *The Modern Olympics: A Struggle for Revival*, Baltimore, MD: Johns Hopkins University Press.

Young, D. C. (2004) *A Brief History of the Olympic Games*, Oxford: Blackwell.

Zarnowski, C. F. (1992) 'A look at Olympic costs', *Citius, Altius, Fortius* 1 (1): 16–32.

Zhang, T. and Silk, M. (2006) 'Recentering Beijing: sport, space, subjectivities', *Sociology of Sport Journal* 23 (4): 438–459.

Zirin, D. (2009) *A People's History of Sports in the United States: 250 Years of Politics, Protest, People and Play*, New York: The New Press.

Zizek, S. (2005) 'The empty wheelbarrow', *Guardian*, 19 February.

INDEX

Note: Page numbers followed by 'f' refer to figures and followed by 'n' refer to notes.

231

Till, Jeremy 186
The Times 16
Tlatelolco Massacre 133
Tokyo 1940 113
Tokyo 1964: architectural projects 191; computer systems 56; political issues 122, 130f, 133; sponsorship 60
Tom Brown's Schooldays 70, 76, 78–9
Tomlinson, Alan 27, 29f, 30f, 34, 36, 43, 44, 60, 104f, 155, 169f, 198
Toohey, Kristine 37–8, 127, 131f
TOP (The Olympic Partner) programme 35, 36, 48f, 49f, 57, 60–2
torch relay 35, 69, 146, 154; Beijing 2008 137, 156–7; Berlin 1936 114, 117–18; London 1948 100; sponsor promotional opportunities 60f, 156; Sydney 2000 136; uncertain future of 154, 157
Torino 2006 136, 152
transnational capitalist class (TCC) 187, 188, 192, 198, 199
transport infrastructures 6, 7, 37, 45, 86; British Empire Exhibition 1924/25 98; London 1908 95; London 2012 11, 16, 19, 157–8, 160; Rio de Janeiro 2016 141; Westfield White City 160–1
transportation of VIPs at Olympics 157
Tudor, Andrew 177
Turnen Societies 70, 102
Turner, Ted 9, 56, 132
Turner, Victor 152

UK Sport 167
United States of America: mega construction projects 187; sporting culture 71, 72, 77, 79; stadium building in 193, 199
urban development 180–3; mega events and generating shock and awe 183–5, 203; producing material infrastructure 185–91; social distribution of supposed benefits 201, 203–4; spatial and political impacts in sports architecture 195–9; and sports mega-events 191–5; and urban boosterism 134–5, 136, 137

Vancouver-Whistler 2010 40–1; dispute over women's ski jumping 170, 171; planning procedures 183
Veal, Anthony 27, 29f, 30f, 34, 37–8, 104f, 127, 131f, 169f
Vertinsky, Patricia 172, 173

video streaming 57–8
Vila Autódromo 138–45, 194f, 195f, 210n

Wahle, Otto 90
'Water Cube' 19, 147f, 181, 182f, 191
websites 56, 57, 58
Welch, David 12
Wembley Arena 93, 96, 99
Wembley Park 96–7, 103
Wembley Stadium 93, 97, 98, 100, 101, 105, 158; programme on architecture of 197
'Wenlock Olympian Society' 72
Westfield: Stratford City shopping mall 23f, 24, 93, 101, 105, 148, 157–61; White City shopping mall 105, 160–1
Whannel, Garry 36, 43, 44, 50, 58, 60, 79, 137, 145, 146, 153, 156, 174, 177, 185
White City shopping mall 105, 160–1
White City stadium 93, 95, 96, 98, 101, 103
Williamson, Theresa 138, 141, 210–11n
Winter Olympics 2018 39, 41f, 42
Wintour, Ulick 98
women: in boxing 170; Coubertin's views on women in sport 79, 169, 170; media coverage of female athletes 174; membership of IOC 162, 169; in Olympic Games 89, 90, 162, 169–74; ski jumping 170–2
Women's Olympics 32, 102, 103f
Women's Sports Foundation (WSF) 173, 174
Workers' Gymnastic Association 114
Workers' Olympics 32, 102, 103f, 115, 116f
workers' sports movements 102, 114–15, 116f
World Cup 33, 40, 47, 76, 81, 103, 103f, 112, 142, 153; 1966 101; 1982 59; 2006 55, 180; 2010 142; 2014 44, 141, 194; 2018 43, 142, 203; Brazil 2014 141; Russia 2018 43, 142; sponsorship 59, 60
World Fairs 85–7, 111, 204; and early modern Games 88–92; London Games and exhibitions 92–101
Wyatt, Derek 18

Yankee Stadium 193
YouTube 57

Zappas, Evangelos 75, 80
Zappas Olympic Games 75–6
Zeus 67
Zirin, Dave 193
Žižek, Slavoj 201, 202

239